GLOBAL HAPPINESS

*A Guide to
the Most Contented (and Discontented)
Places around the Globe*

Roman Adrian Cybriwsky

An Imprint of ABC-CLIO, LLC

Santa Barbara, California • Denver, Colorado

Library of Congress Cataloging-in-Publication Data

Names: Cybriwsky, Roman A., author.
Title: Global happiness : a guide to the most contented (and discontented) places
    around the globe / Roman Adrian Cybriwsky.
Description: Santa Barbara, California : Greenwood, an Imprint of ABC-CLIO, LLC,
    [2016] | Includes bibliographical references and index.
Identifiers: LCCN 2015026006 | ISBN 9781440835568 (alk. paper) |
    ISBN 9781440835575 (eISBN)
Subjects: LCSH: Quality of life—Cross-cultural studies. | Well-being—Cross-cultural
    studies. | Social indicators—Cross-cultural studies. | Cities and towns—Ratings
    and rankings.
Classification: LCC HN25 .C93 2016 | DDC 306—dc23 LC record available
    at http://lccn.loc.gov/2015026006

ISBN: 978-1-4408-3556-8
EISBN: 978-1-4408-3557-5

20 19 18 17 16   1 2 3 4 5

This book is also available on the World Wide Web as an eBook.
Visit www.abc-clio.com for details.

Greenwood
An Imprint of ABC-CLIO, LLC

ABC-CLIO, LLC
130 Cremona Drive, P.O. Box 1911
Santa Barbara, California 93116-1911

This book is printed on acid-free paper ∞

Manufactured in the United States of America

With prayers for peace and prosperity in a Ukraine that is whole and in all the conflict zones in the Middle East.

With prayers as well for a peaceful and prosperous Africa, for a Russia that is democratic, friendly, and contented, and for safe and happy lives for Palestinians and all Israelis, for trans-Mediterranean migrants from Africa, the beleaguered Rohingya people of Burma, the Tatars of Crimea, and Tibetans and Uyghurs in China.

I dedicate the book as well to my son Alex, the great experimenter about where to live in the world, and to his older brother Adrian and younger sister Mary, both of whom are also accomplished global travelers.

Contents

Chapter 2: The Most and Least Contented World Cities

Chapter 3: The Most and Least Contented U.S. States and Cities

PREFACE

I was asked by Kaitlin Ciarmiello, the Senior Acquisitions Editor at ABC-CLIO for Geography and World Cultures, if I would be interested in writing this book, and I happily agreed. She signed me for the first project I did with ABC-CLIO, the 2013 book *Capital Cities around the World*, which I enjoyed writing, and thought that I would enjoy taking on a study of the geography of happiness across the world. It turned out that she was right. Even though I know my world geography well, I was happy to learn more and felt privileged to be able to make judgments about countries and cities in the world where people seem to be most contented versus those places where there is widespread discontentment. Kaitlin and I began with the fact that I have a lot of experience in the geography profession and have traveled the world unusually widely. I then undertook study of the related literature in order to identify the 20 most contented countries in the world, the 20 most contented cities, the 20 least contented cities, the 20 least contented countries, and separately, the 5 most contented states in the United States, the 5 least contented states, the 10 most contented American cities, and the 10 that are least contented. That literature included many data-based rankings of countries, cities, and states that employ wide ranges of criteria that somehow touch on happiness. It was an interesting and challenging task to do this. I think that I undertook the task responsibly, and that the ensuing text explains the choices of happy and unhappy places that I settled on. I want to thank Kaitlin for her advice and support throughout the project, and for thinking of me when she needed an author. I also want to express by thanks to two members of the production team for this book, Gordon Hammy Matchado and Paul Wells. Both worked tirelessly and professionally to make this book better.

I am a senior citizen, although I was not always, and I am also a big person, although again I wasn't always. In fact, I used to run marathons, but now for exercise I simply hobble around a pool table with an expensive 19 oz. cue in hand. When I travel internationally, customs officials sometimes ask why I have so much luggage. They understand my answer when they look at me and I tell them that it is because my clothes are so much bigger, and because the longer suitcase contains a case with my cue sticks. That almost always elicits a smile, which I hope that the reader is doing at this moment too. The reason that I say all this is to explain why this book employs the word "we" from here on, instead of the first-person singular pronoun. The "we" is in fact me, your senior professor-geographer author, and the plural pronoun is simply a literary device to avoid the singular "I." Call it the "royal we" if you will; I accept the promotion with enthusiasm and thanks. Just don't think that the "we" is because I am big enough for two people.

INTRODUCTION

A GEOGRAPHY OF HAPPINESS AND DISCONTENT

In 1985, French writer Dominque Lapierre published a novel called *City of Joy* (*La cité de la joie*) about life in a slum neighborhood in Kolkata, India (then Calcutta), and the enormous hardships endured by the poor. It won numerous awards and was translated into many languages. In 1992, it was made into a Hollywood film directed by Roland Joffé. The production starred the late Patrick Swayze as a doctor from the United States and a popular Indian actor, Om Puri, who played the role of a transplanted farmer from the drought-ridden countryside who struggles to feed his family from income as a rickshaw puller in the giant metropolis. The story is based on real people in a real neighborhood inhabited by the poorest of the poor, and is replete with tales of poverty, disease, vice, prejudices, and human exploitation. Yet, the setting is also a "city of joy," *Anand Nagar*, as residents refer to their slum in the local Bengali language, because it is here that people live, love, make love, share joy at weddings, and celebrate when a new baby is born. Also, the book tells us that no matter how hard life is, the people of Anand Nagar believe that life is worth living. The book is certainly inspiring (the film less so), much like the life of Mother Theresa, the sainted missionary nun who is identified with the same Calcutta slum, and has lessons for everyone.

We see something similar from another part of the world, the poor and violent Central American country of Nicaragua. In this case, the observations are not from a years-old novel-turned-Hollywood film, but from a very recent scientific study by professional social workers that was published in the prestigious and strictly refereed professional journal *Social Work in Public Health*. The study used structured interviews in order to examine happiness among 136 women who live in poverty and are victims of intimate partner violence (IPV). Their situation, of course, is tragic, but more than one-half of the women in the sample claimed to be happy despite the hardships that they face. Despite pressing economic issues and brutal husbands or partners, the women found support from family members, friends, and neighbors who were a basis for "overall happiness," and the "vast majority" expressed optimism about the future (Vázquez, Panadero, and Rivas, 2015).

For us, these insights to places of appalling poverty are a reminder of just how difficult the concept of happiness is, and the shaky ground that we stand on as we try to differentiate places in the world where people are contented from places where they are not. There are objective truths, to be sure: places ravaged by war are less happy than those at peace; good health is better than hunger and disease; clean air is better than pollution; and government by and for the people is better than dictatorship, repression, and kleptocracy. But even in the worst conditions, people find occasions for genuine joy and can be optimistic that tomorrow will be better. On the other hand, it often seems that those people who have apparently everything, have everything but happiness. Such paradoxes have confounded serious thinkers throughout the ages, and have been the subject of probing literature in many languages. The paradoxes are also integral to the teachings of religious faiths around the world, and to the lessons that are offered to the world by the lives of spiritual leaders from Jesus Christ to the Prophet Mohammed to Buddha and the Dalai Lama.

It is with such observations that we begin to sort out a geography of happiness around the world. What are the countries where people are most contented, and what are the countries where they are not? From the lessons from Anand Nagar and Nicaragua, as well as from religious values and great literature, we know that this geography is not likely to be the familiar map of the globe in which countries are shown by income level, level of economic development, or anything else that smacks of familiar "First World"—"Third World" dichotomies. There are already plenty of rankings of countries that employ such data, with the result that Scandinavian and other western European countries, as well as North America and Oceania, almost always occupy all the top slots, and the poorest countries of Africa almost always comprise a long list at the bottom. But these are not rankings of happiness as much as they rankings of material well-being. Our position is that while the richer countries of the world have more of the goods and services that money can buy, that does not necessarily mean that they are the happiest countries as well. Happiness is elsewhere too, we know, and discontent is everywhere too. The same logic applies to cities as well. Because ours is an urban world, we look at cities in this book too and ask the same questions: what are the most contented cities on the planet, and which cities are least contented? Are the happiest cities the ones with the tallest skyscrapers, the greenest suburbs, the best highways, and the cleanest streets, or could the list include places that are totally different?

Our topic is enormous and is complicated by the great diversity of countries and cultures on the planet, the enormous population of the world (now estimated to be about 7 billion), and by the many thousands of cities of different kinds and population levels that exist on the planet (more than 500 urban agglomerations worldwide have populations of 1 million or more, and their numbers are growing). Our challenge is compounded as well by problems of availability of comparable data, even for straightforward variables that deal with health, incomes, housing conditions, and so on. Not every country takes a census, and even among those that do, there are differences with definitions and timing, as well as reliability. An even greater challenge is the great puzzle of how to define and measure happiness and personal contentment. Good health, sufficient income, and decent housing conditions, among other similar variables, are almost certainly ingredients for happiness, but not always so, and not always in the same proportions. For some, happiness can be simply having someone to love and to be loved, with or without good health, a good income, or a good place to live. Or, happiness can be—and is for a great many people—having a close relationship with God. For many people, nothing else is needed. And, of course, there is the problem that no matter how we define or measure happiness, and no matter what the country or city, there are varying levels of happiness and contentment within, with some fractions of the populations being happy, at least for today, and other fractions being unhappy, also at least only for today. Furthermore, happiness can come and happiness can go.

One could easily throw hands up into the air and surrender to the topic, saying that measuring happiness and ranking countries and cities according to happiness and unhappiness is an impossible task. Yet, there is a powerful human impulse to make comparisons, as well as a companion impulse to make note of the comparisons that are put before us. Advertisers on the Internet know this well, as they bombard us continually with enticements to read this "top ten" list or another, and then slip one advertisement after the other before our eyes as we scroll through the promised information. That is, they know that a sure-fire way to get people to see their ads is to affix them to tantalizing lists of the best this, the worst that, and so on. People are receptive to lists if only to see how they stack up against others or, as in the case in this book, to see how where we live stacks up in comparison with other places. Where does my country rank? How about my city? Are there lessons to learn from happier countries and happier cities? What do they have in those places that we do not? Indeed, sometimes we even gauge our own happiness by making implicit comparisons with what we see from the lives of other people, be they friends or relatives whom we know well, or the "the people" in general in some distant and unfamiliar place. We can feel thankful about where we live, because of observations that people elsewhere have it worse, or alternatively, we might be envious of the residents of some other place. People who move voluntarily from one town to another, or who migrate to a new country, can sometimes be considered to be chasers of happiness: in one way or another, they have made the comparison between the old place and the new, and have decided that they will be more contented if they make the move. The reasons can be a better job, a better climate, an escape from harsh circumstances, or some other grass-is-greener ingredient for a happier future.

We expect that readers of this book will look first to see if their own country (or city or state) is mentioned herein, and in what light. They will compare what is written with that they themselves think, and either agree, disagree, or think something in between. What does this book or this supposed expert (i.e., the author of this book) *think* about my country or my city in comparison to what I myself truly *know*? Did the author get it right? Do the criteria that are used to distinguish between happy places and unhappy ones make sense to me? Do I agree that my country (or city) is among the global top 20 (or the bottom 20)? Others will ask, why is my country or city not among the places that are featured? I don't feel middle-of-the-pack. We also expect that many readers from outside the United States specifically will take an especially critical position as they familiarize themselves with this book. It has often been said that it is winners in war who get to write world histories; it could be said as well that it is such winners—if not winners at war, then winners at accumulation of the world's wealth and winners in access to mass media—who get to conduct studies and write reports about the condition of the world such as this book. Here is a book from the United States of America, foreign readers will say, one of the world's richest and most influential countries, by an author who is also an American, albeit one with an ethnic name. Is this book an American viewpoint? Or has the author found a way to write as a global citizen more so than as someone with connections to a winner's corner? Has this American author portrayed my country or city fairly and authoritatively?

We need to steel ourselves for criticism and develop a thick skin, because even when we get it right, we know in advance that there will be disagreements with whatever we come up with. There will be disagreements about methodology, the criteria that we use to represent happiness or lack thereof, our choices of countries and cities (and U.S. states) to put into the various categories of contented and not contented places, and what we say about these various places in our write-ups. We also know that many opposite opinions will be strong and angry, both from the heart and from a sense of competition and self-interest. "That blockhead! What does he know? I can't believe that he didn't put [my place] at #1!" Or conversely, "That blockhead! I can't believe that he listed [my place] in the good category! What does he know? This place is a dump!"

Thus, it is truly a maze of challenges, issues, and pitfalls that we must negotiate as we wade into this project. Yet, despite the difficulties, we have undertaken our own study of the world's most contented and least contented countries and cities. We think that there is a need for a book such as this because there is indeed a wide public interest in knowing the best and the worst places, and because we think that the myriad rankings of countries, cities, and states that exist to this point measure something other than contentment with place. We also think that too many of the existing rankings are biased in favor of Western societies and industrialized nations, and do not take into account that happiness and discontentment exists in all cultures and all levels of economy. In the following paragraphs, we explain our approach to this topic and discuss details of methodology.

SCOPE OF THE STUDY AND METHODOLOGY

This book, *Global Happiness*, is a geography of the most and least contented places in the world. As we have been doing already, the word's happiness and contentment are used interchangeably as exact synonyms. The focus is on countries, of which there are approximately 196 in the world today, and on cities, of which there are literally thousands. The United States is excluded from this global analysis, and is treated in a separate section where we discuss the most and least contented cities in the country and the most and least contented states. We depart from the conventional practice of ranking countries, cities, and states, 1 though n, and instead present *groups* of countries, cities, and states that we have identified as most contented and groups that are least contented. We avoid rankings because we know that accurate rankings in full detail are impossible. Really, what is the difference between, say, the world's 143rd happiest country from #142 and #144, and how would one determine which country is exactly #143, exactly #142, and exactly #144, and so on, anyway from among the nearly 200 countries that are recognized in the world? Therefore, we confine ourselves to identifying the countries and cities that are at the very top and those that are at the very bottom of a happiness-contentment scale. Specifically, we list the 20 countries that we consider to be *representative* of a "most contented" category and 20 that are *representative* of those that are "least contented," as well as the 20 cities at the top and 20 cities at the bottom of a similar scale. Within any of these groups, we do not rank 1–20, but simply list and discuss the countries and cities as they appear in alphabetical order. This avoids some common problems with other rankings: nit-picking about specific position on a scale and dealing with the fact that specific positions can inch up or down from year to year without meaningful differences in what those countries and cities are really like. The number 20 was chosen as a round number that represents about 10% of the countries in the world. For cities, the number 20 was chosen to be parallel with the number of countries.

The word "representative" is in italics in the previous paragraph for a very important specific reason. Our assessment of happiest and least happy countries and cities differs from other rankings in that we make it a point to represent all parts of the world in our lists, be they the top lists or the bottom lists. That is, if happiness can be found among the destitute of Anand Nagar, and if happiness existed in the worlds that victims of slavery in the Americas built for themselves during their dark centuries, as well as in the worlds of oppressed miners, factory workers, and landless serfs in other times and places, then happiness can be and is everywhere in the world. It is *within* human beings, and not without. Likewise, there is discontent everywhere, perhaps even *especially* among the rich if one considers the worlds of envy, competitiveness, and insecurity that seem to mark places like Beverly Hills, yacht marinas along the Mediterranean, and the haunts of China's spoiled *nouveaux riches*. Consequently, our global geography of happiness needs to have both rich and poor countries and cities at the top, and other groups of rich and poor countries and cities at the bottom. In this way we differ from studies that measure countries and cities mostly according to wealth or what wealth can buy: for example, better health, higher degrees of education, cleaner water, and more time for fun. So, do not expect to see only northern Europe and North America at the top and hapless Africa at the bottom in the pages ahead: expect instead a mix of places at both extremes. Look forward, as well, to seeing our specific choices of countries and cities, which in some cases might be surprising, and to reading our reasons for them.

Because happiness is an elusive concept, we think that no single measure and no index made of combined measures will yield an accurate assessment. Furthermore, we believe that while it might be possible for trained specialists to measure individuals' levels of happiness via personal interviews and specially constructed questionnaires, it is impractical to apply such a method on a global scale in which we want to consider every country in the world and all of their cities. In addition, we recognize that data of even quality and reliability do not exist for all countries of the world, and even less so for the majority of the world's cities. What is more, there are huge gaps in data across the globe, as many countries have very little statistical information available about their populations that is reliable, accurate, or current. There are even more data gaps with respect to individual cities, and many cities in the world where one can only guess at even the population totals, much less know anything in detail about those populations. Thus, we are faced with the challenge of an elusive concept—happiness—combined with a lack of hard data that could somehow stand for happiness.

This means that our methodology has to be unique and special-made. At the same time, we need to maintain rigor with respect to the canons of social science research, and rely as much as possible on hard data from reliable sources. The result is that only a combination of approaches can work. After considerable consideration, we settled on a strategy that incorporates and blends quantitative results from existing rankings of countries and cities according to various criteria related to quality of life, and that adds qualitative data about countries and cities from as many sources as possible: authoritative studies and readings about these places, documentaries, information from various news media about current events, and our own considerable travel experience around the globe, among other sources. What we call the "hopper" of data and other information is not equal in weight for all countries and for all cities, as there are more and better data available for some places than for other countries and cities, but we worked with what we had in the hoppers of data to get closer and closer to lists of top 20 and bottom 20 countries and cities. We winnowed. We started with long lists, say 50 or 60 countries out of the 196 countries that exist as candidates for the top list and 50 or 60 other countries as candidates for the bottom list, and then progressively narrowed the lists by looking at details within or data, and by researching deeper, reading more, and seeking advice. As we worked toward lists of 20, we strived for the diversity that we seek: a representation of cities and countries of all types and from all regions of the world. That often resulted in difficult choices, for example, not having room for an obviously prosperous country on the contented list because we wanted its place to be taken by a different kind of country from a different part of the world.

Since there is no one measure of happiness that is possible for a study such as this, we need to use surrogate measures that, to one degree or another, and then in combination, can stand for how contented places are. Thus we need not only to identify what data go into our "information hoppers" for countries, cities, and states, but also to weigh those ingredients one against the other in a way that gives more weight to variables that are closer to what we think underlies true happiness and less weight to happiness/quality-of-life measures that are further away. Therefore, over all, the challenge was to consider as much information from as many sources as possible, but to be judicial as to how we weighed them. Thus, we made note of gross national product and per capita income statistics in our analysis, as well as measures of the health of a population or the quality of public infrastructure, because they are important ingredients to the quality of life a public enjoys, but we give more attention to other measures that are less about money and more about human relations and personal freedoms. For example, political freedoms and free and fair elections, freedoms of the press, and evidence of tolerance with respect to religious differences, ethnic and racial minority rights and inclusion, equal rights for sexual minorities, and political and economic progress for women were all weighed more than income levels. The scores that countries are assigned on previously published indexes of corruption are also in this mix, because while corruption is about money, the absence of corruption indicates that people in responsible positions value something more than money.

In addition to sources based on quantitative data and standardized rankings, our analysis of the world's countries and cities took current events into account. We marked places down on our scale of contentment and discontentment if they were scenes of warfare, revolution, and other strife, as well as in cases of environmental crisis and calamities such as destruction by major earthquakes or storms. We also marked down for conditions of oppression such as dictatorial government, slavery, and other gross violations of peoples' rights, although these problems were reflected as well in some of the indexes that were also part of the analysis. We were especially critical in cases of oppression of women, sexual minorities, and ethnic-religious minorities. Conversely, we "curved" upward where we saw peace and stable government, and government leadership that was widely popular and demonstrably competent. Negative-side examples for this paragraph include lowered marks for Syria and Yemen because of current wars, for Haiti and Nepal because of recent earthquakes, and various countries on the Arabian Peninsula such as Saudi Arabia and the United Arab Emirates because of social intolerance. Examples on the positive side include the recent transformation of Uruguay to stability and prosperity, the success of the Estonia, Latvia, and Lithuania in becoming democratic and increasingly prosperous after the fall of the Soviet Union, and emergence of Tunisia, Senegal, and Botswana as model nations for their respective regions of Africa.

There was a separate issue about how to cover the United States. Since this book is written by an American and published in the United States, there could be a perception of a conflict of interest about comparing the country with others. Moreover, there are simply much more data available for the United States than for most other countries and cities, which can skew comparisons. Also, we know also that many Americans expect the United States to be ranked at the top in global comparisons, firmly #1 in the opinions of many proud citizens, and that anything less than #1 means to them that the study is biased against their country. By contrast, other Americans would be suspicious of a study that gives their country and cities rankings that are too high in global comparisons. Which side, if any, is right or wrong is beside the point. We want to reach all sides of the cultural divide in the United States with our book, as well as readers from other countries, and have decided to treat the country separately from the rest of the world, and to not compare it with other countries. Therefore, after our presentations of most contented and least contented countries and cities around the world, we turn to the United States and its top and bottom states and cities. It would not make sense to talk about top 20 and bottom 20 states, since the total is only 50, so we identify only the 5 most contented states and 5 least contented states. As for cities, instead of two groups of 20, we offer the 10 most contented American cities and the 10 that we found to be least contented, again because the total pool is smaller. As with countries and world cities, we strive for wider representation of all regions of the United States in our presentation at both ends of our happiness scales.

A technical issue that we have had to deal with concerns "double counting" of countries and cities within them and of U.S. states and cities with them should be allowed, whether we are considering places that are most contented or those that we regard as being least contented. For example, should a city that we might consider to be one of the 20 most contented in the world be included on our list if we have already included the country that it is in on our list of 20 most contented countries? And could there be two most contented cities or two least contented cities listed from the same country, or should we spread the recognition to more parts of the world? The same questions apply to U.S. states and their cities. If, for example, we already have, say, Alaska as a most contented state, should, say, Anchorage still be eligible for consideration for the top cities list? Or what about Anchorage and, say, Fairbanks too? We answered this issue after examining the data, and decided that yes, indeed, such double counting should be allowed because we saw cases where separate recognition for country and city or for state and city seemed to be fair and appropriate. We also envisioned that it should be possible for one or more cities in a country (or in a U.S. state) to be on a most contented list and another or city in the same country or state to be on least contented list. Also, there is nothing to say that a country could not be contented as a whole, but one or more of its cities are not, or vice versa. However, in practice, the amount of "double counting" is limited, as we generally found it sufficient to discuss given cities within their respective country or state essays, leaving more opportunity for recognition, positive or negative, for more places.

There are 110 short essays in the pages ahead: one each about the 20 countries that we have chosen as representative of the most contented countries; 20 more for the least contented countries; another 20 for the most contented cities in the world; and 20 more cities that we have chosen to represent the 20 least contented cities in the world. The remainder of the 110 essays are in the separate section about the United States: 10 essays for the 10 most contented U.S. cities; 10 for the least contented cities; and 5 each for the most contented and least contented U.S. states. The essays about places outside the United States all begin with a basic orientation as to geographic location and the type of country or city that this is, followed by paragraphs that explain or justify our choice for listing the country or city where we do. These justifications include references to other rankings or studies that accord with our own observations, as well as information that we have gathered from expert analyses of these places, and from the media about current events. We also have personal experiences with many of the places that we write about, as we have traveled unusually widely, and discuss what we have observed where appropriate.

While *we* know in advance that each of the happiest places we introduce later will have plenty of people who are not happy, and that the least happy places named later will each have plenty of residents who are perfectly content, we believe that we did in fact arrive at arguably accurate lists of the most representative places at both of the extremes. Furthermore, we take pride in the fact that unlike other rankings, we recognize that happiness is everywhere, as is sadness, and that our lists represent all major parts of the world and all major culture areas in our geographies of both happiness and sadness. In the pages that follow, we introduce in turn the 20 most contented countries in the world, the 20 least contented countries, the 20 most contented prominent cities in the world, the 20 least contented, the 5 most contented states in the United States, the 5 least contented states, the 10 most contented prominent American cities, and finally the 10 least contented American cities. Except for the U.S. states, for which we have written abbreviated essays, we provide some suggested readings and references at the end of the essays. There are photographs for many of these places to support our text, and at the end there is an appendix that summarizes key rankings that have been published by other sources and a bibliography. Enjoy!

SOME KEY SOURCES

As we have said, our research employs a combination of approaches and data from a variety of sources. This is the place to list the various rankings and quantitative studies that we consulted as a matter of course in selecting the countries for this book and, separately, in selecting the non-U.S. cities. For each of these key sources, we will provide information about what is being measured and how, as well as the links that we used to access the data. Key rankings about the United States are described in the introduction to that part of the book. The following list is not exhaustive of our outside sources for rankings, but it does include those that are key. Note that the number of countries that are included varies from source to source, as not all data are available for all countries, and some sources include some non-countries (e.g., Hong Kong) in their studies.

Human Development Index: The Human Development Index (HDI) is produced annually for countries of the world by the United Nations Development Program. The most recent report was published in July 2014 and covers 187 countries. It reflects data for 2013. The HDI is a summary measure of what the U.N. refers to as "average achievement in key dimensions of human development." This includes a health dimension that is measured by life expectancy at birth; an education dimension that is measured by the mean years of schooling for adults aged 25 and expected years of schooling for children of entering school age; and a standard of living dimension that is measured by gross national income per capita. Website: http://hdr.undp.org/en/content/human-development-index-hdi.

Life Expectancy. Data about life expectancy at birth by country come from the World Health Organization. The most recent data are for 2012, and are presented clearly and accurately on the interactive map that is in the following link. A total of 199 countries are listed. Data about life expectancy often stand as surrogates for the overall health of a population. Website and interactive map: http://gamapserver.who.int/gho/interactive_charts/mbd/life_expectancy/atlas .html.

Infant Mortality. Infant mortality is another commonly used indicator of the overall health of the population. The most common measure is the number of deaths of infants under one year of age per 1,000 live births. The source that we used is a United Nations Population Prospects report and the *CIA World Factbook* as presented by the following link. A total of 188 countries and other entities are listed in that source. The data that we used are for 2013 as estimated by the CIA. Website: https://www.cia.gov/library/publications/the-world-factbook /rankorder/2091rank.html.

WHO Rankings of Health Systems. The World Health Organization ranks the health systems of its 191 member states. The rankings are based on an index of four factors: overall or average health of the population (25%); distribution or equality of health care (25%); speed of service, protection of privacy, and quality of amenities (25%); and fair financial contribution (25%). The data that we examined were for 2000. Website: http://www.who.int/whr/2000/en/ whr00_en.pdf.

Gross Domestic Product (at Purchasing Power Parity) per Capita. GDP(PPP) per capita is a commonly used measure of per capita income and standard of living in a country. The Purchasing Power Parity component enhances comparisons between countries because it takes into account differential rates of inflation between the countries and differences in costs of living. The data that we used are available here. There were three different measures of GDP(PPP) per capita: one by the International Monetary Fund for 2014 and 187 countries; a second by the World Bank for 2011–2013 and for 185 countries; and the third by the CIA for various years between 1993 and 2013 and for 195 countries. We recognize that happiness and money income are not the same. However, high income does have the ability to increase happiness by making it possible for individuals to live comfortably and securely, and to pay for the various ingredients of good health. Websites: International Monetary Fund: http://www.imf.org/external/pubs/ft/weo/2015/01/ weodata/index.aspx; World Bank: http://data.worldbank.org/indicator/NY.GDP .PCAP.PP.CD; CIA: https://www.cia.gov/library/publications/the-world-factbook/ rankorder/2004rank.html.

Legatum Prosperity Index. This index is calculated annually for 142 countries in the world by the Legatum Institute, a private investment firm that is headquartered in Dubai, United Arab Emirates. The company is affiliated with the Legatum group of companies based in London, England. The index was especially helpful to this study because it incorporates 89 variables in the analysis and covers many topics that contribute to people's happiness. The 89 variables are grouped into eight sub-indexes, which are averaged using equal weights in the calculation of the Legatum Prosperity Index. The eight sub-indexes are as follows: economy, entrepreneurship and opportunity, governance, education, health, safety and security, personal freedom, and social capital. The most recent ranking was for 2014. Website: http://www.li.com/docs/default-source/publications/2014-legatum-prosperity-index.pdf

Literacy Rate. The literacy rate of countries is a common surrogate used in combination with other measures to stand for standard of living. The higher the literacy rate, the better the quality of life in the country, as literacy correlates positively with variables such as income levels, good health, and good infrastructure. The data that we used include those collected by the *CIA World Factbook* and the *United Nations Human Development Report* and self-reporting by individual countries. The most common measure of literacy is the percentage of population aged 15 and older who are able to read and write. For a great many countries that percentage exceeds 99%. However, there are quite a few countries that are quite far down the scale. Literacy and happiness are not synonymous, of course, but we did consider that if a high percentage of a country's population is not able to read and write, that country is likely one that is poor, and that prospects for upward mobility by its poor people are dim. Also, we consider being able to read and write a source of many joys and regret that people who are illiterate are missing out. The global literacy rate for people aged 15 and over is 84.1%. Websites: CIA: https://www.cia.gov/library/publications/the-world-factbook/fields/2103.html #136; UN Human Development Report: http://hdr.undp.org/en/content/adult-literacyrate-both-sexes-ages-15-and-older.

Corruption Perceptions Index. A corrupt government is a demoralizing force, be that corruption at the lowest levels of authority and bureaucracy, at the very top, or simply everywhere in the whole system. We consider living with corruption to be a source of discontentment. Conversely, we think that it is a source of public satisfaction if citizens perceive that their government is honest. The extent of corruption is monitored on a country-by-country basis by the organization Transparency International (TI), an International Non-Governmental Organization (INGO) that was founded in Germany in 1993 and is based in Berlin. TI defines corruption as "the misuse of public power for private benefit," and regularly publishes reports about corruption, as well as an annual country-by-country ranking of corruption that is based on their Corruption Perceptions Index. The index places countries on a 100–0 scale, in which a score of 100 is "very clean" and 0 is "highly corrupt." The latest date are for 2014, and provide rankings for 175 countries. Website: http://www.transparency.org/cpi2014.

Index of Economic Freedom. This index is calculated and published annually by the Heritage Foundation, a conservative research think-tank based in Washington, D.C. The definition of economic freedom according to the Heritage Foundation is "the right of every human to control his or her own labor and property." The index is based on 10 quantitative and qualitative factors grouped into four categories of economic freedom: rule of law, limited government, regulatory efficiency, and open markets. The most recent list is for 2015 and covers 178 countries. Website: http://www.heritage.org/index/ranking.

Democracy Index. The Democracy Index is a product of the Intelligence Unit of *The Economist,* and compares countries according to whether or not their governments are democratic. It is based on 60 indicators that are grouped into five categories that measure pluralism, civil liberties, and political culture in 167 countries. The 167 countries are classified into four regime types: full democracies; flawed democracies; hybrid regimes; and authoritarian regimes. The first index was produced in 2006, and the most recent is for 2014. In 2014, there were 24 countries that were identified as full democracies and 52 that were authoritarian countries. We believe that there is more contentment with democracy than with life under authoritarian rulers. Website: http://pages.eiu.com/rs/eiu2/images/Democracy-Index-2012.pdf.

World Press Freedom Index. The organization Reporters without Borders monitors freedom of information worldwide and produces that annual World Press Freedom Index. It notes that even some countries that are democracies have seen erosion in freedoms of information because of a tendency to interpret national security needs in an overly broad and abusive manner to the detriment of rights to inform and to be informed. The most recent data are for 2014 and cover 180 countries. Website: http://rsf.org/index2014/en-index2014.php.

Satisfaction with Life Index. This is a lesser-known index that offers a country-by country comparison of subjective well-being. It is meant to approximate happiness. The index is the work of Adrian G. White, a psychologist at the University of Leicester in England, and takes in a broad range of variables from many sources. It is based on 2006 data and covers 178 countries. We used the Satisfaction with Life Index as an additional source of information when we were stuck with a close-call decision about whether or not to include a given country in either the top 20 or bottom list. Website: http://www.eurekalert.org/pub_releases/2006–07 /uol-uol072706.php.

Level of Happiness Index. This index is based on a detailed statistical analysis of a wide range of data, including survey data from the Gallup World Poll about how people in countries around the world see their own lives. The research distinguishes between happiness as an emotion and happiness as an evaluation, and takes into account the levels of social support that people have available to them, their life expectancies, freedoms to make one's own life choices, and perceptions about levels of corruption in people's own governments. The index uses data for 2010–2012, and is published in the *World Happiness Report, 2013* edited by researchers John Helliwell, Richard Layard, and Jeffrey Sachs. The number of countries covered is 156. We found some of the results to be counter-intuitive, and in conflict with other surveys, so this index was a fresh and independent view for us to consider in making our decisions about which countries to highlight. Website: http://unsdsn.org/wp-content/uploads/2014/02/WorldHappiness Report2013_online.pdf.

Best Countries for Business. This index is calculated regularly by the business magazine *Forbes.* The topic is somewhat removed from most people's understandings of happiness, but we used the results as for confirmation of our own observations because they correlate quite closely with other country rankings. The most recent data are for 2014 and for 146 countries. Website: http://www.forbes.com /best-countries-for-business/list/#page:1_sort:0_direction:asc_search.

Global Competitiveness Index. The Global Competitiveness Index is a key part of the *Global Competitiveness Report* that is produced on a regular basis by the World Economic Forum. The index compares 144 countries worldwide according to indicators of productivity and prosperity. Website: http://reports.weforum.org /global-competitiveness-report-2014–2015/.

Sustainable Society Index. The Sustainable Society Index is produced by the Sustainable Society Foundation (SSF), a nonprofit organization that was established in the Netherlands in 2006 to assist countries in their development toward sustainability. SSF published three different rankings: Human Wellbeing; Environmental Wellbeing; and Economic Wellbeing. The most recent data are for 2014 and for 151 countries. Website: http://www.ssfindex.com/.

Mercer's Quality of Living Rankings. Mercer is a global consulting firm that deals with human resources, health, retirement, and investments. Its Quality of Living Survey provides detailed rankings of cities around the world based on a broad range of quality of life indicators. The most recent survey is for 2015 and covers 230 prominent cities around the globe. Website: https://www.imercer.com/con tent/quality-of-living.aspx.

Economist Intelligence Unit's Livability Rankings, World Cities. The *Economist* ranks 140 of the world's most prominent cities according to livability as measured according to five dimensions: stability, health care, culture and environment, education, and infrastructure. Cost of living is not one of the criteria. The ranking has been criticized by the *New York Times* as being overly anglocentric, because it seems to favor cities in English-speaking countries. The bottom list has a large lumber of African cities. The most recent data were published in August 2014. Website: http://www.eiu.com/public/topical_report.aspx?campaignid=Liveability2014.

Monocle's Quality of Life Survey, World Cities. The lifestyle magazine *Monocle* has monitored livability in cities around the world since 2006, with the most recent ranking being for 2014. The most important criteria in this survey are safety/crime, international connectivity, climate/sunshine, quality of architecture, public transportation, tolerance, environmental issues and access to nature, urban design, business conditions, proactive policy developments, and medical care. Website: http://monocle.com/film/affairs/quality-of-life-survey-2014/.

1

THE MOST AND LEAST CONTENTED COUNTRIES

We have identified the 20 most contented countries in the world and the 20 least contented countries, and list them here. As we explained in the introduction, they are listed not in rank order, but alphabetically within the two groups. Even though most other comparative rankings of countries present their results in rank order, we think that doing so is inappropriate given the imprecise nature of our topic and the impossibility of accurately measuring national contentment and discontentment, so we are satisfied with simply identifying the top and bottom 20s. As we also explained in the introduction, we wanted our two lists of countries to be diverse in terms of regions of the world, major world cultures, and types of countries. We were never comfortable with the comparative rankings that are stacked at the top with prosperous and/or Western countries and heavy at the bottom with countries from the developing world, most especially from Africa. Happiness has a different geography, we think and believe, and we are happy to say that our research confirmed this, as we do indeed have a range of countries within both the most contented and least contented groups.

As can be seen, our list of the most contented countries includes representation from all the inhabited continents of the world, as well as from subregions within continents such as the Middle East, and Central America and the Caribbean. In addition, the list includes some of the world's largest countries (Canada, Australia), some of the smallest (Seychelles, the Bahamas), some of the richest (Singapore, Switzerland, Norway), and some countries that are fairly poor (Senegal, Tunisia). The least contented group is also diverse. Although there is no representation from North America and Oceania, as these are the two continents with the fewest countries, there is a balance from much of the rest of the world: Europe, Asia, Africa, Central America, and the Middle East, as well as the world's largest

Table 1.1

20 Most Contented Countries	20 Least Contented Countries
Australia	Afghanistan
Bahamas	Cambodia
Botswana	Democratic Republic of the Congo
Canada	El Salvador
Chile	Equatorial Guinea
Costa Rica	France
Denmark	Greece
Estonia	Haiti
Japan	Honduras
Netherlands	Liberia
New Zealand	Maldives
Norway	Mauritania
Oman	North Korea
Senegal	Russia
Seychelles	Saudi Arabia
Singapore	Sudan
Sweden	Syria
Switzerland	Turkmenistan
Tunisia	Uganda
Uruguay	Yemen

country (Russia), some small ones (Maldives, El Salvador), some prosperous countries (France, Saudi Arabia), and some poor countries (Haiti, Afghanistan, Equatorial Guinea). Both groups include representation from among the countries that are mostly Islamic (Senegal and Tunisia from the most contented group, and Yemen and Mauritania as examples from the least contented group). We are pleased to have this diversity, although disappointed that our research showed that the sources of discontentment in some countries are tied to prejudices against ethnic, religious, and other minorities and lack of social tolerance rather than to any poverty or lack of resources. In alphabetical order, we take France, Russia, and Saudi Arabia to task for this.

Even though we do not rank the top and bottom countries in detail, and decided to list the two groups of countries alphabetically, there is still the issue of which countries came close and may have been 21st or 22nd had there been a ranking.

We think that readers might be curious about this and want us to elaborate if only to extend credit to some other contented countries. In response, we say that if there had been a top 25 list of contented countries instead of just a top 20, prime candidates for consideration for the five new slots would have included Luxembourg, Latvia, Lithuania, Poland, Slovakia, and Finland from Europe, and Panama, Belize, Suriname, Morocco, Namibia, Mauritius, Taiwan, South Korea, and Palau. As we worked to winnow, we would have wanted to minimize the number of new entrants from Europe, because Europe is already well represented on the top 20 list, and would have been cautious in not having too many countries from the former Soviet Union and the former Soviet satellite countries in Eastern Europe. Our top 20 list already has Estonia, a former Soviet republic, as a representative of this group, so maybe any addition should come from the former satellite countries group, either Poland or Slovakia. Both countries are doing well in transition to a market economy, democracy, and formal affiliation with the European Union and NATO. Finland had been a top candidate for the top 20 list, but was edged out because there were other countries from the region such as Sweden and Norway already on the list. Our solution was to include Finland's capital Helsinki on the list of most contented cities in the world, but not to have Stockholm and Oslo, the capitals of Sweden and Norway, respectively, on that list even though they too are great cities with contented populations. However, our data did persuade us to list both country and major city on the respective most contented lists in the case of the Netherlands (Amsterdam) and Denmark (Copenhagen).

Readers might also be curious about which countries just missed the list of 20 least contented countries. Here, we can say that the People's Republic of China would be a prime candidate for an expanded list because of its discontented ethnic minorities such as Tibetans and Uyghurs, it abysmal pollution and environmental recklessness, and its various repressions and assaults against personal freedoms. China, however, is well represented on the list of 20 most discontented cities, with three cities: the capital Beijing, Chongqing, and Ürümqi. We also would have considered additional European countries for this list. The prime candidates would have been from the politically fragile Balkans region such as Albania, Kosovo, Macedonia, or Bulgaria, but since Greece is in the group of 20 least contented countries, the region is already represented. Other discontented countries include Israel (for its internal conflicts among Jewish citizens with different perspectives about the country, and for the poverty and plight of the country's many Palestinian residents), Nepal (especially in light of the massive earthquake that occurred on April 25, 2015, just before this writing), Myanmar (especially for the plight of its Rohingya minority), and Thailand (for its political unrest). African countries to be considered for any expanded bottom list would include Angola, Burundi, Rwanda, Guinea, and Togo, among others, while from Latin America we would look at Guatemala, Guyana, and perhaps even Brazil, which we see to be increasingly discontented with the current government, as well as discontented with recent drops in economic performance. Other problems in Brazil include heightened tensions related to problems of poverty and a widening social divide, as well as various environmental issues in the country's frontier regions, rainforests, mines, and overcrowded cities.

The pages ahead list each of our 20 most contented countries, followed by the 20 countries that we consider to be least contented. The reasons for our choices are given in the accompanying essays. First there is a definition of the country and its location in the world, and then paragraphs that explain why the country was selected for one or the other list. In many cases, we have our own observations about the countries from what we know about current events and from our own travels, but we also cite other rankings as appropriate to back up our choices. For some of the countries, the editors of this book have selected photographs to help illustrate our text. There are also some references and/or additional readings that are given for each of the countries.

THE 20 MOST CONTENTED COUNTRIES

AUSTRALIA

Australia is a large island country in Oceania in the Southern Hemisphere between the South Pacific and Indian Oceans, and south of the islands of Southeast Asia. Its nearest neighbors are New Zealand, Papua New Guinea, and Indonesia. It consists of a main island, also named Australia, that is large enough to be called a continent, plus Tasmania, a smaller island to the southeast of main part of the country, and numerous islands that are still smaller. The population is highly urban and is concentrated in coastal cities, especially in the southeast, while the interior, a large part of which is arid and is called the Outback, is sparsely populated. All told, Australia is the sixth-largest country in the world in area and the 51st largest in population, with a total of 23,786,400 inhabitants. The country once consisted of six crown colonies of Great Britain, led by New South Wales in the southeast where the city of Sydney was founded in 1788 as a penal settlement, but the six united into a federation in 1901 and declared independence. The country is officially called the Commonwealth of Australia. The country is an increasingly diverse society, with population with origins in many parts of the world, but it maintains particularly close cultural ties with the United Kingdom, and English is the de facto national language.

Australia is widely regarded to be one of the wealthiest and most livable countries in the world. It ranks second in the world after Norway in the United Nations Human Development Index 2014, and second in the world after Switzerland in average wealth. Furthermore, Australia has the world's 5th highest GDP per capita (nominal) and is the world's 12th largest economy. It was ranked #1 in the world in the Legatum Prosperity Index in 2008. Other notable rankings include #3 in the world in the 2010 Index of Economic Freedom by the Heritage Foundation, #9 out of 167 countries in the Democracy Index by the *Economist*, and #11 in the world out of 177 countries in the Corruption Perceptions Index by Transparency International. Australians feel closely engaged with the workings of government, and consistently turn out in high numbers to vote in elections. A recent turnout was an amazing 93% of eligible voters.

Australia also ranks highly in health care and education. Universal health care was introduced in 1975 and is now funded by a surcharge on income tax that provides citizens with access to excellent hospitals and clinics. The country has the fourth-highest life expectancy in the world, after Iceland, Japan, and Hong Kong: 79.5 years for males and 84.0 years for females. Schools are excellent too, and education is compulsory from age 5 to about age 16. The adult literacy rate in Australia is 99%. The country's universities have excellent reputations around the globe. A comparison of 34 countries in 11 wide-ranging categories of quality of life by the international Organization for Economic Cooperation and Development has ranked Australia in first place for at least two recent years in a row.

Australia's major cities are consistently ranked among the most livable in the world. Melbourne often tops global lists or is not far behind the #1 position. The city was ranked first in livability in the world by the *Economist* in 2011, 2012, and 2013. The *Economist* also considered Adelaide, Sydney, and Perth in its global top 10. All cities have excellent public services and infrastructure, parklands, hiking and biking trails, and wide varieties of good housing and fine neighborhoods. Residents can choose between urban lifestyles based on walking, bicycles, and public transit, or they can live in lower-density settings in suburbs and depend on personal automobiles. Sydney, Perth, and some other cities have superb beaches too. Canberra is an exceptionally beautiful planned capital city. In this book we discuss Melbourne and Perth as two of the world's 20 most contented cities. Water supply has become a problem in a number of cities because of growing demands and localized drought, and it has been necessary to enforce rationing of water and reduce waste.

One of the key strengths of Australia is that is a large country that is rich in resources, and that is still lightly settled. There is a frontier mentality that sees the future with optimism, growth, and boundless opportunity, and that believes that the best days for this already very fine country are yet to come. There are wide open spaces that have not yet been developed, and could potentially contain great resources. Australians are very proud of their land, and know that it has brought them a high standard of living and considerable wealth. The country has trading partners around the globe, but in recent decades it has profited especially from exports to Japan, and then in much great amounts to China. The main exports include iron ore, coal, and other mining products, as well as manufactured goods and products from the farms. The country is the world's fifth-largest exporter of wine. Tourism is increasing in Australia, especially from East and Southeast Asia, and also adds to the economy. In addition to the beaches, there is the spectacular Great Barrier Reef off the coast in the northeast, the world's biggest and most diverse reef ecosystem, as well as tropical and equatorial environments in the far north, deserts in the west-center, and lush forests and temperate climate in the southeast.

FURTHER READING

Bryson, Bill, *In a Sunburned Country* (New York: Random House, 2007).
Hughes, Robert, *The Fatal Shore: The Epic of Australia's Founding* (New York: Vintage, 1988).
McLean, Ian W., *Why Australia Prospered: The Shifting Sources of Economic Growth* (Princeton, NJ: Princeton University Press, 2012).

BAHAMAS

The Bahamas is a country of about 700 small islands and cays in the North Atlantic Ocean to the east of the state of Florida in the United States and north of Cuba, its nearest neighbors. It is part of the British Commonwealth of nations and shares many cultural characteristics with islands in the Caribbean that still are or once were also parts of the British Empire, although technically the islands are located outside the Caribbean Sea. The country is one of only two in the world whose official name begins with "The," although simply "Bahamas" is also an accepted form. (The other "the" country is the Gambia, also once part of the British Empire.) More formally, the Bahamas is named the Commonwealth of the Bahamas. The word "Bahamas" is said to be from the Spanish *baja mar*, or "shallow sea."

It is believed that Columbus landed on one of the Bahamas Islands during his historic 1492 voyage. The indigenous inhabitants were called Lucayans, a branch of the Taino people, but they were shipped to be slaves on Spanish Hispaniola and succumbed to European diseases. The islands were then very sparsely populated for more than 100 years until 1648 when British settlers began to arrive. Because pirates, including the notorious Blackbeard, were using the islands as a base for their raids, the British Crown took an interest in securing them and made the Bahamas into a colony in 1718. After the American Revolution, many British Loyalists settled on the islands, bringing their African slaves with them. Other settlers included Africans who had been captives on illegal slave ships, runaway slaves and freed slaves from the United States, and Black Seminoles from Florida. Slavery was abolished on the islands in 1834, almost 20 years before the 1863 Emancipation Proclamation in the United States. The Bahamas achieved independence from Great Britain in 1973.

Today, about 90% of the population of the Bahamas are the descendants of slaves or free Africans. Afro-Bahamians, as they are called, comprise the large majority of this population and are the main ethnic group, but the 90% figure also includes a large minority of immigrants from Haiti and their offspring, numbering about 80,000, who had arrived from that poor Caribbean country much more recently. There is also a large minority with European origins living in the Bahamas, including descendants of British settlers who had arrived in 1648, and more recent immigrants from the United Kingdom, other European countries, and Americans of European origin. Their numbers include many people who are well-off financially, prosperous retirees, and famous celebrities who were attracted to islands that offer extra measures of privacy. The term "White Bahamians" applies to those who are citizens or long-term Bahamas residents. All told, the population of the Bahamas is about 319,031 (2013 estimate). The largest settlement is the capital city Nassau, population 254,132 (2009 estimate), located on the island of New Providence, while Freeport and West End on Grand Bahama Island (populations 47,085 and 13,004, respectively) account for most of the rest of the nation's total. Most of the other 700 islands of the Bahamas are very lightly populated or are completely uninhabited.

The Bahamas is a relatively prosperous country, ranking at #32 out of 183 countries in GDP per capita as reported by the International Monetary Fund, #39 out of 187 countries as reported by the World Bank, and #38 out of 193 countries and territories as reported by the United Nations. By all measures, the Bahamas is the wealthiest country in the Americas after the United States and Canada. The economy of the country depends heavily on tourism, which accounts for about 60% of the GDP and employs about one-half of the labor force, and secondarily on banking and finance, which account for about 15% of GDP. The country offers various tax incentives and other benefits to foreign financial concerns in order to have them open office in financial companies, particularly in Nassau. Tourism in the Bahamas is based on a pleasant climate year-round, nice beaches, unspoiled and very private islands, and sparkling clear ocean waters that are perfect for snorkeling and other activities. There are many unspoiled coral reefs. Sport fishing is also a popular attraction. There are many marinas on the island, with impressive yachts and smaller pleasure craft from ports in Florida and elsewhere on the U.S. Atlantic Coast and Gulf coasts, as well as from other countries. Nassau is a very popular cruise ship harbor for the approximately 60% of all international visitors who arrive by boat. Whenever a large ship arrives, Nassau becomes crowded and hectic, as tourists take over the center of the city for shopping and snapshots during the relatively short time that their ship is in port, while vendors and shop-keepers work with extra diligence to not miss an opportunity for a sale.

Contentment in the Bahamas is based on the nice weather and beaches, even for the locals, but also on a strong and growing economy, stable, democratic government, and a high standard of living as compared to many countries around the world that were once foreign colonial possessions. According to a study by Adrian G. White at the University of Leicester, the Bahamas ranks at #5 in the world out of 178 countries in the Satisfaction with Life Index. The United Nations Human Development Index ranks the Bahamas at #51 out of 187 countries and fourth-highest in the Americas after the United States, Canada, and Cuba. Nearness to the United States and Canada and their flows of tourists who stay for short periods only but spend money with energy has been helpful, as has the appeal of the Bahamas to some of the world's rich and famous, who not only contribute to the local economy via their spending, but also by adding the kind of prestige to the islands that attracts other visitors. However, high-end tourism drives up prices, especially for land and housing, which brings strain to local population and produces dual economies between visitors and residents. The country enjoys good schooling and health care, has a high literacy rate of 95.6%, and a high-side

The Bahamas depends on tourism and visitors from large cruise ships for a big part of its economy. The photo was taken off Nassau, the island country's capital, on January 13, 2013, and shows the *Carnival Dream*, the largest ship in the fleet of Carnival Cruise Lines, as it enters port. (fallbrook/iStockphoto.com)

life expectancy (76.5 years for both genders combined, ranking #56 in the world out of 198 countries). Local tradition and passions combine African, Caribbean, British, and American influences, for example, as participants and fan bases in cricket and baseball alike, as well as for soccer-football and American football. The culture also includes rich storytelling traditions, and a colorful street festival of music, dance, costumes, and art called Junkaroo that is held on various holidays in the year.

FURTHER READING

Collinwood, Dean, "Terra Incognita: Research on the Modern Bahamian Society," *Journal of Caribbean Studies*, 1, 2–3, Winter 1981, pp. 284–297.

Smith, Larry, *The Bahamas: Portrait of an Archipelago* (Oxford: Macmillan Education, 2004).

BOTSWANA

Botswana is a landlocked country in southern Africa that is bordered by South Africa, Namibia, and Zimbabwe, and with a very short border with Zambia in the north. Much of the country is part of the Kalahari Desert, and most territory is very sparsely settled. According to the 2011 census, the total population is 2,038,228. It was estimated to be about 2.16 million in 2013. Most of the population is concentrated in the south of country near the border with South Africa, where climate is more humid. The capital city, Gaborone, is in this zone and, with a population of approximately 232,000, is the country's largest urban center. Gaborone's metropolitan area population is nearly double that total. The country was previously a British protectorate called Bechuanaland. It took its present name with independence in 1966. Citizens of the country are called Batswana, while one citizen is a Motswana in the Setswana language where prefixes are very important. The main ethnic group, comprising about 80% of the population, is the Tswana people. The official languages are English and Setswana.

Botswana is not a country without serious problems, but we include it in our list of 20 most contented countries in the world because it stands out in Africa as a country with a stable, democratic government, and as one that has made considerable economic progress since independence. Poverty still haunts too many Batswana, but the economy is growing rapidly and economic well-being is spreading within the population more than in most other African nations. The United Nations Human Development Index for Botswana ranks at #109 out of 187 nations in the world (2013). While this is below the global median, the country is #1 in HDI in continental Sub-Saharan Africa (the Sub-Saharan island nation of Seychelles ranks ahead of Botswana, as do four countries in the north of Africa).

The per capita GDP at purchasing power parity has risen rapidly, and is ranked at #74 in the world out of 187 countries by the International Monetary Fund, #70 in the world out of 185 countries by the World Bank, and #65 in the world out of 195 countries by the U.S. Central Intelligence Agency (all for 2013). In each of these cases, Botswana is ahead of most developing countries in the world and among the leaders in Africa.

We also note that Botswana ranks highly in economic freedom as measured by the Heritage Foundation in cooperation with the *Wall Street Journal*: in 2014 the country was #27 in the world on this index out of 178 countries that were ranked, and #1 in continental Sub-Saharan Africa, second in the region only to the small island country of Mauritius. Other Botswana pluses are that it is the least corrupt country in Africa and #30 out of 177 countries worldwide as measured by Transparency International (2013), and the best governed country in Africa as measured by the Legatum Prosperity Index (also 2013). For the people of Botswana, such plusses have resulted in great improvements to education nationwide, and significant increases in rates of literacy, improvements to public health. There are also infrastructure improvements such as better roads, wider distribution of electricity, fresh water, and other public services. However, the HIV/AIDS epidemic has hit Botswana especially hard, with an estimated infection rate of 24% for adults in 2006, the second-highest rate in the world after that in nearby Swaziland. As a result, life expectancy at birth is only about 54.06 years (2011 census), although that number represents an increase from the recent past when the AIDS crisis was even more devastating.

The economy of Botswana is tied to the unique riches of the land. Mining is the single largest contributor to the economy, especially of diamonds, and accounts for about 40% of national GDP. The country has four diamond mines in operation and produces more gem diamonds than any country in the world, accounting for about 25% of the world's supply. Other minerals available are nickel and copper. The country also has a strong tourism sector. It accounts for about 12% of GDP and is growing as Botswana strives to diversify its economic base. There are many national parks and game reserves, with the main safari destinations being Moremi Game Reserve, Chobe National Park, and the spectacular Okavango Delta, a large inland delta within the Kalahari Desert that is especially rich in wildlife. Ecotourism and sustainable development of the tourism economy are increasingly important projects for Botswana. The goals are to protect natural ecosystems as tourism grows and for economic benefits to reach local populations. The small village of Khwai, population 400, near the Moremi Game Reserve in the north of the country is a well-known example of enlightened tourism planning in practice. Despite the importance of mining and tourism, as well as the growth of Gaborone as a prosperous center of finance and other services, more than one-half of all Batswana still depend on agriculture for a living, especially subsistence farming and herding on marginal lands. Only about 0.7% of the total land is arable, so available farmlands are crowded and overused, requiring investment in soil and water conservation practices, and most farmers are poor. Agriculture contributes about 2.8% of total GDP, most by exports of beef.

According to many experts, much of Sub-Saharan Africa has turned a corner in economic development and is now beginning a happy rise out of poverty, and Botswana has been a leading light in the region. More countries need to follow Botswana's example of honest, transparent government, political stability, democracy, and opportunities for citizens to better their lives. It helps a lot to have diamonds in your economy, but it is more important to share a nation's wealth across the population, as Botswana has been doing more and more, no matter what the basis of the nation's economy.

FURTHER READING

Hillbom, Ellen, "Botswana: A Development-Oriented Gate-Keeping State," *African Affairs*, 111, 442, January 2012, pp. 67–89.

Jerven, Morten, "Accounting for the African Growth Miracle: The Official Evidence—Botswana 1965–1995," *Journal of South African Studies*, 36, 1, 2010, pp. 73–94.

Muchapandwa, Edwin and Jesper Stage, "The Economic Impact of Tourism in Botswana, Namibia, and South Africa: Is Poverty Subsiding?" *Natural Resources Forum*, 37, 2, 2013, pp. 80–89.

CANADA

Canada is the world's second-largest country in total area and fourth-largest in land surface area, as well as the country with the largest surface area of water within its territory, as it contains many lakes and the huge Hudson Bay. It is the largest country in North America, and shares the world's longest international border with the United States, its neighbor to the south and in the northwest where the country borders the state of Alaska. It is comprised of 10 provinces and three territories, and has many coastal islands in its three oceans, the Atlantic, the Pacific, and the Arctic, including some of the world's largest. Canada's population is 35,675,834 (2014 estimate), and grows rapidly because of a generous immigration policy. Most of this population resides in the southern part of the country near the border with the contiguous 48 states of the United States because the climate is more temperate. To the north, Canada is very lightly settled because of long and harsh winters and unfavorable ground conditions during the warm months. The country ranks as the 37th most populated country in the world, but because of vast empty spaces in the north and the mountainous west, it ranks only 228th in population density out of 242 sovereign states and dependent territories.

Canada is widely acclaimed as one of the world's most livable countries. It has a high standard of living, excellent services, honest democratic government, and a tradition of tolerance and opportunity for all. It ranks #8 in the world out of 187 countries in the United Nations Human Development Index, #5 out of 142 in the Legatum Prosperity Index, #10 in nominal per capital income, #15 out of 144 countries in global competiveness as reported by the World Economic Forum, and #6 in the 2015 Index of Economic Freedom by the Heritage Foundation. Income inequality is relatively low. The country is one of only ten in the world with an AAA rating by Standard & Poor's. The Reputation Institute, a global consulting firm that works out of New York and Copenhagen, ranked Canada as the most reputable country in the world from the 50 that were considered, meaning that it scored at the very top in "people's trust, admiration, respect and affinity."

In 2015, the economy of Canada ranked as the 11th largest in the world, with a nominal GDP totaling US$1.79 trillion. The country was once a nation of farmers, but the national economy has been transformed into one that is highly globalized and dependent on trade. Exports of food products, including grain from the vast farmlands of the prairie provinces in the interior and fish from both the Atlantic and Pacific coasts, are still important exports, but so too are various mineral resources, timber, and many manufactured products. Most importantly, Canada is one of a few developed nations to be a net exporter of energy resources, including oil, gas, and hydroelectricity. The Canadian Arctic is a vast storehouse of natural resources that can supply Canada's needs and its export economy for a long time into the future. Canada has planned its resource development more carefully than most other countries in terms of environmental impacts and the impact of development on the lives and cultures of its people, particularly vulnerable indigenous populations in the north, than most other resource-rich countries. The largest economic sector in Canada is services, which employs about three-quarters of the workforce. High educational standards prepare the population for the economy of the future, and can be considered to be yet another of Canada's resources. The population is reportedly the most educated in the world, with about 51% of all adults having college or university degrees.

Canada has one of the most diverse populations of any country in the world. Its citizens come from every country, and comprise a wide spectrum of ethnic, religious, and racial categories. The country has a reputation not just for tolerance, but also for being welcoming. It has one of the highest per capita immigration rates in the world, with about one in five residents being foreign-born. Many immigrants are visible minorities, especially South Asians, Chinese, and blacks from Africa, the Caribbean, and the United States. Cities such as Toronto, Montreal, and Vancouver are some of the most diverse cities in the world in terms of population makeup. In addition to poor immigrants looking for building a better life for themselves, Canada attracts wealthy immigrants from poor or unstable countries looking to lead a better life. A fascinating book on this subject tells about Chinese "millionaire migrants" to Vancouver. Unfortunately, the poorest citizens in Canada are the descendants of the original Canadians, the nation's aboriginals or First Nations people as they are called in the country. They comprise about 4% of the population and about 600 recognized First Nations governments or bands. Canada has been especially generous in accepting refugees from parts of the world that were torn by war or other strife, and accounts for about 10% of global refugee resettlements.

Canadians take great pride in their country and its fine reputation around the globe. When they travel, many wear the national maple leaf symbol to show that they are proud to be Canadian. The Canadian passport is one of the most respected in the world. Canada attracts international tourists too, as it is renowned for great natural beauty in the Rocky Mountain West, the Atlantic and Pacific Coasts, and historic Quebec, Nova Scotia, and Prince Edward Island, and its safe, lively, and richly diverse urban centers. Favorable global attention on Canada was heightened when the country hosted the Summer Olympics in 1976 in Montreal and the Winter Olympics in 1988 in Calgary and in 2010 in Vancouver and Whistler, British Columbia. Many people around the world also respect Canada for its principled stands in recent decades with respect to wars and troublesome dictators

First Nations dancers perform for the National Aboriginal Awareness Celebration at Canada Place, Vancouver, British Columbia. These particular performers are from the Kwakwaka'wakw Nation of northern Vancouver Island. (Howesjwe/Dreamstime.com)

around the world, most recently against aggression by Vladimir Putin's Russia against its independent neighbor countries.

FURTHER READING

Adams, Susan, "The World's Most Reputable Countries, 2013," *Forbes*, June 27, 2013, http://www.forbes.com/sites/susanadams/2013/06/27/the-worlds-most-reputable-countries-2013/.

Bone, Robert, *The Regional Geography of Canada* (Don Mills, Ontario: Oxford University Press, 2010).

Cohen, Andrew, *The Unfinished Canadian: The People We Are* (Toronto: McClelland & Stewart, 2007).

Ley, David, *Millionaire Migrants: Trans-Pacific Lifelines* (Malden, MA: Wiley-Blackwell, 2010).

Thomas, David M. and David N. Biette, *Canada and the United States: Differences That Count*, 4th edition (Toronto: University of Toronto Press, 2014).

CHILE

Chile is a country on the west coast of South America's southern cone that has a famously long and narrow shape. The country extends north to south for some 2,670 miles (4,300 km) from the border with Peru to the southern tip of the continent and Isla Grande de Tierra del Fuego, a large island that it shares with Argentina, and measures only about 217 miles (350 km) at its widest point east to west. The unusual shape is because the boundary is drawn along the high crest of the Andes Mountains, which it also shares with Argentina, and the eastern shores of the South Pacific Ocean. The coastline is deeply indented with fjords and other inlets, as well as countless islands. The famous Easter Island located some 2,291 miles (3,687 km) from Chile's shore is also part of the country. The northern reaches of the country are part of the Atacama Desert, a difficult terrain with great mineral wealth, especially copper and nitrate. The population of Chile is 18,006,407 (2015 estimate), and its capital and largest city is Santiago, located in the north-center of the country, with a population of more than 5.1 million.

Chile was part of Spain's colonial empire in the New World until after it declared independence in 1818 and was recognized as a sovereign state in 1844. The country was settled by Spaniards who displaced and intermarried with the indigenous inhabitants, and later by other immigrants from Europe, although not in the same large numbers as European immigration to Argentina or Brazil. Much of the country's history since independence has alternated between periods of stability and periods of conflict, including a war in 1879–1883 with Peru and Bolivia and a near-war later with Argentina, and with periods of democracy and periods of dictatorial rule during which there was undue favoritism for a class of wealthy elites. The period 1973–1990 was especially difficult in Chile, as strong-armed ruler General Augusto Pinochet Ugarte took power in 1973 in a United States–aided coup against country's elected president Salvador Allende, the first democratically elected Marxist leader of a Latin American nation, and then consolidated his grip on the country. Under Pinochet, many Chileans were murdered by the army's helicopter-borne "caravan of death" that traversed the country to root out political adversaries, and more than 2,000 others were killed later. Tens of thousands of opponents of the right-wing government were victims of state-sponsored torture. Pinochet remained in office until 1990, after which Chile returned to an elected government. At the time of his death in 2006, Pinochet was facing as many as 300 criminal charges against him for human rights violations, corruption, and tax evasion.

Happily, Chile is now democratic and stable, as well as one of Latin America's most prosperous nations. It ranks at #1 in Latin America in the United Nations Human Development Index for 2013 (and #40 out of 187 countries worldwide); #1 in Latin America in quality of life as reported by the *Economist*; #1 in Latin America and #31 out of 111 countries worldwide in *Newsweek's* "word's best countries" reportage; and #1 in Latin America in the Index of Economic Freedom for 2014 by the Heritage Foundation. Likewise, *Forbes* rated the country as the best in Latin America for doing business in 2013 (and 22nd out of 145 countries worldwide). Freedom House rates the country as "free." Other high rankings are #3 in Latin America in the Democracy Index for 2014 by the *Economist* and #32 out of 162 countries worldwide; #2 in Latin America in the 2013 Corruption Perceptions Index by Transparency International and #22 out of 175 countries worldwide; and #2 in Latin America and #33 out of 191 countries worldwide in overall performance of the country's health systems as reported by the World Health Organization.

Chile's early wealth came from exploitation of nitrate resources, but now it is copper that generates the most wealth. The largest copper mine in the world is Escondida in the north of the country; it produces about 5% of global copper ore supplies. Copper mining accounts for about 20% of Chilean GDP and 60% of exports. The economy has also been based on agriculture and ranching, making use of different climate regimes that vary with latitude north-south and with elevation. Leading agricultural exports include wool, fruits, and wine. There is also a large fishing industry. The country's bigger cities, specifically the capital Santiago, the nearby city of Valparaíso where the National Congress is located, and Concepción, are among the most livable in South America, and have excellent services, good public transportation, and relatively low crime rates. These cities do have poor neighborhoods, however. Santiago's metro system is the most extensive in Latin America, while its modern financial district sports a number of impressive new high-rises and has the clever moniker "Sanhattan." Valparaíso is on the coast and has exceptionally beautiful architectural ensemble for which it has been

A street market in downtown Santiago, Chile's capital and largest city. On certain days of the week, certain streets in the cities of Chile are closed to vehicular traffic and become day-long farmers' markets where urban residents can buy fresh foods at lower prices. (Francisco Javier Espuny/Dreamstime.com)

designated as a UNESCO World Heritage Site. We discuss this city elsewhere in this book as one of the world's 20 most contented urban centers.

Chileans have exceptional recreation opportunities, as no one in the country lives far from the sea and no one is far from high mountains. Hiking and camping in the highlands is a popular pastime, while the highest peaks attract some of the world's most demanding climbers. There are excellent ski resorts that attract skiers from the Northern Hemisphere during their warm months. Tennis is a very popular sport, while the country's greatest passions are for football (soccer). The Chilean national team has been a frequent participant in FIFA World Cup tournaments, and often achieves success.

FURTHER READING

Constable, Pamela and Artur Valenzuela, *A Nation of Enemies: Chile under Pinochet* (New York: W.W. Norton & Company, 1993).

Han, Clara, *Life in Debt: Times of Care and Violence in Neoliberal Chile* (Berkeley: University of California Press, 2012).

Wheeler, Sara, *Travels in a Thin Country: A Journey through Chile* (New York: Modern Library, 1999).

COSTA RICA

Costa Rica is a small, beautiful country of a little more than 4.5 million people in Central America that faces both the Caribbean Sea (Atlantic Ocean) and the Pacific Ocean. Its name, which dates to the quest for gold and other wealth by Spanish explorers in the early 16th century, means "rich coast." The country is technically classified as a developing country because its average income levels fall somewhat below the conventional cutoff (US$11,905 per capita Gross National Income in 2012) that distinguishes between wealthier countries and poorer ones, and because it has a high poverty rate estimated to be about 23%. However, Costa Rica has a great many pluses in other areas and qualifies easily for our list of the 20 most contented countries in the world. It ranks #12 in the world and #1 in Latin America and among developing countries worldwide in the World Happiness Report published by the United Nations Sustainable Development Solutions Network (2013).

Costa Rica is a rich land indeed. Its volcanic soils are highly fertile and well watered, and support a strong rural economy based on growing coffee beans, bananas, and pineapples for export. Its mountains and tropical rainforests are a paradise of biodiversity and beauty. A full 25% of the country's land area is set aside as a national park land or other protected areas, a higher fraction than in

Costa Rica is known for its natural beauty and spectacular vistas. This is the volcano Arenal, one of 15 volcanoes in the country, and one of the six that are known to be active. (Roman Cybriwsky)

any country in the world. As a result, Costa Rica is a leading destination for ecotourism and a pioneer in this relatively new field. Costa Rica also has spectacular seashores and beautiful beaches, especially on the Pacific Ocean coast. This too contributes to the tourism economy, which has grown recently to be bigger in the national economy than agriculture. The country is the most visited country in Central America, with the largest numbers of tourists coming from the United States and Canada. Other than Caribbean island nations, Costa Rica is also the most heavily visited country in Latin America in proportion to size and population. Mountainous Corcovado National Park and the spectacular Tortuguero ("full of turtles") National Park on the coast are the country's leading national parks. Other emerging aspects of Costa Rica's economy include various growth industries: for example, the manufacture of pharmaceuticals, financial outsourcing, and software development, as well as retirement communities for expatriates, again mostly from the United States and Canada.

Costa Rica pays extraordinary attention to protection of its environmental treasures. Not only is much of the country designated national park land, the country is also a world leader in environmental sustainability. In 2007, it was the first country in the world to embark on a program to become carbon-neutral. More than 90% of Costa Rica's electricity is generated by renewable energy sources, most notably from hydropower. Another progressive characteristic is a total ban since 2012 on recreational hunting. Because of its progressive environmental policies, Costa Rica is ranked first in the Americas and fifth in the world on the Environmental Performance Index (2012), and first in the world on the New Economic Foundation in its Happy Planet Index (2009 and again in 2012). In 2010, the Environmental Performance Index that is calculated at Yale University ranked Costa Rica third in the world among 163 nations and first in Latin America. Ticos, as Costa Rican natives call themselves, take pride in the beauty and richness of their country, and enthusiastically support strong environmental legislation and sustainable living.

Another plus for Costa Rica is its health care system. The national Social Insurance Administration provides comprehensive health care coverage for most Costa Ricans, including those living in isolated rural areas, and manages a wide network of hospitals and medical clinics across the country. Immunization levels for children exceed 90%, and life expectancy has been on the rise. In 2010, the country's life expectancy at birth was 79.3 years, the highest rate in Latin America, the second highest in the Americas (after Canada), and therefore higher (but not by much) than that for the United States. Costa Rica's Nicoyan Peninsula (Pacific coast) has been identified as one of only five localized "Blue Zones" in the world where an unusually large number of residents lives to be more than 100. Life style and diet appear to be the principal contributing factors for such longevity. Because of excellent medical services at lower cost, Costa Rica has become an important destination for medical tourism.

Costa Rica is also known for its political stability and democracy, especially in comparison to other Central American nations where coups and counter-coups have occurred again and again. The lone violent blemishes in Costa Rica's modern history were the rebellions in 1917–1919 against an unpopular dictator and a 44-day civil war in 1948 about a disputed presidential election that left 2,000 dead, but other than those events Costa Rica has been peaceful and stable. Immediately after the conclusion of the civil war, Costa Rica abolished its military forces and is now one of only 15 countries in the world without an army, among which it is by far the largest and by far the most populous, as all of the other army-less countries are micro-states and small island nations. A constitution written in 1953 protects citizens' rights and guarantees democratic processes. Voter turnouts are high for elections, even though much of the population lives in small rural settlements. In 2010, the *Economist's* Intelligence Unit ranked Costa Rica 24th in the world out of 167 countries in democracy and 26th out of 149 in global peace. Also in 2010, Reporters without Borders ranked the country 29th out of 178 countries in freedoms of the press.

Costa Rica's capital and largest city is San Jose. Its population is just under 300,000 (2011). It is the hub of a sprawling metropolitan area in the Central Valley that has a population of nearly 2 million, nearly half of the country's total. San Jose is a pleasant city with beautiful mountain views and green neighborhoods, but it suffers from traffic congestion, air pollution, and high crime. It is, however, a safer capital than most others in Central America and a popular destination for international travelers. In addition to being the center of Costa Rican government, the city is the hub of the country's economy and transportation systems, and a leading cultural center. It was founded by Spanish colonists in 1738, and still has an historic, Spanish ambience in its older neighborhoods.

FURTHER READING

Miller, Andrew P., *Ecotourism Development in Costa Rica: The Search for Oro* Verde (Lanham, MD: Lexington Books, 2012).

Palmer, Steven and Iván Molina (eds.), *The Costa Rica Reader: History, Culture, Politics* (Durham, NC: Duke University Press, 2004).

DENMARK

Denmark is a small, prosperous country between the North and Baltic Seas in north-central Europe that ranks at or very near the top on virtually all rankings of countries of the world according to measures of quality of life and general happiness. One could arguably make a case that it is the world's best country. In 2010, it was ranked #1 among the world's happiest countries in a survey by

Gallup Poll survey, and in 2013 it was # 1 again in the United Nations "World Happiness Report." Other distinctions are that the United Nations Development Program ranks Denmark as first out of 182 nations in its Gini index of equality of incomes (2010); the Gallup World Poll has it first among 155 countries in its World's Happiest Countries ranking (2009); and a University Leicester study has the country first out of 178 countries in terms of residents' satisfaction with life (2006). In addition, the country is #8 out of 179 countries in Index of Economic Freedom (Heritage Foundation, 2011); #3 out of 167 in Democracy Index (the *Economist*, 2010); #1 out of 180 in Corruptions Perception Index (i.e., the world's least corrupt country as measured by Transparency International, 2010); and #4 out of 153 countries in the Global Peace Index (Institute for Economics and Peace [2011]). There are many other examples from other rankings as well. Denmark never gets even a middle score, much less a bad one, as for this country the grades are always straight As.

Perhaps the most impressive distinction is that even though Denmark is a small country, it is a recognized world leader in efforts to live sustainably and protect the global environment. The country was one of the first to establish a cabinet-level ministry for environment (in 1971), and in 1973 was the first nation in the world to pass sweeping legislation for environmental protection. There are many environmental research institutions in Denmark with funding from the national government, the European Union, and Danish corporations; and Copenhagen and other cities are frequent venues for international conferences on environmental topics. The country ranks highly on the Yale University Environmental Sustainability Index, although at #26 from 146 countries (2005), it is not at the very top. This is probably because Denmark has its own deposits of oil and natural gas, which it exploits as well as exports, and because a sizable fraction of its electricity is derived from the burning of coal. Even so, the country is a world leader in renewable wind energy and produces more than one-quarter of its electrical power from wind turbines. Power derived from wind is integrated into the national electricity grid, and helps to run electric motor vehicles, where Denmark is once again among the world leaders. Also with respect to environment, Denmark is one of the world's leaders in bicycle usage per capita, and Copenhagen, its capital and largest city, which we recognize elsewhere in this book to be one of the world's most content urban centers, is acknowledged to be the world's #1 bicycling city.

Likewise, Denmark is world leader in global peacekeeping and efforts to advance democracy and human rights. As a member of the European Union, NATO, and the United Nations, the country has contributed more than its share to efforts in trouble spots around the globe, including Afghanistan, Iraq, Kosovo, and Lebanon. Danes are justifiably proud of their international efforts, and consider that the financial and human sacrifices that they make are appropriate given the high standard of living they enjoy in comparison to most other countries.

The social services that Danes enjoy are first-rate. Health care is considered to be a basic human right, and is available free to everyone, funded by taxes. As a result, life expectancy is high (79.5 years at birth, ranking 37 among 193 nations in 2012), although not as high as other Nordic countries because of higher rates of smoking and obesity. According to a study of Copenhagen residents, those who bicycle an average of 30 minutes per day extend their life expectancy by a full two years. There are generous benefits for mothers and fathers at the birth of the child, including paid leaves from work, return access to previous jobs for new mothers, even years after parental leave, and free or low-cost child care. Denmark was one of the first countries in the world to recognize women's rights to vote (in 1915), and is at the very top among nations in the world in gender equity in access to employment and rates of pay. There is also a culture of tolerance in Denmark for religious and ethnic differences, sexual orientation, and other aspects of lifestyle and personal identity. The strong sense of social responsibility that Danes exhibit with respect to the environment and global security is also evident in a culture of participation at local levels to make community life better, and for neighbors to take care of one another. The sense of neighborliness is enhanced by local gatherings such as community meetings, festivals, and other events, and effective public spaces such as neighborhood parks and shopping streets where neighbors routinely see one another and pause for greetings and conversation. Not surprisingly, voting participation among Danes is extraordinarily high: in a recent national election (September 2011), voter turnout was 87.7%! Such a high number indicates that people feel connected to government and that they have a voice in their country's affairs.

Other sources of contentment in Denmark are the country's general wealth and high income levels, low unemployment, and opportunities for individual to change jobs, advance in chosen careers, and succeed in business. Additionally, Danes enjoy long paid vacations and travel the world widely. Their country ranks fourth among 174 countries in the world in per capita Gross National Income, US$59,870 (2012). It also enjoys clean, beautiful, and efficiently run cities, an efficient transportation system (both by rail and by road), ample coastline and many beaches (Denmark consists of an irregularly shaped peninsula named Jutland that is the body of the country and an archipelago of 407 nearby islands, 70 of which are inhabited), and a picturesque and productive agricultural landscape. The climate is temperate, with mild winters and summers that are never too hot. The northerly location of the country means that summer days are very long and can be savored, but that winter days are correspondingly short. The abbreviated winter sunlight can cause depression, but Danes have cultivated a "culture of coziness" that they call *hygge* that elevates people's moods when darkness is long. This includes attention to warmth, comfortable settings, and quality time with family, friends, and lovers, as well as enjoyment with good wine, chocolate, coffee, or tea, and nice, long baths.

FURTHER READING

Kingsley, Patrick, *How to Be Danish: A Journey to the Cultural Heart of Denmark* (New York: Marble Arch Press, 2014).

Russell, Helen, *A Year of Living Danishly: My Twelve Months Unearthing the Secrets of the World's Happiest Country* (London: Icon Books, 2015).

ESTONIA

Estonia is a small country on the Baltic Sea that is bordered by Russia to the east and Latvia to the south, and that neighbors Finland across the Gulf of Finland to the north. Its population is only about 1.3 million, nearly 70% of whom are ethnic Estonians and about 25% Russians. The capital and largest city is Tallinn, with a population of about 434,000. The country was a reluctant part of the Soviet Union from the time of a hostile takeover in 1939 until the Soviet Union collapsed and independence was restored in 1991. The United States and many other democratic countries never recognized Estonia and the other two Baltic republics of the Soviet Union, Latvia and Lithuania, as legally parts of the USSR. A landmark event in the process of restoring independence was the so-called Singing Revolution of 1989 in which hundreds of thousands of Estonians, Latvians, and Lithuanians formed a human chain to express collective opposition to Soviet rule. Estonia became a member of the United Nations in 1991 and joined both NATO and the European Union in 2004. In 2011, the country adopted the euro as its official currency. The country's principal language, Estonian, is closely related to Finnish.

One reason for listing Estonia as an especially content country is, very simply, that it is no longer part of the Soviet Union. It has successfully integrated with the Europe and the West since independence, turning its back on its neighbor and former occupier, Russia. Estonians never accepted Soviet rule and the forced russification that accompanied it, and are fully content to be independent. This is one of the main points of the fascinating and highly educational Museum of Occupations in Tallinn. Surveys indicate that the large Russian minority in Estonia is generally content too, and that despite the fact that they or their parents or grandparents were made to emigrate to Estonia in order to russify the country, the vast majority of them have no desires to leave or to live in Russia. Estonia's closest links are now with the West. For example, the country's leading trade partners are Finland, Sweden, and Germany, and it is via the West that the country had achieved new levels of prosperity and freedoms. Many Estonians feel threatened anew by Russia during this time (2014–2015) of Russia's war of aggression in Ukraine and general saber-rattling by Russia's President Vladimir Putin, but the common enemy draws them closer as a nation and closer to powerful allies in the West.

Even though Estonia is small and not especially rich in natural resources, it has managed to attain a high standard of living and is referred to as a "tiger" in the Baltic Sea region because of an expanding economy. Its major mining resource is oil shale, which produces about 90% of the country's electricity, albeit with substantial environmental disruption. The country exports food products, wood and paper, textiles, and machinery. Other sources of income are tourism to the beautiful Baltic coast and beaches, and to Tallinn, a modern and comfortable city with a large and intact historic medieval urban center and many museums and cultural attractions. Tartu, Estonia's second-largest city and home of the historic and prestigious University of Tartu, is also a popular tourist destination. Estonia is famous as well as an especially Internet-savvy nation, thanks largely to the Tiigrihüpe project ("Tiger's Leap") project that the Estonian government initiated in 1996 to extend computer usage and information technology network infrastructure as widely as possible in the country. More than other countries, the government of Estonia works electronically, that is, via e-government. The globally popular Skype software is a product of Estonia. According to speedtest.net, Estonia has one of the fastest Internet download speeds in the world.

Estonia has achieved many other favorable rankings in comparisons with other countries. The country is ranked 1st in the world out of 47 countries by Freedom House in Internet Freedom (2012); 11th in the world out of 157 countries in the Index of Economic Freedom (2014); 11th in the world out of 187 countries by Reporters Without Borders in the Press Freedom Index (2011–2012); and 1st in the world out of 159 countries in the State of the World Liberty Index (2006). Furthermore, Estonia is 33rd out of 110 countries in the Legatum Prosperity Index (2011), #33 out of 169 countries in the United Nations Human Development Index (2013), and #28 out of 176 countries in the Corruption Perceptions Index that is calculated by Transparency International (2013). In terms of public health, Estonia ranks #59 in the world out of 193 countries in life expectancy at birth, 76.1 years overall, and #39 out of 188 countries in infant mortality rate (2013). The country also ranks near the top in citizens' facility with English as a second language, ease of doing business, and UNICEF's State of the World's Children Index (#10 out of 165 countries in 2012). Democracy and civil society are strong in Estonia, as are popular movements to protect the environment and live in a sustainable manner. All this places Estonia comfortably within the high standards of countries in Western Europe and far above those of neighboring Russia, once Estonia's colonizer but now on our list of world's least contented countries.

FURTHER READING

Lieven, Anatol, *The Baltic Revolution: Estonia, Latvia, Lithuania, and the Path to Independence* (New Haven, CT: Yale University Press, 1993).

Smith, David J., *Estonia: Independence and European Integration* (London: Routledge, 2001).
Subrenat, Jean-Jacques, ed., *Estonia: Identity and Independence* (Amsterdam; New York: Rodopi, 2004).

JAPAN

Japan is a prominent island country in the western Pacific Ocean off the Asian continent. Its nearest neighbors are China, the Korean Peninsula, and the Far East of Russia. It was a bit of a close call as to whether or not the country should be included on our list of 20 most contented countries in the world, because the Japanese economy, once the envy of the world because of its size relative to population and fast growth from devastating defeat in World War II, has floundered in recent times, bringing new social woes to a country that once prided itself on harmony and contentment, and because competitor nations, especially China and Korea, have risen in influence as exporters of durable manufactured products. Japan has also experienced the trauma of a major earthquake and deadly tsunami in 2011, and continues to be burdened by a nuclear power facility in Fukushima, north of the capital city Tokyo, that was badly damaged during that natural disaster. Yet, despite these setbacks, there are enormous strengths in Japanese society and, for most people, a very high standard of living, which has led us to conclude that the country belongs in our elite category after all.

We can begin with the country itself, which, despite risks from earthquakes and other natural hazards, and with no spectacular endowment of mineral resources or fossil fuels as various other prosperous countries have, is remarkably beautiful and varied, and a source of great pride and enjoyment by Japanese citizens. There are mountains, forests, and clean streams, as well as spectacular coastlines, beautiful beaches, and idyllic islands. Most of Japan's 126.4 million residents (2014) live in a handful of giant cities in lowlands near the coast, especially on the Pacific side of the country, which leaves much of the interior and other regions sparsely populated and, in many places, even rugged. Furthermore, the shape of Japan is elongated in the north-south dimension, meaning that its landscapes range from those of icy winters in Hokkaido to the north to the warmth of tropical Okinawa and other islands with sandy beaches, palm trees, and exotic fruit to the south. Japanese are in love with their countryside and believe that they are blessed on their own land.

Second, we can say that Japan's cities and urbanized areas are highly livable despite enormous populations, extremely high levels of crowding, and the taxing routines of hard work and long commutes. Even Tokyo, which is the world's most populous urban area with an astounding 35.7 million residents, is clean, safe, and orderly, and extremely well served by services of all kinds, including utilities, public transportation, medical service, schools, recreation centers, senior citizen centers, and despite the crowding, areas of greenery and solitude. The rate of crime is very low and people feel safe at all times of day and night. For these and other reasons, we discuss Tokyo elsewhere in this book as one of the world's 20 most contented urban centers. Other Japanese cities have high standards of living too, including Kyoto, the country's previous capital. Commutes on trains and subways in large cities can be long and uncomfortable because of intense crowding, but schedules are punctual and the crowds are orderly.

Next, we can point to the richness and beauty of Japanese culture, and to the great pride that Japanese citizens take in their country's long history and distinctive traditions, festivals, arts, and cuisine. The Japanese language is also distinctive, and rich with nuances, politenesses, and poetic possibilities. Citizens of other countries take pride in their own cultures too, but Japan is unusual in citizens' perceptions that their society is unique and their traditions are truly special. These differences are due, in part, to Japan's history of isolation from the rest of the world for some 250 years during the rule of the shoguns until 1868, and because the Japanese islands are unusually homogeneous in the ethnic-racial makeup of the population, providing an extra sense of "oneness" to the country. The fact that many foreign tourists come to Japan to experience and enjoy its differentness is an added source of pride for Japanese, as is the recent globalization of things Japanese, such as the culture of sushi and the creative world of anime. The blossoming of cherry trees every spring and *Obon* festivals every summer to honor one's ancestors are times of great happiness that are unique to Japan.

Japan has the longest life expectancy of any country in the world: 84.6 years as expressed for 2012 by the World Health Organization. The reasons have to do with healthy diet and excellent medical care, as well as perhaps genetic factors. The country ranks highly as well in other comparative studies: #12 out of 187 countries in the United Nations Human Development Index; #6 out of 144 countries in the Global Peace Index; #15 out of 174 countries in the 2014 Corruption Perception Index by Transparency International; #17 out of 157 countries in the *Wall Street Journal* Index of Economic Freedom (2008); and #29 out of 173 countries in the Worldwide Press Freedom Index calculated for 2008 by Reporters without Borders. The country also ranks very highly in education, including mathematics, sciences, and reading, and in technological advances and applications. It is #1 in the world in patent applications and patents granted. On the down side, however, Japan has a shrinking population because of low birth rates, leading to labor shortages and financial stress on social security programs for the aged, and resistance to increasing foreign immigration to supplement the labor force because of fears that Japanese culture will be diluted as a result. There is also considerable stress in Japanese workplaces and schools, which has produced an unusually high suicide rate, as well as extra measures of social stress to conform to public norms.

FURTHER READING

Silverberg, Miriam, *Erotic Grotesque Nonsense: The Mass Culture of Japanese Modern Times* (Berkeley: University of California Press, 2007).
Sugimoto, Yoshio, *An Introduction to Japanese Society*, 4th edition (Cambridge: Cambridge University Press, 2014).
Varley, H. Paul, *Japanese Culture*, 4th edition (Honolulu: University of Hawaii Press, 2000).

NETHERLANDS

The Netherlands is a small and crowded country in Western Europe that is bordered by Germany, Belgium, and the North Sea. Along with Belgium and Luxembourg, it is one of the three "Low Countries" of Europe, so named because of low elevation and flat terrain where the waters of Rhine and other important European rivers flow into the North Sea. The word "Netherlands," in fact, means "low lands." The country is also referred to as Holland, even though technically that term should apply only to 2 of the Netherlands' 12 provinces that once comprised a country of that name. Its people are "Dutch" as is the name of the country's principal language. The population of the Netherlands is nearly 17 million. Increasingly, these numbers include immigrants from abroad.

As much as 50% of the land surface of the Netherlands no higher in elevation than 1 meter (3.3. feet) above sea level, and 17% is actually below sea level in the form of man-made land surfaces reclaimed from the sea that are called *polders*. The farmlands of the Netherlands are extraordinarily productive, and despite the country's small size and high population density, and despite the fact that about 90% of its population is urban and only about 4% of the workforce is engaged in agriculture, the Netherlands is second in the world, after only the United States, in exports of food and other agricultural products. Fruits, vegetables, cheeses, and flowers are among the main categories of exports from the country's farms. The largest city is the capital, Amsterdam with a municipal population of 813,562. We discuss this city elsewhere in this book as one of the 20 most contented cities in the world. The second-largest city is Rotterdam, municipal population 619,879, which has by far the largest port in Europe. In addition to farming, the economy of the Netherlands is based on manufacturing, shipping, trade, and banking, among other sectors. The country is considered to be the first in the world to have developed a fundamentally capitalist economy. The first stock exchange in the world was opened in Amsterdam in 1602 by the Dutch East Indies Company. Overall, the Netherlands has the 17th-largest economy in the world.

The Netherlands is consistently ranked among the top countries in the world across any number of criteria. For example, it ranks at #4 in the world among 187 countries after Norway, Australia, and Switzerland in the 2014 United Nations Human Development Index, #9 out of 142 countries in the 2014 Legatum Prosperity

Index, and #13 in the world out of 187 countries in GDP(PPP) per capita as measured by the International Monetary Fund. In addition, the Netherlands ranks as the 8th best country in Transparency International's Corruption Perceptions Index for 2014; #17 out of 178 countries in economic freedom as determined by Heritage House for 2015; 4th in the world out of 156 countries in the World Happiness Report (2010–2012 data) by the U.N. Sustainable Development Solutions Network; #10 in the world out of 167 countries in the Democracy Index as reported for 2014 by the *Economist*; #17 out of 146 countries in the world as best for doing business as determined by *Forbes* for 2014; and #15 in the world out of 176 countries in the Satisfaction with Life Index (2006) that was developed at the University of Leicester. In 2000, the World Health Organization put the Netherlands at #17 out of 191 countries in its ranking of overall health systems. The Sustainable Society Foundation has ranked the Netherlands at #14 out of 153 countries in human well-being and at #28 out of 158 countries in economic well-being.

Dutch society places high values on democracy, consultation, pluralism, openness, and social tolerance. The country was one of the first in the world to have an

Dutch residents protesting strict immigration policies at the national parliament building in The Hague. The girl on the left is from Sudan and is at risk of being deported because she is in the country illegally. Her classmate on the right offers support, asking for a pardon and a grant of asylum. Immigration is a sticky issue in many European countries. (AP Photo/Fred Ernst)

elected parliament, and it continues to be strongly democratic as seen in its high ranking on the Democracy Index. The political culture includes consultation with both trade unions and employers before decisions that affect the economy are made in government. The country is tolerant of all religious faiths even though it is one of the world's most secular societies. It has done much better at integrating recent immigrants from Islamic countries than many of its European neighbor countries. Many of its Muslims come from Indonesia, a distant country that was once part of the Netherlands colonial empire. The Netherlands, and especially Amsterdam, was a haven from persecution for Europe's Jews from the late 16th century onward until the Nazi invasion in World War II and the Shoah. Amsterdam's population was 10% Jewish before that tragedy. The Jewish community in the Netherlands has been rebuilding since, and is now thriving again.

Dutch tolerance is also seen in permissive attitudes with respect to prostitution, which is licensed, abortion, women's rights, gay and lesbian rights, and soft drugs. The country's gay pride parades and festivals are some of the world's largest and most famous. In 2001, the Netherlands became the first country in the world to legalize same-sex marriage. Euthanasia is legal under certain conditions. Most Dutch consider openness and tolerance to be integral parts of the national psyche. They also have an international culture that dates back to the days of Dutch explorers and colonial ventures. The Netherlands does business around the world, and more than in most societies its people are bilingual and multilingual. The majority of the population knows English very well in addition to Dutch, and many also speak other languages. Finally, we note that Dutch culture places a high value on healthy lifestyle. Adults and children alike belong in large numbers to sports or fitness clubs, and exercise regularly. There is a culture of bicycle-riding to work or school, both as a form of exercise and to have less impact on the environment. Even though it is a crowded country, city planners and landscape architects make sure that there are many bicycling and jogging trails, parks, and skating rinks for the public to enjoy.

FURTHER READING

Bolt, Rodney, *Xenophobe's Guide to the Dutch* (London: Oval Books, 2008).
Shorto, Russell, *Amsterdam: A History of the World's Most Liberal City* (New York: Vintage Books, 2014).
White, Colin and Laurie Boucke, *The UnDutchables: An Observation on the Netherlands, Its Culture, and Its Inhabitants* (Oakhurst, CA: White-Boucke Publishers, 2013).

NEW ZEALAND

New Zealand is an island country in the southwestern Pacific Ocean about 900 miles (1,500 km) east of Australia. It consists of two main islands, North Island

and South Island, plus numerous smaller ones, and is known for having a rich and beautiful natural environment that includes a great diversity of natural landscapes and biota, high and rugged mountains, lush farms and pasturelands, dense green forests, and picturesque coastlines, among other features. The original settlers were Māori people who arrived from South Pacific islands in about the 13th century. European colonization followed after Dutch navigator Abel Tasman sighted the islands in 1642. In 1840, New Zealand became a British colony. Independence came afterward, but in stages with no fixed date as in the case of other former colonies. The Māori population became a minority because of deaths from disease and inter-tribal warfare in the 19th century, and the rising tide of European settlers, mostly English. In 1893, New Zealand became the first country to allow all women the right to vote. As of 2013, the total population of New Zealand was about 4.5 million, about 74.0% of whom are identified ethnically as European, 14.9% as Māori, 11.8% as Asian, and 7.4% as Pacific islanders. The population of the country is becoming increasingly diverse. In contrast, in 1961 Europeans accounted for 92% of the total and most of the remainder were Māori (7% of the total).

The economy of New Zealand economy centers on agricultural exports. Wool was the most important commodity from the 19th century to the 1960s, but since then that commodity has been surpassed in value by dairy products, which continue to be the #1 export item, and by wine, which entered into second place in 2007. Sheep farming, however, is still closely identified with the landscape and culture of New Zealand. Kiwis, as New Zealand's citizens fondly refer to themselves, are proud to point out that there are more sheep in their country than people. The ratio is now about 7 sheep per person, but once it was as high as 30 per person. The country also identifies strongly with its sports culture. Mountaineering and hiking are popular participation sports, as are sailing, windsurfing, and surfing in the country's waters. In addition, New Zealanders give avid support to favorite cricket and rugby teams as spectator sports. The New Zealand All Blacks, the national rugby team, has been especially successful in global competition. It has come to be identified around the world with the *haka*, a traditional Māori war dance and challenge to opponents that was first introduced to the team by Māori players, as well as by uniforms that are all black.

By all accounts, New Zealand is one of the most livable countries in the world. It has a very high standard of living, high environmental standards, a strong economy, and strong democratic institutions. It is ranked #1 in the world in both political rights and civil liberties, #1 as the least corrupt country in the world, #2 in the world in the Global Peace Index, #3 in the United Nations Human Development Index and the Fraser Institute Ease of Doing Business Index, #4 in the world in economic freedom, and #5 in the Global Prosperity Index and in the strength of democratic institutions. Also, New Zealand is ranked 8th in the world in press freedom and 10th in literacy rate, which is at 99%. The Organization for Economic

Cooperation and Development ranks the country's educational system as seventh best in the world, citing particular strengths in reading, mathematics, and science. The OECD also commends New Zealand for high voter turnout (recently 79% as compared to an OECD average of 72%) and for having a high level of trust by citizens in their governmental institutions (67% in comparison to the OECD average of 56%). Life expectancy is 13th highest in the world at 80.2 years, owing to excellent medical care and an active, outdoors lifestyle for many citizens. The Failed States Index that is calculated annually by the Fund for Peace ranked New Zealand at #173 out of 178 countries in 2013, meaning that 172 countries ranked worse across an array of 12 key social, economic, and political variables.

The majority of New Zealand's population resides in cities, with more than half of the total living in the four largest urban centers: Auckland, Christchurch, Wellington, and Hamilton. All cities compare favorably with urban centers in other countries, with Auckland ranking #3 in the world in the 2014 Mercer Quality of Life Survey and Wellington #12. Auckland is the largest city with 1,413,700 people, about 31% of the nation's total. It is on North Island and lies on and around an isthmus, giving it two harbors. It is often referred to as the "City of Sails" because sailing is such a popular sport. About one in three households in the city own a boat, with the total number of registered yachts and launches being about 135,000. Aucklanders also enjoy beautiful parks and beaches in their city. Wellington, population 393,600, is the second-largest city. It is near the southern tip of North Island, and was chosen to be the national capital because of central location between the two main islands. It, too, has a long and beautiful waterfront and a fondness for sailing. Because of strong winds in the region, its nickname is Windy Wellington. All four of the largest cities are popular tourist destinations in their own right, as well as departure points for visitor attractions in their respective parts of the country. Despite remoteness from most of the rest of the world, New Zealand is increasingly being regarded globally as a "clean, green adventure playground" and has been gaining over the long run each year in numbers of foreign visitors. There were 2.84 million visitor arrivals to New Zealand in the year that ended November 2014, the highest ever for a 12-month period, and 5% higher than in the year that ended November 2013 (2.70 million). The leading source countries are Australia, China, the United States, the United Kingdom, and Japan, in that order. Most visitors come for outdoor activities and scenery tourism, including most spectacularly the Southern Alps on South Island. Since the filming of *Lord of the Rings* based on the novel of the same title by J. R. R. Tolkien, there has been a spike in tourism to see landscapes that were backdrop for the popular movie.

FURTHER READING

Mein Smith, Philippa, *A Concise History of New Zealand* (Cambridge: Cambridge University Press, 2005).

Scherer, Jay, *The Contested Terrain of the New Zealand All Blacks: Rugby, Commerce, and Cultural Politics in the Age of Globalization* (New York: Peter Land, 2013).

NORWAY

Norway is a country in northern Europe that consistently ranks at or very near the top among countries in the world in quality of life. It is very prosperous, has outstanding public services, and is extremely beautiful. The main part of the country occupies the western part of the Scandinavian Peninsula, where it faces the North Atlantic Ocean, but there are also numerous sparsely populated islands offshore, as well as in the Barents Sea in the far north. The Atlantic coastline is marked by steep mountain slopes interspersed by majestic, deep fjords. Inland, the country is mountainous with picturesque narrow valleys and scattered small plains. There are glaciers on the highest peaks. The Arctic Circle crosses Norway more than halfway up the coastline, and much of the land to the north is covered in permafrost. The south of the country is heavily forested, but there are also many agricultural villages and much farm land. Oslo, the national capital and largest city, is in the southeast at the northern end of Oslofjord, where the climate is more benign and the topography less rugged.

The population of Norway is a little more than 5.1 million (2013). The country is fairly homogeneous ethnically, with about 86% of the population being ethnic Norwegians, but the north of the country is the territory of indigenous Sami, Kvens, and Forest Finns, while in Oslo and other urbanized areas, there are increasing numbers of immigrants from various European countries, North Africa, and Asia. Northern ethnic groups who live off the land and many newer immigrants have lower incomes, but the population of Norway as a whole is among the most prosperous in the world. According to the International Monetary Fund, Norwegians have the world's second-highest GDP per capita (after Luxembourg; 2013: $100,318). In 2013, the country was ranked #4 after Qatar, Luxembourg, and Singapore in GDP and purchasing power parity (GDP(PPP); $54,947). The United Nations Human Development Index, which is based on various measures of life expectancy, literacy, education, standards of living, and quality of life, placed the country as #1 in the world each year between 2001 and 2006, and then again from 2009 through 2013. The Global Gender Gap Report by the World Economic Forum consistently ranks Norway at or very near the top in gender equality. That index includes measures of gender equality in economic opportunity and salaries, educational attainment, political empowerment, and outcomes from health care services. Norway also scores very highly on income equality between highest-paid and lowest-paid workers, without the enormous gaps that are seen in the United States and other countries where CEOs tend to have extremely high salaries.

The economy of Norway is closely linked to the sea. Historically, the country was the land of Viking seafarers and fishermen. Fishing is still a major part of the national economy, and the country ranks in the top 10 in the world in total harvests from the seas. The country was once one of the major whaling nations of the world, but it no longer harvests whales except for select species in small quantities. Norway is also one of the world's leading shipping countries, having one of the world's largest merchant fleets. There are also many Norwegian cruise vessels and passenger ferries, and lucrative tourism businesses by cruise ships that move along the coast and among the country's fjords. However, the single largest part of the economy of Norway is offshore oil and gas exploitation, particularly from the North Sea. Drilling started in the 1960s, and quickly turned Norway into a wealthy country. Exports of oil and gas account for more than one-half of all exports from the country by value, and for about 20% of the GDP. The country is the world's fifth-largest oil exporter and third-largest gas exporter. Other notable resources include timber, which is also exported, and farm products, particularly livestock, grains, and potatoes. The snowy mountains of Norway are popular destinations for skiers. In 1952 and 1994 Norway hosted the winter Olympics, first in Oslo and then in Lillehammer.

Because the economy depends on extraction and dissemination of fossil fuels, Norway does not rank as highly as other European nations on indices of environmental sustainability. However, in other respects Norwegians have a culture of resource conservation and are generally environmentally conscious. The country has a long history of managing its fishing and forestry industries, and of protection of all categories of land (e.g., mountains, coast, farmland, cities, and the far north) from inappropriate land use development. Architecture and construction techniques emphasize energy efficiency, as well as harmony with surroundings. About 95% of the country's electricity comes from renewable hydropower.

According to a 2013 survey by the Organization for Economic Cooperation and Development, Norway ranks especially highly among the 36 countries that were considered in satisfaction with work, recreation, and home life. In addition to high wages, Norwegians enjoy high job security, low unemployment, and outstanding working conditions. Most workers have the equivalent of five weeks of paid vacation. Furthermore, both mothers and fathers enjoy generous parenting leaves with the birth of a child, as well as other benefits: mothers get up to 10 months of full pay after the birth of a child and fathers get the equivalent of 10 weeks away from work with pay during that child's first year. There is a flexible policy regarding age of retirement starting with age 62, with state pensions payable at age 67. Health care is excellent, with the result that Norway's life expectancy is one of the highest in the world, 81.5 years (2012; 83.5 years for women and 79.5 for men). The country ranks third in the world (after Switzerland and Australia) according to the *Economist's* "Where-to-be-born Index" for 2013. The overall Legatum Prosperity Index ranks Norway at #1 in the world from 147 countries for each year 2009–2013, and #1 in both economy and social capital in 2013. The Failed States

Index that is calculated annually by the Fund for Peace ranked New Zealand at #175 out of 178 countries in 2013, meaning that 174 countries ranked worse across an array of 12 key social, economic, and political variables.

The housing conditions of Norwegians are excellent, although rents and purchase prices have been rising faster than incomes, putting new pressures on first-time buyers and young renters. Oslo is especially expensive, ranking as one the highest cost of living cities in the world. Other cities in Norway are expensive too. According to the Intelligence Unit of the *Economist*, Norway's capital ranks as the world's third-most expensive city, after Singapore and Paris (2014). Taxes are high too, in order to support the country's outstanding social services. The high costs of living in Norway have been hard on immigrants who arrive poor in the country and struggle to find a financial footing. Many of the social benefits that Norwegians enjoy routinely do not kick in immediately, but require specific periods of gainful employment and costly pay-ins to the social welfare system, so new arrivals are often disappointed and sometimes return home. As elsewhere in Europe, there is a rising tide of anti-immigrant sentiment in Norway, although not as much as in France or Austria, or in some other countries in Western Europe, perhaps because of ingrained Scandinavian cultural beliefs of social equality and collective responsibility. Most Norwegians are generally welcoming and helpful to immigrants, so there are many happy stories as well.

FURTHER READING

Almaas, Ingerid Helsing, *Made in Norway* (Berlin: Birkhäuser Architecture, 2010).
Nina, Berglund, "Norwegians Still Satisfied with Life," *News in English.co*, May 28, 2013, http://www.newsinenglish.no/2013/05/28/norwegians-still-satisfied-with-life/.
O'Leary, Margaret Hayford, *Culture and Customs of Norway* (Santa Barbara, CA: Greenwood, 2010).

OMAN

Oman, formally the Sultanate of Oman, is a country on the southeastern corner of the Arabian Peninsula, where it is bordered by Saudi Arabia, the United Arab Emirates, and the Gulf of Oman and Arabian Sea. The country also includes two very small exclaves named Madha and Musandam that have land borders only with the United Arab Emirates. It is a lightly settled country of gravel deserts and rugged terrain, and has a total population of about 3,219,775 (2014 estimate). Most of the population resides along the coasts, with Muscat, population 1,208,114, being the capital and largest city. The country is overwhelmingly Muslim, with most people belonging to the Ibadi sect of Islam, and Arabic is the official language. Oman is an absolute monarchy. Its leader is Sultan Qaboos bin

Said al Said (born 1940), who took office after a palace coup against his father in 1970 and is now the longest-serving ruler in the Middle East.

We have included Oman in this list of 20 most contented countries in the world with some reservation. Sultan Qaboos has absolute power in the country, issues laws by decree, and has little tolerance for criticism. Freedom House categorizes the country as "not free." Furthermore, there are serious human rights abuses, including torture in prisons and poor working and living conditions for foreign laborers, as well as restrictions on the press and criticisms of government on the Internet. Therefore, the country is quite far from ideal. However, Oman is by far the most contented country in its region, specifically the Arabia Peninsula and countries to the east of the Persian Gulf, albeit the other countries are a bad lot. Moreover, Oman continues to make much more positive strides than its neighbors in giving more voice to its citizens, improving the rights of women, and allowing freedoms of religion. If we want to represent the Middle East on these pages, it has to be Oman, because the country does have many positive aspects and the other countries in the region are, sad to say, significantly worse.

Even though he took power in a coup and rules more or less as he wishes, Sultan Qaboos is viewed as a modernizer, although again the context is a region where modern ideas are often taboo. When he took power, Oman was experiencing a civil war, and was so backward and badly poised for the future that there were only two primary schools and one secondary school in the whole country. He promptly invested in education, health care, and infrastructure, raising standards to those of Oman's neighbors and beyond, even though the other countries are much richer in oil than Oman and have more resources to work with. In 1992, the Consultative Assembly of Oman, the Majlis al-Shura, was established to give people a forum for participating in government, and in 1997 women were given the right to vote and to be elected as members to this body. Two women were voted in straight away. Then, in 2002 voting rights were extended to all citizens aged 21 and older. Sultan Qaboos was also influenced to invest in education, opening schools throughout the country, as well as universities. Women have equal access to schooling, and indeed comprise about one-half of all students. In stressing education, the sultan acknowledged that the country's future would depend on a having a well-trained workforce. The economy has been diversified, and includes not just a share of the Middle East's oil production, but also trade, finance, and tourism. Advances in irrigated agriculture, animal husbandry, and fishing have propelled the country toward self-sufficiency in food. The country is classified as having a high United Nations Human Development Index, and ranks at #56 out of 187 countries across the world. Several Middle Eastern countries nearby rank higher, but they are leaders in oil exploitation and typically have bad human rights records.

Oman is stable and has a very low crime rate. It is also very interesting culturally, with multiple ethnic groups, religious sects, and traditional tribal loyalties, and a fascinating blend of old and new lifestyles and old and new landscapes. Consequently, the country is finding its way successfully onto global tourism paths, sometimes as a refreshing alternative to the skyscraper worlds of Qatar and the United Arab Emirates nearby where traditional culture has been distorted too much and too fast by sudden wealth. The Omani inland town of Nizwa is a well preserved oasis settlement at the base of high mountains, but yet it is only two hours away on fine highways from Muscat and the ocean. It has one of Oman's new universities. Muscat is also a gem for tourists, combining history such as the Muscat Gate Museum and old fortifications with modern comforts, and with spectacular new architecture such as the Sultan Qaboos Grand Mosque and the Muscat Royal Opera House. The city is also the gateway to strings of beach resorts both up the coast and down. Although there are now complaints that some beaches have become dirtied by too many tourists, the environment as a whole in Oman is beautiful and well preserved, as Sultan Qaboos values the outdoors and is a leader in environmental protection.

FURTHER READING

Beasant, John, Christopher Ling, and Ian Cummins, *Oman: The True-Life Drama and Intrigue of an Arab State* (Edinburgh: Mainstream Publishing Company, 2014).

Nielsen, Stig Pors, *Oman: Stories from a Modern Arab Country* (Bloomington, IN: Author-House, 2014).

Valeri, Marc, *Oman: Politics and Society in the Qaboos State* (Oxford: Oxford University Press, 2014).

SENEGAL

Senegal is a small country at Cape Verde at the westernmost tip of Africa. It borders Mali, Mauritania, Guinea-Bissau and Guinea, and envelopes the Gambia, an even smaller country that follows the course of the Gambia River. The capital and largest city of Senegal is Dakar, population about 2.4 million. Senegal itself totals 13,567,338 inhabitants (2013). The country was once a colony of France and Dakar was the capital of the entirety of French West Africa. Senegal gained its independence in 1960, but French is still the official language and is widely spoken, as is Wolof. The most numerous ethnic populations are Wolof (43.3%), Fula (23.8%), and Serer (14.7%). Islam is the predominant religion, accounting for about 92% of the population.

Our main reason for selecting Senegal for this list of 20 most contented countries in the world is because since independence, it has been a model for Africa and elsewhere in the Third World in democratic institutions and market economy. All of the country's presidents have been democratically elected in free and fair balloting, and without undue tensions. In 2000, the presidency was handed over peacefully after 40 years of power by the Socialist Party, when an opposition politician, Abdoulaye Wade, won the election. There have been no coups or attempted coups. In comparison to most African governments, Senegal is relatively corruption-free. According to the *Economist*, Senegal was ranked #74 in the world out of 167 countries in its Democracy Index for 2014, not among the highest-ranking countries, but comfortably within the top 50% and among the better scores for Africa.

Even though Senegal is not especially well endowed with natural resources or fertile lands, it has managed to avoid widespread poverty. The economy is based on agriculture, in which cotton and groundnuts are main exports, fishing, food processing, and light manufacturing. There are also many Senegalese who work abroad, particularly in France, and who support families back home through remittances. Our personal observations in Senegal confirmed that most Senegalese, most critically the younger generations, are optimistic about their futures, if cautiously so, and believe in the benefits of education and hard work for getting ahead. Indeed, we were impressed with the dedicated energy that we saw in the population, be it among street vendors and taxi drivers in Dakar, fishermen at the

Children playing their beloved sport on the street in Dakar, Senegal. The scene is from the Yoff neighborhood, and the street is sand. (Roman Cybriwsky)

shore, or goat herders and farmers in the countryside. Our visits to schools, too, showed enthusiasm for the tasks at hand.

Senegal has excellent prospects to become a major tourism destination. International tourism is important already, including in the form of shopping and medical tourism by Africans from nearby countries where options are not as good for either need, and by sun-seeking Europeans who are drawn to the country by warm weather, beaches, and low prices. There are also American tourists, especially African Americans, who visit Senegal for an experience in history or heritage because the country was one of the places on the African coast from which slaves were shipped to the Americas. Gorée Island off the coast from Dakar is a UNESCO World Heritage Site that memorializes the evils of the slave trade. A highlight is a building called the House of Slaves, where slaves were kept in chains until (reportedly) going through "the door of no return" to board a slave vessel for the Atlantic Crossing. U.S. president Barack Obama visited Gorée in June 2013 and stood for photos at the infamous doorway. In addition to being of interest to him personally, the visit was a sign of America's friendship with Senegal and good publicity for further development of tourism to the country. Other Dakar highlights are the Dakar Grand Mosque, the French-built Dakar Cathedral, and the African Renaissance Monument, the tallest statue in Africa. There are excellent beaches outside Dakar and growing numbers of comfortable places to stay, as well as spectacular national parks and nature preserves in the country's interior. Senegal has excellent prospects to be a magnet for ecotourism.

Senegal is also a fascinating blend of cultures. The majority of the country's Muslims are Sunnis with strong influences from Sufism, and their communities are generally organized around one of several Sufi brotherhoods headed by a direct descendant of the group's founder. For Senegalese, these religious organizations are like extended family. The country is also well known for its traditions of storytelling by professionals called *griots*, who relay the details of local history from generation to generation. We also enjoyed Senegalese food, music, and dance. All in all, we were impressed with Senegal as a very welcoming and friendly country. There are smiles from everyone and friendly greetings. The country has very low crime rates and is quite safe. Hospitality is deeply ingrained in the culture, so much so that the name of the Senegal national football (soccer) team is the Lions of Teranga, with *teranga* being the Wolof word for hospitality. These qualities are also important for promoting tourism and building a national economy.

FURTHER READING

Balzone, John M. and D. Balouziyeh (eds.), *Street Children in Senegal* (Paris: GYAN FRANCE, 2005).

Diouf, Mamadou (ed.), *Tolerance, Democracy, and Sufis in Senegal* (New York: Columbia University Press, 2013).

SEYCHELLES

Seychelles is an archipelago country of approximately 116 small islands in the Indian Ocean north of Madagascar and east of Kenya and Tanzania on the African mainland. It is considered to be a part of Africa, and at a total of 177 miles (459 kilometers) is the smallest country in Africa and one of the smallest in the world. Its population is 90,024, also the smallest in Africa. It ranks at #195 in the world in population. Because it is small and relatively remote, it gets little attention globally. During the colonial period, the islands became a possession of France from 1756 and were named after Jean Moreau de Séchelles, the French Minister of Finance under King Louis XV. They came under British control in 1810 when they were administered as part of Mauritius, and became their own Crown Colony in 1903. Independence was achieved in 1976. The first president, the erudite Sir James Mancham, was overthrown by a coup in 1977 by France Albert René. Other coup attempts and a failed army mutiny followed, but René held onto power until 2004 when he stepped down in favor of his vice president, James Michele, who has since won two elections and is still in office. At first, René governed Seychelles as a one-party socialist state, but he changed the country to a multiparty democracy in the early 1990s, reportedly because of pressure from international aid donors. The country has been stable since. The so-called Seychelles Affair in 1981, in which there was an attempted coup by 43 South African mercenaries who entered the country by posing as rugby players on holiday, exemplifies the unhappy and unstable government during René's first years in power.

Today, Seychelles (the spelling of Séchelles had been anglicized; the term "the Seychelles" is also used to refer to the country, but more properly it is used to refer to the island group) is not only stable politically and democratic, but also relatively prosperous. Its United Nations Human Development Index for 2013 is 0.756, which is classified as "very high" and is in a tie for 71st place in the world out of 187 countries with Mexico. It is the third-highest HDI in Africa. Its GDP per capita (PPP) is fairly high too: #47 out of 187 countries as calculated by the International Monetary Fund; #43 out of 185 countries as calculated by the World Bank; and #42 out of 195 countries as calculated by the U.S. Central Intelligence Agency. The country enjoys good health care and good education. Literacy rates are very high, reportedly approaching 100% for the adult population because of adult learning programs that were targeted at older persons who had grown up without formal schooling. In order to stop a brain drain outmigration by talented young Seychellois and keep them home, the government opened the University of Seychelles in 2009 in cooperation with the University of London.

Seychelles has traditionally relied on agriculture and fishing as mainstays of the economy. Since the colonial era and its plantation economy, the main crops for export have included vanilla and cinnamon. In 1971, the Seychelles International Airport was opened near the capital city Victoria on the island of Mahé, opening the way for the rise of international tourism as a major part of the economy. Tourism now employs about 30% of the labor force (15% directly and another 15% indirectly), while agriculture employs only 3%. The major attractions are the islands' beaches such as the beautiful Beau Vallon beach on the northwestern coast of Mahé, and clear turquoise waters. The climate is warm year-around, although somewhat humid. The largest numbers of tourist arrivals are from France, the United Kingdom, Germany, and South Africa. The islands also offer unspoiled natural beauty and great varieties of flora and fauna. Giant and sea turtles and tortoises are protected in nature reserves. About one-half of the territory of Seychelles is under natural conservation, more than any nation on earth. Tourism usually entails significant negative impacts on environment and local culture, but the Seychelles government has been more watchful than most developing countries, and requires that detailed impact studies be made and reviewed in advance of any new construction for the tourism economy. Environmental impacts are reduced by increasing reliance on wind as a source of electrical energy.

The people of Seychelles are a blend of nationalities and cultures, with many Seychellois being multiracial of mixed African, Asian, and European descent. The cuisines of the country are also a fusion from different continents, as are other various aspects of local culture such as the music of Seychelles. The official languages of the country are French, English, and Seychellois Creole, which incorporates French along with borrowings from English.

FURTHER READING

Hoare, Mike, *The Seychelles Affair* (Boulder, CO: Paladin Press, 2008).
Mancham, James R., *Seychelles: The Saga of a Small Nation Navigating the Cross-Currents of a Big World* (St. Paul, MN: Paragon House, 2015).

SINGAPORE

Singapore is a small island country in Southeast Asia just to the north of the equator and off the southern tip of the Malay Peninsula. However, it is not just a country, but is also a city-state as "Singapore" is also the country's only city and national capital. The boundaries of the two are coterminous. Therefore, Singapore could be discussed in this book as either one of the most contented countries in the world or one of the world's most contented cities. We list it here under countries, if only to leave space for discussion of one additional top city.

The population of Singapore is 5,399,200 (2013). The country is one of the smallest in the world (710.2 km²; 274.2 mi²), and because of its urbanized character, is also one of the most densely settled, ranking second only to tiny Monaco. Its nearest neighbors are Malaysia, of which it was once a part and to which it is connected by bridges across the narrow Johore Strait, and the islands of Indonesia's Riau Archipelago which lie across the Singapore Strait, an important shipping lane. The country has virtually no natural resources to speak of, including fresh water, arable land, and timber, but yet it has managed to develop an extremely high standard of living. Moreover, it is one of the world's wealthiest countries. According to calculations by the International Monetary Fund, in 2013 Singapore had a per capita (nominal) GDP of $54,775 (ranking #8 in the world) and a per capita GDP at purchasing power parity (GDP [PPP]) of $64,584, #3 in the world after Qatar and Luxembourg. There is very little poverty, and almost everyone lives comfortably in terms of financial resources. Unemployment is among the lowest in the world. Singapore has the world's highest percentage of millionaires, with about one in six households having at least US$1 million in disposable wealth. If other wealth such as the value of property is added into the calculation, then Singapore has even more millionaires, as values of owned businesses and real estate are extremely high in the country.

Singapore's extraordinary success is attributed to investment in its own people, that is, its human resources, and especially in education, as well as to smart business decisions for the country. Considerable credit for decisions to do so is given to Dr. Lee Kuan Yew (1923–2015), who led Singapore as its first prime minister from 1959 to 1990, and who continued to serve for many years afterward, first as senior minister and then as minister mentor, two titles that were developed specifically for him. His strong leadership was instrumental in turning a small city-state into one of the world's most educated and most IT-savvy populations, and its economy into one that is significantly disproportionate in wealth and influence, given the nation's smallness. An excellent harbor and location of Singapore at the intersection of natural shipping channels has helped make Singapore into a major center of international trade, a refining center for foreign oil, and a center for ship repair. It is also a manufacturing center that processes imported resources and parts into products for export. In addition to refined oil and gasoline, exports include chemicals, electronics, biomedical supplies, and offshore oil rigs. The port is one of the five busiest in the world. The financial sector in Singapore is enormous too, ranking fourth in the world. Singapore's downtown presents one of the most impressive skyscraper skylines in the world.

Singapore has been ranked first in the world by the World Bank for ease of doing business for seven consecutive years (to 2012). It is also ranked first in the world for protection of intellectual property, and second in the world by the *Wall Street Journal* in its Index of Economic Freedom (2008). Transparency

International ranks Singapore as fifth in the world out of 177 countries on its Corruption Perception Index, meaning that the country is #5 in absence of corruption. Other distinctions are a #6 ranking out of 111 countries by the *Economist* in its Where-to-be-born Index for 2013, a #8 ranking out of 144 countries in the United Nations Human Development Index for 2014, and a #10 ranking out of 133 countries in the World Economic Forum's Travel and Tourism Competiveness Index for 2009.

Singapore is a very popular destination for international tourism, attracting more than 10 million foreign visitors each year. Highlights include a spectacular waterfront with dazzling new buildings and greatly innovative architecture, excellent shopping in beautiful enclosed shopping malls, interesting historic ethnic neighborhoods, a picturesque riverfront with fine restaurants and pubs, a great zoo, a botanic gardens, and many parks and beaches. Everywhere, the island is clean, green, and lush. There is also outstanding food, including local cuisines and foods from around the world. The country is a very popular international convention center, as well as a staging point for air travelers who pass through Singapore on their way to or from destinations throughout Southeast and South Asia, Oceania, other places.

Singapore is a clean, orderly, and safe city. The photo shows part of the downtown business district and, in the foreground, a part of its historic Chinatown. Even though more than three-quarters of the population are of Chinese descent, there is still a Chinatown neighborhood. It is a vestige of the colonial period when the British controlled the city and determined which ethnic groups would live where. (Roman Cybriwsky)

Singapore is one of the world's safest, cleanest, and most orderly cities. The population is well housed, mostly in well-planned public housing apartment blocks provided by the Singapore Housing Development Board, and is served by an outstanding mass rapid transit system (the Singapore MRT) that totals 153 kilometers (95 miles) and 108 stations. The health system is excellent. The World Health Organization ranks Singapore as #6 in the world in overall quality of health care. Infant mortality rates are consistently the lowest in the world, and life expectancy is #4 in the world at 80 for males and 85 for females. Schools and universities are also excellent. The language of instruction is English in this multiethnic, multiracial country, even as languages spoken at home in are Chinese, Malay, and Tamil, as well as other languages. There is freedom of religion and a tradition of social tolerance. There is little tolerance, however, for violations of law or, say, rules in school as Singaporeans understand that the smooth working of this small, crowded country depends on strict enforcement and strict penalties for violations. A popular slogan about Singapore that is seen often on T-shirts that are for sale as tourist souvenirs is that "Singapore Is a Fine City," meaning that is a fine place because it imposes sure fines for violations of each of its many rules. Freedoms of speech and of the press were problematic in the first decades after Singapore's independence (1963 from the United Kingdom and 1965 from Malaysia), as the government of Lee Kuan Yew exerted a strong hand in order to set the country on the course of development that it wanted, but once Singapore succeeded and the public was in step, restrictions on free speech and the media were loosened. Singaporeans travel widely across the globe for pleasure and business, and the Singaporean passport is probably the most widely accepted at international borders of all world passports.

FURTHER READING

Kong, Lily and Brenda S.A. Yeoh, *The Politics of Landscapes in Singapore: The Construction of "Nation"* (Syracuse, NY: Syracuse University Press, 2003).

Lee, Kuan Yew, *From Third World to First: The Singapore Story—1965–2000* (New York: Harper, 2000).

Turnbull, C. M., *A History of Modern Singapore: 1819–2005* (Singapore: National University of Singapore Press, 2010).

SWEDEN

Sweden is a Scandinavian country in northern Europe that is bordered by Norway and Finland and is connected to Denmark by bridge. It is elongated north-south, with the south having a temperate climate and an agricultural economy, while the north is forested and has long, cold winters with limited hours of daylight. The majority of the country's 9.7 million citizens live in the south, especially in the capital city Stockholm and its environs. About 85% of the country is urbanized, one of the highest totals in the world. The country is recognized globally for a high standard of living and considerable wealth, as well as for having some of the most liberal social programs in the world and correspondingly high taxes. It consistently ranks among the top countries in the world in terms of quality of life. In 2014, it ranked at #5 in the world from 142 countries in the Legatum Prosperity Index and, as a result was listed by *Forbes* as one of the planet's happiest countries. In 2013, Sweden was ranked at #12 out of 187 countries in the United Nations comprehensive Human Development Index. The Reputation Institute, a global consulting firm that works out of New York and Copenhagen, ranked Sweden as the second-most reputable country from the 50 that were considered, meaning that it scored very highly in "people's trust, admiration, respect and affinity."

Sweden ranks as the seventh-richest country in the world in per capita GDP. Furthermore, income inequality between the richest and the poorest workers is lower in Sweden than in most other prosperous countries, as is the gender gap in incomes. The economy ranks as the fourth-most competitive economy in the world, and is both knowledge-based and based on export industries. Exports include timber, hydroelectricity, and iron ore, as well as products manufactured by such globally familiar brands as Volvo, Ericsson, Scania, and IKEA. Sweden is ranked at the top among the world's countries in the 2014 Global Green Economy Index and #1 in Europe by Richard Florida in creativity for business. It has been a global leader in scientific research for several centuries, and now invests heavily in science and technology research not just to strengthen its industries, but also to improve the environment and human well-being. The population is highly educated and technologically savvy. In addition to Swedish, most residents know English well, as it is a compulsory subject in schooling, and in many cases other languages as well.

The social welfare system of Sweden provides universal health care for all citizens. It is publicly funded and administered by county councils, and allows patients to choose their own physicians. The quality of care is excellent, and the population is generally healthy. There are paid paternal and maternity leaves, a government allowance for every child, and free day care from age 1. Schooling is free for the primary and secondary levels, and includes free lunches. University studies and postgraduate studies are free too. Rents are controlled in order to keep housing affordable. Workers receive many vacation days and paid holidays each year, job security protections, and workdays that have been shortened to six hours in some places as an experiment. Bus and rail transit are efficient and affordable too. The costs of these benefits are taxes that are among the highest in the world.

Most Swedes do not complain, however, as the tax system has everyone paying and the welfare system has everyone receiving benefits.

Other pluses about Sweden are a highly developed democratic system of government with multiple political parties and high voter participation, low corruption that ranked fourth-best in the world according to the Corruption Perceptions Index by Transparency International, low crime rates and humane prisons that are geared toward educating convicted lawbreakers and preparing them for an honest living, and a high degree of social tolerance. Sweden takes in immigrants from around the world and helps them assimilate into mainstream society and the workforce, although there is at least one minority political party that has been agitating for restricting immigration. About 15% of the population is foreign-born. Sweden is also known for very liberal attitudes about homosexuality. Its laws permit same-sex marriage and recognize domestic partnerships between unmarried same-sex and opposite-sex couples. Cohabitation is commonplace.

Many Swedes enjoy a way of life that emphasizes outdoor activity and exercise, sports, vacation homes along the coast or beside lakes, the joys of sauna, and international travel. The main cities, Stockholm, Gothenburg, Malmö, and Uppsala, are all safe, clean, and well managed, and offer residents good neighborhoods, tasteful blends of historic and modern architecture, nice parks, and good transportation. All have excellent universities, museums, theaters, and concert halls, as well as many other cultural attractions, and all were contenders for inclusion on our list of 20 most contented cities in the world. Sweden is also known for a disproportionate number of stars in popular music, the film industry, literature, and professional sports. Finally, we note that Sweden is a global leader in environmental protection and education about how to live more sustainably, and in efforts to maintain peace around the globe. Swedes are justifiably proud of their country.

FURTHER READING

Adams, Susan, "The World's Most Reputable Countries, 2013," *Forbes*, June 27, 2013, http://www.forbes.com/sites/susanadams/2013/06/27/the-worlds-most-reputable-countries-2013/.

Bergh, Andreas, *Sweden and the Revival of the Capitalist Welfare State* (Cheltenham, UK: Edward Elgar Publishers, 2014).

Einhorn, Eric and John Logue, *Modern Welfare States: Politics and Policies in Social Democratic Scandinavia* (New York: Praeger Publishers, 1989).

Florida, Richard, *The Rise of the Creative Class: Revisited—Revised and* Expanded (New York: Basic Books, 2014).

Scott, Andrew, *Northern Lights: The Positive Policy Example of Sweden, Finland, Denmark, and Norway* (Melbourne: Monash University Publishing, 2014).

SWITZERLAND

Switzerland is a small, prosperous, landlocked country in Western Europe with a population of about 8 million. It has a reputation for neutrality in conflicts between nations, and has not been engaged in war since 1815. It does, however, maintain a military service and has contributed actively to peacekeeping efforts around the globe. The country also has a deserved reputation for having a very high standard of living, a strong economy that is disproportionately large for the size of the country and its population, and great natural beauty. On the downside, however, is that Switzerland is very expensive—in fact, it is either the most expensive country in the world in costs of living or #2, depending on methodology and the year (the other most expensive country is Norway). We include Switzerland (and Norway) in our top 20 countries because, despite the high costs of living, Swiss people are extremely content with where they live and are proud of the many ways in which their country has achieved a higher quality of life than most other countries. Swiss are also well paid, which makes life affordable for them and the rest of the world seem like a bargain.

Switzerland enjoys many high rankings in comparisons of world nations. The country ranks #1 in the world according to the *Economist's* "Where-to-be-born Index" for 2013. The United Nations Human Development Index, which is based on various measures of life expectancy, literacy, education, standards of living, and quality of life, places Switzerland as #3 in the world in 2013, after Norway and Australia. The country is also #3 in the UN Sustainable Development Solutions Network World Happiness Report (2013), after Denmark and Norway. In terms of economics, Switzerland is ranked #7 from 187 countries, #9 from 191 countries, and #8 from 195 countries in GDP at purchasing power parity (GDP (PPP)), by the International Monetary Fund, the World Bank, and the U.S. Central Intelligence Agency, respectively. Since 2009–2010, the country has been ranked #1 on the Global Competitiveness Index that is published annually by the World Economic Forum. It also ranks #1 in the World Economic Forum's Travel and Tourism competitiveness index (most recently 2013). The Institute for Economic and Peace has the country at #5 in its 2014 Global Peace Index. Other rankings for Switzerland are #8 from 180 countries in the 2010 Corruptions Perceptions Index by Transparency International (i.e., Switzerland is #8 as "very clean"); #1 out of 178 countries in the Press Freedoms Index for 2010 compiled by Reporters without Borders ; and #8 for 167 countries in the 2010 Democracy Index by the *Economist*. In addition, the Organization for Economic Cooperation and Development (OECD) has calculated that Switzerland offers workers the greatest job security in the world, with the chance of any given worker losing her or his job in a given year being only 2.8% (2012).

Switzerland's success is rooted in the nation's political stability and disproportionately large economy given the country's size and population. Leading sectors
are banking, which accounts for more than 11% of the country's GDP and employs
nearly 200,000 workers, insurance, pharmaceuticals, chemicals, biotechnology,
and microtechnology. The country is especially well known for the manufacture
and export of high-quality watches, measuring instruments, and musical instruments, as well as food products such as cheeses and fine chocolates. The two largest banks are UBS (the Union Bank of Switzerland) and Credit Suisse, both with
headquarters in Zürich, the nation's largest city, while the largest insurance company is Zurich Financial Services, also based in Zürich. Other prominent corporations are pharmaceutical manufacturers Novartis and Hoffmann-La Roche, both
with headquarters in Basel, the food and beverage company Nestlé, and watch-
makers such as the Swatch Group. Switzerland's second-largest city, Geneva,
is noted as a headquarters city for many international organizations, including
various agencies of the United Nations, and has the nickname "Peace City." It
is an important global financial center as well, ranking #3 in Europe behind London and Zürich. The nation's capital is Bern. All Swiss cities are clean, safe, and
orderly, with high standards of living (and commensurately high prices). In this
book, we have chosen to discuss Zürich as Switzerland's representative on our list
of the world's 20 most contented urban centers.

Swiss residents enjoy outstanding health care. They are required to purchase
insurance from private companies, which in turn are required to insure every
applicant. The standards of medical know-how and technology are as high as
anywhere in the world, and Swiss hospitals are among the world's best. Total
health care costs are 11.4% of GDP, which compares with those in other leading
European nations, and are cheaper than costs in the United States which are at
approximately 17.6% of GDP. The outcomes of the Swiss health care system are
very successful: the overall life expectancy of the population is 82.8 years, that is,
85.4 years for women and 80.4 years for men, in both cases among the highest in
the world (data for 2013).

The natural beauty of Switzerland centers on its high mountains, the Alps,
and spectacular snow-capped peaks, and beautiful, lush valleys. There are many
picturesque small towns and villages in the countryside, where there is a thriving agricultural and pastoralist economy, as well as a great demand for second
homes by urban Swiss residents and foreigners alike. Mountain climbing, hiking,
biking, and skiing are popular sports that help keep the population healthy. Several of Switzerland's most popular ski resorts rank among the best in the world.
The alpine environments are fragile, and Switzerland does a good job at protecting them by regulating the character and location of construction and development. In order to lessen impact on environment and landscape, as well as to
shorten distances, Switzerland has drilled dozens of tunnels through mountains

A homeowner in a small town in Switzerland near the border with Italy disposes of household trash. The trash containers are hidden below ground and are lifted up when needed by punching a code into an access terminal. The containers then disappear again below ground, to keep the area trash-can free. (Roman Cybriwsky)

for roadways, rail tracks, and water distribution. The 57-kilometer-long (35 miles) Gotthard rail tunnel is nearing completion in the south of Switzerland. It is the world's longest tunnel and will help to make Europe smaller by significantly shortening the travel time for passenger rail service between the north and the south.

FURTHER READING

Bewes, Diccon, *Swiss Watching: Inside the Land of Milk and Money* (London: Nicholas Brealey Publishing, 2012).

Church, Clive H. and Randolph C. Head, *A Concise History of Switzerland* (Cambridge: Cambridge University Press, 2013).

TUNISIA

Tunisia is a small country in the Maghreb region of North Africa and the northernmost country on the continent. It is bordered by Algeria and Libya, and by the Mediterranean Sea to the north. Its population is about 10.9 million (2014), 98% of whom are ethnic Arabs. Independent of ethnicity, 98% of the population again practices the Islamic religion. Arabic is the official language. The capital city is

Tunis, with a population is just over 650,000 (2013). The city is located off the Mediterranean on the Gulf of Tunis and is a port. Nearby, in the suburbs of Tunis, are the ruins of the ancient city of Carthage, now an important archaeological site and tourist attraction.

Tunisia is included in the list of 20 most content countries in the world primarily because of progress that it has made recently toward becoming a fully democratic country, assuring human rights and personal freedoms, and development of the economy. The country is, therefore, a shining light among the Arabic nations of North Africa and the Middle East where dictatorial rule and political repression are all too prominent. The turning point in the country's direction is the Tunisian Revolution of the winter of 2010–2011 which resulted in the overthrow of the corrupt and dictatorial president Zine El Abidine Ben Ali and the banning by a court order of his political party, the Constitutional Democratic Party (RCD) which had ruled Tunisia since its independence from France in 1956. The only previous president before Ben Ali, the RCD's Habib Bourguiba, had also been corrupt and dictatorial. The immediate spark for the mass protests against Ben Ali was the self-immolation by a Tunis fruit vendor, 26-year-old Mohamed Bouazizi, in protest against a highhanded government official who had illegally confiscated his wares. The public protests that followed were in support of this one victim, but were also a mass action by frustrated citizens against a poor economy, rising costs, and official corruption. They were inspiration for the ensuing Arab Spring protests in several other countries in the Arab world. New elections and a new constitution that was enacted in 2014 have since propelled Tunisia on its progressive path.

Among the many changes that have taken place in the country since the revolution is an end to the RCD's "political police" that had been used to stifle dissent and intimidate political activists; a large increase in the number of active political parties (although most are very small); improvements to freedoms of expression and the press; reductions in corruption; and significant increases in women's rights. Women now hold more than 20% of the seats in parliament in Tunisia, a rarity among Arab nations. There is also significant growth of civil society in Tunisia, with many new NGOs having been established. Furthermore, NGOs that had fallen dormant during the difficult years before the revolution have been revived. There has been particular progress with respect to NGOs that have goals of increasing democracy and human rights. Islam remains the state religion, as it was before the revolution, and the new constitution affirms that the president of the country must be a Muslim, but there are guarantees of freedom of worship for all faiths, as well as for those individuals who choose to not practice any religion.

There is still room for improvement in all of these areas in Tunisia, as the country is far from ranking among the top nations in the world in any of these categories, and there has been some slippage as well after initial progress, particularly in freedoms for the media where there have been attempts by government to stifle independent reporting and arrests of journalists for allegedly defaming public officials. On the whole, however, the country has risen recently in comparative rankings of countries, and is at or near the top in a number of categories among the many nations in Africa and the Arab world. For example, we note that Tunisia ranks #90 in the United Nations Human Development Index out of 186 countries (2013), putting it approximately in the middle globally, but is #4 in Africa and #6 among Arab nations on this measure.

Under the Ben Ali dictatorship Tunisia had a secular culture in which religion was separated not only from the state, but it was also expected to be confined to the private sphere. Even Muslims, who constitute the vast majority of the population, were required to not display religiosity in public. For example, women were not permitted to wear the *hijab*, and men were expected to not wear beards. There were thousands of cases where school girls were sent home because they had worn Islamic head scarves. Such repression ended with the revolution, after which the public was free to practice its faith openly. At the same time, there has been a rise in Islamic fundamentalism in the country, and ensuing conflict

Tunisia is a strongly Muslim country, and the Great Mosque in the small inland city of Kairouan is a major landmark. The mosque, like the entire city, is a UNESCO World Heritage Site. The mosque is significant because it dates back to the early years of Islam, is very large, and has had great influence on Islamic culture and religious architecture across North Africa. (Lukasz Janyst/Dreamstime.com)

between fundamentalists' calls for Tunisia to follow Sharia law (strict Islamic law) and more moderate views represented by the Ennahda Movement (also known as the Renaissance Party), a new Islamist political party that is now the country's largest. Ultraconservative groups have attacked Tunisians who sell alcohol and have destroyed Sufi Moslem shrines that they consider to be un-Islamic. More recently, the terrorist movement Islamic State has claimed credit for a March 18, 2014, attack on a Tunis museum that killed 23 people, including 20 foreign tourists, in an apparent attempt to undermine the country's tourism economy.

Despite the new conflicts, there is considerable optimism in Tunisia that the country is on a right path, and that democracy will continue to make gains. Tunisians are proud that their revolution gained global attention and had influence on other countries in the region. The country's elections are now free, open, and fair, and include candidates with opposing viewpoints. Among the advantages that Tunisia has for success with democratic institutions is a homogeneous society, high levels of education and literacy, and considerable close social and economic links with democratic countries in Europe that can serve as standards or models, especially France with which there are historical ties. If democracy does not work in Tunisia, it will be difficult to see how it could succeed in other countries in North Africa and the Middle East.

FURTHER READING

Gana, Nouri, ed., *The Making of the Tunisian Revolution: Contexts, Architects,* Prospects (Edinburgh: Edinburgh University Press, 2013).

Perkins, Kenneth, *A History of Modern Tunisia*, 2nd edition (Cambridge: Cambridge University Press, 2014).

URUGUAY

Uruguay is the second-smallest country in South America after Suriname. It is located on the Atlantic seaboard of the continent where it is bordered on the north and west by Brazil. To the south is the wide mouth of the Rio de la Plata, one of South America's major rivers, and the country of Argentina and its capital Buenos Aires. Uruguay's population is about 3.3 million, about one-half of whom live in the national capital, Montevideo and its urbanized surroundings. We discuss this city separately in this book as one of the world's 20 most contented urban centers. Historically, the land that is now Uruguay was once part of Colonia del Sacramento that was founded by the Portuguese in 1680. The country won its independence between 1811 and 1828 as the outcome of a four-way conflict between Spain, Portugal, Brazil, and Argentina. Its economy is diversified, but has long had exports of beef, wool, soybeans, and other agricultural products as mainstays. The country's main port in Montevideo is one of South America's busiest and most modern, while the city's new (2009) international airport is generally regarded as one of the world's best. Uruguayans love soccer, which is the most popular national sport, and are proud that despite s small population base, their country won the inaugural FIFA World Cup at home in 1930 and again in 1950 in Brazil where the Uruguayan squad defeated the powerful home favorite in the final match.

Uruguay is widely recognized as one of the most liberal and most progressive countries in the world, and certainly as the most liberal and most progressive in Latin America. It has legalized sale, distribution, and consumption of marijuana in order to combat the illicit drug trade and reduce drug-related crimes, and is one of a very few countries in Latin America to have legalized abortion despite the fact that Roman Catholicism is the largest religious denomination. It has also legalized same-sex marriage. The legislation for all three was accomplished in 2012 and 2013. Such steps have caused the *Economist* to name Uruguay as its "country of the year" for 2013. The country is also considered to be first in Latin America in democracy, peace, lack of corruption, and quality of living, as well as in freedoms of the press, the proportionate size of the middle class, prosperity, and security. Along with Chile, it is the only Latin American nation to be ranked in the top group as a high income country by the United Nations. It ranks second in the region in economic freedom, income equality, per capita income, and direct foreign investment, and third in South America in terms of the United Nations Human Development Index, growth in GDP, innovation, and infrastructure. Uruguay contributes more troops to United Nations peacekeeping forces on a per capita basis than any other country. Uruguayans are proud of these distinctions that set their small and lightly populated country apart and ahead of most other nations. In 2010, a poll by Latinobarómetro revealed that Uruguayan citizens are the most supportive of democracy of any nation in Latin America and are by far the most satisfied with the way democracy works in their country. This is quite a change for a country that was run by harsh military rule from 1973 to 1985.

Uruguayans are also contented that their country has enjoyed a buoyant economy for more than a decade, avoiding some of the downturns experienced in neighboring countries and worldwide. It has taken advantage of high prices for its export commodities, invested wisely in technology and infrastructure, and diversified its economy to promote such growth industries as software development, tourism, and banking services. Because of the latter sector, Uruguay has been referred to as the "Switzerland of Latin America." Prosperity has helped to pay down foreign debt, reduce poverty and unemployment, and invest in the future by investing in education. In 2009, Uruguay became the first country in the world to provide a free laptop computer for every elementary school child.

The unique character of Uruguay is exemplified by its current president, José Mujica. Elected in 2009 and in office since March 1, 2010, Mujica is often described as the humblest president in the world because of his personal lifestyle. He and his wife eschewed residence in the official presidential palace, which they consider to be too opulent, and live instead on a small farm outside Montevideo where they grow chrysanthemums for sale. The president also economizes on security details and motorcades, and drives himself to and from work every day in an aging Volkswagen Beetle valued at $1,800. Sometimes he picks up hitchhikers along the way. During the time of military rule, he was a revolutionary in support of the nation's poor people, and spent time in prison for his political activities. He donates 90% of his monthly salary as president to charities that support the poor and small entrepreneurs. In a speech to the United Nations General Assembly in September 2013, Mujica talked at length about the impact of globalization on humanity, and urged that the world return to a life of greater simplicity. He argued that individuals should be guided in their lives by love, friendship, adventure, solidarity, and family instead of by markets and money. For his insights, lifelong commitments to the downtrodden, and progressive leadership as president, Mujica has been proposed as a possible candidate for a Nobel Peace Prize.

FURTHER READING

Mitchell, Shane, "Uruguay: South America's Latest Hot Spot," *Travel + Leisure*, February 2012, http://www.travelandleisure.com/articles/uruguay-south-americas-latest-hot-spot.

Psetizki, Veronica, "Uruguay: South America's Best-Kept secret?" *BBC News*, October 3, 2010, http://www.bbc.co.uk/news/world-latin-america-11397130.

Tremlett, Giles, "José Mijica: Is This the World's Most Radical President?" *The Guardian*, September 18, 2014, http://www.theguardian.com/world/2014/sep/18/-sp-is-this-worlds-most-radical-president-uruguay-jose-mujica.

THE 20 LEAST CONTENTED COUNTRIES

AFGHANISTAN

Afghanistan is a mountainous, landlocked country in the heart of Asia that has been devastated by decades of warfare and civil strife. It is variously described as being part of Central Asia, South Asia, and the Islamic Middle East. The fighting is ongoing in Afghanistan with no end in sight, and the people continue to suffer, which is why we selected this country for our list of 20 least contented countries in the world.

Afghanistan's population is approximately 31 million people. The country has a diverse ethnic makeup. Pashtun people are the most numerous ethnic group, comprising about 40–50% of the nation's total, followed by Tajiks, who are at about 25% of the total. Dozens of other ethnic groups make up the rest of the population. Dari and Pashto are the main languages, comprising about 50% and 35% of the nation's total, respectively. Islam was introduced in Afghanistan in the seventh century, and today some 99% of the population is Muslim. About 80–85% of the population belongs to the Sunni branch of Islam and most of the rest are Shiites. Afghanistan's capital and largest city is Kabul, located in a narrow valley between mountains in the east of the country. Its population is estimated to be about 3.1 million. Kandahar, in the south, is the second city with a little more than 500,000 inhabitants,

Historically, the country has occupied a strategic crossroads location between the cultures of Asia to the east and those of the Mediterranean and European worlds to the west, as well as between the imperial ambitions of czarist Russia to the north and the British Empire in India in South Asia, and has therefore been coveted by various powers for centuries. The storied Khyber Pass through mountains east of Kabul connects Afghanistan and Pakistan, and has long been an avenue for armies, traders, and adventurers between different worlds on the Asian continent. A turning point in the modern history of Afghanistan was a successful Marxist revolution in 1978, followed by more than nine years of war by invading troops from the Soviet Union who fought in support of the communist state. More than 1 million people, mostly civilians, perished in the war and as many as 6 million refugees fled across the borders. The wars have not ceased since. In 1994 the Taliban managed to wrest control of much of central and southern Afghanistan, including the capital Kabul, and after some setbacks, gained even more territory in 1996 and established a very strict religious state called the Islamic Emirate of Afghanistan.

In 2001, the Taliban dynamited the giant Buddhas of Bamiyan. The two statues date back to the fifth century and pre-Islamic history, and were considered to be great treasures of art and national heritage. The Taliban, however, saw them as idols and ordered their destruction. Also in 2001, the United States began war in Afghanistan to root out terrorists in the al-Qaeda network who were behind the September 11 attacks on targets on American soil, and to search for al-Qaeda leader Osama bin Laden. The American war in Afghanistan became the longest in U.S. history. It ended officially on December 28, 2014, but American soldiers are still in the country as NATO troops. The number of causalities in the U.S. War in Afghanistan, as it is formally called, is in the tens of thousands. The country continues to be a tinderbox, with frequent skirmishes between rival forces for power, and terrorist attacks such as car bombings and suicide bombings. Many of the attacks are against populated spots in Kabul.

Constant war has ensured that Afghanistan continues to be a poor country—one of the poorest in the world. The annual per capital GDP is about $1,100, and more than 40% of the population survives on less than $1 per day. The United Nations

Human Development Index for Afghanistan ranks at #168 out of 187 countries surveyed, the lowest rank in Asia, while the Legatum Prosperity Index for the country ranks at #137 out of 142 countries, the second-lowest in Asia after Yemen. An estimated 11% of the economy of the country comes from the cultivation and sale of opium poppies, a crop that the current government and international organizations are working to eradicate. Life expectancy for both genders is only about 60. Afghanistan has one of the highest fertility rates in the world, at 5.64 children born per woman, while infant mortality is the world's highest: 119.41 infant deaths per 1,000 live births. These are devastating statistics. Thankfully, there are many international aid workers who are working alongside dedicated citizens to make a difference in Afghanistan. If only there were peace, their work would be so much easier!

FURTHER READING

Ansary, Tamim, *Games without Rules: The Often-Interrupted History of Afghanistan* (New York: Public Affairs, 2012).

Jones, Seth G., *In the Graveyard of Empires: America's War in Afghanistan* (New York: Norton, 2010).

Rubin, Barnett P., *Afghanistan from the Cold War to the War of Terror* (New York: Oxford University Press, 2015).

Tomsen, Peter, *The Wars of Afghanistan: Messianic Terrorism, Tribal Conflicts, and the Failures of Great Powers* (New York: Public Affairs, 2011).

CAMBODIA

Cambodia is a small country in Southeast Asia that is bordered by Vietnam, Laos, and Thailand, and by the Gulf of Thailand. The Mekong River flows through the country and contributes heavily to livelihoods, as does a large lake in the center named Tonle Sap that greatly expands and contracts its territory with wet and dry seasons. The famous archaeological and UNESCO World Heritage Site Angkor Wat is to the north of the lake in the north-center of the country near today's town of Siem Reap, and attracts tourists from around the world. It was once the focus of a powerful Khmer Kingdom. The capital city today is Phnom Penh, the country's largest city with a population of about 1.5 million by official count. Cambodia itself has a population of about 15.2 million (2013 official estimate), about 90% of whom are ethnic Khmer and 95% of whom practice Theravada Buddhism.

Cambodia was colonized by France in 1863 and became part of what was known as French Indochina. Independence was achieved in 1953, but was followed by exceedingly difficult times with great losses of life when the Vietnam

War spread into the country because of intense bombing by the United States, and from 1975 to 1979 when the Khmer Rouge led by Pol Pot took control of Cambodia and conducted a campaign of genocide that killed up to 3 million of his own countrymen. Now, the country is a constitutional monarchy that is governed by Hun Sen, a highly corrupt and repressive prime minister who came into office in a coup in 1997. He had once been a Khmer Rouge official. It is because the Cambodian people have suffered so greatly for so long, and because a land that has been richly endowed by nature has so many poor people, that we have included Cambodia in our group of 20 least contented countries in the world.

Most Cambodians live in rural areas and derive their incomes from agriculture and related fields, with rice and fish being important staples. Although incomes have been rising, the GDP per capita still ranks among the lowest in Asia and #147 out 187 countries as measured by the International Monetary Fund, #144 out of 185 countries according to the World Bank, and #153 out of 195 countries according to the U.S. Central Intelligence Agency. The 2013 United Nations Human

Dani, age 9 at the time the photo was taken, sells birds to tourists and religious visitors at Wat Phnom, a Buddhist temple in the heart of Phnom Penh, Cambodia. She has braces on her legs because of polio. People purchase the birds in order to say a prayer or make a wish and then release them. Boys with nets catch the birds later, and the cycle continues. (Roman Cybriwsky)

Development Index for the country is at #136 out of 187 countries (tied with Bhutan). Agricultural improvement is hampered by rapid deforestation, which has resulted in problems of soil erosion and flooding, and by changes to water levels in the Mekong River owing to construction of dams in countries upstream. Rural areas are also held back by the tragedy of an estimated 4 to 6 million landmines that are still in place many years after the fighting of the 1970s has ceased. Until these mines are removed one by one with great care, much of the land near the country's villages cannot be put to productive use. Already, some 40,000 Cambodians are amputees as a result of injuries from landmine explosions.

There has been growth in international tourism to Cambodia, opening employment in non-agricultural sectors and stimulating migration to Siem Reap, Phnom Penh, and Sihanoukville, a city near Cambodia's beaches, as a result. Cambodia has also seen growth in industrial production, especially in the manufacturing of textiles and garments for foreign markets. New factories often employ large numbers of young women from the countryside, and are financed by investments from China, Thailand, Malaysia, or other foreign sources. Foreign investment in Cambodia has been a two-edged sword. While it can produce much-needed employment for many Cambodians, it also often results in profits being taken from the country rather than being reinvested locally, as well as inferior or exploitative working conditions.

The problem of corruption is especially acute in Cambodia. On the grand scale, the Hun Sen regime is accused of profiting enormously from sale of land to foreign investors who, in turn, have caused the evictions of many villagers and residents in urban neighborhoods where foreign companies want to build, and from bribes that are paid by foreign businesses in exchange for grants of rights to exploit the country's mineral and timber resources. On a smaller, everyday scale, Cambodian citizens face corruption when trying to gain admission to a better school for their children, seek medical services, deal with traffic police, or need some document from government bureaucrats. A new anticorruption law was put into place in 2010, but it seems to have had little effect. In particular, instead of protecting anti-corruption whistle-blowers, it threatens them with jail sentences if the accusations that they make are not successfully proven in courts that are themselves corrupt. It is no surprise then that Transparency International has given low marks to Cambodia, ranking the country as 156th in the world out of 174 countries in its Corruption Perceptions Index.

Hun Sen's government is also accused of other abuses, including condoning violence against political opponents, extrajudicial killings and torture, widespread abuse of prisoners, conducting dishonest elections, and stifling freedoms of the press. Most recently, on September 22, 2013, several journalists, including foreigners, were assaulted by police as they attempted to cover a story about disputed elections in Phnom Penh. In such a light, Freedom House International has assessed the country as being "not free," and has ranked Cambodia at an abysmal #149 out of 153 countries in freedom of the press.

FURTHER READING

Brinkley, Joel, *Cambodia's Curse: The Modern History of a Troubled Land* (New York: PublicAffairs, 2012).

Freeman, Michael, *Cambodia* (London: Reaktion Books, 2004).

Strangio, Sebastian, *Hun Sen's Cambodia* (New Haven, CT: Yale University Press, 2014).

DEMOCRATIC REPUBLIC OF THE CONGO

The Democratic Republic of the Congo (DRC) is a country in Central Africa that occupies most of the basin of the Congo River, and that stretches from the shores of the Great Lakes in East Africa to a narrow westward extension of sovereign territory along the lower reaches of the Congo River that provides access to the South Atlantic Ocean. The equator extends across the northern part of DRC. From 1971 to 1997 the country was named Zaire. Before independence in 1960, it was a colony of Belgium and was known as the Belgian Congo. As described in the chilling book by Adam Hochschild, millions of Congolese died from forced labor in rubber plantations, mutilations, hunger, and untreated diseases during the harsh rule of Belgian King Leopold II (r. 1865–1909).

The DRC is the 2nd-largest country in Africa in size and the 11th largest in the world, and has a population of about 75 million, the fourth-highest total on the African continent. The population is highly diverse ethnically and linguistically. As a legacy of the colonial period, French is the official language, making DRC the most populous French-speaking country in the world. Its capital city, Kinshasa, has about 9 million people and is the third most populous city in Africa. We discuss Kinshasa elsewhere in this book as one of the world's poorest and least content cities.

The DRC is an extremely rich country in terms of natural resources, but most of the population is impoverished because wealth is grossly unequally distributed due to bad government and corruption. Key resources are cobalt and copper, of which the DRC leads the world in production, diamonds (#2 in the world), and gold. The country also has other minerals, timber, and great hydroelectric potential. Had there been peace and good government, the DRC could have been a prosperous, shining light in Africa, but a succession of dictatorships, kleptocracy, and civil wars have devastated the country and its people. Communications are poorly developed in the interior, with few paved roads and few rail lines except for those that were built specifically to transport resources such as mineral ores to export markets. Wars in 1996 and again in 1998–2003 (the Second Congo War) took as many as 5 million civilian lives, about one-half of them children, mostly on account of disease and malnutrition. The second war involved nine African states and about 20 armed groups, and was the deadliest war in African history. Of those who survived, millions more were displaced from their villages into refugee camps abroad. Thousands of child soldiers known as *kadogos* (Swahili for "little ones who fight") were conscripted to fight in these wars. Some were as young as seven. There is now somewhat better government under the administration of President Joseph Kabila (he took office in 2001 and a new constitution was promulgated in 2006), but "better" is relative and the road out of poverty in the DRC and away from bloodshed is distressingly long.

The DRC does very poorly in standardized comparisons with other countries. For example, the United Nations Human Development Index, which combines measures of life expectancy, access to schooling, and income levels, has the country in 186th place from 187 countries (2012; Niger is last). Key indicators are that life expectancy at birth in the DRC is only 48.7 years, the mean number of years of schooling is only 3.5, and the mean income level is only 31.9% of what the UN has calculated as being needed in DRC for a decent standard of living. Furthermore, the DRC ranks 144th out of 148 countries on the Gender Inequality Index (2012), a measure that combines data about women's reproductive health, empowerment, and participation in the paid labor force. Key indicators here are that for every 100,000 live births, 540 women die from pregnancy related cause, only 8.2% of seats in parliament are held by women, only 10.7% of women have attained a secondary or higher level of education as compared to 36.2% of men, and the rate of labor force participation is 70.2% for women and 72.5% for men. With respect to other measures, Transparency International has ranked the DRC 154th out of 175 countries (2013) in terms of corruption (i.e., 154th most corrupt), and Reporters without Borders has ranked the country 142nd from 179 nations surveyed in its World Press Freedoms Index. With respect to human rights, the DRC is one of 48 countries from 195 that Freedom House has classified as "not free" (most recently 2013), describing the country as one characterized by "violence and insecurity in the context of endemic official corruption."

The health situation in the DRC is acute. In addition to the low average life expectancy mentioned earlier and high mortality rates at childbirth, the country suffers from a high incidence of HIV/AIDS illness (about 4.2% of adults; 1.1 million individuals), as well as from malaria, yellow fever, tuberculosis, polio, cholera, and typhoid. The Ebola virus has afflicted various parts of the DRC in recent years, including in the recent (2014) outbreak. The high rate of HIV/AIDS is attributed to poor knowledge about how the disease is transmitted and poor preventative measures, as well as the disproportionate numbers of high-risk populations in DRC such as refugees and soldiers. Condoms are said to be available only in bigger cities. There is a shortage of medical facilities and supplies in DRC, as well as of trained health professionals. Poverty contributes in many ways to the dire health situation, because in the DRC health care has to be paid for in cash in advance, before treatment.

Perhaps the worst aspect of life in the DRC is the extraordinary dangers that exist in the country for women. The east of DRC in particular has been called the "rape capital of the world." Sexual violence is so prevalent that a United Nations study concluded that a large segment of society perceives it to be normal. The chronic warfare in the country has included the rape and kidnapping of women and children, and their use as sexual slaves. In 2010, Oxfam reported that rapes were on the increase in the DRC rather than decreasing in number, and in 2014 the British organization Freedom from Torture, that provides medical care to victims of torture, reported that rape and sexual violence were being used routinely by Congolese officials in state-run prisons as punishment for politically active women. Although the custom is not as widespread as it is in parts of West and Central Africa, female genital mutilation (FGM) is also practiced in parts of the DRC.

FURTHER READING

Deibert, Michael, *The Democratic Republic of Congo: Between Hope and Despair* (London: Zed Books, 2013).
Hochschild, Adam, *King Leopold's Ghost* (New York: Houghton Mifflin Harcourt, 1999).
Stearns, Jason K., *Dancing in the Glory of Monsters: The Collapse of the Congo and the Great War of Africa* (New York: PublicAffairs, 2012).

EL SALVADOR

El Salvador is the smallest and most densely populated country in Central America. It faces the Pacific Ocean on the south, and also borders Guatemala and Honduras. Much of the interior is mountainous, although there are also broad valleys with fertile volcanic soil and heavy settlement. The country is prone to earthquakes and volcanic eruptions. Its capital city, San Salvador, has been hit by earthquakes numerous times since it was founded in 1525, most recently in 2001 and 2005. Other environmental hazards are alternating periods of drought and heavy rainfall, which often leads to destructive landslides along exposed hill slopes after torrential downpours. The country also experiences hurricanes. Since the 1990s, there has been a marked increase in the number and severity of such storms in El Salvador, including those that form in the Pacific and those that come from the Caribbean and cross the Central American isthmus. Much of El Salvador also suffers from deforestation caused by population growth and the opening of new farm lands. The country is rich in biodiversity, although again the pressure of population on the land has endangered various animal and plant species. Because of its small size, El Salvador is sometimes referred to as *Pulgarcito de America*, "the Tom Thumb of the Americas."

The population of El Salvador is 6,290,420 (2013). The largest city is San Salvador, with a population in 2011 of 567,698 in the municipality and 2,442,017 in the metropolitan area. The country is among the poorest nations in Latin America, although income levels rank somewhat higher than those in nearby Honduras and Nicaragua. That small plus, however, is attributed in significant measure to remittances that are sent home by El Salvadorans working abroad, particularly in the United States. There are nearly 200,000 Salvadorans in the Washington, D.C. area alone, forming the capital area's largest immigrant population. In 2012, El Salvador's income from remittances amounted to $3.9 billion, the fourth-highest total in Latin America behind Mexico, Guatemala, and Colombia, but first in per capita terms as those three larger countries have significantly larger populations. Such money transfers comprise a significant percentage of El Salvador's national economy (16% in 2013), and for many families represent the difference between a life of poverty and better conditions. On the downside is that remittance income tends to drive prices upward in local economies, especially for needs such as housing, putting an added pinch on families without someone working abroad. This, in turn, leads to more labor migration to other countries and a concomitant erosion of economic independence of El Salvador. About one-third of all Salvadoran households receive money from individuals abroad. On average, Salvadoran workers send nearly $3,000 home per year, with the largest remittances coinciding with the Christmas holiday season.

Environmental hazards and economic problems aside, the greatest reason for listing El Salvador among the world's 20 least content countries is its extraordinarily high crime rate, especially murders. According to the United Nations Office on Drugs and Crime, the murder rate in El Salvador was 41.2 per 100,000 population in 2012, the fourth-highest rate in the world. (The highest murder rate was in neighboring Honduras, a country that is also on our list of 20 least contented countries.) In both countries, as elsewhere in Latin America where crime is also high, the problem is attributed to violent gangs, or *maras* in colloquial Spanish, that engage in the trafficking of narcotics, weapons, and people (including labor migrants into the United States), as well as gambling, prostitution, extortion, and other rackets, and to the turf wars that were associated with these illicit businesses. El Salvador's biggest gangs are Mara Salvatruca, which is commonly abbreviated as MS-13, and Barrio 18. When there was a truce between gangs recently, the violence eased somewhat, but it has since escalated once again.

The gang problem in El Salvador has extensions in Salvadoran neighborhoods in the United States, especially in Los Angeles and the Washington, D.C. area, where Salvadoran (and other Central American) gang members have also been engaged in violence and narcotics trafficking. Many gang members have been deported from the United States repeatedly, and earn extra money as they return to the United States by sneaking other Salvadorans (and other Central Americans) into the country. The most ruthless of them kill or leave their human freight to die after collecting payments from them for the northward journey, and rape women clients. In El Salvador, gang members are known to gang rape and kill former girl-friends of gang members if the gang decides that the women know too much about gang activities. Because of gang activity, San Salvador and other Salvadoran cities are among the most dangerous in the world. People in poor neighborhoods seek gangs for protection, while wealthy residents surround themselves with elaborate security systems and private guards. El Salvador is heavily armed. Additional violence in the country comes from vigilante groups that dedicate themselves to ridding the country of its gangs scourge by murdering gang members. The most notorious of these groups is Sombra Negra, meaning Black Shadow in Spanish. It is comprised largely of rouges from police departments and the Salvadoran military.

El Salvador ranks as #115 out of 186 countries in the United Nations Human Development Index. This puts it ahead of several other countries in Latin America, but is still low by standards of the Western Hemisphere. Among the areas where the country comes up short is higher infant mortality than neighboring countries, inadequate sewerage and sanitation systems and the resultant dangerous pollution of waters, high rates of deforestation and soil erosion, underfunded and overcrowded schools, a poor climate for business investment, widening income inequality between rich and poor, poor housing conditions and slum neighborhoods in urban and rural areas alike, and lingering poverty, underdevelopment, and political division that is traced to the country's 12 years of exceptionally brutal civil war (1979–1992).

FURTHER READING

DeLugan, Robin Maria, *Reimagining National Belonging: Post-Civil War El Salvador in a Global Context* (Tucson: University of Arizona Press, 2014).

Moodie, Ellen, *El Salvador in the Aftermath of Peace: Crime, Uncertainty, and the Transition to Democracy* (Philadelphia: University of Pennsylvania Press, 2012).

EQUATORIAL GUINEA

Equatorial Guinea is a small country in Central Africa on the Gulf of Guinea of the Atlantic Ocean. As its name also suggests, the country is tropical and straddles the equator. There are two parts to Equatorial Guinea: a larger one on the African mainland that is called Rio Muni, and two islands in the Gulf of Guinea, Bioko (still referred to often by its former name Fernando Pó) and Annobón. Bioko is the larger island and contains the country's capital city, Malabo, a coastal city located on the rim of a sunken volcano. In 2005, its population was 156,000. The largest city is the Rio Muni port of Bata, 2005 estimated population 173,000. The population of Equatorial Guinea as a whole is about 1.6 million (2012). A new capital city, Oyala, is under construction in Rio Muni.

Equatorial Guinea was once a Spanish colony called Spanish Guinea, and achieved its independence in 1968. It is the only African nation to have Spanish as an official language. Most Equatoguineans are Bantu people, with the main ethnic group, constituting about 80% of the population, being the Fang. The largest ethnic minority are Bubi people. They are indigenous to Bioko Island and comprise about 15% of the national population. Roman Catholicism is the majority religion.

Oil was discovered in Equatorial Guinea in the 1990s and has since transformed the economy. Previously, the most highly valued exports had been cocoa, coffee, and timber, but since the start of petroleum exploitation the nation has grown to become a major exporter on the world market and the richest country in Africa on a per capita basis. In 2013, the per capita GDP was $25,700, the 58th highest in the world from among 228 countries. While this represents an impressive increase from before the oil production years, the oil wealth is grossly unequally distributed, with most of the country's residents remaining poor. It is because of this inequality and the failure of Equatorial Guinea's government to assure that the country as a whole benefits from the resource bonanza that we list Equatorial Guinea among the 20 least contented countries of the world.

We are not alone in offering a negative assessment. Despite the wealth, Equatorial Guinea is ranked as #47 out of 178 countries in the Failed States Index (2013) as calculated by the Fund for Peace, and receives especially low marks for three categories: legitimacy of the state, uneven economic development, and violations of human rights and rule of law. Likewise, the Freedom House "Freedom in the World" rankings for 2015 include Equatorial Guinea as among the 10 "worst of the worst" countries in the world from 195 countries surveyed, and Reporters without Borders considers the country's president, Teodoro Obiang Nguema Mbasogo, to be a "predator" of press freedom. Furthermore, Equatorial Guinea is considered to be a major violator of proscriptions against human trafficking, and is accused as both a source and a destination for women and children who subjected to forced labor and exploited for sex. The government is also accused of allowing inhumane conditions in the nation's prisons, as well as the torture of prisoners and unexplained prisoner deaths.

Teodoro Obiang assumed the presidency in 1979 in a coup against his uncle, the despotic and murderous Francisco Macias Nguema, and is now the world's longest-serving nonroyal head of state. While some conditions may have improved in Equatorial Guinea during his rule, such as termination of a campaign of genocide against the Bubi minority, Obiang is far also from being a good president. He has enriched himself greatly from the national treasury, and has taken personal control of the country's finances reportedly so that the country's lower-level bureaucrats would not have an opportunity to steal for themselves. As reported by Human Rights Watch and other sources, Obiang's relatives and other inner circle members have also become fabulously wealthy as a result of oil corruption, and enjoy lavish lifestyles. Furthermore, Obiang has encouraged a cult of personality in the country, with his image appearing not just on posters and billboards, but also on T-shirts worn by the country's citizens. In 2003, state-operated radio broadcasts declared that Obiang was "the country's god" and that he wielded "all power over men and things." It was also announced that he "can decide to kill without anyone calling him to account and without going to hell." Obiang is himself on record as saying that he is a god. Among the titles that he has given to himself is the pretentious-sounding "gentleman of the great island of Bioko, Annobón and Río Muni."

A constitution that was drawn up for Equatorial Guinea in 2011 limits the president to two terms in office, but Obiang, who has already been elected at least four times, has said that the first of his allowed two terms would begin in 2016. Understandably, this president is widely considered to be among the worst rulers in the world, and is faulted, along with his predecessor uncle, for the state of poverty and repression that the citizens of Equatorial Guinea face on a way of life. As reported by the international humanitarian organization IRIN, "Equatorial Guinea is the dictatorship that no one talks about. The government earns billions in oil every year, yet 60% of its population lives on US$1 a day."

FURTHER READING

"Equatorial Guinea: Poverty Rife in Africa's 'Kuwait,'" http://www.irinnews.org/report/80768
/equatorial-guinea-poverty-rife-in-africa-s-kuwait.
Klitgaardd, Robert, *Tropical Gangsters: One Man's Experiences in Development and Decadence in Deepest Africa* (New York: Basic Books, 1991).
Roberts, Adam, *The Wonga Coup: Guns, Thugs, and a Ruthless Determination to Create Mayhem in an Oil-Rich Corner of Africa* (Cambridge, MA: PublicAffairs, 2007).

FRANCE

France is an influential country in Western Europe that borders the English Channel in the north, the Mediterranean Sea in the south, and the Bay of Biscayne to the west, as well as eight European countries, most prominently Belgium, Germany, Switzerland, Italy, and Spain. As such, it is squarely in the heart of Western Europe and the European Union, and in fact houses the European Parliament in its charming eastern city Strasbourg. Its own capital, Paris, is one of the most romanticized and most visited cities in the world, as well as a giant metropolis (population 2,273,305; metropolitan area approximately 13 million) of global economic and political importance. France itself is the largest country that is wholly within Europe and has a population of 66,109,000, the 3rd-largest total in Europe and 20th-largest in the world. The country ranks fifth in the world after the United States, China, Japan, and Germany in the size of its economy as measured by GDP, and fourth in the world in numbers of *Fortune* 500 companies as compiled for 2014.

France has a long and proud history. Its people have made innumerable contributions to global cultures and civilization, including contributions to fundamental principles of freedom, democracy, human rights, as well as to the arts, literature, science, and many other fields. The country has its own language, French, which is spoken as well in many former colonies of the country around the globe, as well as many distinctive cultural traditions such as its cuisine and wonderful wines that are also admired globally. Most citizens enjoy a very high standard of living, with decent housing, excellent health care, excellent schooling, and excellent public infrastructure. The country is relatively safe from crime, advanced technologically, and progressive with respect to many aspects of women's rights, labor law, and personal freedoms. The Human Development Index for the country is classified as "very high" by the United Nations and ranks as 20th in the world out of 187 countries surveyed. The Legatum Prosperity Index for the country is 21st-highest among 142 countries surveyed. The Transparency International Corruption Perceptions Index for France ranks 26th-best from among 179 countries. Freedom House gives the country its highest rating in each of three categories: freedom, political rights, and civil liberties.

Why then is France listed here among the 20 least contented countries in the world and not among the 20 most contented countries? While we acknowledge that France almost always ranks highly on data-based measures related to quality of life, as do most of the other countries of northern and western Europe, we single this country out for criticism because, unfortunately, it epitomizes many of the major problems that affect European society today that these measures have not yet picked up. Specifically, we see France as an especially sad example of a nation's failure to successfully integrate immigrant populations into wider society, and as well as an all-too-prominent example of increasing prejudices against immigrants. Sadly, these prejudices have ugly racial, religious, and cultural overtones. Because France has been such a leader in human rights and democratic values in the past, we think that the country could and should be a bastion of tolerance and enlightened social policy today. However, what we see instead is a descent into a Europe with increasing racism and hatreds, and the rise of intolerant, ultra-right wing political parties and movements. In good conscience, we cannot ignore this aspect of Europe, which we find in every country on the continent (and in Europe's island countries too), and single out France because it has been especially disappointing in these regards.

Many of the poorest citizens in France are immigrants from former French colonies in North, West and Equatorial Africa, and their offspring. They tend to reside in peripheral suburbs of cities such as Paris, Marseille, and Lyon in large public housing blocs called *banlieues* that concentrate poverty and related social problems outside the main parts of cities. Examples near Paris include Clichy-sous-Bois, Bondy, and Sevran. Residents feel excluded from mainstream French society and its economic opportunities. In Sevran, the unemployment rate is 18%, and 40% among the young. Some 36% of the population lives below the poverty line, approximately three times the national average. The frustrations of residents occasionally boil over into conflicts, including mass rioting that sometimes sweeps the country, as happened quite famously in both 1981 and 2005 when young *banlieusards* showed their anger by burning cars in cities across the country.

In many *banlieues*, the majority of residents are Muslims. In addition to those of African heritage, Muslims in France come from Turkey, the Levant, and other regions, with the result that the country now has a Muslim population of more than 6 million, which is significantly more than any other country in Europe other than Turkey and Russia, and nearly 10% of the country's total population. There has been considerable religious conflict such as about the *hijab* worn by many Muslim women and insults against Islam such as derogatory cartoons of the Prophet Mohammed in French publications such as those in the satirical magazine *Charlie Hedbo*. On January 17, 2015, 12 individuals were shot to death in the magazine's Paris offices by two Islamist gunmen who were outraged over recently published drawings. Discontentment is also reflected in new waves of anti-Semitic violence in France, this time often perpetrated by anti-Israel Muslims and radical Islamists, that echo the dangers that Jews faced in Europe with the rise of Nazism, and that have raised questions for France's Jews about whether or not it is time to flee the country for safety. We also note that today's France has a poor record of human rights related to its Roma minority. There have been attacks by racist French against Roma (or "Romani") camps near Paris, and deportations of Roma people by the French government that have resulted in international condemnations, including by the United Nations. The extreme-right National Front Party has considerable support among French voters for its anti-Islam and anti-immigration positions. We see France as being highly fracture and increasingly dangerous, and see no choice except to list it as one of the world's 20 least contented countries.

FURTHER READING

"Forgotten in the Banlieues: Young, Diverse and Unemployed," *The Economist*, February 23, 2013, http://www.economist.com/news/europe/21572248-young-diverse-and-unemployed-forgotten-banlieues.

Goldberg, Jeffrey, "Is It Time for the Jews to Leave Europe?" *The Atlantic*, 315, 3, April 2015, pp. 62–75.

Moran, Matthew, *The Republic and the Riots: Exploring Urban Violence in French Suburbs, 2005–2007* (Bern: Peter Land AG, 2012).

Thomas, Dominic, *Africa and France: Postcolonial Cultures, Migrations, and Racism* (Bloomington: Indiana University Press, 2013).

GREECE

Greece is a small country at the southern tip of the Balkan Peninsula in southeastern Europe that faces the Ionian, Aegean, and Mediterranean Seas. In addition to the mainland, the country includes more than 10,000 offshore islands, about 227 of which are inhabited. The coastline is highly irregular in shape and therefore very long. It has the longest coastline in the Mediterranean Basin and the 11th longest in the world. About 80% of the country is mountainous, with Mt. Olympus, the legendary home of gods in Greek mythology, being the highest peak. The country has a very long and decorated history that dates back to the eighth century B.C. and the rise of classical Greek civilization and the once-powerful Greek Empire. Over time, the country has made enormous contributions to Western culture. It is recognized as the birthplace of democracy, as well as for foundations in Western philosophy, science, mathematics, literature, and theater, among other fields. The historic Greek Orthodox Church has been influential far beyond the borders of Greece, with fundamental impact on the Orthodox faith as it is practiced in the Balkans, in Russia, and in other countries. The country gave birth to the Olympic games, which date back to the eighth century B.C., and hosted the first modern-era Olympics in 1896 in the national capital, Athens. According to the census of 2012, the population of Greece is 10,816,286.

We acknowledge that Greece is a beautiful country with a rich and proud culture, and that its contributions to the world have continued since ancient times. Who doesn't like Greek food, for example, or the exuberance of a Greek wedding as popularized in some unforgettable Hollywood films? We also acknowledge that Greece continues to be one of the world's most popular international tourism destinations, drawn by history, scenic beauty, and idyllic island villages and beaches, as well as a global leader in maritime shipping. Yet, we feel compelled to include Greece on our list of 20 least contented countries in the world because of a long period of economic crisis in the country and the many social and political problems that have ensued. We see dark pessimism among many Greek citizens about the future stability of their country and its economy, and fears about how they will survive the strains on them that are caused by the enormous debt crisis that Greece faces. The country has overspent and overborrowed, has failed to collect much of the tax revenue that it is due from its own citizens and their businesses, and has a notoriously poor record of paying back the debts that it owes. There has been corruption too. Creditors include numerous banks and other financial institutions in Greece and other European countries, most notably France and Germany, the European Union, and others. The total debt is about €315.5 billion (about $333 billion), which is a huge amount for any country, much less one that is small and with only 11 million residents, and more than enough to have brought the country to the edge of bankruptcy and spread economic crisis throughout Europe and the Eurozone.

For ordinary Greek citizens, the financial crisis has meant elevated levels of unemployment, higher prices, higher taxes, and a loss of confidence in government, banks, and other institutions. There have been cuts in wages and major reductions in social benefits such as housing subsidies and health insurance. People's pensions for old age have taken a massive hit, homelessness has increased markedly, as have social problems such as crime, alcoholism, and drug addiction. Suicide rates have also risen dramatically. Not surprisingly, the economic mess has also caused a large emigration from Greece in search of employment abroad. The exodus of talented and energetic citizens has added to the national gloom. The government's austerity measures were met with anger and public protests, and have resulted in the recent election of a new Greek government led by Prime Minister Alexis Tsipras (assumed office on January 26, 2015) and his left-wing

Tensions have been high in Greece because of the country's high public debt and poor economy. This photo, taken in the national capital Athens, shows a scuffle between angry citizens and riot police at the office of an important government official. (AP Photo/Petros Giannakouris)

political party Syriza in coalition with politicians from the Far Right. Their platform is to push back against austerity measures that bring hardship to Greek citizens, and to strive instead for debt forgiveness and bailouts. In early April 2015, the Tsipras government announced a plan to seek an amount of €279 billion ($305 billion) from Germany, a major creditor, as reparations for killings in Greece and other suffering that occurred during the brutal Nazi German occupation of the country in World War II.

The economic crisis aside, we are compelled to note that the major cities of Greece, the capital and largest urban center Athens in particular, as well as the second city Thessaloniki, suffer from serious urban problems such as poorly regulated growth, impossible traffic, and chronic air pollution. Visitors to Athens often express surprise and great disappointment to see that this city that displays monuments to a proud history is so badly littered and filled with graffiti, that smog affected their breathing and irritated throats and eyes, and that old neighborhoods are crumbling with disrepair. Motor vehicles have been the main source of air pollution. Unfortunately, Greek cities have recently seen new spikes in air pollution levels, reportedly to record-worst levels, because increases in the costs of home heating during the financial crisis have caused residents to burn wood instead. Not only is wood inefficient as a heating fuel, it adds a distinctive smell to the city and toxins to the air because much of the burned wood is painted scrap material.

FURTHER READING

Leontidou, Lila, *The Mediterranean City in Transition: Social and Urban Development* (Cambridge: Cambridge University Press, 2006).

Matsaganis, Manos, "The Greek Crisis: Social Impact and Policy Responses," *Friedrich Ebert Stiftung: Study*, 2013, http://library.fes.de/pdf-files/id/10314.pdf.

Mitsopoulos, Michael and Theodor Pelagidis, *Understanding the Crisis in Greece: From Boom to Bust* (New York: Palgrave Macmillan, 2012).

Sarrinikolaou, George, *Facing Athens: Encounters with the Modern City* (New York: North Point Press, 2004).

HAITI

The Republic of Haiti is a country in the Caribbean Sea that occupies the western part of the island of Hispaniola that it shares with the Dominican Republic. It was the second country in the Americas after the United States to gain its independence, that being 1804 from France as result of a violent rebellion by slaves. All of the first leaders of the country were former slaves. Haiti has had a troubled history from the start, with numerous internal conflicts and political coup d'états, conflicts with the Dominican Republic, occupation by U.S. troops from 1915 to

1934 (to protect American business interests), and poor government by corrupt, autocratic, and sometimes incompetent political leaders.

Haiti has a population of nearly 10 million and, with more than 80% of citizens living below the poverty line, ranks as the poorest country in the Western Hemisphere. It is also the lowest-ranking country in the Western Hemisphere in public health. Malnutrition affects half of the country's population, and more than half of all Haitians do not have access to safe drinking water. Half of all Haitian children are undersized because of inadequate diet and diseases, and only 43% of the population has been immunized. According to World Health Organization data for 2014, life expectancy at birth in Haiti is 63 years (62 years for males and 64 years for females). Out of 193 countries in the survey Haiti ranks #155, the lowest ranking for countries in the Americas and lower than all countries outside the African continent except for Afghanistan. Likewise, Haiti ranks poorly with respect to infant mortality. United Nations data for the period 2005–2010 show that there are 63.10 infant deaths for every 1,000 live births, putting Haiti at #150 out of 188 countries on this variable. Again, it is at the bottom for nations in the Western Hemisphere, among the worst of all countries that are not in Africa. Furthermore, the country has the highest incidence of HIV/AIDS infection outside Africa. The Human Development Index for Haiti ranks #168 out of 186 countries (2013), again ahead of only a handful of countries in Africa and Afghanistan, which ranks barely behind Haiti. Haiti's Legatum Prosperity Index ranks #134 out of 142 countries.

There are many causes for Haiti's poverty. To be sure, the country's history of bad government and political instability is to blame, as is a legacy of corruption and despotism. In addition, we can cite greed and a lack of caring by the nation's elite, as well as discrimination by the elite according to skin color. Although most people in Haiti are descendants of African slaves, political and economic powers in the country are concentrated to a greatly disproportionate degree among the 5% of the population that is considered to be mulattoes, that is, lighter-skinned descendants of mixed African and European parentage. Indeed, even language is to blame for economic and social marginalization. While all Haitians speak Creole, a distinctive language that takes much of its grammatical structure from African tongues and considerable vocabulary from French, only the elite minority speaks French, which is the official language of government in the country. Unequal access to education also helps to perpetuate poverty. Other causes of poverty are exploitation of Haitian land and workers by foreign companies, especially those from the United States for whom Haitians are no more than cheap labor. We can also cite overpopulation in Haiti and the destructive pressures on land resources as another factor behind Haiti's woes. There has been considerable deforestation and soil erosion in Haiti, as population has pushed onto steeper slopes to open new farmland, as well as an increase in devastating floods by unstable rivers.

On Tuesday, January 12, 2010, Haiti was rocked by an enormous magnitude 7.0 earthquake that was centered just west of the capital city, Port-au-Prince. It caused enormous damage in the most densely settled part of the country, and well over 100,000 deaths. In Port-au-Prince, not only was the main government building, the National Palace, collapsed, but there was destruction as well of city hospitals and medical clinics, the airport, and the port, making it difficult to bring in relief supplies and workers. The city still has considerable rubble from the quake that has not been cleared. Many residents are still in temporary shelter, as progress in rebuilding the city has been painfully slow. There have been outbreaks of disease, including cholera, as well as violence. The economy of the country, weak as it was, has also not recovered. Consequently, Haiti still depends on foreign aid for day-to-day needs, and on the good work of foreign and Haitian volunteers who staff medical clinics, schools, and various community development programs.

There was once more foreign tourism to Haiti, but the political instability, fear of crime, and damage from the earthquake has significantly eroded this branch of the economy. The major exception is a large private resort called Labadee on the north coast of the country that has been leased for the exclusive use of cruise ships from the Royal Caribbean line. Tourists are required to stay within the walls of the property and may not venture into Haiti beyond, while Haitians are excluded from the tourist zone altogether except for those who work there or are licensed to operate concessions. Almost all the financial benefit leaves the country. In recent years, a number of foreign-owned garment factories have opened in Haiti in order to take advantage of cheap labor. In 2012, the Caracol Industrial Park was opened with great fanfare near Cap-Haitien on the north coast of Haiti. It is expected to become the largest industrial park in the Caribbean, with some 65,000 jobs.

Emigration from Haiti had been on the rise before the earthquake and then increased still more afterward. Most of those who leave go to the United States where sizable Haitian communities have formed in Miami and New York City, but there are also Haitians in Canada, France, and elsewhere. Some Haitian Americans arrived in the United States as so-called boat people who, since 1972, have set out in crowded, rickety boats from Haiti's shores to ride ocean currents to Florida. There are frequent disasters at sea with many lives lost. Especially since the earthquake, survivors in Haiti depend on emigrant relatives in the United States and other countries for remittance income and relief packages of clothing and other necessities.

FURTHER READING

Bell, Beverly, *Fault Lines: Views across Haiti's Divide* (Ithaca, NY: Cornell University Press, 2013).

Farmer, Paul, *Haiti after the Earthquake* (New York: Public Affairs, 2011).

Farmer, Paul, Noam Chomsky, and Jonathan Kozol, *The Uses of Haiti* (Monroe, ME: Common Courage Press, 2005).

HONDURAS

Honduras is a small country in Central America with coastlines on both the Caribbean Sea and the Pacific Ocean and boundaries with Guatemala, Nicaragua, and El Salvador. Its population is 8,249,674 (2010 estimate), comprised mostly of *mestizo* people (mixed Amerindian and European heritage). The country was once a colony of Spain, and Spanish is the national language. The majority religion is Roman Catholic, also a legacy of the Spanish period, but church membership is falling and membership in Protestant churches is increasing. We include Honduras in our list of 20 least contented nations because of its poverty, environmental problems, and the highest rate of crime in the Western Hemisphere.

According to data compiled by the United Nations, Honduras had a nominal GDP per capita of US$2,339 in 2012 (#135 out of 193 countries in the survey) and a GDP per capita at purchasing power parity (GDP(PPP)) of US$4,800 in 2013 (#135 out of 195 countries). The only Western Hemisphere countries with lower incomes were Nicaragua and Haiti. Honduras ranked #129 out of 186 countries in the United Nations Human Development Index for 2013, again ahead of only Nicaragua and Haiti, and #96 out of 142 countries in the 2013 Lagatum Prosperity Index, ahead of only Haiti among the countries in the Americas. According to data for 2012, nearly two-thirds (66.5%) of Hondurans live in poverty and 46.0% in what the National Statistical Institute of Honduras defines as extreme poverty. A 2013 study by the Center for Economic Policy Research reveals that poverty rates had been in decline in the country from 2006 through 2009, but that subsequent political instability highlighted by a coup d'état in 2009 has made the situation worse and that poverty is once again on the rise. Income inequality has long been a characteristic of Honduran society, but the same study has shown that it has worsened in step with the increases in poverty and that the country is now (i.e., through 2011, the most recent year for which data are available) the most unequal in Latin America. Furthermore, Honduras is one of only three Latin American countries in which income inequality has been rising in recent years, the others being Paraguay and Panama. Moreover, the inequality index has risen much faster for Honduras than indices for the other two countries. Between 2009 and 2011, 100% of the real income gains in the country went to the wealthiest 10% of the population.

Rural poverty is especially acute in Honduras. The best land is given to large-scale plantation agriculture, especially bananas, coffee and, more recently, palm oil, while *minifundistas*, or subsistence farmers, are relegated to small land plots with soils that are less productive, and to steep slopes that are difficult to

A woman is cooking rice on a stove fueled by wood in rural Honduras, where it is common for home kitchens to be open to the outdoors. (Phototrip/Dreamstime.com)

cultivate and prone to soil erosion. There are often conflicts over access to land between poor villagers and corporate agriculture. There are few alternatives to farming in the countryside of Honduras, so many unemployed poor people have migrated to cities or to other countries, most notably the United States, from where remittances prop up rural economies.

The most critical environmental problem in Honduras is deforestation caused by population pressure on farmland, illegal logging, and dependence on firewood as a critical energy resource. Between 1990 and 2005, 37.1% of the country's forests were cut down, the highest percentage loss of forest resources of any country in Latin America. What is worse, the rate of deforestation seems to be increasing rather decreasing, owing to both increasing poverty and a high rate of corruption in government. Some 85% of the country's timber harvest is said to be illegal. The loss of forests contributes to soil erosion, which exacerbates rural poverty and colonization of marginal lands, and increases flooding in densely populated valleys. Recent tropical storms have caused greater damage in the country than they would have otherwise because of deforestation and greater silt loads in streams. In 1998, Hurricane Mitch caused enormous damage in all parts of the country, including approximately 14,600 deaths and the destruction of most bridges and roads, and other infrastructure. Rebuilding is still not completed. The worst damage was from landslides in areas that were most severely deforested. The capital city, Tegucigalpa, was also very heavily affected. Another major environmental problem is pollution of water resources by mining activities. The most famous example is the Canadian-owned San Martin gold mine northeast of the capital that caused many grotesque skin and eye ailments downriver in the Siria Valley before it was forced to close.

In addition to having the highest rate of crime in the Western Hemisphere, Honduras has the highest homicide rate of any country in the world. According to the United Nations Office on Drugs and Crime, the country had 6,239 intentional homicides in 2010, a rate of 82.1 killings per 100,000 of population, a rate significantly higher than the 66.0 per 100,000 rate in the world's second-ranking homicide country, neighboring El Salvador. In both counties the violence is attributed to poverty, dislocation of population from the countryside to urban areas, high rates of unemployment among young males, gang activity, and the trafficking of drugs and international migrants. All parts of Honduras are at risk, but the border area with Guatemala and the area of Tegucigalpa are especially dangerous. The country's second-largest city, San Pedro Sula, located in the northwest corner of the country near the border with Guatemala, recorded a murder rate of 159 per 100,000 residents in 2011. It has been called "the murder capital of the world," and is arguably the most dangerous city on the planet where there is not a war. It is a center of cocaine trafficking for markets in the United States and of trafficking in unaccompanied minors. Some of the most dangerous criminals in Honduras had been gang members in Los Angeles where they lived as undocumented immigrants, and were deported from the United States. The gang problem in Honduras is said to have slowed recovery efforts from damage by Hurricane Mitch and discouraged foreign investment and foreign tourism.

FURTHER READING

Johnston, Jake and Stephan Lefebvre, *Honduras since the Coup: Economic and Social Outcomes* (Washington: Center for Economic and Policy Research, 2013).

Kerssen, Tanya M., *Grabbing Power: The Struggles for Land, Food, and Democracy in Northern Honduras* (Oakland: Food First Books, 2013).

Pine, Adrienne, *Working Hard, Drinking Hard: On Violence and Survival in Honduras* (Berkeley: University of California Press, 2008).

Reichman, Daniel R., *The Broken Village: Coffee, Migration, and Globalization in Honduras* (Ithaca, NY: ILR Press, 2011).

LIBERIA

A number of the world's poorest and most unstable countries are in Africa, and Liberia is one of them. It is located on the Atlantic coast of West Africa and is bordered as well by Sierra Leone, Guinea, and Côte d'Ivoire (Ivory Coast), all countries that could also find a place on these pages as least contented countries. We single out Liberia because its recent history has been especially violent and unstable, and because this otherwise beautiful and potentially prosperous corner of Africa is depressingly poor. Its Human Development Index is near the bottom for the world, ranking #175 from 187 countries surveyed, while its income statistics are equally abysmal. For example, the GDP(PPP) per capita ranks at #183 out of 197 countries as calculated by the International Monetary Fund (2013), #181 out of 185 countries as calculated by the World Bank (2011–2013), and #191 out of 195 countries as calculated by the U.S. Central Intelligence Agency (1993–2013). More bluntly, some 85% of the population lives below the international poverty line.

The word "Liberia" comes from the Latin for "freedom" or "liberty," and originated with a unique chapter of history when this western shore of Africa was settled beginning 1822 by former slaves from the United States who were eager to

Soccer is the world's sport and is especially popular in many African countries such Liberia, where this photo was taken. (MissHibiscus/iStockphoto.com)

return to the continent of their origins. The migration was organized by a back-to-Africa movement called the American Colonization Society, and resulted in formation of the Republic of Liberia in 1847. The Americo-Liberians, as they came to be known, became a dominant minority where previously the lands were ruled by tribal groups, and patterned their government and institutions after those in the United States. The flag of the country resembles that of the United States, and the capital city that was established for this free country was named Monrovia, after James Monroe, the fifth president of the United States and an ardent supporter of the American Colonization Society. Today this capital city is the country's largest urban center, having a population of nearly 1 million, about one-quarter of Liberia's total of 4,092,310 residents (2014 estimate). The country's official language is English, but there are also many tribal languages spoken.

Liberia's descent into what one author referred to as a modern-day Heart of Darkness (after the famous novel by Joseph Conrad that was set in colonial Belgian Congo) began with a military coup in 1980 that was led by Master Sergeant Samuel Doe that ousted the government of President William R. Tolbert and executed him and his entire government. Doe was later elected president in an election that is widely regarded to have been fraudulent, and ruled the country with violence. He, in turn, was ousted by a coup led by Charles Taylor in 1989, and was himself executed. There were successive civil wars after both coups, costing the country somewhere between 250,000 and 520,000 civilian lives. Taylor was also a ruthless leader, even worse than Doe, and was eventually ousted from office and found guilty in an international court of war crimes and crimes against humanity. He is serving a 50-year prison term in Great Britain. During his rule, he profited from blood diamonds and illegal timber harvesting, and Liberia was branded a pariah state. In 2005, Ellen Johnson Sirleaf was elected president in an election that was hailed as Liberia's first truly open and fair one. She is the first female ruler of an African country as well as a Nobel Prize winner. The government has become more democratic and more stable under her leadership, but major economic and human rights problems remain.

Among the many problems that Liberia continues to face is endemic corruption. Bribery is a way of life in the country, and reaches all institutions and walks of life, although there are now many more countries that are worse, as one of Ms. Sirleaf's priorities while in office has been to combat corruption. As reported by Transparency International in 2010, a shocking 89% of Liberians reported that they had to pay bribes in order to obtain public services, the highest percentage in the world. As of 2013, Liberia ranked #83 out of 177 countries in Transparency International's Corruption Perceptions Index. Other problems in Liberia are a short life expectancy of 59 years for men and women combined, ranking 166th from 198 countries surveyed, a literacy rate that is barely above 60%, high rates of infant and maternal mortality, and widespread diseases such as tuberculosis, malaria, and diarrhea. In 2007, more than one in five children under age 5 were malnourished, and in 2008 only 17% of the population had access to adequate sanitation facilities. Also in 2008, there was only 1 doctor and 27 nurses for every 100,000 people in Liberia. Nearly two-thirds of Liberian women are victims of female genital mutilation. In March, 2014, Liberia became one of the countries that were affected by the Ebola virus, which had entered the country via Guinea. On August 16, 2014, an Ebola quarantine center in Monrovia was attacked by a panicked mob, causing infected patients to flee into the general population. In addition, we note that Liberia has a very high crime rate. Rape and sexual assault are especially prevalent, with adolescent girls being the most frequent victims.

Finally, we note that Liberia is experiencing an environmental crisis. Monrovia and other cities are filthy and unhealthy, while in the countryside, there is illegal logging that cuts back the rainforest, and additional deforestation because of slash-burn agricultural practices and the use of firewood for fuel. A 2004 study by the United Nations reported that 99% of Liberians use firewood or charcoal for cooking and heating. Also there are threats to many plant and animal species in Liberia from illegal harvesting and hunting, including the hunting of endangered elephants, pygmy rhinoceroses, leopards, and chimpanzees for meat.

FURTHER READING

Moran, Mary, *Liberia: The Violence of Democracy* (Philadelphia: University of Pennsylvania Press, 2013).
Pham, John-Peter, *Liberia: Portrait of a Failed State* (Gainesville, FL: Reed Press, 2001).
Williams, Gabriel I. H., *Liberia: The Heart of Darkness* (Bloomington, IN: Trafford Publishing, 2006).

MALDIVES

Maldives, officially the Republic of the Maldives, and sometimes referred to as "the Maldives" and "the Maldives Islands," is a country of 1,192 small coral islands, only 200 or so of which are inhabited, in the Indian Ocean to the southwest of India and Sri Lanka, its nearest neighbors. It is considered to be part of Asia, and is Asia's smallest country both in land area and in population. The former measures approximately 298 km² (115 mi²) spread out over an ocean territory of roughly 90,000 km² (35,000 mi²), while the population totals 328,536. Because the country is so small, we would have been tempted to exclude it from our select list except for the unusually serious problems that it faces as a result of global warming and rising sea levels. Specifically, Maldives is the lowest country in elevation in the world, with an average elevation of only 1.5 meters (4'11") above sea level, and a maximum elevation of only 2.4 meters (7'10") above sea level, and is likely to be permanently flooded by the sea unless global warming is reduced sharply and soon.

There is some controversy about data and projections, but in general it seems that at current rates of sea level rise, Maldives could be totally inundated by 2100, and that large parts of the country would be covered sooner. Consequently, the Maldives government has embarked on a serious quest for land that could be purchased elsewhere to relocate the country should that become necessary. Sites in India, Sri Lanka, and Australia are among those that have been considered. However, this is not just a problem for the future in this country, as rising sea levels have caused low-lying coastal areas and small islands to be lost to the sea already. Moreover, the country's coasts are battered increasingly frequently by high waves and storm surges, rendering them dangerous for habitation. Nearly one-half of the inhabited islands experience annual flooding, and the number of environmental refugees in the country is increasing accordingly. In addition, livability is imperiled by shrinking supplies of fresh water on the islands, especially during the dry season when stored rainwater is depleted and increased amounts of water are withdrawn from the shallow water table which, in turn, is being increasingly contaminated by saltwater incursion. The country has had to devote ever more of its resources to building up the land with dredged sand and other materials and construction of sea walls, which is only a temporary fix at best, that drains investment from other needs such as schooling, health care, and non-flood construction. In 2009, Maldives gained global attention for its predicament when, dressed in scuba gear, then-president Mohammed Nasheed, who is an environmental scientist by profession, and other officials of the national government held an underwater cabinet meeting accompanied by the sight and sounds of divers' bubbles, and signed a document that urged countries around the world to cut carbon emissions. Maldives itself contributes just a tiny fraction of the pollutants that cause global warming, but has announced a goal of becoming carbon-neutral by 2019.

The crisis in the Maldives has been made worse by domestic political and social instability, some part of which can be attributed to the rise of Islamic fundamentalism in this officially Islamic country. There have been cases of severe punishment for having had sex outside marriage, homosexuality and the consumption of alcohol by Muslim residents, including flogging. There are also complaints of police brutality and other abuses, as well as of corruption by police and the courts. Migrant workers from abroad, who tend to work in construction and in resort hotels, are often poorly treated by employers and suffer sexual harassment and other wrongs. Freedoms of speech, the press, and religion are restricted. The national constitution stipulates that all citizens of Maldives must be Muslim. Maldivians with other faiths or with atheist convictions have been imprisoned or forced into exile, while foreigners of other faiths are required to keep their religious practices private. Many of these restrictions were enacted during the 30 years between 1978 and 2008 when Maldives was ruled by President Maumoon Abdul Gayoom, whose administration grew increasingly autocratic with every successful reelection to office. His successor, Nasheed, who was once a prisoner of conscience in the country, attempted reforms and liberalization when he took office, but was forced from the presidency in 2012 by large-scale protests by police and military personnel, and was placed under arrest. Since then, human rights abuses have increased again in the country, to the point where the international watchdog group Amnesty International has issued a report citing a new "human rights crisis" in Maldives.

The economy of the Maldives has traditionally depended on the seas, and fishing continues to play a major role, contributing some 15% of the national GDP and employing about 30% of the workforce. There is also a small manufacturing sector, with the garment industry being most prominent, but lack of space makes expansion of manufacturing and other enterprises difficult. Far and away, the biggest part of the Maldivian economy is foreign tourism. It accounts for approximately 28% of the country's GDP and more than 60% of its foreign exchange receipts, and contributes more than 90% of the country's tax revenues. Maldives hopes to use receipts from tourism to pay expenses of responding to the sea level change crisis. The country's international airport is in Male, the capital, and tourists then go to designated resort islands that have little or no Maldivian resident population. The beaches and clear waters are ideal, but tourists, especially those who are not Muslims, have little interaction with Maldivians and usually enjoy their holidays oblivious to their host nation's cultures or its problems. The country's tourism policies favor such segregation in order to protect local cultures and values from the corrupting influences of other cultures, and to allow tourists a space where they can be free to enjoy themselves in ways that are otherwise prohibited in the country. This includes the consumption of alcohol and the wearing of skimpy attire on the beach or less. Tourism is on the rise in Maldives, as the country advertises widely for foreign visitors in order to increase revenues.

FURTHER READING

Amnesty International, *The Other Side of Paradise: A Human Rights Crisis in the Maldives*, September 2012, http://www.amnesty.org/en/library/asset/ASA29/005/2012/en/6d93c0bb-67f0–4688-b22a-b8c115e83f52/asa290052012en.pdf.

Henley, John, "The Last Days of Paradise," *The Guardian*, November 10, 2008, http://www.theguardian.com/environment/2008/nov/11/climatechange-endangered-habitats-maldives.

U.S. Department of State, *2013 Human Rights Reports: Maldives*, February 27, 2014, http://www.state.gov/j/drl/rls/hrrpt/2013/sca/220399.htm.

MAURITANIA

Mauritania is a country in the western part of North Africa that borders the Atlantic Ocean, and also Algeria, Mali, Senegal, and Morocco-controlled Western Sahara. Most of the country is part of the Sahara Desert, and population is heavily concentrated in the south where there is more rainfall. According to a census in 2013, the population of the country is a little more than 3.5 million, almost all of whom are Muslims. About one-third of the population is Arab, another third is black with origins in nearby Sub-Saharan Africa, and the remaining third is mixed. Many languages are spoken in the country, with Arabic being the official language. Before independence in 1960, Mauritania was a colony of France. The capital city of Mauritania is Nouakchott, located on the Atlantic coast. According to the 2013 census, its population is about 960,000, the country's largest city.

Mauritania is rich in mineral resources. Iron ore is the main export, but there are also reserves of gold and copper. There is offshore oil as well, although it is not yet certain how much and what impact oil exploration could have on the country's economy. Still, Mauritania is very poor, with most people who are not in the capital city living as nomadic herdsmen and subsistence farmers, and most people in Nouakchott living in untidy squatter slums to which they were driven by persistent drought on their lands. About 20% of the country's population subsists on less than the equivalent of $1.25 per day. According to independent calculations of GDP at purchasing power parity per capita (GDP(PPP)) for 2013, Mauritania is ranked #152 out of 187 countries by the International Monetary Fund, #142 out of 185 countries by the World Bank, and #161 out of 195 countries by the U.S. Central Intelligence Agency. The country ranks #161 out of 186 countries in the United Nations Human Development Index.

We have listed Mauritania as one of the 20 least contented countries in the world not just because of the poverty, but also because of chronic political instability and an abysmal human rights situation. On the former count, Mauritania had a military coup in 2005 that ended the 21-year rule of Colonel Maaouya Sid'Ahmed Taya while he was out of the country attending a state funeral, its first presidential election in 2007, and then another military coup in 2008 that resulted in the arrest of newly elected president Sidi Ould Cheikh Abdallahi and the start of another contentious period in national politics, this time under the administration of coup leader Mohamed Ould Abdel Aziz. Abdel Aziz was formally (and narrowly) elected president in 2009, but critics assail the voting as dishonest. He nevertheless remains in office and has been recognized as president by an increasing number of countries. The Failed States Index that is calculated annually by the Fund for Peace ranked Mauritania at #31 out of 178 countries in 2013, meaning that 147 countries ranked more highly across an array of 12 key social, economic, and political variables.

With respect to human rights, the country is one of the few in the world where slavery is still practiced, as well as a country in which female mutilation and child labor are common. An estimated 150,000 people are enslaved in Mauritania at minimum, with higher estimates ranging from 340,000 to 680,000, that is, approximately 10% to 20% of the population. Even at 150,000, the percentage of people who are enslaved exceeds the percentage in any country in the world. A great many of the slaves met their fate because they were political enemies of leaders in power. Although slavery was officially outlawed in 1981, to date only one person in Mauritania has ever been prosecuted for being a slave owner. The odious practice persists in Mauritania for three main reasons: (1) it is difficult to enforce laws across the vastness of desert territory; (2) the poverty of the country would make it difficult for slaves to support themselves if freed; and (3) there are common beliefs in Mauritanian culture that slavery is part of the natural social order.

In a practice that is rooted in gender inequality and intended to suppress female sexuality, young girls in Mauritania are forced to undergo genital mutilation. According to the United Nations Children's Fund (UNICEF), in 2013, 69% of females in Mauritania had undergone the painful procedure, a higher proportion than in many North African countries where the procedure is also practiced, but not the highest. However, female genital mutilation might soon be on the decline in Mauritania because in January 2011, the nation's Islamic leaders issued a *fatwah*, a formal interpretation of Islamic law, that the practice is to be banned. Another common practice in gender-unequal Mauritania is the force-feeding of pre-pubescent daughters with enormous quantities of food, especially milk, in order to make them obese. Called *leblouh* or *gavage*, the practice dates to Berber society in the 11th century, and is a response to cultural beliefs that very fat women are the most attractive (and that slim ones are sickly). It requires that young girls be fattened in order for their fathers to be able to arrange a good marriage partners for them. Betrothal is typically between ages of 8 to 10, meaning that girls are put into an unhealthy situation at an early age. This is one factor underlying a low life expectancy at birth for Mauritania's population: 57.5 years in 2013 according to the World Health Organization, #162 out of 198 countries.

Other human rights issues in Mauritania include child labor, human trafficking, and torture of political prisoners and prisoners who were found guilty of criminal offenses. The human rights group Amnesty International has accused the country of operating with little regard for the rule of law and for humane imprisonment. In addition, the Arab population of Mauritania routinely discriminates against the nation's black population, which is concentrated primarily in the southern part of the country. Among other affronts, blacks are denied equal access to education and employment and are treated unequally in the justice system and by lending institutions. Unfortunately, there is little evidence that Mauritania will make strides soon for improvement, and every reason to believe that the country will be poor and unequal for years to come.

FURTHER READING

Foster, Noel, *Mauritania: The Struggle for Democracy* (Boulder: Lynne Rienner Publishers, 2010).

Pazzanita, Anthony G., *Historical Dictionary of Mauritania* (Lanham, MD: Scarecrow Press, 2008).

Sene, Sidi, *The Ignored Cries of Pain and Injustice from Mauritania* (Bloomington, IN: Trafford Publishing, 2011).

NORTH KOREA

North Korea is a country that occupies the northern part of the Korean Peninsula in East Asia. Its formal name is the Democratic People's Republic of Korea (DPRK), although as well will see, it is neither democratic nor a republic, nor is it very much for the people. Instead, it is a repressive dictatorship. The country's northern border is with China and, for a short length, with Russia, while to the south the border is disputed and with the Republic of Korea (ROK), commonly called South Korea. The two countries are separated by a Demilitarized Zone (DMZ) that was set in 1953 as part of a Korean War armistice agreement, and that runs more-or-less along the 38° N. parallel. Neither country recognizes the other, and for more than six decades their respective military forces have faced one another in enormous numbers and sophisticated weaponry from opposite sides of the DMZ.

Ironically, the Korean Peninsula as a whole is one of the most ethnically homogeneous parts of the world, with more than 99% of the population in both Koreas being ethnically Korean. Koreans describe their territory as *dan-il minjok guk ga*, "the single race society." The division of the peninsula came about with the defeat of Japanese colonialism in World War II, and concurrent conflict about whether the country should ally itself with the communist world to the north or the democracies of the West led by the United States. This led to war in 1950, and then the formalization of two rival governments on the peninsula. North Korea has its capital in Pyongyang, while that of South Korea is in Seoul. The two cities are about 121 miles (195 km. apart, with the most heavily fortified parts of the DMZ almost equidistant between them. North Korea is generally a very poor country, although government secretiveness and manipulation of data for propaganda purposes precludes specific information about incomes, housing conditions, and other sociological data, while South Korea is democratic and ever more prosperous because of a manufacturing economy that is focused on global exports. After more than

60 years of living apart, the cultures of the two Koreas have diverged. Even the once-unitary language has become different in accent and vocabulary between north and south. However, in North Korea and South Korea both, as well as among ethnic Koreans in a global diaspora, there is agreement that Korea should be one: the conflict is about the kind of government that the country should have, and about the self-serving influences on the divided peninsula by Cold War and post–Cold War global superpowers.

North Korea has been ruled with an iron hand by three successive members of the same family since before the country was formally established: Kim il-Sung, a national hero who helped liberate Korea from Japanese colonial rule and who ruled until his death in 1994; his eccentric son Kim Jong-il, who ruled until his own death in 2011; and Kim Jong-il's third son, Kim Jong-un, who took over in 2011 and is still in power. Foreign observers have referred to North Korea's government as a hereditary dictatorship and something akin to an absolute monarchy. The citizenry is taught to revere the Kim family, particularly Kim il-Sung who is glorified as the "Great Leader" and the country's "Eternal President." There is an unusually strong cult of personality that surrounds all three Kims, but again more so for the first Kim, whom many citizens had thought to be immortal. Some even credit him with creating the world. His birthday, April 15, is celebrated each year as the "Day of the Sun," and throughout the country there are statues and other monuments that honor him. The country is guided by an ideology called "Juche" that emphasizes economic self-sufficiency, military self-reliance, and independence in foreign policy, and domestic policies that subordinate citizens' needs to those of the military, including basic needs such as food.

Data about North Korea are hard to come by because of the government's secretiveness, and foreign visitors are tightly controlled as to where they may go in the country and with whom they may speak. Therefore, the country is often not included in the indices and rankings that we use here in comparing countries. For example, there is no United Nations Human Development Index for North Korea, nor is there a Legatum Prosperity Index ranking. However, where there are comparative rankings, North Korea typically comes in dead last in the world. For example, the conservative Heritage Foundation has the country at #178 out of 178 countries surveyed in its 2015 Index of Economic Freedom; the *Economist* has the country at #167 out of 167 countries in its 2015 Democracy Index; and the country is in a tie with Somalia for #174 out of 174 countries in the Corruption Perceptions Index by Transparency International. Furthermore, the country does not permit freedoms of religion or the press, nor are North Koreans free to leave the country at will. Satellite images and testimony by defectors from North Korea indicate that there are six large prison camps in the country that hold a total of as many as 200,000 political prisoners who are made to toil in slave-like conditions. There are also reports of starvation, torture, rape, and medical experimentation applied to political prisoners. Because of North Korea's horrible record of human rights abuses, the United Nations Commission of Inquiry has accused the country's leadership of crimes against humanity.

We had promised to not rank countries or cities in this book as we include them on our respective lists of those 20 that are most contented and those that are least contented, but we can say here with confidence, that were there a 1–20 ranking, North Korea would be first on our list of least contented countries.

FURTHER READING

Demick, Barbara, *Nothing to Envy: Ordinary Lives in North Korea* (New York: Spiegel & Grau, 2010).

French, Paul, *North Korea: State of Paranoia* (London: Zed Books, 2014).

Lankov, Andrew, *The Real North Korea, Life and Politics in the Failed Stalinist State* (New York: Oxford University Press, 2014).

RUSSIA

Russia is the largest country in the world, covering about one-eighth of the world's inhabited land area and stretching across nine time zones from eastern Europe across Eurasia through the farthest reaches of Siberia to the Pacific Ocean. Its population is just under 145 million, the ninth-highest total in the world. The country is officially known as the Russian Federation, as it is an amalgamation of numerous ethnic and national territories that Russia had conquered over the centuries from its historical heartland in the Grand Duchy of Muscovy (the area of Moscow). According to the Russian census, 81% of the population is Russian, with the rest of the population comprising 160 ethnic groups speaking about 100 different languages. Russia was the leading republic of the Soviet Union from the time of its founding in 1922 until it fell apart in 1991, and is recognized today as its sole successor state, as all the other republics chose independence. Russia's capital is Moscow, the former Soviet capital.

Russia is a country with a proud history and culture, and many beautiful places. The country has produced many greats in literature such as Leo Tolstoy and Alexander Pushkin, musical composers such as Pyotr Tchaikovsky, Sergei Rachmaninoff, and Igor Stravinsky, and geniuses of science such as Mikhail Lomonosov and Ivan Pavlov. The country has been a world leader in space exploration, sending the first artificial satellite, Sputnik 1, into earth orbit in 1957, as well as a great military power with nuclear capability. There are also many proud achievements by Russian and Soviet athletes, including dominant performances in various summer and winter Olympics. Russia's historic capital city, St. Petersburg is one of the world's most spectacular cities for its palaces, churches, and art.

Lake Baikal in southern Siberia is spectacularly beautiful and is the deepest lake in the world. It contains about 20% of the world's unfrozen fresh water.

We could continue for many pages about the greatness of Russia, but our attentions here are on unhappiness and why we chose Russia for the list of 20 least contented countries in the world. We focus not on the cruelties of the past that also define Russia's history such as the reigns of Ivan the Terrible and Catherine the Great, or the murderous years of communism under Vladimir Lenin and Joseph Stalin, but instead on the deficiencies of Russia today. We can begin with the lack of democracy. Whereas most other former Soviet republics and the former Soviet satellite states in East Europe have embraced democracy, Russia is an autocratic state. It ranks at #132 out of 167 countries in the 2014 Democracy Index that is calculated by the *Economist*. It places the country precisely between Cameroon and Angola in the ranking. The situation has worsened under the current presidency of Vladimir Putin, as independent and opposition television, radio, and print media outlets have been shut down and oppressed, and prominent independent journalists such as Anna Politkovskaya in 2006 and political opposition leaders such as Boris Nemtsov in 2015 have been assassinated. Furthermore, the government is corrupt, with Russia being in a tie for 136th place with Nigeria and Cameroon (among some other countries) out of 174 countries in the world in the 2014 Transparency International Corruption Perceptions Index. We described a recent example of this corruption in another part of this book when discussing the construction for the winter Olympics games that were held recently in the Russian resort city of Sochi. Furthermore, under Putin Russia has once again become an imperialist aggressor. It waged war and annexed territory from the neighboring country of Georgia in 2008, snatched Crimea from Ukraine in 2013, and then initiated a war in that country's eastern region that is still ongoing. In addition, Russia continually threatens the three Baltic countries, Estonia, Latvia, and Lithuania, that were once part of the Soviet Union but that are now members of both the European Union and NATO. There has been widespread condemnation of Russia for its aggressions, and the country is becoming increasingly isolated in world diplomacy. Its economy has been badly hurt by sanctions that the Western world has imposed on the country because of its adventures in Ukraine, as well as by declines in income that have resulted in recent worldwide declines in oil prices.

As soon as it became possible to do so when the Soviet Union collapsed, many Russians emigrated abroad. This has resulted in net population losses for the country in the millions, and an enormous brain drain. Many of those who left were best able to mount an opposition against autocracy. One indicator of Russia's decline in independent thinking and talent is that only one university in the entire country is rated among the top 400 universities in the world (2013–2014), that being Lomonosov Moscow State University, which is in the #226–250 group. There are many millionaires and even billionaires in Russia, but most of them

Russia is a land of contrasts. The suburban scene here from Moscow shows new cars and residential towers, and billboards that advertise choices for middle-class consumers. However, the city also has many people trapped in poverty, and the Russian countryside is generally very poor and backward in terms of infrastructure. (Roman Cybriwsky)

have footholds abroad too, with second or future homes in other countries, mostly in Europe. Moscow and St. Petersburg have some very fine neighborhoods, glitzy shopping centers, and other landmarks of wealth, but in most cities and certainly in the small towns and countryside, Russia is a mostly backward and poor country. Industrial cities are badly polluted, the housing developments that the Soviets had built for workers and their families are fast turning into slums, and many communities still have unpaved streets and outhouses out back. There are many social problems, including alcoholism, drug abuse, prostitution, and crime. Successful businesses are pressured for money by mobsters or are stolen altogether. There is widespread animosity in Russia against gays and lesbians, and open discrimination against many non-Russian nationalities, especially those from north of the Caucuses in the Russian Federation such as Chechens. Many young people see little future for themselves, and either dream of moving abroad or joining Putin in a quest to restore Russia's imperial glory.

FURTHER READING

Gessen, Masha, *The Man without a Face: The Unlikely Rise of Vladimir Putin* (New York: Riverhead Books, 2012).

Krainova, Natalya, "Only One Russian University Makes Latest World Rankings," *The Moscow Times*, October 3, 2013, http://www.themoscowtimes.com/news/article /only-one-russian-university-makes-latest-world-rankings/487013.html.

Petrou, Michael, "Putin's Unhappy Russia," *MacLean's*, October 19, 2011, http://www .macleans.ca/news/world/putins-unhappy-country/.

Sperling, Valerie, *Sex, Politics, & Putin: Political Legitimacy in Russia* (Oxford: Oxford University Press, 2015).

SAUDI ARABIA

Saudi Arabia, formally the Kingdom of Saudi Arabia, is a Middle Eastern country of some 31 million inhabitants that occupies about 80% of the land area of the Arabian Peninsula. It is comprised mostly of desert, and is the second-largest country in the Arab world after Algeria. Its territory includes the birthplace of the Islamic faith, as well as the pilgrimage city of Mecca, Islam's holiest site. Islam is the official religion, embracing nearly 100% of the country's citizens as well as a great many foreign residents.

Saudi Arabia is the world's largest producer and exporter of oil. Its proven oil reserves are second only to those of Venezuela. Because of oil wealth, the country is classified as a high-income economy. Per capita incomes were $53,935 in 2014, the 11th highest in the world, although the income distribution is skewed by extraordinarily high incomes for privileged citizens and very low incomes for millions of other Saudis and for most of the many millions of foreign workers in the country. However, precise data about income distribution within Saudi Arabia are hard to come by, as the government strives to project a glowing image of the country and "hides the poor very well," according to an article about poverty in Saudi Arabia in the *Guardian*. The Saudi capital and largest city, Riyadh, population 5.7 million, reflects the nation's oil wealth via a soaring skyline of showy skyscrapers, wide, modern roads, and other state-of-the-art infrastructure. The country has a high Human Development Index, ranking #34 out of 195 countries in 2014.

Despite the pluses, there are good reasons to list Saudi Arabia among the 20 least contented countries in the world. For one thing, there is very little democracy in the country, as Saudi Arabia is an absolute monarchy that was ruled with a stern hand from 2005 until his death in early 2015 by a king, Abdullah bin Abdulaziz, a member of the hereditary House of Saud that has ruled the country continuously since 1741. There are thousands of members of the royal family living in posh residences in Saudi Arabia and/or abroad. All of them enjoy great wealth and privileges. National elections and political parties are not allowed, so the country is rated as "not free" by Freedom House, and as the world's fifth most authoritarian state by the *Economist* (2012). Adult male citizens are allowed to petition the king directly through a traditional format called the *majilis*, but women have no voice. According to the Basic Law of Saudi Arabia adopted by royal decree in 1992, the king must make his decisions in accordance with *Sharia* (Islamic Law), the Quran, and the Sunnah, that is, the traditions of the Prophet Muhammad.

Second, we note that Saudi Arabia has an especially poor human rights record. Indeed, the *Freedom in the World* report for 2014 by Freedom House lists it as among the 10 "worst of the worst" nations in both political rights and civil liberties. Likewise, both Amnesty International and Human Rights Watch have condemned the country for a justice system that has no jury trials, no presumption of innocence, no rights to legal representation, and no fair chance for an accused person to mount a defense. Many trials are held in secret and sometimes the accused is not even informed of the charges. Judges (or a single judge) decide the case and usually mete out very harsh punishment, including the death penalty. Homosexuality, atheism, and perceived affronts against Islam are among the capital crimes in Saudi Arabia, as is the conversion of a Saudi citizen to a faith other than Islam. Moreover, Saudi Arabia does not allow the practice of any religion other than Islam, even for foreign visitors. About 85–90% of Saudi citizens are Sunni Muslims, with the rest being Shias who face discrimination in employment, education, and legal rights by the Sunni majority. Foreigners who are brought to Saudi Arabia to work in occupations such as construction and domestic service are poorly paid, have no legal rights or recourse, and are often to victims of abuse by employers.

We note as well that women have an inferior status in Saudi Arabia and have few rights. In 2010, the Global Gender Gap Report by the World Economic Forum ranked the country as #129 out of 134 countries in gender parity. Most telling is that every woman in the country, adults included no matter how old or how well educated, must have a male legal guardian who is empowered with making decisions for her about her own life and may grant or deny permission to work, travel, or study, open a bank account, opt for elective surgery, among other normal activities. Although King Abdullah announced in 2011 that women would gain the right to vote (the country has local elections), it would still be necessary for a woman to obtain permission from her male guardian in order to do so. Very famously because of recent controversies, Saudi women are not allowed to drive. They gained the right to ride bicycles only in 2013, although only in parks and other designated places, and they must be dressed in full body coverings and be accompanied by a male relative when doing so. Likewise, women are confined to certain sections in restaurants and other public places, and must come and go via women-only doorways. Women are also disadvantaged in the justice system: for example, it takes the testimony of two women to equal that of one male, while in matters of inheritance, women heirs automatically receive only one-half of that given to male counterparts.

Finally, we note that Saudi Arabia suffers from many social problems. Unemployment is high, at about 10% in 2010, despite the nation's overall wealth, leading to anger and dissatisfaction among many young people, as well as to previously unthinkable criticisms of the Royal Family. Rates of drug abuse, alcohol consumption, and juvenile delinquency are rising. A dangerous type of car racing by young drivers called *Tafheet* or Arab drifting shows disregard not just for one's own safety, but also for the public on the roads at large and for driving laws, and is said to be an emblematic of social tensions in Saudi society. Furthermore, although crime rates in Saudi Arabia are generally low, the rate of child abuse is reportedly extraordinarily high, with an estimated 45% of all children in the country having been victims of some sort of abuse or domestic violence. There are also various genetic disorders in the Saudi population that are traced to inbreeding that stems from traditional cultural practices to marry close relatives.

FURTHER READING

House, Karen Elliott, *On Saudi Arabia: It's People, Past, Religion, Fault Lines—and Future* (New York: Vintage, 2013).

Lacey, Robert, *Inside the Kingdom: Kings, Clerics, Modernists, Terrorists, and the Struggle for Saudi Arabia* (New York: Penguin, 2010).

Sullivan, Kevin, "Saudi Arabia's Riches Conceal a Crowing Problem of Poverty," *The Guardian*, January 1, 2013, http://www.theguardian.com/world/2013/jan/01/saudi-arabia-riyadh-poverty-inequality.

SUDAN

Sudan is a country in the Nile River Valley in North Africa to the south of Egypt and east of Chad. Ethiopia is to the southeast and the Red Sea borders the country to the east. To the south is South Sudan, which broke off from Sudan after a long period of civil war and became the world's newest country in 2011. Until the separation of South Sudan, Sudan was Africa's largest country. It now ranks third in size after Algeria and the Democratic Republic of the Congo. The population of Sudan is 37,289,406 (2014 estimate). The capital city is Khartoum, population 639,598 (2008 census), and the largest city is Omdurman, population 2,395,159 (also 2008). The two cities are opposite to one another on the eastern and western banks of the Nile, respectively. About 97% of the population of Sudan is Muslim.

Sudan achieved independence in 1956, but instead of prosperity based on its fertile farmlands and rich oil reserves, the country tumbled into political chaos and poverty. A civil war that had started in 1955 lasted until 1972 and took a half a million casualties. A second civil war raged from 1983 to 2005. It was one of the longest civil wars in history and took approximately 2 million lives. As many as 200,000 people were enslaved during this conflict. Furthermore, we note that Sudan has experienced several coups, attempted coups, and counter-coups, a brief period of rule by the Sudanese Community Party, famines brought on by warfare, desertification, and climate change, and considerable environmental degradation. In 1989, Colonel Omar al-Bashir took control of the country in a bloodless military coup, and banned opposition political parties, introduced an Islamic justice system, and imprisoned or executed his political opponents and independent journalists. He has been elected president three times since, but always in elections that are widely considered to be corrupt. He remains in office today.

It was during al-Bashir's tenure that South Sudan was established as a new sovereign state after the Second Sudanese Civil War. A small region called Abyei that sits at the boundary between Sudan and South Sudan is also a candidate for breaking away. Like South Sudan, it is rich, it has been an important oil-producing region, and its loss would be another economic blow to the parent country. Since 2003 Sudan has engaged in a major conflict against rebel armies in Darfur, a poor and famine-prone region in the western part of the country. The conflict is ongoing and has resulted in nearly half a million dead and millions of refugees. The United Nations has described events there as one of the worst humanitarian disasters in the world. The word "genocide" has been applied often in discussions about the tragedy of Darfur. According to UNICEF, there are as many as 6,000 child soldiers in Darfur. In 2009, President al-Bashir became the first sitting president in history to be indicted by the International Criminal Court for war crimes. The charges include responsibility for mass murders and rapes, and the pillaging of civilian settlements.

Not surprisingly, Sudan has an abysmal human rights record. The Democracy Index for the country as determined for 2014 by the *Economist* has the country at #153 out of 167 countries surveyed, while Reporters without Borders has ranked the country in 172nd place out of 180 countries in freedoms of the press. Sharia law applies nationwide. People who are convicted of crimes are flogged, and those found guilty of more serious offenses are stoned to death or crucified. Prisoners are routinely tortured. Police have the right to publically flog any woman that they think is not dressed modestly. Slavery continues to be practiced, and according to some reports, it targets the country's non-Muslim population. There are documented cases of the flogging of Christians and other persecution. Homosexuality can be punished by death. Child marriage is allowed. An estimated 80% of the adult female population has been subjected to genital mutilation.

By every measure, Sudan is one of the world's most troubled countries. The country ranks in a tie with Togo for #166 out of 187 countries in the 2013 United Nations Human Development Index and is ranked in the bottom 20 in the world at #130 out of 142 countries in the 2014 Legatum Prosperity Index. Nearly one in five Sudanese live on incomes that are below the international poverty line of $1.25 per day. The International Monetary Fund ranked Sudan at #137 out of 187 countries in GDP per capita for 2013, while the World Bank has the country at

#140 out of 185 countries on this measure. While these are not among the lowest rankings, they would be lower except that Sudan happens to have considerable oil income, which raises the total national GDP. That income is unevenly distributed, however, and overall poverty rates are distressingly high. According to the Global Hunger Index that was developed by the Washington, D.C.-based International Food Policy Research Institute, Sudan has an "Alarming Hunger Situation" and is the fifth-hungriest nation in the world. The country is also among the world's most corrupt nations. The 2013 Corruption Perceptions Index by Transparency International has the country at a near-bottom #173 out of 175 countries surveyed. Other problematic indicators are that overall life expectancy is only 63 years, ranking at #158 out of 193 countries as measured for 2012 by the World Health Organization, the infant mortality rate is 63.75 per 1,000 live births over 2005–2010 as reported by the U.N. Population Division and ranks 151st out of 188 countries surveyed, and the country's health systems are ranked at #134 out of 190 countries by the World Health Organization. The 2014 Fragile States Index that is compiled by the Fund for Peace has only five countries in its "Very High Alert" category: South Sudan takes first place and Sudan is #5.

FURTHER READING

Cockett, Richard, *Sudan: Darfur and the Failure of an African State* (New Haven, CT: Yale University Press, 2010).

Copnall, James, *A Poisonous Thorn in Our Hearts: Sudan and South Sudan's Bitter and Incomplete Divorce* (London: C. Hurst & Co., 2014).

Natsios, Andrew S., *Sudan, South Sudan, and Darfur: What Everyone Needs to Know* (New York: Oxford University Press, 2012).

Prunier, Gérard, *Darfur—The Ambiguous Genocide* (Ithaca, NY: Cornell University Press, 2005).

SYRIA

Syria is a country in the Levant in the Southwest Asia that is squeezed between Turkey, Iraq, Jordan, Israel, and Lebanon. It also has a coastline to the west on the Mediterranean Sea. According to an estimate for 2014, its population is 17,957,639, but that total is questionable because the country is engaged currently on many fronts in a very costly civil war and there are millions of refugees. The largest concentrations of population are in the valley of the Euphrates River whose waters irrigate Syria's farmlands, and along a green strip of land along the coast. Otherwise, the country is an arid plateau. Since 1974, Syria has exported oil from fields in the east near the city of Deir ez-Zor. Oil is the single largest branch of the economy. The capital is Damascus in the southwest near the border with Lebanon. With about 1.7 million inhabitants, it is Syria's second-largest city. The largest city is Aleppo in the northwest. It is also richly historic like Damascus, and has a population of about 2.1 million inhabitants. Largely because of the traumas of the current war, we list Aleppo in this book as one of the world's 20 least contented cities.

The land that is Syria has been settled since earliest antiquity, and has had a long history of rule by successive empires and kingdoms, interspersed with invasions and periods of war. An entire Who's Who of Middle Eastern history has at one time or another laid claim to Syria: Assyrians, Babylonians, Persians, Alexander the Great's Macedonian Empire, the Roman Empire, various Arab dynasties, Egyptians, Mongols, Crusaders from Europe, and Ottoman Turks, among others. The country is, therefore, a great repository of history and its culture blends countless traditions from many places over many centuries. In the seventh century A.D., Islam became the dominant religion in Syria and Arabic replaced Greek and Aramaic as the principal language. Modern Syria emerged after World War I and the fall of the Ottoman Empire, and was a French mandate until gaining its independence as a parliamentary republic in 1946. It was unstable for some years afterward, with numerous coups and attempted coups, and even a brief period (1958–1961) of union into one country with Egypt. A coup d'état by the Arab Socialist Ba'ath Party succeeded in 1963, leading to autocratic rule that has continued since. During that time, Syria had exchanged hostilities with Israel on the 1973 Yom Kippur War, and its army occupied Lebanon for nearly three decades from 1976 to 2005. Hafez al-Assad was president from 1970 until his death in 2000, and was succeeded in a one-candidate election by his son Bashar al-Assad who is still in office.

There were hopes during a period in 2000 called the Damascus Spring that Syria might become more democratic after three decades of dictatorship. However, within months the new government of Bashar al-Assad had suppressed the movement and imprisoned its leaders. The civil war began in 2011 as part of the Arab Spring protests that swept the Middle East. The protests were peaceful at first, but a crackdown by al-Assad escalated into all-out conflict. The opposition is determined to overthrow him, and al-Assad is equally determined to stay in office. A religious dimension to the conflict is that most of the rebels are Sunni Muslims, while Assad and his closest supporters are Alawites. As many as 100,000 people have been killed in the fighting, including 11,000 children, and more than 2.1 million refugees have fled Syria to take shelter in Jordan, Iraq, Lebanon, and Turkey. Also, an estimated 450,000 Syrian Christians have fled their homes. A geopolitical map of Syria shows the country to be fragmented into unstable zones controlled by opposing forces. Syrian government forces control much of the west of the country, the radical Islamic State of Iraq and the Levant controls most of the west, Kurdish forces hold sections in the north adjacent to Turkey, the al-Nusra Front, a

Syrian branch of al-Qaeda, holds scattered territory in the northwest, and Syrian Opposition has a stronghold in the northwest near Aleppo. The fighting is active, and no one knows how or when it will end.

The Ba'athists in Syria has a very poor record with respect to human rights. The organization Human Rights Watch refers to Syria's record as being among the worst in the world, and the organization Freedom House classifies the country as "not free." There is no freedom of the press, the Internet is heavily censored, and opposition politicians and activists are routinely arrested. There are many reports of torture and murder of prisoners, and attacks by government forces against civilian targets. The government of the United States has accused the al-Assad forces of deploying chemical weapons against its own civilians. The United Nations has estimated that about 9.5 million people (equivalent to about one-half of the total population of the country) have been displaced from their homes during the crisis, including the 2.1 million referred to earlier who have fled abroad, and has referred to the situation in Syria as "the biggest humanitarian emergency of our era."

FURTHER READING

Hokayon, Emile, *Syria's Uprising and the Fracturing of the Levant* (New York: Routledge, 2013).

McHugo, John, *Syria: A Recent History* (London: Saqi Books, 2015).

Schner, Christian, *Among the Ruins: Syria Past and Present* (London: C. Hurst & Company, 2014).

Van Dam, Nikolaos, *The Struggle for Power in Syria: Politics and Society under Asad and the Ba'th Party* (London: I.B. Tauris & Company, 2011).

TURKMENISTAN

Turkmenistan is a newly independent nation in Central Asia that is bordered by the Caspian Sea to the west, Iran to the south, and three other "stan" nations in the other directions: Afghanistan, Uzbekistan, and Kazakhstan. From 1924 through the fall of the Soviet Union and Turkmenistan's declaration of independence in 1991, the country existed as the Turkmen Soviet Socialist Republic. Before then, from 1881 when imperial Russian took over the territory, it was part of the Russian province of Transcaspia. In medieval times, the territory of Turkmenistan was on the Silk Road between China and Europe. The ancient oasis city in the Karakum Desert of Merv was an important trade center along this route. It is now a UNESCO World Heritage Site. The city has been renamed Mary because local tradition holds that Mary the mother of Jesus was buried there.

The population of Turkmenistan is 5,171,943 (2014 estimate). About 85% of the people are ethnic Turkmen, and 89% are Muslims. There are numerous minority groups in the population as well, the largest of which are Uzbeks and Russians. The country's capital city is Ashgabat, population 1,031,992 (2012). It is located on the Karakum Canal, an enormous Soviet-era engineering project that carries precious water from the Amu Darya River across the deserts of Turkmenistan and irrigates what were then newly opened farmlands. Ashgabat is known for exorbitant monuments and grand buildings that were erected during the 1990–2006 rule of Turkmenistan's first president, Saparmurat Niyazov, and is nicknamed the "White Marble City" because of the construction material that was widely used, even for telephone booths. Niyazov built a cult of personality around himself, and spent extravagantly on architecture to build national pride in Turkmenistan and, more importantly, to shower himself with glory. In addition to spectacular mosques, Ashgabat showcases lavish government buildings and giant monuments, most of which, such as Independence Monument, Neutrality Monument, and Turkmenistan Tower, are eccentric in form and greatly challenged aesthetically. Also, Niyazov did not hold back in erecting gold statues of himself (at least one of which rotated), and with oddball decrees such as the renaming of months of the year to honor his family members, the banning of dogs from the capital because he said they smell, and the outlawing of opera, ballet, and circus because they were said to be "decidedly unturkmen-like."

We include Turkmenistan in our list of 20 least contented countries in the world because most citizens are very poor despite the great natural resource wealth of the country, and because the country has had very poor government and a miserable human rights record. We are not alone in our assessment. While the 2013 United Nations Human Development Index places Turkmenistan in a tie with Maldives and Eritrea for 103rd ranking out 186 countries, which is low-middle in this survey, the country is #177 out of 179 countries in freedoms of the press according to Reporters without Borders (2013: ahead of only North Korea and Eritrea); #168 out of 177 countries in absence of corruption as measured by Transparency International (2013); and #57 out of 58 countries that depend heavily on export of hydrocarbons or minerals on the 2013 Resource Governance Index that was compiled by the National Resource Governance Institute. Furthermore, Turkmenistan was assigned all failing scores—consistent 7s on a 1–7 scale in which 1 is the best and 7 is the worst—in the 2013 the scoring of personal freedoms by Freedom House International, and was declared to be "not free." Similarly, the organization Human Rights Watch has taken the country to task for lack of personal freedoms: the text of its report concludes that "Turkmenistan remains one of the world's most repressive countries. The country is virtually closed to independent scrutiny, media and religious freedoms are subject to draconian restrictions, and human rights defenders and other activists face the constant threat of government reprisal."

Turkmenistan's wealth comes mostly from natural gas. The country has the fourth-largest reserves of gas in the world, as well as considerable oil. Its Galkynysh

Turkmenistan has especially large deposits of natural gas, which it sells to China, Russia, and many other countries. The photo shows a fire in a natural gas field in the village of Derweze in the Karakum Desert. It has been burning since 1971 when it was set ablaze by Soviet engineers, and there seems to be no way to extinguish the flames. The fiery crater is called the "Door to Hell." (Antonella865/Dreamstime.com)

gas field is the world's second-richest. The country also produces considerable cotton for export, in which it ranks ninth in the world. Citizens benefit from free or heavily subsidized electricity, natural gas, water, and salt until 2030, and vouchers for free gasoline each month. There is also improved infrastructure, such as in Ashgabat which has wide roads, attractive landscaping, and good public services. However, the country's over-the-top construction projects and endemic corruption has meant that the economic benefits of the gas industry are, in the net, not equitably shared across the population. In much of Turkmenistan, living conditions are primitive and there is scant evidence of the nation's wealth. In fact, conditions regressed under Niyazov when he inexplicably canceled or severely cut back pensions for the elderly, closed all medical clinics and hospitals outside Ashgabat, saying the sick people should come to the capital for treatment, and shut all libraries in the country, saying that the only books that Turkmen needed to read were the Quran and *Ruhnama* ("Book of the Soul"), a tome that Niyazov himself had authored. There are also serious environmental problems, not the least of which is at a place in the very center of the country called the Door to Hell where a smelly natural gas fire has been burning continually in a 230-foot-wide (70 meters) crater since it was ignited accidentally in 1971.

Conditions have improved a bit under Niyazov's successor, Gurbanguly Berdy-mukhamedov, who has taken down at least one extravagant monument and the rotating statue of Niyazov in gold, and restored some of the services that citizens had lost, but the country is still poor, corrupt, and autocratic.

FURTHER READING

Human Rights Watch, "World Report 2014: Turkmenistan," http://www.hrw.org/europecentral-asia/turkmenistan.

Peyrouse, Sebastien: *Turkmenistan: Strategies of Power, Dilemmas of Development* (Armonk, NY: M.E. Sharpe, 2011).

Righetti, Nicolas, *Love Me Turkmenistan* (London: Trolley Books, 2008).

Taylor, Alan and Amos Chapple (photographer), "The City of White Marble: Ashgabat, Turk-menistan," *The Atlantic*, June 5, 2013, http://www.theatlantic.com/infocus/2013/06/the-city-of-white-marble-ashgabat-turkmenistan/100528/.

UGANDA

Uganda is a landlocked country of nearly 36 million inhabitants on the north shore of Lake Victoria in East Africa. It is ethnically and linguistically diverse, with only one tribal group, the Baganda who comprise about 17% of the total, exceeding 10% of the population. Most other groups number well below 5% of the total. English and Swahili are the official languages, with the former being a vestige of colonialism. Lugandan is widely spoken too. Uganda gained its independence from Britain in 1962. The country's capital and largest city is Kampala, with nearly 1.7 million inhabitants, but most of the population (86.7% in 2010) lives in rural areas where farming and herding are the mainstays of livelihoods. Christians make up 84% of the population, with Roman Catholics being the largest denomination (41.9%), followed by adherents of the Anglican Church of Uganda (35.9%).

We list Uganda among the 20 least content countries in the world because most of its people are very poor, because the government is highly corrupt, because there is considerable social strife and political unrest, and because there are intolerable abuses of human rights on a routine basis. The United Nations ranks Uganda as #164 out of 186 countries in the world in its Human Development Index for 2013, lower than every country that is not in Africa other than Haiti. Likewise, the country is ranked #114 out of 142 countries on the Legatum Prosperity Index, and #168 out of 187 countries, #172 out of 185 countries, and #174 out of 195 countries in gross domestic product at purchasing power per capita (GDP(PPP) per capita) for 2013 by the International Monetary

Fund, the World Bank, and the U.S. Central Intelligence Agency, respectively. The World Health Organization lists Uganda as #175 out of 193 countries in life expectancy: 56 years. Furthermore, the country has the 27th-highest infant mortality rate out of 221 countries as reported for 2012 by the CIA World Factbook: 61.22 infant deaths per 1,000 live births. Rates of HIV/AIDS infection are also disappointingly high, having spiked anew after an encouraging downturn in the 1990s. With respect to corruption, Transparency International has ranked Uganda #140 out of 170 countries in its Corruption Perceptions Index for 2013, a measure that says that 139 countries are less corrupt than Uganda and only 30 are more corrupt. The problem is pervasive and involves high government officials, members of the national parliament, local officials, run-of-the-mill bureaucrats and police.

Yoweri Museveni has been Uganda's president since 1986. At first, he was considered to be a reform-minded, new generation type of African leader, but his rule has since become increasingly autocratic and less democratic. Opposition political parties have had their activities severely restricted, opposition candidates have been harassed and arrested, mass gatherings and political rallies are no longer allowed, and press freedoms have been curtailed. Presidential term limits have been abolished, allowing Museveni to stay in power longer. He won an election in 2011 that many say was rife with fraud. Other criticism is that Museveni has led Uganda into needless wars in East Africa and across the border in the Democratic Republic of Congo with a cost of more than 5 million lives. In addition, his policies have detracted from economic development efforts in Uganda, helping to keep the nation poor. Uganda has had other poor leaders, most notably the horrific dictator Idi Amin who ruled the country with an iron fist and a greedy hand from 1971 to 1979.

Since the late 1980s, Uganda has been involved in a civil war against the so-called Lord's Resistance Army (LRA) headed by a Ugandan religious zealot named Joseph Kony who says that his aim is to govern the country as a theocracy according to the Ten Commandments. The fighting has been sporadic, with times of greater conflict alternating with times of relative quiet, but the war has cost tens of thousands of lives and displaced at least a million citizens. Many of Kony's soldiers have been children. Other accusations against the LRA include murder, mutilation, abduction, and child sex slavery. Irrespective of the civil war, human rights violations against children in Uganda have included forced labor, especially on farms, denial of education, trafficking, and sexual abuse when working as domestic servants. They become especially vulnerable to such abuses because of extreme poverty, a situation that is exacerbated because of the country's violence and political instability. Young girls face extra problems because poverty often leads them to become sex workers where they become subject to violence from clients and are at high risk of HIV infection.

There are also serious human rights abuses in Uganda against LGBT (lesbian, gay, bisexual and transgendered) persons. Homosexuality was made illegal in Uganda in January 2014, and may be punishable for a term of life in person. There have even been calls by prominent Ugandan politicians for death penalties for "repeat offenders." Gays and lesbians face widespread discrimination and harassment on a daily basis, and are thereby forced to be secretive about sexual orientation. At least two newspapers in Uganda have published names and photographs of Ugandan citizens that they believe to be homosexuals, along with calls to violence against them. One man on such a list, a gay rights activist named David Kato, was murdered on January 27, 2011. Other similarly exposed individuals are missing and are feared to be dead, while others still had to flee abroad. There are few countries as hostile toward homosexuals as Uganda.

Uganda has also been a dangerous place for people of Indian and other South Asian extraction. During colonial times, the British had encouraged South Asians to settle in Uganda because they were seen as a more dependable source of labor than Africans, but then after independence and during the rule of Idi Amin, considerable violence was unleashed against this population and tens of thousands fled the country. Conditions are better now for Indians in Uganda, but the memories of ethnic hostility are still painful.

FURTHER READING

Rice, Andrew, *The Teeth May Smile but the Heart Does Not Forget: Murder and Memory in Uganda* (London: Picador, 2010).

Tripp, Aili Mari, *Museveni's Uganda: Paradoxes of Power in a Hybrid Regime* (Boulder, CO: Lynne Rienner Publishers, 2010).

YEMEN

Yemen is a mountainous desert country at the southwestern corner of the Arabian Peninsula that has land borders with Saudi Arabia and Oman, and shorelines on the Red Sea, the Gulf of Aden, and the Arabian Sea. There are also numerous offshore islands, the largest and most notable of which is Socotra to the southeast, an island that has been referred to as the "Galapagos of the Indian Ocean" because of flora and fauna and that can be found nowhere else in the world. Yemen also stands out for a long history and ancient ruins, including those of the enormous Great Ma'rib Dam that was constructed with ingenious design as far back as the eighth century B.C. to irrigate farmlands. The capital city, Sana'a (population approx. 1.7 million) is remarkably intact from centuries past, and is known for its 14,000-plus "tower houses"—buildings that reach six to eight stories in height and that are referred to as the world's first skyscrapers. Arabs comprise the dominant ethnic group in Yemen, and Islam is the religion of about 99% of the population, with some 60–65% of citizens being Sunni Muslims and 35–40% Shiites. The Sunnis dominate the south and southeast of Yemen. Yemen's total population is about 24 million.

Yemen could be an interesting country to visit for unique vistas and cultural encounters, but unfortunately it is very unstable and unsafe, and travel is not advised for anyone. We include the country as one of the 20 least contented countries in the world because it has been beset with continuing conflict and violence over recent decades, and because the country is poor, corrupt, and lacking in many basic freedoms and human rights. While there have been recent strides in bringing some normalcy to people's lives, the bottom line, unfortunately, seems to be that inevitably one conflict is replaced by another, with the result that Yemenis are still far from enjoying peace and are certainly not prosperous. Indeed, at the moment of this writing, the bloodshed is escalating again and there is a prospect for all-out warfare. This second-largest country on the Arabian Peninsula is the region's poorest, with nearly one-half of the population living below the poverty line of US$2 per day. Some 25% of GDP and 63% of government revenue derive from oil revenues, but oil reserves are rapidly dwindling and may run out as early as 2017. At present, the country ranks #80 out of 188 countries in GDP(PPP) per capita as calculated by the International Monetary Fund, and #89 out of 179 countries as calculated by the World Bank, but these ranks will certainly drop as the petroleum economy contracts and the country's patterns of violence continue. Increasingly, Yemen depends on foreign aid and development money to keep functioning. However, the country is highly corrupt, and much of the aid that is received fails to reach the intended targets. In 2012, Transparency International ranked the country at #156 out of 174 countries in its Corruption Perceptions Index.

Yemen has been politically unstable for centuries. In the 20th century, there was a war every seven years on the average, with periods of bloody civil wars and political insurrection from the 1990s onward. Much of the conflict has involved North and South Yemen, which were two countries with disparate populations and different historical experiences until they were unified in 1990, but disagreements between the regions continue. During the 1990–1991 Gulf War, Yemen sided with Iraq, alienating not just the governments of the United States and Kuwait, but also that of Saudi Arabia where many Yemeni citizens were working. The result was the summary expulsion of 1 million Yemeni guest workers from Saudi Arabia and a crushing blow to Yemen's already poor economy. The Arab Spring of 2011 inspired protests in Sana'a against poverty, corruption, and an attempt by the then-president to abolish term limits for the office, which then resulted in a violent response by government with many deaths and arrests. The political situation is complicated by the fact that a sense of national identity is poorly developed among most Yemeni citizens, as loyalty is given first to tribes and tribal federations, and much of the country's territory is controlled by tribal leaders and not the government. In addition, there are long-standing conflicts between tribal groups, and seemingly endless histories of feuds and bloodshed. Even though Yemen has only 24 million people, including women and children, there are an estimated 60 million firearms in the country. Kalashnikovs are the weapon of choice, and are sold quite openly, as are other automatic weapons, machine guns, and grenades. There have been attacks against American targets in Yemen, most notably an October 2000 suicide attack against the naval vessel USS *Cole* in the harbor off the city of Aden that killed 17 American military personnel. Al-Qaeda is particularly strong in the country and controls considerable territory. The U.S. government considers al-Qaeda on the Arabian Peninsula (AQAP), which is based in Yemen, to be especially threatening, and has launched missile strikes and attacks by drones against suspected terrorist targets. An American antiterrorism strike in December 2009 hit a village by mistake and killed many civilians.

Yemen is a source region for many men, women, and children who are trafficked abroad as forced labor and involuntary sex workers, and the country is classified by the U.S. Department of State as a Tier 3 country, meaning that it does do enough to try to stop human trafficking. Although slavery is outlawed, it still persists and often involves children. Furthermore, there are migrants from the Horn of Africa who have been tricked into coming to Yemen with promises of good jobs who then find themselves exploited in slave-like conditions. Child labor is common in Yemen, with an estimated 23% of children aged 5–14 in the labor force. In contrast to accepted practices around the world, Yemeni law says that men may marry young girls as soon as they reach puberty. Yemen's women are frequent victims of discrimination and violence, and the country ranks last in the world in the Global Gender Gap as calculated by the World Economic Forum. There are restrictions on speech, the press, and religion, and many reports of inhumane conditions and torture in prisons and extrajudicial executions. Homosexuality is illegal and is punishable by death.

FURTHER READING

Brehony, Noel, *Yemen Divided: The Story of a Failed State in South Arabia* (London: I.B. Tauris, 2013).

Johnsen, Gregory D., *The Last Refuge: Yemen, al-Qaeda, and America's War in Arabia* (New York: W.W. Norton & Company, 2014).

Mackintosh-Smith, Tim, *Yemen: The Unknown Arabia* (New York: Overlook Books, 2014).

2

THE MOST AND LEAST CONTENTED WORLD CITIES

In addition to the 20 most contented and least contented countries in the world, we have identified the 20 most contented cities in the world and the 20 least contented cities. We list and discuss them on the pages ahead. As with the countries, the cities are listed not in rank order, but alphabetically within the two groups. Even though most other comparative rankings of cities present their results in rank order, we think that doing so is inappropriate given the imprecise nature of our topic and the impossibility of accurately measuring the degree of contentment and discontentment in any given city, so we are satisfied with simply identifying the top and bottom 20s. Also as for countries, we wanted our two lists of cities to be diverse in terms of regions of the world, major world cultures, and types of cities. We were never comfortable with the comparative rankings that are stacked at the top with prosperous and/or Western cities and heavy at the bottom with cities from the developing world, most especially from Africa. Happiness has a different geography, we think and believe. As you will see later, our research confirmed this, but only to a point.

One of the issues that we faced as we made our choices was about whether or not there should be a cutoff to exclude cities that are smaller than a certain population. Most of our top and bottom cities, as you will see, are "millionaire cities," meaning that their population is over 1 million, but what about smaller places? In the end, we decided to include them in the analysis too, especially if they are famous or have been recently in the news. The result is a huge range in city size, from Tokyo, Japan, at one extreme (metropolitan area population 36 million; a contented city) and the polluted city of Dzerzhinsk, Russia, at the other extreme (about 240,000; a discontented city).

As can be seen, our list of the most contented cities does indeed include representation from all parts of the world, but Europe is especially well represented

Table 2.1

20 Most Contented Cities	20 Least Contented Cities
Accra, Ghana	Aleppo, Syria
Amsterdam, Netherlands	Baghdad, Iraq
Bangalore, India	Beijing, China
Barcelona, Spain	Cairo, Egypt
Bogotá, Colombia	Caracas, Venezuela
Cape Town, South Africa	Chongqing, China
Copenhagen, Denmark	Cuidad Juarez, Mexico
Curitiba, Brazil	Dhaka, Bangladesh
Hamburg, Germany	Donetsk, Ukraine
Helsinki, Finland	Dubai, United Arab Emirates
L'viv, Ukraine	Dzerzhinsk, Russia
Melbourne, Australia	Jakarta, Indonesia
Montevideo, Uruguay	Karachi, Pakistan
Ottawa, Canada	Kinshasa, Democratic Republic of the Congo
Perth, Australia	Lagos, Nigeria
Tokyo, Japan	Marseille, France
Valparaiso, Chile	Port Moresby, Papua New Guinea
Vancouver, Canada	Sochi, Russia
Vienna, Austria	Ürümqi, China
Zürich, Switzerland	Venice, Italy

with as many as 8 of the 20 cities. Put simply, this is a continent with many countries and many prominent cities, as well as a part of the world that is generally prosperous, progressive, and democratic. Furthermore, Europeans have the financial and technical wherewithal for designing cities and residential districts that are conducive for good living. Our results reflect these facts; anything less than a strong European representation would have been dishonest. The second most cities in the top 20 come from Latin America, where there are a number of progressive cities with rising standards of living. Our four cities from this region are Bogotá, Colombia; Curitiba, Brazil; Montevideo, Uruguay; and Valparaiso, Chile. We were surprised that we could list only two cities from Asia on out top 20 list: Bangalore, India, and Tokyo, Japan. We had considered other Japanese cities too, including Kyoto, Yokohama, Sapporo, and Fukuoka, but held back because Japan itself is listed as one of the top 20 countries. Singapore, also an Asian city, would certainly have been one of our top 20 cities but the country Singapore, which is essentially coterminous with the city, was chosen as one of the top 20 countries.

Other Asian cities that ranked high in our estimation in contentment include Hong Kong and Taipei. From the Middle East part of Asia, we gave considerable points to Muscat, the capital of Oman, which is one of our top 20 countries, and to Tel Aviv, the largest city in Israel. Although it has problems too, it stands somewhat apart from the dispiriting impoverishment that is seen in Palestinian zones, the religious conflicts that have plagued Jerusalem, and the heated conflicts for space between Palestinians and Jewish settlers in the West Bank.

The alphabetical list of 20 least contented cities includes representation from most parts of the world, but not North America where there are few countries other than the United States, which is treated separately in this book. Oceania has only one representative on this list, and that is Port Moresby in Papua New Guinea. No cities in Australia or New Zealand are on this list. Europe has five cities on this list, but three are in the former Soviet Union, Dzerzhinsk and Sochi in Russia and Donetsk in the current war zone in Ukraine. The other two are Venice (surprise!) and Marseille, a poster city that represents the tensions and racism that characterize much of Europe in conjunction with immigration from south of the Mediterranean. Asia has the largest number of the least contented cities: 9. Three of these cities are in China, the only country with as many cities on either of the two lists. Dubai, the largest city in the United Arab Emirates is also on our list despite being one of the world's most dazzling cities. This is because a large fraction of residents are exploited foreign workers. A similar situation exists in other cities in the region, including Abu Dhabi, Doha, Kuwait, and Riyadh, all of which could also have been on our list. A number of African capitals could have been on the list too, but in a number of these cases the country itself was on the list of least contented countries.

The pages ahead list each of our 20 most contented cities, followed by the 20 cities that we consider to be least contented. The reasons for our choices are given in the accompanying essays. First there is a definition of the city and its location, and then paragraphs that explain why the city was selected for one or the other list. In many cases, we have our own observations about the cities from what we know about current events and from our own travels, but also we cite other rankings as appropriate to back up our choices. For some of the cities, the editors of this book have selected photographs to help illustrate our text. There are also some references and/or additional readings that are given for each of the cities.

THE 20 MOST CONTENTED WORLD CITIES

ACCRA, GHANA

Accra is the capital and largest city in Ghana, a rapidly developing country on the Gulf of Guinea and the Atlantic Ocean in West Africa. The city is on the coast in the country's south, and is an important port and rail hub, as well as Ghana's principal business and financial center. Its population is about 2.27 million, while that of the Greater Accra Metropolitan Area is approximately 4 million. From 1877 to independence in 1957, the city was capital of the British Colony of Gold Coast. Ghana was among the first of Europe's colonies in Africa to gain independence, and Accra was one of the key centers of African nationalist movements and decolonization politics. Kwame Nkrumah, the leader of Ghana's struggle for independence, became the country's first president. He worked to develop Accra as a city for all citizens, and a symbol of African rule in a former colony. Nkrumah's mausoleum and a memorial park in downtown Accra honor his memory. Today, Ghana is one of Africa's most developed and most stable countries, and Accra has emerged as one of the continent's most prosperous and most livable cities.

Accra has a highly diversified economy that combines its roles as the government center of Ghana, and one of the largest manufacturing and financial centers in Africa outside the Republic of South Africa. It is home to numerous banks, the Ghana Stock Exchange, and various financial concerns, as well as one of the continent's leading centers of higher education, health care, the media, and the arts. Its manufacturing base includes processing food products from the Ghana's countryside, including the country's historic mainstay of cocoa production, timber and wood products, garments, and assembly plants such as electronics and automobiles. The city also has numerous retailing centers, and serves not just the local population, but travelers from other African countries on shopping trips. There is also considerable tourism. There are a number of fine hotels, good restaurants, and streets in the city that are known for nightlife. One of the attractions for tourists is the city's main beach, Labadi Beach, also known as La Pleasure Beach, and its resort hotels. The city is one of Africa's leading conventions and expositions centers, with many of the larger events being held at the Accra International Convention Center. The city's main football (soccer) team, the Accra Hearts of Oak, and the national team of Ghana, the Black Stars, play in the Accra Sports Stadium and have enthusiastic fan followings.

The vibrancy of Accra is revealed especially well in a district called Osu. It is located to the east of the Central Business District, but is known locally as the "West End" as a reference to London, and its main street, Cantonments Road, is referred to as "Oxford Street." The area reflects the many layers of history that have shaped Accra from the construction of the Danish fort of Christiansborg in the 17th century onward, and is a mix of architectural styles and land uses. Oxford Street and other commercial streets are lined with shopping centers, supermarkets, and restaurants, as well as pubs and nightclubs that stay busy well into the night. An engaging recent book by a Ghanaian émigré scholar in Canada, Ato Quayson, focuses on Oxford Street in order to encapsulate the historical experiences of Ghana and its people, and to tell the story of the development of Accra as a diverse and vibrant global metropolis.

Like other cities in Africa, Accra has more than its share of urban poverty and injustice. Economic growth has stimulated considerable migration of poor people to the city, not just from the countryside of Ghana but also from neighboring countries where job prospects are not as good. As in many other cities, the result is generally more migrants than jobs available, and inadequate housing to meet rising demands. This in turn leads to the creation of informal squatter settlements wherever people can find space, and the emergence of a large informal economy that provides services for growing migrant populations. Housing conditions are often ramshackle, at least initially until a squatter community gets established, and there is typically inadequate supply of fresh water, sanitation systems, and transportation, among other services. In Accra, the Mensah Guinea slum neighborhood was recently demolished reportedly because of an outbreak of cholera, but residents say that there was no cholera, but only a plan to remake their neighborhood near the beach into an upscale district. These are not usually the characteristics of a contented city, but in Accra we see an overall atmosphere of optimism about the future and a pattern of long-term development that is encouraging, and think that the city can be a model for other urban centers in developing countries that are emerging from histories of colonialism and poverty.

FURTHER READING

Grant, Richard, *Globalizing City: The Urban and Economic Transformation of Accra, Ghana* (Syracuse, NY: Syracuse University Press, 2009).

McTernan, Billie Adwoa, "Accra Slum Dwellers Suspect Cholera Demolitions a Pretext for Profit," *The Guardian*, October 20, 2014, http://www.theguardian.com/global-development/2014/oct/20/accra-cholera-ghana-mensah-guinea-slums-demolished-commercial-profit.

Pellow, Deborah, *Landlords and Lodgers: Socio-Spatial Organization of an Accra Community* (Chicago: University of Chicago Press, 2008).

Quayson, Ato, *Oxford Street, Accra: City Life and the Itineraries of Transnationalism* (Durham, NC: Duke University Press, 2014).

AMSTERDAM, NETHERLANDS

Amsterdam is the capital and largest city in the Netherlands. It has a population of 813,562 within municipal limits and 1,575,263 for the metropolitan area. It is the main urban center of the Randstad, a densely built-up conurbation in the heart of West Europe that numbers about 7 million inhabitants. The city dates back to a fishing village in the 12th century, and is named after a dam that was constructed across the Amstel River. In the so-called Dutch Golden Age of the 17th century, Amsterdam became one of the world's most important ports and business centers. The world's first stock exchange was opened in the city in 1602. During this time, the Netherlands prospered from empire in Europe, the Americas, and Southeast

Asia. The city continues as one of Europe's leading financial centers and as a major hub of the international diamonds trade. Amsterdam is also one of Europe's leading tourist destinations, attracting an estimated 3.7 million international visitors each year. Popular attractions include the city's 17th-century network of canals, several significant art and history museums, the Anne Frank House, and the famous Amsterdam Red Light District, a zone of legalized prostitution.

Amsterdam is known as a progressive city with liberal social policies and a tradition of tolerance for racial, ethnic, and religious minorities. The city has had a diverse population since the 16th and 17th centuries, when the native Dutch in the city were joined by Huguenots, Flemings, and Sephardic Jews, among other immigrants. The Jewish population grew to more than 10% of the city's total before being decimated by the Nazi invasion in World War II and the Holocaust. Immigrants from Indonesia began to arrive in large numbers after the after the 1940s collapse of the Dutch East Indies, while after 1975, many Surinamese immigrants migrated from the former Dutch Guyana after it had gained independence. The city's population also includes people from Turkey, Morocco, Spain, and Italy who arrived as labor migrants, and more recently, Poles and other East Europeans who have also come in search of jobs. There are Chinese and Indian migrants as well, and new residents from throughout Europe, North America, and all other corners of the globe. The result is an exceptionally diverse city in which people of Dutch ancestry are now a minority: as of 2012, people with Dutch heritage comprised 49.5% of the population and residents of foreign background 50.5%. However, most of the population, 88%, has Dutch nationality. It would be incorrect to say that everything is peaceful with this mix, as ethnic and religious tensions do exist, and more than a few Dutch are guilty of Islamophobia in particular, as are too many people in the United States and in other European countries with fast-changing populations. Furthermore, a vastly disproportionate number of the poor people in Amsterdam are immigrants or the children of immigrants. However, it is fair to add that the Dutch in Amsterdam and elsewhere in the country are adjusting more admirably to the social changes around them than many of the citizens of nearby countries, and that if Europe is to become truly diverse and tolerant, it will find models in Amsterdam and the Netherlands.

Amsterdam's tradition of tolerance extends as well to sexual minorities. It is one of the most gay- and lesbian-friendly cities in the world, and its annual Pride Parade on boat-floats along the city's canals is one of the world's largest and most boisterous of such festivals anywhere. Indeed, Amsterdam is a city of many festivals, by one count as many as 300 per year. In addition to gay pride events, the city hosts various ethnic and religious holiday festivals, arts and music festivals, food fairs, beer festivals, festivals on national holidays, festivals in local neighborhoods, garden festivals. There are also various truly unique events such as the High Times Cannabis Cup every November that features marijuana tasting in the city's many cannabis cafés, and the 5 Days Off Amsterdam festival that is usually held in March and features nonstop electronic music performed extremely loudly. There is never a shortage of things to do in Amsterdam, and no one has ever called the city dull.

Another reason for us to recognize Amsterdam on this list of 20 most contented cities in the world is that it is in the forefront among the word's cities in environmental awareness and goals for sustainable living. Most Amsterdam residents strive to conserve energy and reduce waste, are diligent about recycling, and think not just about the here and now, but also about global responsibilities and the future. Many people are also committed to healthy living and spend as much time outdoors as schedules allow, no matter what the season. There is no better example of Amsterdam residents' commitments to staying fit and maintaining a clean environment than their love affair with their bicycles. The vast majority of city residents are bike owners and more than one-half of all workers in the city use bikes for daily commuting. This is measurably more than in other "green" cities of Europe, with the possible exception of Copenhagen. Bicycles are popular also for shopping errands, recreation, and other uses. Consequently, one can recognize Amsterdam by its many bike lanes and bike trails, and by the profusion of parked bikes on seemingly every street, sidewalk, and canal bridge in the city, and by the crowded, large bicycle parking lots at metro stations and shopping centers. Automobile ownership is high too, as the Netherlands is a prosperous society, but many residents of Amsterdam and other cities prefer to use them sparingly. The city also has a dense network of mass transit lines, so for many people driving where you could otherwise walk, bike, or use public transit would be unthinkable. Such attitudes about transportation put people on streets and sidewalks at all times of day and night, so the city is made safer as a result. Additionally, there is a greater sense of community and common experience in Amsterdam than in many other cities in wealthy countries. Immigrants who come from societies where bike-riding is not part of the culture are less prone to bicycling, as some had always associated owning a car as a symbol of wealth and higher social status. There are programs in Amsterdam to acculturate immigrants to the ways of the city, and to teach adults who never learned to ride that biking can be for them too.

FURTHER READING

Jordan, Pete, *In the City of Bikes: The Story of the Amsterdam Cyclist* (New York: Harper Perennial, 2013).

Mak, Geert and Philip Blom, *Amsterdam: A Brief Life of the City* (London: Vintage Books, 2010).

Shorto, Russell, *Amsterdam: A History of the World's Most Liberal City* (New York: Vintage Books, 2014).

BANGALORE, INDIA

Bangalore is a city in the Deccan Plateau region of south-central India and the capital of Karnataka State. Its official name became Bengalūru in 2006, but the old spelling remains in common use. The city has a population of 8,425,970 (2011), the third-highest total among India's many cities, while the Bangalore metropolitan area has 8,520,345 residents, the fifth-highest total in India. The city is the center of India's booming information technology industry, and is one of the fastest-growing cities in the country. The population of the metropolitan area more than doubled in the 20 years from census year 1991 to census year 2011, from approximately 4.1 million to the aforementioned 8.5 million. As India continues to expand economically, the population of Bangalore will doubtlessly grow accordingly.

The modern history of Bangalore is traced to a mud fort that was built by Kempé Gowda I in 1537. He also ordered a regular grid plan for the city's streets and artificial lakes to provide a water supply. During the British colonial period, the city was a regional administrative center and garrison town. It was divided into a cantonment for the British population and a separate district for the local Kannada people. There were beautiful buildings such as Bangalore Palace that was modeled after Windsor Castle in England, fine public buildings such as schools and hospitals, many parks, and a botanical garden. The city developed a reputation as the "Garden City of India." The city also developed as an industrial center. In 1906, Bangalore became the first city in Asia to have electricity. During the movement for Indian independence, Bangalore was the scene of numerous protests and civil disturbances. In 1956, nine years after India won its independence, Bangalore's imposing legislature building for Karnataka State was completed. Called the Vidhana Soudha, this spectacular granite structure is described as being "Mysore neo-Dravidian" in architectural style. It was built at great cost specifically to outdo the beautiful court building that the British had built in the city.

Our choice of adding Bangalore into this list of the 20 most contented cities in the world is guided by a desire to include representation from India, which is enormously rich culturally and is a fast-rising global economy, and by the fact that the city is especially prosperous in that it has evolved into one of the world's leading IT centers. The city also reflects the old stereotype of a poor India, in that there are impoverished slums and street beggars as well, but on the whole, Bangalore is "New India" on the rise. In comparison to Mumbai, where about one-half of the population resides in neighborhoods that are officially classified as slums, the parallel figure for Bangalore is only about 10%. The city is dotted with modern office buildings, industrial parks, and state-of-the-art campuses for research. The GDP of Bangalore is some $83 billion, the fourth-largest contribution to India's economy by a single city. Many Indians from all over the country

Chicken meat for sale at Russell Market in Bangalore, India. The market was built by the British in 1927. (ElenaMirage/iStockphoto.com)

see Bangalore as a city of opportunity, and migrate there in search of a better life. Consequently, the city is one of India's fast-growing urban centers, as well as a city that increasingly reflects the vast cultural, linguistic, and religious diversity of India as a whole.

Because of the IT economy that now dominates Bangalore, the city's nickname has become the "Silicon Valley of India." Major Indian technology companies that are headquartered in Bangalore include Wipro Limited and Infosys, a giant locally born corporation that provides business consulting, information technology, software engineering, and outsourcing services to its clients. Other prominent concerns in the city are Bharat Electronics Limited, Hindustan Aeronautics, the National Aerospace Laboratories, the Indian Space Research Organization, the Indian Institute of Science, and the National Institute of Mental health and Neurosciences. The city's Bangalore University was opened in 1886 and is one of India's oldest institutions of higher learning. It has some 500 colleges and an astounding 300,000 students. In 1985, Texas Instruments became the first foreign multinational company to open operations in Bangalore, but now the city houses research and development center for a who's who of foreign technology and manufacturing companies: Airbus, Bosch, Boeing, General Electric, Google, Microsoft, Nokia, Oracle, Philips, Shell, Toyota, and Tyco, among others. It also has a large call centers business because the population is highly educated, technologically savvy, and fluent in English.

The prosperity of Bangalore is reflected in the city's many fine neighborhoods and new housing developments, modern highways, its modern, tree-lined city streets, many attractive green spaces, and the city's new Kempegowda International Airport. Bangalore Palace, which is now owned by the Mysore royal family, has a large amusement park called Fun World on its grounds. Attractions include rides, a water park, and a room with artificial snow. The grounds also host concerts, often by some of the most famous music stars from around the world. The city has a booming nightlife, and is referred to as the "Pub Capital of India" and the "Rock/Metal capital of India," in addition to being a "Garden City" and India's Silicon Valley. Finally, we note that Bangalore is home to a thriving Kannada film industry, many theaters, and is a great sports town in which cricket is the most popular sport and the Bangalore Royal Challengers the most popular team.

FURTHER READING

De, Aditi, *Multiple City: Writings on Bangalore* (London: Penguin, 2008).

Mascarenhas, R. C., *India's Silicon Plateau: Development of Information and Communications Technology in Bangalore* (Hyderabad, India: Orient Blackswan, 2010).

Nair, Janaki, *The Promise of the Metropolis: Bangalore's Twentieth Century* (Oxford: Oxford University Press, 2005).

BARCELONA, SPAIN

Barcelona is located on the coast of the Mediterranean Sea in the northeast of Spain, where it is the capital and largest city of the autonomous commune of Catalonia. Its population is 1,620,919 (2011), making it Spain's second-biggest city after Madrid. The urban area of Barcelona totals 4,604,000 inhabitants, while the larger metropolitan region numbers 5,375,774 inhabitants. It is the largest metropolitan area on the Mediterranean. There are two official languages, Spanish and Catalan, and among many Catalan speakers there is a strong desire to be independent from Spain and for Catalonia to be its own country. This desire is driven by feelings of Catalan pride and nationalism, as well as a measure of anger about how Spain has treated the region at specific points in history. In addition, Catalans are aware that both Barcelona and Catalonia are very wealthy in comparison to all other cities and regions in Spain, and are among the wealthiest places in Europe. Many of them think that Spanish rule holds them back economically, and are eager to live in a smaller, more prosperous country.

There is no question that Barcelona is one of the most charming, enjoyable, and most livable large cities in the world. Residents and visitors alike adore it for its climate, architecture, cultural life, nightlife, public spaces, cuisine, and sun-soaked beaches, as well as for vibrancy, friendliness, tolerance, and sophistication. In many people's opinions, the city is large enough to offer everything that an urban resident could want and to be genuinely a global city, but not so big as to be oppressive. It is hard to find anyone who dislikes the place, as here is one city in the world about which there seems to be universal acclaim. Barcelonans know that they are lucky.

One could be perfectly contented in Barcelona with only the climate and the beaches. The city has a Mediterranean-type climate regime in which winters are mild and it is never truly cold, and summers are warm but not humid. There is sunshine year-round, and it is warm enough to enjoy beach life for at least half the year. The city has about 3 miles (4.5 km) of wide beaches, plus many more beaches nearby both up the coast and down the coast from city limits. The beach in the historic central neighborhood of Barceloneta is especially popular. There are pleasant cafés and restaurants along the beaches, and lively bars for partying after dark. Indeed, for many people, Barcelona is something of a mecca for nightlife, good music, and dancing. Other pluses about Barcelona include nearness to the Catalan Pyrenees, where there are charming mountain villages, beautiful farming valleys, and winter ski slopes to visit, and to Spain's beautiful wine country.

Barcelona gained considerable favorable attention around the globe when it hosted the summer Olympics in 1992. Its reputation for tourism grew as a result, and now the city ranks as the world's 10th most visited city, and the third most visited city in Europe after London and Paris. Tourism is, therefore, a mainstay of the economy. There are many museums and cultural events in Barcelona for international visitors to enjoy, as well as excellent shopping streets and glamorous shopping malls, historic districts led by the Barri Gòtic (the Gothic Quarter or old Barcelona), and spectacular architecture, both new and old. Several of the most famous sites for visitors are the highly original and fanciful buildings designed by architect Antoni Gaudi (1852–1926), the most notable of which is the soaring church named Sagrada Familia. Indeed, Barcelona seems to be overrun with tourists, especially in summer, and some locals complain. Desirable neighborhoods near popular beaches and tourist landmarks have seen a disruption in the real estate market, as apartments that had been occupied by Barcelonan families are converted by profit-minded landlords to short-stay and higher-priced spaces for a tourist clientele. Other advantages of the city are a tradition of tolerance, relative safety from crime, and a great environment for families and children. The city is one of the most gay-friendly in the world, and its annual gay pride parade is among the world's largest and most joyous.

The strong economy of Barcelona is exemplified by a GDP of $177 billion, or nearly $35,000 on a per capita basis. This is 44% more than the average for the European Union. The GDP of Barcelona is the 4th-highest among European cities, being outpaced only by cities with much more population, and the 35th-largest among world cities. The city's economy is based not only on the tourism and hospitality industries, but also on conventions and global expositions, and manufacturing (which is led by the manufacture of automobiles), as well as banking and finance, health care, higher education, the media, the arts, and fashion. In fact, the city is considered to be one of the world's leading centers of style and fashion, and is home to many trendsetters in the design of high-end clothing, accessories, and other goods. There is also a strong high-technology sector in Barcelona with many promising start-up businesses in cutting-edge fields. Quite a few talented young people from all over Spain and from countries abroad choose to settle in Barcelona, knowing that the networks they encounter in the city can be good for creativity and for getting started in business. Both *National Geographic* and the *Discovery Channel* have reported that Barcelona is one of the world's top 10 cities, while the lifestyle magazine *Monocle* has ranked the city as #14 in the world in livability. We agree enthusiastically that the city is among the best.

FURTHER READING

Busquets, Joan, *Barcelona: The Urban Evolution of a Compact City* (Cambridge, MA: Harvard University Press, 2006).

Marshall, Tim, ed., *Transforming Barcelona* (London: Routledge, 2004).

Ramon Resina, Joan, *Barcelona's Vocation of Modernity: Rise and Decline of an Urban Image* (Palo Alto, CA: Stanford University Press, 2008).

BOGOTÁ, COLOMBIA

Bogotá is the capital of Colombia, a country of nearly 48 million inhabitants located in the northwestern corner of South America where it has coastlines on both the Pacific Ocean and the Caribbean Sea. The city is in highlands in center of the country at an elevation of about 8,660 feet (2,640 meters), making it South America's third-highest capital city after Quito, Ecuador, and La Paz, Bolivia. The population of Bogotá was counted in the census of 2005 at 6,778,691 and is now estimated to be nearing 8 million. The metropolitan area of Bogotá has a population of about 12 million. The city ranks among the 25 largest in the world and is among the leading financial and business centers of Latin America. It was founded in 1537 by the Spanish conquistador Gonzalo Jiménez de Quesada, and later became capital of New Granada, the Spanish colonial territory that preceded Colombia. The country's independence was declared in 1810 during a long and bloody struggle against the Spanish crown that was led by Simón Bolivar. Today the main plaza in the city is named Plaza Bolivar after the celebrated liberator.

Only a few years ago, Bogotá may have been a candidate for designation as one of the world's least contented cities, rather than most contented. It was mired in poverty and governmental corruption, had extremely high crimes rates, and was a major center of production and distribution of illicit narcotics to other countries, including to Europe and North America. It was known around the world for gangland murders and for kidnappings of innocent civilians and foreign visitors by gangs and to collect ransom monies. Also, there was open warfare between Colombia's military forces and a shady guerilla army known as FARC from the Spanish words for Revolutionary Armed Forces of Colombia that was responsible for much of the bloodshed and spate of kidnappings. Bogotá was also hopelessly clogged with traffic and badly polluted. These problems still exist, although there is a kind of peace with FARC and the worst of the kidnappings seems to be over, and Bogotá is still not a safe city by any means. Furthermore, bad traffic and air pollution continue as well. The city still has a way to go before it is truly one of the world's 20 most contented cities, but there has been so much progress recently and such promise for the future that citizens can now breathe more easily and are feeling ever more contented. It is primarily because the city has ascended so successfully from the depths of being one of the violence capitals of the world that we recognize Bogotá on these pages.

The London-based Economist Intelligence Unit (EIU) might agree with our assessment. In 2013, its researchers calculated that livability had improved in Bogotá much more over the previous five years than in any of the other 139 cities in its worldwide survey, and commended Bogotá especially for a significant drop in crime rates. This success is attributed to an improved policing strategy called *Comunidad Segura* that was adopted in 1995 and that has been expanded and upgraded ever since. The numbers of murders in the city have plummeted from 4,352 in 1993 (81 per 100,000 inhabitants) to 1,401 in 2007 (19 per 100,000 inhabitants), to 1,283 in 2013 (approximately 16 per 100,000 inhabitants). Other Colombian cities have also seen marked improvements in public safety.

Likewise, the city has also made progress on other problems, most especially traffic congestion. Like many fast-growing large cities, Bogotá had come to be choked by the automobile. A pall of air pollution hung over the metropolis and traffic became so congested on an inadequate street network that commuting became a nightmare. However, instead of focusing on construction of superhighways and widening roads to ease traffic flow, as many cities have done to end congestion, the strategy that Bogotá introduced in 1998 centered on discouraging automobile usage according to a three-pronged approach: (1) the introduction of very specific restrictions on automobile usage in the city; (2) construction of an innovative new mass transit system; and (3) successful transition of Bogotá into a bicycle-friendly city. The motor vehicle restrictions, called *pico y placa*, regulate access to key streets during morning and evening commuter rush periods according to day of the week and the last digit of a car's license plate and force car owners to seek alternative means of transportation on the days they are not allowed to drive. The new mass transit system is called TransMilenio. It is an integrated bus network that consists of large buses that move rapidly on dedicated "busways"

Bogotá, Colombia is discouraging automobile usage in the city as a way to fight traffic jams and reduce pollution. The *TransMilenio* public bus system is an effective alternative. It allows the city's various districts to be equally accessible to more people, including the poor, and is, therefore, a way of fighting poverty. (Jesse Kraft/Dreamstime.com)

along major streets, and smaller feeder buses and minivans called *colectivo* that operate in residential neighborhoods to bring passengers to major stops along the busways. The new bicycle network employs safe bicycle paths that have been constructed throughout the city, as well as dedicated bicycle lanes along major roads that have replaced thousands of curbside parking spaces. These dedicated bike lanes are called *ciclorrutas*. They now total more than 234 miles (377 km) and serve as many as 400,000 riders each day. On Sundays, many of Bogotá's major streets are closed to motor vehicles altogether, and are given to pedestrians and bicyclists. These Ciclovía Sundays, as they are known, are a further way to increase interest in bicycling among the public as an alternative to automobiles. As a result, the city has become noticeably quieter, the air is cleaner, and citizens benefit from good exercise. A side benefit is that many residents of Bogotá have gotten to know their city better, which in turn increases civic mindedness and feelings of neighborliness between different communities.

The city has also made strides in addressing housing and other problems in its poorest neighborhoods, the *barrios*, such as the squatter district known as Ciudad Bolivar. A key part of the approach is to empower residents by way of participatory politics and "bottom-up" communications strategies such as "*Bogotá, Como vamos?*" (Bogotá, How are we doing?) in which poor people are asked to speak up to city government about their needs. The makeover of Bogotá is far from complete, but great strides have been made already, with the result that the city is now considered to be a model for improvements in other poor, overgrown urban centers in the developing world.

FURTHER READING

Abel, Ann, "South America's Next Capital of Cool: Bogotá," *Forbes*, April 29, 2013, http://www.forbes.com/sites/annabel/2014/04/29/south-americas-next-capital-of-cool-bogota/.

Hernandez-Garcia, Jaime, *Public Space in Informal Settlements: The Barrios of Bogotá* (Cambridge: Cambridge Scholars Publishing, 2013).

Sendoa Echanove, Matias, "Bogota at the Edge: Planning the Barrios," 2004, http://www.bogotalab.com/articles/bogota_edge.html.

CAPE TOWN, SOUTH AFRICA

Cape Town is a large city in South Africa on the Cape of Good Hope at the southern tip of the African continent. It has a population of 433,688 and a metropolitan area population of 3,740,026 (2011), and is the second-largest urban center in the country after Johannesburg. The population is diverse and reflects all segments of South Africa's complex society. As reported in the census, which asks respondents to describe themselves according to racial identity, about 42.4% of the population is "Coloured," 38.6% is "Black African," 15.7% is "White," and 1.4% is "Indian" or Asian." In terms of first language, 35.7% of the population speaks Afrikaans, 29.8% Xhosa, and 28.4% English. As seat of the National Parliament, Cape Town is the legislative capital of South Africa. The city is sometimes referred to as "the most European city on the African continent," although the precise meaning of such a term is hard to fathom.

The city is remarkably beautiful and is typically among the first cities mentioned when knowledgeable travelers talk about the world's most spectacular urban settings and most benign climate. Cape Town faces the sea and is rimmed with many beaches, and has as a backdrop the 3,558-foot (1,085-meter) high Table Mountain, a high, level plateau above steep cliffs that is about 2 miles (approximately 3 km) across from which visitors gain panoramic views of the city. There are popular hiking trails to the top as well as a cable car route, and diverse worlds of flora at various elevations along the way. Indeed, Cape Town is noted for the rich biodiversity of its region, a unique natural area that botanists have labeled as the Cape Floral Kingdom. The climate is a warm-summer Mediterranean-type climate, characterized by mild and moderately wet winters and warm, dry (Southern Hemisphere) summers. The city's maritime location assures low levels of air pollution. Because of these attractions, Cape Town is an extremely popular destination for both domestic and international tourists. It ranks first in tourism in South Africa and is also among the top tourist destinations on the entire African continent. The city is also noted for outdoor lifestyles and sports, including hiking, sailing, and biking, as well as team sports such as rugby, cricket, and soccer.

Cape Town had a troubled recent past. As a result of 1948 elections that led to the establishment of the Group Areas Act in South Africa, the city became notoriously segregated according to the official South African racial categories. Formerly multiracial districts were either demolished or became strictly segregated by race, with the most desirable neighborhoods being assigned as whites-only districts. Black Africans were evicted from their homes by the tens of thousands. Such racial engineering was especially heavy-handed in a part of Cape Town known as District Six. Consequently, the city became one of the main centers of protest by Black Africans and their supporters against apartheid, and experienced many conflicts during the decades of struggle for racial equality. Robben Island, a former penitentiary island off the Cape Town coast, once confined many political-prisoner opponents of apartheid, including Nelson Mandela, a national leader who was to become the country's first democratically elected president. The situation has changed significantly since 1994, when South Africa's discriminatory apartheid rules were at last dismantled and the country became a democracy based on majority rule. Although there is still a strong legacy of spatial residential segregation based on race, racial barriers have fallen one after the other, and Cape Town is to be commended for continual progress in the integration of once-segregated neighborhoods and equality of access to employment, schooling, and other aspects of city life. Significantly, the gap in income levels between Whites and Blacks in Cape Town has fallen over the post-apartheid period, and is now the lowest among large cities in South Africa (although it is still high by global standards). However, the vast majority of large businesses in the city (and in South Africa as a whole) are still white-owned, and the most prestigious neighborhoods are still overwhelmingly white, so there is still much to do before genuine equality is achieved.

Cape Town has a diversified economy that includes financial services, manufacturing, tourism, and fishing as key sectors. The city is Africa's leading information technology city as based on the numbers of successful companies in the field, and has been identified as the South Africa's most entrepreneurial city. The University of Cape Town, which was founded in 1829 and is South Africa's oldest university and is one of the oldest in Africa, ranks quite highly in educational quality and research among universities around the globe. In 2010, the city was one of the host venues for the FIFA World Cup tournament, which brought it considerable favorable attention around the world as well as considerable urban renewal and redevelopment in preparation. There has also been a recent real estate boom associated with the World Cup and with the city's increasing popularity as a place for South Africans and African and European expatriates to retire.

Rising prosperity levels have led to significant physical improvements in the city's poorest neighborhoods, such that now there are comparatively few squatter areas remaining that lack basic city services, and electricity, water lines, and sanitary sewers now reach all parts of the city. However, a negative effect has been displacement of poorer residents to marginal neighborhoods because of increased rents and property prices in better and more conveniently located areas. Also, there are pockets of urban crime, drug addiction, and other social problems, although again we acknowledge that Cape Town has made much progress in quality of life for all citizens since the fall of apartheid.

FURTHER READING

Besteman, Catherine, *Transforming Cape Town* (Berkeley, CA: University of California Press, 2008).

Hammer, Joshua, "Inside Cape Town," *Smithsonian Magazine*, April 2008, http://www.smithsonianmag.com/people-places/inside-cape-town-31497119/?no-ist=&page=1.

Samara, Tony Roshan, *Cape Town after Apartheid: Crime and Governance in the Divided City* (Minneapolis: University of Minnesota Press, 2011).

Western, John, *Outcast Cape Town* (Berkeley: University of California Press, 1997).

COPENHAGEN, DENMARK

Copenhagen is the capital and largest city in Denmark, a small country in north-central Europe that we discuss elsewhere in this book as one of the world's most content countries. The city is located in the east of the country on the eastern coast of the Danish island of Zealand, and has a population of 1,246,611. The metropolitan area population is 1,975,361 (both figures 2014). An additional part of the city is on the small island of Amager, to which it is connected from Zealand by five bridges. In addition to being national capital, Copenhagen is Denmark's leading economic center, as well as an important cultural center, center of higher education, and a leading tourism destination. Among the major companies with headquarters in Copenhagen are A. P. Møller-Maresk, which is most known for container ships around the world, the pharmaceutical company Novo Nordisk, the Carlsberg Group (a brewing company), and Novozymes, a global biotechnology company. A mix of old and new, leading landmarks in the city include the Børsen (the stock exchange building completed in 1640), Frederiksberg Palace (16th and early 17th centuries), the prestigious, historic University of Copenhagen that was founded in 1479, and Tivoli Gardens Amusement Park (opened in 1843). Kronborg Castle, which dates originally to the 1420s and that was immortalized as Elsinore in William Shakespeare's *Hamlet*, is near Copenhagen in the town of Helsingør. Modern landmarks are the national library's dramatic Black Diamond Building that was opened on the waterfront in 1999, the spectacular Øresund Bridge (also 1999) that connects Copenhagen with southern Sweden, transforming the shape of the metropolitan area, and the Copenhagen Opera House, also on the waterfront and dating to 2004. A popular icon of the city is the bronze Little Mermaid sculpture (1913) on the waterfront that is based on Danish writer Hans Christian Andersen's fairy tale of the same name.

We include Copenhagen among our 20 most content cities in the world because it is just that—widely acclaimed as one of the world's most livable cities, with a healthy, happy, and generally prosperous population. Among the many recognitions that the city has received is a #1 ranking by the London-based magazine *Monocle* in its global Quality of Life Survey for 2014, #9 ranking in the Mercer Quality of Living Index for 2014, and recognition as the European Commissions' European Green Capital for 2014. On the negative side, but perhaps reflecting the adage that you get what you pay for, the city is terribly expensive in cost of living. For example, the Intelligence Unit of the *Economist* has ranked Copenhagen as #9 in the world in cost of living for expatriate employees in 2014, and the management consulting firm ECA International has ranked it #11 globally in a similar survey in 2013.

Perhaps the most distinctive aspect of livability in Copenhagen is that, arguably, the city ranks #1 in terms of being bicycle-friendly and in commuting by

Many European cities have excellent public spaces and lively neighborhoods, and Copenhagen, Denmark, is no exception. The photo shows tourists and locals enjoying themselves in an historic waterfront district named Nyhavn, or "New Harbor." (fotoVoyager/iStockphoto.com)

bicycle. (Another of our top cities, Amsterdam, can also claim to be #1 in bicycling.) With respect to the former point, bikers can take advantage of the city's flat terrain and compact form, as well as an extensive network of bicycle paths, dedicated lanes for bicyclists, and other cycle tracks that serve all parts of the city. There are also many facilities for bicycle parking. On the second point, we report that every day 750,000 miles (1.2 million km) are cycled in Copenhagen, and that 36% of the population regularly commutes to and from work, school, or university by bicycle. In fact, every day more commuters bicycle in Copenhagen than in the entire United States. Because cycling is better for the environment than other forms of transport, cheaper, and because it improves human health, there are plans to increase Copenhagen's commuting-by-bicycle percentage to 50%. While automobile ownership is quite high in this prosperous society, Copenhagen also sports an efficient public transportation system that is widely used. It includes a metro, as well as bus and railway networks designed on the principle that all residents should be within 350 meters (1,148 feet) of public transit.

Copenhagen is a green city in other ways too. The city has a great many parks of all sizes and types, and a municipal policy that says that there needs to be a park or beach with 15 minutes walking time from every residence in the city. That goal is almost fully attained. Three of the city's beaches are within 30 minutes cycling distance from the city center. One of the city's newest parks, opened in 2012, is Superkilen in the ethnically diverse and sometimes tense immigrant district of Nørrebro. It is a unique and fun urban space that incorporates in its design various plants, signs, and other artifacts brought in from countries around the world: palm trees from China, picnic tables from Armenia, a fountain from Morocco, benches from Brazil, and manhole covers from Zanzibar, among other surprises. Another goal of Copenhagen is to become totally carbon neutral by 2015. If successful, the city would be the first in the world to achieve this distinction. An important step toward this goal is to make sure that every building in the city, even old ones built long before much attention was paid to environmental issues, is as energy efficient as possible. Space is used very efficiently in Copenhagen, and new construction favors brownfield sites to put them to good use.

Health care is another strong point. In addition to having excellent hospitals and clinics and an admirable national health insurance system, Copenhagen residents benefit from a "Long Live Copenhagen" program that is administered by city government to increase longevity by encouraging weight loss and exercise, and cutbacks in consumption of alcohol and tobacco products. Healthy eating is also encouraged, including fresh fruits and vegetables in place of processed foods. The city is known for good restaurants and fine dining, and a vibrant cultural life that includes museums, concerts, and theater, among other enjoyments. There is an excellent library system, as Danes love to read. The Copenhagen Marathon is one of the most popular long-distance runs in the world. Danish workers get comparatively much time off for holidays and vacation periods, and travel abroad quite often.

FURTHER READING

Andersen, Hans Thor and John Jørgensen, "Copenhagen," *Cities: The International Journal of Urban Policy and Planning*, 12, 1, 1995, pp. 13–22.
Kadushin, Raphael, "Copenhagen: Tidings of Good Cheer," *National Geographic Traveler*, 26, 8, 2009, pp. 38–43.

CURITIBA, BRAZIL

Curitiba is the capital of Paraná State in southeastern Brazil, and an important business center in a part of the country where agriculture and ranching are important mainstays of the economy. Although the city was founded as far back as 1693, it was growth of the agricultural frontier in Brazil starting in the mid-19th century that caused the early, very small settlement to grow into one of Brazil's most important cities. It was populated mainly by poor immigrants from Italy, Germany, Poland, and Ukraine who were looking for farmland and a chance at a life better than the poverty that Europe offered. The city also has sizable populations of Japanese-Brazilians and Jews. Although the city is not as large or well known around the world as Brazil's giant cities Sao Paulo and Rio de Janeiro, it is a populous place nonetheless, having a total of 1,764,540 residents (2010). It is Brazil's eighth-largest city. The Curitiba metropolitan area has 3,209,980 inhabitants, the seventh-largest total in Brazil.

We include this lesser-known city as one of the world's most contented cities because it is a model of sensible city planning, not just in the context of Brazil, but also globally. Its goals are to increase social equality and to be a sustainable city. People in the know about city planning and innovative approaches to urban problems are familiar with Curitiba, and applaud it for successes that provide lessons for cities worldwide. In fact, the city receives a constant flow of scholars and experts in city governance from around the world who are eager to observe how this Brazilian city addresses its problems, so that solution can be found for cities back home. Curitibans know that their city is special, and are justifiably proud that it has such a fine reputation. A reported 99% of Curitiba residents are happy with the city, according to at least one survey, although we admit that such a high number does seem a bit suspicious. Among the nicknames that Curitiba has earned are *Cidade Modelo* (Model City), *Capital Ecológica do Brasil* (Ecological Capital of Brazil), and *Cidade Verde* (Green City). UNESCO has proposed Curitiba as a model for the rebuilding of urban areas in war-torn Afghanistan.

City planning in Curitiba has emphasized providing the public with affordable public transportation, especially by buses on dedicated bus lanes, as opposed to highways and automobiles, and keeping the urban center free from traffic congestion by discouraging cars and converting key thoroughfares into pedestrian zones. Some 2 million people ride the city's buses every day. It is ironic that the city should favor mass transit, because one of the most important industries in the city is automobile assembly. Moreover, rates of automobile ownership are higher in Curitiba than in any other city in Brazil. Yet, even though the city's population has skyrocketed in recent decades, the amount of automobile traffic has actually declined over the same period. The result of the city's transportation policy is a cleaner and quieter city, and atmospheric pollution that is the lowest in the country. Furthermore, emphasis on mass transit has increased face-to-face contact among the city's residents, leading to a friendlier, people-oriented way of urban life that people in many other cities do not even know is possible. The city has also enacted strict controls on urban sprawl, which not only preserve undeveloped land outside the metropolis, but also force everyone to be more careful about how land that is available for urban uses is developed and utilized. Building at higher densities than may have been the case otherwise economizes on land, supports mass transit, and frees up space for parks. Accordingly, Curitiba has more parkland per capita than most other cities of its type. These and other pluses about Curitiba originated with a bold plan for the city that was first put forth in the 1960s by architect Jaime Lerner, who developed the Curitiba Master Plan and later became mayor of the city.

Other creative approaches in Curitiba include a program called "Garbage? That's not garbage!" that has made recycling into a way of life in the city, and that applies revenue from the sale of recycled materials to social programs for the needy. Residents of poor shanty towns can exchange trash for bus tickets and food, while another program allows children to get school supplies and sweets in exchange for recyclable garbage. On a different front, the city operates an open university to provide residents with jobs skills, as well as various other programs to train people for the labor market and to stimulate economic growth, for example, by nurturing small businesses. A program called Faróis do Saber ("Lighthouses of Knowledge") sets up libraries and computers for public use in local neighborhoods so that residents can improve literacy and be better trained for jobs. This has helped Curitiba to have the lowest illiteracy rates in Brazil as well as the country's highest levels of educational attainment. Furthermore, there are extra measures of tolerance for the homeless in Curitiba, who have been allowed to camp in the parks and squares in the city center, although there are complaints from some residents that this harms the public image of an otherwise prosperous city.

Curitiba's economic performance is excellent in comparison to that of Brazil as a whole, which itself is a fast-growing economy. The economic growth rate for the city over a recent 30-year span has been 7.1%, significantly exceeding the national average for the same period of 4.2%. Moreover, economic growth levels in Curitiba are some 66% higher than the average for Brazil. Such numbers account for a rapid population growth rate in the city, as Curitiba attracts migrants from elsewhere in Brazil, and helps keep its well-employed and well-paid citizens happy indeed. In 2014, Curitiba gained additional international exposure as one of the cities in Brazil to host the FIFA World Cup tournament.

FURTHER READING

Macedo, Joseli, "Curitiba," *Cities: International Journal of Urban Policy and Planning*, 21, 6, 2004, pp. 537–549.
Soltani, A. and E. Sharifi, "A Case Study of Sustainable Urban Planning Principles in Curitiba (Brazil) and Their Applicability in Shiraz (Iran)," *International Journal of Development and Sustainability*, 1, 2, pp.120–134.

HAMBURG, GERMANY

Hamburg is a city near the mouth of the Elbe River in northern Germany, as well as one of Germany's 16 states. It has a population of over 1.8 million, making it Germany's second-largest city and the ninth-largest city in the European Union. The population of the Hamburg Metropolitan region is more than 5 million. The official name of the city is the Free and Hanseatic City of Hamburg, referring to its status as a free imperial city during the Holy Roman Empire and its membership in the Hanseatic League of trading cities from the 13th through the 17th centuries. The city's port is still vitally important to the local economy, and ranks as the 2nd-largest port in Europe after the Port of Rotterdam (Netherlands), and the 10th largest in the world. It is an exceedingly prosperous city that is both rich in history and very current, and has a very high quality of life. The city is included here as one of the 20 most contented cities in the world not just because of its own many merits, but also as a representative of Germany and its many other very livable cities such as Berlin, Frankfurt, Munich, Düsseldorf, and Cologne. And, yes, Hamburg residents really are called Hamburgers, and the hamburger is so named because it really did originate there.

The economy of Hamburg is highly diversified. The port is the single largest component, but the city is also an important financial and manufacturing center, as well as a cultural and media center, and a popular destination for domestic and international tourism. Prominent manufacturing activities include steel and aluminum industries, shipbuilding, and aircraft assembly for the French company Airbus. Several of Germany's most prominent television stations and book publishers are located in Hamburg, as are the main offices of the popular national newspapers *Der Spiegel* and *Die Zeit* ("The Mirror" and "The Time"). There are 17 universities in Hamburg with a total of 70,000 students. The University of Hamburg is the largest. In 2013, the GDP of Hamburg was 97.7 billion euro ($129.8 billion), one of the highest totals for any German city and in the top 10 among cities in the European Union.

Hamburg is rated as one of the world's most livable cities. The *Economist* has ranked the city within its global top 20 for five years running, most recently at #14 in 2014. The city's strengths include its many cultural and leisure opportunities, its universities, and a low crime rate. Also, the 2015 Mercer Quality of Living Survey has put the city in a tie with two other of our own top 20 cities, Melbourne and Ottawa, for #16 in the world out of 221 cities surveyed. Interestingly, the Mercer study rated Munich, Düsseldorf, Frankfurt, and Berlin ahead of Hamburg, while the ranking by the *Economist* has Hamburg ahead of all other German cities. Hamburg is also reported to be one of the world's "smartest" cities in terms of information technology, and a "green" city. It is sometimes called the greenest city in Europe. In 2011, Hamburg was awarded the designation European Green Capital. A very large urban redevelopment project called HafenCity has won accolades for Hamburg with respect to design. It is the city's old port district. Its old warehouses and industrial buildings are being converted in stages into modern office and residential uses. Some of the world's best-known architects are involved. A new landmark in HafenCity is the Elbe Philharmonic Hall, which is being built as a 361-foot (110-meter) tall high-rise atop an old warehouse structure, albeit with some highly publicized cost overruns and construction delays.

The new philharmonic hall will add to the already-rich assortment of cultural venues in Hamburg. All told, the city has a reported 40 theaters, 60 museums, and 100 music venues and clubs. The Laeiszhalle Hamburg has been the city's main venue for classical music since 1908. There is also the Hamburg State Opera, which has its own philharmonic orchestra. The Deutsches Schauspilhaus (the German Playhouse), opened in 1901, has seating for 1,192 spectators, and is the largest theater in Germany. It is one of three state-owned theaters in the city. Leading museums include the Kunsthalle Hamburg, the Museum for Art and Industry, and a maritime museum in HafenCity. The city is also known for contemporary music and arts, and well as a broad range of arts and film festivals, street fairs, and sporting events such as the Hamburg Marathon and the Vatenfall Cyclassics, a popular cycling event. The Dockville Arts and Music Festival is a large annual event in the city's Wilhelmsburg district, while the city's annual Christopher Street Festival is one of Europe's largest gay pride events.

These various events and cultural institutions contribute to a growing tourism industry in Hamburg. In addition to having much to do, visitors enjoy a uniquely picturesque city. Instead of a landscape of high-rise office towers, as one might expect from a prosperous and modern city in a prosperous and modern country, Hamburg has a low profile and a skyline that is punctuated by church spires more than by skyscrapers. The city still has an historic ambience even though it was very heavily destroyed by Allied bombing in World War II, and is unique in that it is a city of a great many rivers, streams, and canals, and the bridges that cross them. There are reportedly more than 2,400 bridges, which is more than London, Amsterdam, and Venice combined, and more than any city in the world, and more canals than Venice and Amsterdam combined. Hamburg's City Hall is a beautiful Neo-Renaissance structure from 1897 that is marked by a 367-foot (112-meter) high tower, while the historic Church of St. Nicholas that dates back to 1189 is one of the city's two tallest buildings. It was destroyed in World War II but the spire, which reaches to 482 feet (147 meters), still stands as an historical treasure. In 1874–1876, the church was the tallest structure in the world.

FURTHER READING

Jefferies, Matthew, *Hamburg: A Cultural History* (Northampton, MA: Interlink, 2011).
Nossack, Hans Erich and Erich Andres, *The End: Hamburg 1943* (Chicago: University of Chicago Press, 2004).

HELSINKI, FINLAND

Helsinki is the capital and largest city of Finland, a country in northern Europe that borders Norway, Sweden, and Russia, as well as the Baltic Sea. The city is located in the southern part of the country on the tip of a peninsula that juts into the Gulf of Finland, an arm of the Baltic. The city also includes 315 offshore islands. Tallinn, the capital of Estonia, is about 50 miles (80 km) across the gulf to the south. The population of Helsinki is 623,135, while that of the metropolitan area is approximately 1.4 million. At 60° N. latitude, Helsinki is the northernmost metropolitan area in a world with a population of over 1 million, as well as the northernmost capital of a country in the European Union.

We selected Helsinki for this list of 20 most contented cities in the world because it is, indeed, a highly livable city, with good neighborhoods, excellent public services, and a full array of cultural and recreational opportunities that enrich people's lives and keep them healthy and happy. The Quality of Life Survey by the lifestyle magazine *Monocle* agrees, and has ranked Helsinki at #5 in the world for 2015, while the Intelligence Unit of the *Economist* had put the city at #8 in the world in Global Livability for 2014. In 2011, the city claimed the world's top spot in the *Monocle* ranking. The 2015 Mercer Quality of Living Survey has Helsinki a bit lower, at #31 from 221 cities, but that still within the top 15% of cities surveyed. The city has also been ranked highly as a place to do business, in sustainability and environmental quality, and as a destination for international tourists.

Our own observations in Helsinki revealed a city that was very much focused on the outdoors during perfect summer weather and long hours of daylight. During the summer solstice, it is light out for nearly 19 hours. Be it the center of the city, or residential neighborhoods nearby or in suburban-ring towns such as Espoo and Vantaa, it seemed that all of Finland was enjoying fresh air, sunshine, and lingering light. People were relaxing in parks, sunning at one of the urban area's many beaches, window shopping along trendy commercial streets, or sitting in outdoor cafés or restaurants. We also attended outdoor concerts as dusk finally arrived, and watched Helsinki residents as they expertly danced a jitterbug in a downtown square. There are outdoor flea markets, food fairs, and crafts exhibitions. Many people own small boats and enjoy sailing or fishing offshore among the islands of the Helsinki archipelago. There was also a particular day when we saw a parking area downtown and all the nearby city streets clogged with vintage automobiles, many of them American models from the 1960s that were heavy with polished crone and sleek tail fins, as collectors cruised and showed off. Top-down convertibles seemed to be especially numerous. There were joggers and bicyclists everywhere, as well as dedicated trails through parks and along city streets. We also joined locals and tourists alike on a cruise to the offshore island of Suomenlinna, a UNESCO World Heritage Site that centers on an 18th-century fortress that once protected the city's harbor and shipping channels. It's a great place for hiking and picnics, and for finding a secluded cove for a swim in the crystal clear, cool waters of the Baltic.

Winter, of course, is cold, long, and dark, but Finns also enjoy the outdoors while cross-country skiing in parks, or skating, playing ice hockey, or ice fishing. A rich sauna culture keeps people warm and invigorated. The city is beautiful in the snow, with architectural masterpieces such as Helsinki Cathedral and the Government Palace that evoke another winter-wonderland city, nearby St. Petersburg, Russia. And like St. Petersburg, Helsinki has many theaters, concert venues, and museums. The Helsinki Music Center is home to the Helsinki Philharmonic Orchestra and the Finnish Radio Symphony Orchestra. Other music venues are the Finlandia Concert Hall and the Finnish National Opera. Major museums include the National Museum of Finland, the Ateneum Art Museum, and the Design Museum. The University of Helsinki is one of Europe's better universities and has many museums, theaters, and concert halls of its own. The Sibelius Monument which honors the famous Finnish composer Jean Sibelius and the spectacular Church in the Rock are two of Helsinki's most popular tourist attractions.

Helsinki residents benefit from excellent public education, excellent health care, and excellent public transportation. Their city is prosperous, and is the center of Finland's economy, accounting for about one-third of the country's GDP. Eighty-three of the 100 largest companies in Finland are headquartered in Helsinki or its surroundings, including the giant Finnish multinational communications and information technology company Nokia Oyj, which has its main offices in nearby Espoo. The city is generally safe from crime, clean, and free from litter, and there is plenty of fresh air from over northern forests and open seas. The tap water in Helsinki is of outstanding quality and is sometimes bottled to be sold as drinking water abroad.

FURTHER READING

Kent, Neil, *Helsinki: A Cultural History* (Northampton, MA: Interlink, 2014).
Kolbe, Laura, "An Eastern or a Western Capital City? The Spirit of Helsinki," *International Review of Sociology*, 16, 2, July 2006, pp. 329–346.

L'VIV, UKRAINE

L'viv is a city in western Ukraine, about 43 miles (70 km) from the country's border with Poland. It is the leading city of Ukraine's Halychyna region, formerly known as Galicia, and a major center of Ukrainian cultural life. The city had very close ties to be Poland in history, and was essentially a Polish city from the mid-19th century until boundaries were redrawn in the wake of World War II and the city was annexed into the Ukrainian S.S.R. in the Soviet Union. Between the two world wars, it was Poland's third-largest city after Warsaw and Łódź. When the Soviet Union fell apart in 1991, L'viv became part of independent Ukraine. It is the capital of L'viv Oblast (province). The city is widely known for strong feelings of Ukrainian nationalism and as a bastion of Ukraine's struggles to free itself from the legacies of the Communist U.S.S.R. and from the current ambitions by Vladimir Putin's Russia to reintegrate Ukraine into Russia's sphere of political and cultural dominion. L'viv is also known for its great historical diversity and mix of cultural and architectural traditions, and as a fast-emerging international tourism destination in Central Europe.

The population of L'viv is 729,842, making it the seventh-largest city in Ukraine. The ethnic composition has shifted dramatically over the last century or so, and now as much as 90% Ukrainian if not more. This contrasts with the early 20th century when Ukrainians comprised less than 20% of the total. Russians are now the second-most numerous population at under 9%, but there were very few Russians in the city before western Ukraine was annexed to the Soviet Union, and then within five years their numbers zoomed to nearly one-third of the total as the Soviet government resettled Russians in the region in an effort to weaken its Ukrainian identity. Now that Ukraine is independent and in renewed conflict with Russia, the Russian population has been declining by emigration. Poles accounted for more than one-half of L'viv's population in the early 20th century and as much as 63% of the total in 1944 during World War II. However, after the war the Soviets resettled the Polish population to the west of the redrawn international boundary, their total quickly plummeted to less than 2%. The most tragic story, however, concerns the region's Jewish population. Before World War II, about one-third of L'viv's population was Jewish and the city was one of Europe's most important centers of Jewish life and culture, but all that ended with the Holocaust, which left very few Jewish survivors. The tumultuous social history of L'viv is reflected in the city's changing names. The Ukrainian word "L'viv" means "city of the lion" in honor of Lev (meaning "lion") the son of the city's 13th-century King Danylo, but the city has also been known as Lvov from the Russian, Lwów from Polish, and Lemberg from German and the Austro-Hungarian Empire.

We include L'viv in our list of the world's 20 most contented cities for a number of reasons. For one, we see a hidden gem of a city whose intact historic architecture and landmarks speak volumes about various epochs of European experience, both tragic and joyous. UNESCO has recognized this fact and has placed the entire city center on its list of world heritage sites. As global tourists discover the city, we have another reason for L'viv's contentment: tourism is a fast-rising sector in the city's economy, providing jobs and opportunity in a country where both are much too scarce. Tourism to L'viv also helps to link the city, and by extension Ukraine more generally, much more closely to Europe, thereby steering the global perception of both the city and the country away from the Russian past, and placing them both within the democratic West. This brings great satisfaction to the overwhelming majority of L'viv's residents. This was seen very clearly in 2012 when L'viv was one of the successful host cities for the UEFA Euro football (soccer) championship along with three other cities in Ukraine and four in Poland. Indeed, L'viv is a contented city even as Ukraine is at war with Russia in the country's east, because its residents are convinced that the end of Russian domination in Ukraine is coming, and that Ukraine will finally be allowed to prosper as a truly

The charming city of L'viv in western Ukraine is known for its architecture and beautiful parks. Ivan Franko Park in the city center is named after a beloved Ukrainian writer. (Roman Cybriwsky)

independent, democratic, and fully European country. Their wish and prayer is that the war will end with as few casualties as possible.

L'viv has many advantages that can result in a very bright future. It is more European in culture and outlook than the rest of Ukraine. Its population is well educated and highly literate, and not only bilingual, but also multilingual. In addition to Ukrainian, most residents have familiarity with Russian, and most young people study English and/or other European languages such as German, French, Polish, or Italian. Although many Leopolitans (as L'viv residents are sometimes known) and other Ukrainians have emigrated abroad over the two decades-plus that their country has been nominally independent, representing something of a brain-drain, the city now has as a resource of a highly educated and generally successful émigré population in many countries around the globe. This is potentially a great plus as a source of contacts for business and trade, a source of investment funds, and a population to argue for Ukrainian interests in capitals abroad. Furthermore, L'viv has excellent universities (there is a total of 12), considerable scientific expertise because of its many research institutes, many cultural institutions such as the beautiful L'viv Opera in the city center, and a strong industrial base that has focused on machinery manufacture, electronics, and motor vehicles, particularly buses. It is the information technology center of Ukraine. The city is safe, and is continually being brought up to European standards with respect to infrastructure, housing, and public services. Its pubs and restaurants have attracted notice in the European tourism media, and the city is emerging as a hub of new popular music, film, and other arts, and a vibrant nightlife. As a gateway to Ukraine's Carpathian Mountains region, L'viv was preparing a bid to host the 2022 Winter Olympics, but because of the war and its weight on the Ukrainian economy, it hopes to try for the 2026 games instead.

FURTHER READING

Czaplicka, John, *L'viv: A City in the Crossroads of Culture* (Cambridge, MA: Harvard Ukrainian Research Institute, 2005).

Narvselius, Eleanora, *Ukrainian Intelligentsia in Post-Soviet L'viv: Narratives, Identity, and Power* (Lanham, MD: Lexington Books, 2012).

Reid, Anna, *Borderland: A Journey through the History of Ukraine* (Boulder, CO: Westview Press, 2000, pp. 74–92).

Risch, William Jay, *The Ukrainian West: Culture and the Fate of Empire in Soviet L'viv* (Cambridge, MA: Harvard University Press, 2011).

MELBOURNE, AUSTRALIA

Melbourne is one of several cities in Australia that were strong candidates for our list of 20 most content cities in the world, including in alphabetical order Adelaide,

Brisbane, Canberra, Perth, and Sydney. Indeed, we discuss the county as a whole in a different part of this book as one of the 20 most content nations in the world. As for cities, our goal of spreading urban accolades around the globe limits us to listing no more than two cities from any given country. With all due respect to the other very fine cities in Australia, each of which we know would have rapid supporters for inclusion of their cities here, we have selected Melbourne and Perth as Australia's representatives here. The reason we have singled out Melbourne specifically is because the city consistently outranks in-country competitors on global indices of urban livability. For example, Melbourne is the current (2014) #1 ranked city in the world in livability as determined by the Intelligence Unit of the *Economist* (EIU). It was also ranked #1 by EIU in 2013, 2012, and 2011, when it nudged Vancouver, Canada, another one of our top 20 cities, from nearly a decade of residence at the top spot. Moreover, Melbourne is the current #3 ranked city in the world in the *Monocle* Quality of Life survey (after Copenhagen and Tokyo, two cities that are also on our top 20 list).

Melbourne is located in southeastern Australia at the north end of a bay off the Bass Strait that is called simply Port Phillip. The Yarra River flows through the city and empties into the bay. The city is the capital of the state of Victoria and has a population of 4,347,955 (2013), a close second in Australia to Sydney (4.6 million). It is a major business center, being the headquarters city for several of Australia's largest banks and other corporations, as well as an important cultural and media center, and center of higher education. The port of Melbourne is Australia's busiest. The city was founded in 1835, making it one of the oldest of Australia's large cities (Sydney was established in 1788). Its architecture includes a mix of historic buildings from the 19th and early 20th centuries, as well as soaring skyscrapers of recent construction. Prominent older building include the 1879–1880 Second Empire-style South Melbourne Town Hall in one of the city's inner suburbs, the 1879–1880 Royal Exhibition Building that was built to host the 1880–1881 Melbourne International Exhibition, and the 1909 Flinders Street Railway Station, once the busiest passenger rail station in the world, while examples of prominent newer structures are the Rialto Towers office building (1986) and Eureka Tower (2006), one of the tallest residential structures in the world. Among Melbourne's many pluses is that it is a green city with many parks and gardens, including the Royal Botanic Garden, Fitzroy Gardens, and Flagstaff Gardens, all in the very center of the city. One of Melbourne's nicknames is "garden city." There are beaches in Melbourne too, particularly in suburbs along the eastern shores of Port Phillip.

Other reasons why Melbourne ranks highly in livability are that it scores highly as being family-friendly with good schools, has many well-equipped neighborhood playgrounds and sports fields, hospitals and public healthcare, and has low crime rates. The city is tied for first with Canberra for the highest male life expectancy in

Australian cities (80.0 years) and ranks second behind Perth in female life expectancy (84.1 years). Furthermore, Melbourne is rich in street art. This beautifies the surroundings and creates enjoyment for locals and visitors alike. Melbourne also has many cultural and entertainment events, as well as popular festivals such as the Melbourne International Arts Festival, the Melbourne International Film Festival, the Melbourne International Comedy Festival, and the Melbourne Fringe Festival, an alternative arts festival. The most popular festival of all, however, is Moomba, the largest community festival in Australia and a Melbourne tradition since 1955. It is run by the city of Melbourne and attendance regularly exceeds 1 million. The events are led along the Yarra River, and include parades, water floats, fireworks displays, and live music, as well as a birdman rally in which competitors vie to fly with homemade human-powered devices. Studies by QS, a consulting firm, placed Melbourne in a tie with Zürich, Switzerland, for fifth place in 2013 among 50 prominent cities around the world as a good environment for students, and in second place in 2015, behind only Paris.

Melbourne has a highly diverse population, more so than most other Australian cities. About 63.3% of its inhabitants were born in Australia, with the remainder coming from countries around the world, led by England, India, China, Italy, and New Zealand in numerical order. English and Australian were the most common ethnic ancestries as reported by Melbourne residents in 2011, followed by Irish, Scottish, and Italian. Other ancestries include Vietnamese, Sri Lankans, and Malaysians. Melbourne has the largest Greek-speaking population outside Europe. The mixed population is reflected in a distinctive ethnic character in some of the city's residential neighborhoods, in a mix of ethnic restaurants and cuisines, and in various ethnic holiday celebrations and festivals. The presence of ethnic neighborhoods and institutions such as places of worship and community centers makes adjustment to life in Australia easier for new immigrants.

Despite the high rankings that Melbourne achieves in comparative rankings, and despite the fact that most Melbourne residents are content with the city in which they live, Melbourne falls on some important criteria that rankings typically overlook. Most significantly, the city is not especially sustainable in how it is laid out and how people live, and can be criticized for being overly automobile-oriented, like many American cities, and too spread out. Many Australians prefer to live in single homes with large private yards (the so-called Australian Dream), with the result that there is a sprawl pattern of urban development that depends on private automobiles and freeways for transportation. Melbourne is said to have an oversized carbon footprint, larger than that of New York City and London, both of which are substantially larger in population. This is mostly because even though Melbourne has good public transport and the wherewithal for improvements and additions, a much higher percentage of residents choose to drive to where they need to go. There are also concerns about water supply, as there have been drought conditions in the city's watershed in recent years, as well as concerns about water pollution. The Yarra River is polluted with *E. coli*, grease, and oils, as well as by heavy metals from 19th-century industrialization that have been disturbed by dredging to deepen the port of Melbourne for use by larger ships.

In 2015, Melbourne hosted the ICC World Cup Cricket Final, which was won by Australia over New Zealand by 7 wickets.

FURTHER READING

Collins, Jock, Letizia Mondello, John Breheney, and Tim Childs, *Cosmopolitan Melbourne. Explore the World in One City* (Rhodes, New South Wales: Big Box Publishing, 1990).

Cunningham, Sophie, *Melbourne* (Sydney: University of New South Wales Press, 2011).

James, Paul, "Melbourne, the World's Most Livable city? Not Exactly," *The Conversation*, http://theconversation.com/melbourne-the-worlds-most-liveable-city-not-exactly-17677.

MONTEVIDEO, URUGUAY

Montevideo is the capital and largest city of Uruguay, a small country in South America that is bordered by Argentina and Brazil and that faces the Atlantic Ocean to the south and southeast. The country is discussed elsewhere in this book as one of the world's 20 most contented countries. The city is contented as well. It is situated on the southern coast of the country at the mouth of the Rio de la Plata. Upriver and on the opposite bank of the Rio de la Plata is the capital of Argentina, Buenos Aires. According to the census of 2011, the population of Montevideo is 1,319,108, about one-third of the population of the entire country. The metropolitan area totals more than 2 million inhabitants, pushing Montevideo's share of the Uruguayan population to nearly two-thirds. The overwhelming majority of residents are of European extraction, especially immigrants and their descendants from Spain, Italy, France, Germany, and the Netherlands. In addition to being the capital, Montevideo is the economic and cultural hub of Uruguay, as well as one of Latin America's more prominent business centers. It is also important in Latin America as the headquarters city of Mercosur and ALADI (from the Spanish for Latin American Integration Association), two regional trade associations. This has prompted comparisons of Montevideo to Brussels, Belgium, the main administrative city of the European Union.

Montevideo was founded in 1724 by a Spanish soldier named Bruno Mauricio de Zabala as a counter by Spain to a settlement named Colonia do Sacramento that the Portuguese had established in the 1680s upriver opposite Buenos Aires. The city competed with Buenos Aires for economic primacy during the Spanish colonial period, and was in conflict at various times with Portuguese Brazil and with Spain before Uruguay became independent in 1830 and Montevideo became its capital. In the late 19th century Uruguay prospered from its farm lands and attracted many immigrants, and Montevideo grew into a handsome city with fine buildings, modern street lighting, and public transportation at European standards. The early 20th century was also a prosperous period for Montevideo. In 1930, the city hosted the first FIFA World Cup tournament, which Uruguay won. Economic difficulties set in during the 1950s, leading to social unrest and a left-wing urban guerilla movement in the 1960s and 1970s that attempted to unseat the government via political kidnappings and assassinations. From 1973 to 1985, the country was a military dictatorship. Democracy was eventually restored, and both Uruguay and its capital city have recovered. Montevideo is considered to be one of the most pleasant and most prosperous cities in Latin America. Interestingly, the former president of Uruguay, José Mujica, elected in 2009, is a former member of the Tupamaros guerillas. He has been described as the humblest head of state in the world because of the exceptionally modest lifestyle that he and his wife have chosen to lead, as well as a very progressive leader because his attention to the needs of Uruguay's poor, matters of equality and justice, and to environmental quality and sustainable living.

Montevideo is now regarded to be the most livable of all cites in Latin America. The Mercer Quality of Living Survey has awarded the city first place in Latin America every year since 2005. In 2015, the city was ranked at #78 in the world out of the 230 cities studied (top one-third), and still best in Latin America. The economy is generally strong and diversified, and unemployment is no longer the problem that it once was. In 2015, the GDP of Montevideo was $40.5 billion, while the per capita GDP was $24,400. The city is an important port, a manufacturing and food processing center, a center of higher education, and a major banking and financial center. Because of the latter, Montevideo (or Uruguay more generally) has been referred to as the "Switzerland of the Americas." The downtown of the city has a prosperous, "corporate" look, with modern new skyscrapers, shopping malls, and fine hotels.

There is a growing tourism economy too. For many visitors, the focus is on the historic old city, Ciudad Vieja, and its landmarks, old churches, museums, and places to eat and drink. The Solis Theater is a beautiful and historic (from 1856) landmark that is venue for various concerts, operas, and ballet performances. Nearby is fabulous neighborhood called Pocitos that faces the city's main beach, and the Rambla, a fashionable boulevard along the beach with popular restaurants, cafés, and nightclubs. The city's several gracious parks include Parque Prado and Parque Rodó. There is a causal and relaxed atmosphere in much of the city that also reflects the high degree of contentment that many Montevideans hold. The city has a reputation for ethnic and religious tolerance, and is known as one of the most gay-friendly cities in the world. Finally, we note that the city is in love with football, and gives undivided attention whenever the national team plays against teams from Argentina, Brazil, and other rival squads.

FURTHER READING

Garcia Ferrari, Maria Soledad, "Montevideo," *Cities: International Journal of Urban Policy and Planning*, 23, 5, 2006, pp. 382–399.
Pintos, Graciela, "Territorio y políticas sociales en Montevideo" (in Spanish: "Territory and Social Politics in Montevideo"), *Prisma*, 22, May 2008, pp. 215–263.

OTTAWA, CANADA

Ottawa is the capital of Canada. It is located in the province of Ontario on the Ottawa River, across which is Gatineau, Quebec. The Rideau River and Rideau Canal enter the Ottawa River near the city's historic district and government area. The city was established in 1826 as a sawmilling town named Bytown, and the waterways were used to float timber from forests upstream. The city was renamed Ottawa in 1855, and was designated capital of Canada in 1857 by Britain's Queen Victoria. The government area is called Parliament Hill, or simply the Hill, and overlooks the rivers and the canal. Construction of government buildings took place in the 1860s, but fires in the city in 1900 and 1916 caused considerable damage and required reconstruction. The distinctive Gothic revival Centre Block of the Parliament buildings was rebuilt in 1922 and the iconic Peace Tower on Parliament Hill was added in 1927. The ensemble of government buildings, monuments, and landscaping on Parliament Hill is beautiful, and is a great source of pride for Canadian citizens.

According to the 2011 census, the population of Ottawa was 883,391 and that of the Ottawa-Gatineau metropolitan area 1,236,324, making both the city and the metropolitan area the fourth largest in Canada. The city is genuinely bilingual, reflecting Canada's two official languages of English and French, as well as the city's location at the boundary between mostly English-speaking Ontario and French-speaking Quebec. About 37% of the population knows both languages. In recent years, the population has become increasingly diverse with growing immigration from abroad. Now, about one in five Ottawa residents are foreign-born, with Caribbean-Canadians, African-Canadians, Chinese, South Asians, and Lebanese among the principal ethnic groups.

An industrial economy no longer dominates the city as it did in the sawmilling days, and it is now government that is the major employer. The city also has a growing high-tech industry and world-class research centers. This is in part because Ottawa is home to two fine research universities, Carleton University and the University of Ottawa, and has a highly educated population. Some 51%

of the adult population has a college degree, the highest rate in Canada. Ottawa has been called "Silicon Valley of the North." Some 26.4 % of the workforce in Ottawa is engaged in the knowledge field, a higher proportion than in any other Canadian city, and one in seven employees work in science and technology. Tourism is also an important part of the economy, as is the health sector. In addition to the government buildings, the main tourist attractions include the city's outstanding national museums: the National Gallery of Canada, the Canadian Museum of Nature, and, in Gatineau, the Canadian Museum of History, which is the most visited museum in the country. Unemployment is low in Ottawa, and income levels are high, with the city ranking third in Canada among major urban centers. In a 2013 survey by the Toronto-based think-tank Martin Prosperity Institute, Ottawa placed #1 in the world out of 61 cities studied in the combination of ingredients for a "creative economy:" talent, technology, tolerance, and "quality of place."

Even though Ottawa is a city with very cold winters, it is a very livable city with indoor and outdoor activities to enjoy year-round. One of the most distinctive features of the city is winter of the Rideau Canal, when the waters are frozen and the canal becomes a Skateway, as it is known, that is more than 4 miles (7 km) long. Not only is it used for recreation, but during the morning and afternoon rush, the frozen canal is used by commuters who skate to and from work. The city also has more than 105 miles (170 km) of bikeways that area also used for both recreation and transportation. There are hundreds of small parks in the city, meaning that every resident lives within quick reach of a place to rest or exercise outdoors, as well as a place for neighbors to interact. The city also has four public beaches. In addition, there are large parks such as Gatineau Park, a greenbelt zone at the city's edges, and unspoiled natural areas of forests, lakes, and streams nearby. Fishing, skating, skiing, nature walks, and biking are popular seasonal leisure time activities for Ottawans.

Other outstanding characteristics that make Ottawa one of our top 20 cities include an excellent public education system, a fine library system with many branches, good public transit, and outstanding health care with state-of-the art technology and outstanding medical specialists. The city also has a low crime rate, even in comparison to most other Canadian cities, which as a group also have crime rates much lower than cities in the neighboring United States. The neighborhoods are clean and safe, and except in winter, green. Many Ottawans enjoy gardening and maintain flower gardens and rose bushes. The city has theaters, a busy nightlife, and fun festivals such as the Ottawa International Jazz Festival, Bluesfest, the Folk Music Festival, the Canadian Tulip Festival, and celebrations of Canadian national holidays. The fact that Ottawa has 130 foreign embassies means that the city has a truly global population and many events that honor other countries and cultures.

Ottawa is consistently ranked among the top cities in the world on comparative surveys that use standardized quantitative data. For example, in the Mercer Quality of Living Survey, which considers 39 variables that cover health, education, transportation, economy, environment, and public services, the city was ranked #14 in the world and #2 in North America (after Vancouver) out of 221 cities in 2010, 2012, and 2014. It is seen as an especially good city for the raising of a family. For example, Ottawa came out first on this question in an opinion survey that was carried out in five Canadian cities (also Halifax, Calgary, Winnipeg, and Edmonton) by Prairie Research Associates, Inc. What Ottawans liked most, the survey found, was the city's scenery, greenery, and clean air, the city's size and its associated comfort level, and the many things for children to do, including sports.

FURTHER READING

Keshen, Jeff and Nicole St-Onge, *Ottawa: Making a Capital* (Ottawa: University of Ottawa Press, 2001).
McLennan, Rob, *Ottawa: The Unknown City* (Vancouver: Arsenal Pulp Press, 2007).
Prairie Research Associates, Inc., "Ottawa the Place to Raise Children: Survey," n.d., http://www.pra.ca/releases/Release&backgrounder_OttawaV2.pdf.

PERTH, AUSTRALIA

Perth is the major metropolis of Western Australia and the capital of the state of Western Australia. Its population is 1,972,358 (2013), the country's fourth-largest city. It is located in the far southwest of the country where the Swan River empties into the Indian Ocean, and along with the neighboring smaller city of Fremantle is a maritime port. Because it is far from any other sizable metropolis (the nearest big city is Adelaide, South Australia, more than 1,300 miles [2,104 km] to the east), Perth has been called the most isolated city on earth, with the exception of perhaps Honolulu, Hawaii. The city has a Mediterranean-type climate with hot and dry summers and winters that are rainy and mild, and enjoys as many as 19 white-sand beaches on the Indian Ocean. Inland behind Perth is the vastness of the Great Australian Desert.

We include Perth in our list of 20 most contented cities in the world because it scores highly across the board on key ingredients related to a high quality of life. Not only is there a pleasant climate and ample beachfront, the city also enjoys a strong, growing economy; beautiful neighborhoods and parks; good public services such as schools, health care, and roads; and opportunities for a wide range of indoor and outdoor cultural and recreational activities. The city is safe, with lower crime rates than other Australian cities (where crime is also low as compared to cities in other countries), as well as less polluted than most other cities

A group of students waiting for surfing lessons at Cottesloe Beach in Perth, Australia, which is noted for fine beaches and sunny weather. Surfing is very popular in Australia. (Jan-Otto/iStockphoto.com)

in Australia and elsewhere. The city seems to be an especially fine place to raise a family. The Intelligence Unit of the *Economist* ranks Perth as #9 in the world (and #4 in the Australia) in quality of life. However, as it seems to be the case in urban areas around the globe, many residents bemoan what they see to be increases in crime, social conflict, traffic congestion, and other urban problems, as well as rising prices for homes and apartments. Some residents like that Perth is far from a hectic world, but others think that Perth is too isolated or complain that the city is itself becoming increasingly hectic. Whichever is the case, it is true that Perth is becoming more populous. It has grown with every census count since the first official tally in 1854, with increases between counts that are quite impressive. Whereas the city now has almost 2 million people, its population in 2006 was about 1.6 million, in 1996 1.3 million, and in 1986 just over 1 million. That is, every decade about 300,000 new residents are added to the population! This does indeed bring new pressures on urban infrastructure and increases in the price of housing, but is also strong testimonial that Perth is popular and that people want to move there.

The transformation of Perth into a major city was sparked by growth of Western Australia's mining and petroleum and natural gas industries. The state is rich in various minerals and fossil fuels, including aluminum ores, iron ore, coal, gas, and other commodities, which it processes and sells not just across Australia, but to other countries as well, most notably the large economies of Japan, China, and increasingly, India. While mines and drilling sites may be distant from Perth, company offices are in the city, giving Perth a rather dramatic, tall skyline in the center. Western Australia's industries tend to pay well, with the result that Perth is a prosperous city. The industries have done well in recent times, creating continual shortages of skilled labor, which in turn drives wages upward and stimulates labor migration to Perth and other job sites. Indeed, the city needs to actively recruit labor in order to keep up with the expanding economy, and does so energetically especially in Great Britain and Ireland. In doing so, the recruiters point to not just the promise of good jobs for talented workers, but also to the possibilities of a charmed life in a warm climate under blue skies, and near beaches. Simultaneously, the population of the city is becoming increasingly diverse ethnically, with newer waves of immigrants arriving from China, Vietnam, South Asia, and elsewhere. Perth is also supported by tourism, which tends to be outdoors oriented, taking advantage of the weather and the beaches, and by an agricultural economy that likewise takes advantage of the area's Mediterranean climate. Wine is one of the city's key exports.

Perhaps because Perth is so far from other population centers, it has developed into a greatly diversified city that is, let us say, self-sufficient with attractions and facilities for almost every need and taste. For many residents, this is a special plus about their city, allowing them to argue that they have everything that one could possibly want from a place to live, so why go elsewhere? Well, there are no snowfalls or winter storms, no outdoor ice skating facilities, and no Alpine peaks to climb, but the point is about the diversity and high quality of public services and cultural/entertainment attractions that are found in this remote urban center. Examples include a very fine system of health care that includes at least 10 large hospitals with up-to-date equipment and know-how, good schools; five universities, of which the University of Western Australia is a leader; a full range of museums, libraries, theaters, concert halls, and other venues for performing arts, including ballet, symphony orchestra, and opera; various arts and music festivals; many parks, a zoo, a large aquarium, and a great many other attractions. There is also a variety of sporting activities available in Perth, both on land and in the sea, as well as range of spectator sports for local fans to follow, including Australian rules football, soccer, cricket, and rugby.

FURTHER READING

Duncan, Jeremy, *Perth: A City Again* (Edinburgh: Luath Press, 2014).
Whish-Wilson, David, *Perth* (Sydney: University of New South Wales Press, 2013).

TOKYO, JAPAN

Tokyo, formally Tokyo Metropolis (*Tōkyō-to*), is the capital and largest city in Japan, as well as the world's largest metropolitan area. It is located on the Pacific coast of the country's largest island, Honshu, at the end of Tokyo Bay, and occupies Japan's largest plain, the Kantō Plain. The city itself is actually equivalent to a prefecture (state or province) of Japan in administrative status and not technically a city, and has a population of 13,047,446 according to the 2010 census, while the metropolitan area includes three other prefectures in addition to that of Tokyo (Chiba, Kanagawa, and Saitama) and has total 2010 population of 35,623,327. In addition to Tokyo, the Tokyo metropolitan area includes three other cities with more than a million population: Yokohama, which is technically Japan's largest city (population 3,689,603), Kawasaki, and Saitama, plus the city of Chiba which has a population of 962,310.

In addition to an enormous population, Tokyo has the largest economy of any metropolitan area in the world. According to a study by PricewaterhouseCoopers, the urban area had a total GDP(PPP) of US$1.9 trillion in 2012. It is a financial center of global proportions, as well as headquarters of many of the most famous Japanese manufacturing companies such as Sony and Honda, construction firms, insurance firms, airlines, advertising companies, national newspapers and other print media, television and film studios, and most of the companies in the Japanese fashion industry, among other sectors of economy. A total of 51 global 500 companies are headquartered in the metropolis, more than in any other city in the world and almost double that of the #2 city, Paris. The Tokyo Stock Exchange is the largest in Japan and the third largest in the world. The city is also a major center of higher education, having several of Japan's largest and most prestigious universities. As every student who studies globalization knows, Tokyo is one of the three so-called global cities or "command centers" for the world economy, along with New York City and London.

We know Tokyo extremely well, and hesitated as to whether or not to include it on this list. It is notoriously crowded, most famously on the trains and subways that most residents use for commuting, and is very expensive. Because of the high cost of land, most housing units are comparatively small, even in distant suburbs. The city also has long and demanding workdays for many employees, in addition to the long and unpleasant commutes. Consequently, one sees many people who are plain and simply exhausted. We also note that Tokyo has had a weakened economy in recent years, and that the city has been imperiled by the Fukushima Daiichi nuclear power plant in the outer reaches of the metropolitan area that was heavily damaged in the March 11, 2011, earthquake and tsunami disaster. As we deliberated, we considered listing a different Japanese city on these pages, perhaps Yokohama or Sapporo or Fukuoka, but in the end settled on Tokyo after all, because despite the drawbacks, it is truly a remarkable place. Both city and metropolis work extremely well, and are clean, safe, and highly efficient. Despite the drawbacks, we see a very high quality of life in Tokyo overall, and in the end decided to list this monster of a metropolis as one of the 20 most contented cities in the world.

We are not alone in this assessment. For example, the lifestyle magazine *Monocle* rated Tokyo as #2 in the world behind only Copenhagen in its Quality of Life Survey for 2014, while the Intelligence Unit of the *Economist* has the city at #19 in the world in its Global Livability analysis for the same year. There is a lower ranking for Tokyo in the 2014 Mercer Quality of Living Survey: #44 in the world of 221 cities. That, however, is just enough to be in the top 20%. We observe that the Mercer ranking has generally favored European cities, and note that Tokyo is at #2 in Asia after #26-in-the-world Singapore, which also gets higher scores in other rankings. The World City Survey for 2014 by *TripAdvisor* concluded that Tokyo offers the "best overall experience," and ranked it first in the world in a number of categories including the quality of local public transportation, the cleanliness of streets, and helpfulness by locals.

Our observations about the city include that although commuter lines get impossibly crowded at peak times, the trains are clean, safe, and punctual, and that there is frequent service to every part of the metropolis. Every neighborhood has excellent public services: trash is picked up on schedule; police patrol neighborhoods on bicycles and know many of the residents personally; schoolchildren walk or bicycle to schools safely or ride public transit; there is almost no litter and no graffiti in most parts of the metropolis; and everyone knows to respect their neighbors by being quiet, unobtrusive, and cooperative with respect to rules about trash, recycling, bicycle parking, and other potential sore points. There are also many neighborhood parks and playgrounds, neighborhood gyms, swimming pools, and community centers. Because Japan has a disproportionate number of senior citizens, there are many senior citizen centers and various programs that keep seniors physically and socially active. Although there are many large shopping malls and supermarkets in the city, much of Tokyo life still revolves around small neighborhood shopping streets that are closed to traffic at peak times, and become places for neighbors to see and greet one another as they make their daily purchases. In this way, the much of city resembles an amalgamation of many closely-knit villages.

At a different scale, we note that Tokyo is also a major cultural center with many museums, theaters, and musical venues, the locus for many popular festivals and street parades, and a city that is simultaneously cutting edge with respect to virtually every fashion and trend imaginable, and also a keeper of Japanese traditions and values. Tokyoites move seamlessly in their lives from glitzy shopping emporia to traditional festivals at neighborhood shrines and temples, from the best Italian or French cuisine to traditional Japanese foods, and from wearing

Buyers of a fresh tuna that was just bought at auction begin cutting it for resale in the world's largest fish market in the Tsukiji district in Tokyo, Japan. (Roman Cybriwsky)

the trendiest global fashions to traditional *kimono* and *yukata*. That is, Tokyo is a global powerhouse, and yet it is also very Japanese. For many residents, this in itself is reason for contentment.

FURTHER READING

Bestor, Theodore, *Neighborhood Tokyo* (Palo Alto, CA: Stanford University Press, 1990).
Cybriwsky, Roman, *Tokyo: The Shogun's City at the Twenty-First Century* (New York: Wiley, 1998).
Mansfield, Stephen, *Tokyo: A Cultural History* (Northampton, MA: Interlink, 2009).
Seidensticker, Edward and Donald Richie, *Tokyo from Edo to Showa, 1868–1969: The Emergence of the World's Greatest City*, 2 volumes (North Clarendon, VT: Tuttle Publishing, 2010).

VALPARAISO, CHILE

Valparaiso is a port city in central Chile, a country that runs along South America's southern Pacific Coast. It is called Valpo for short. The city is located some 70 miles (112 km) west of Santiago, the country's capital and largest city. Valparaiso has a population of 284,630 (2012), and ranks sixth in size in Chile. The Valparaiso metropolitan area totals 930,220 inhabitants, and is Chile's second-largest urban area. Although Santiago is the capital of Chile, Valparaiso is the seat of Chilean National Congress.

We selected Valparaiso for inclusion here because it is an exceptionally charming historical city that is now staging a remarkable recovery from a series of economic setbacks. We were also impressed with the high quality of life in the city. We like Santiago too, and recognize it as one of Latin America's leading economic centers and an exceptionally exciting city, but were put off by the larger city's notorious air pollution and traffic congestion. Valparaiso is smaller, more laid back, and cleaner, and it is not quite as soaring in skyline. One of its nicknames is "Little San Francisco," because both Valparaiso and the city in California are West Coast port cities at somewhat the same latitude from the equator (33°S and 37°N, respectively), are notable for their hills and charming neighborhoods on slopes, and share similar temperate climates with sunshine and blue skies alternating with chills and fogs. Another of Valparaiso's nicknames is the Jewel of the Pacific. This is because the city is so picturesque, again perhaps like San Francisco. We like Valparaiso, too, because it is in Chile, a country that we discuss elsewhere in this book as one the world's 20 most contented countries.

The Plaza Echaurren in Valparaiso, Chile, and some of the historic architecture in the neighborhood nearby. Many Latin American cities are centered on public plazas with fountains, monuments, and places to sit and relax. (Imre Cikajlo/iStockphoto.com)

Valparaiso dates back to 1536 with the arrival of Spanish explorers off the Chilean coast. It was named "Paradise Valley" because of the natural beauty of the site. The settlement remained a small village until Chile gained its independence in 1818, when the site was chosen to be a base for the country's new navy and as a trading port. It prospered as a stopover point for ships traveling between the Atlantic and Pacific Oceans via the Strait of Magellan and Cape Horn at South America's southern tip. In another tie-in to San Francisco, the city did a booming business in supplying the California Gold Rush of the 1850s. It attracted European immigrants as well, and became a cosmopolitan city with English, German, Italian, and other ethnic districts. In 1906, like San Francisco the same year, Valparaiso was destroyed by an earthquake. And then just as it was beginning a recovery, the Panama Canal was opened in 1914, diverting shipping from around the tip of South America to the much shorter route between the oceans. Valparaiso lost business, Santiago emerged as the more prosperous city, and Valparaiso became its port. Many residents of Valparaiso left the city for better opportunities in the capital. The port thrived, however, and evolved into a modern facility for container cargo and large vessels. Cruise ships dock in Valparaiso too. Another major earthquake struck the city on February 27, 2010, and on April 13, 2014, a huge brush fire swept through the hills of the city, destroying some 2,800 homes and taking 16 lives.

Despite the setbacks, Valparaiso has much going for it and keeps rebounding. Residents have a great pride in the city and a will to move it forward. At the same time, there is also will to preserve townscapes and traditions from the past. As a result, Valparaiso's revitalization is rooted in the uniqueness of the city and historic preservation. An organization called Fundación Valparaiso (the Valparaiso Foundation) has taken the lead in many neighborhood redevelopment projects that modernize and update the city, while at the same time extolling local history. Not only is there preservation of historic architecture and infrastructure, there are also programs to educate the public about Valparaiso's social and economic history. A fast-growing and creative arts community has brought new life and color to the city with music, art galleries, and various popular festivals. There are graffiti murals throughout Valparaiso that illustrate local history and build civic pride, while the vistas of hillslope neighborhoods are splashed with creative combinations of pastel shades on brightly painted houses. The *cerros* (hills) are remarkable for the variety of housing and unique ways that builders have anchored their structures into steep slopes, and for their labyrinth of winding streets, cobbled walking paths, outdoor stairways, and panoramic lookout points. Also, there are several *ascensores* (funiculars or cable cars) that are still in operation in the city and that are protected by the National Monuments Council as historical monuments. They are not just for enjoyment by tourists, but also a part of Valparaiso's commuter transit routes. A light rail system called Valparaiso Metro opened in 2005.

Valparaiso has four universities, a vibrant nightlife, and many pleasant cafés and public parks. Warm temperatures year-round with no scorching heat and scant rainfall make Valparaiso an outdoors city. In 2003, Valparaiso was declared to be Chile's "Cultural Capital" by the national congress and was designated to be the home of the country's new Ministry of Culture. In the same year, the historic district of Valparaiso was declared to be a UNESCO World Heritage Site. Not surprisingly, tourism is an ever-bigger part of the city's economy. There are no good beaches in Valparaiso, as the waterfront was transformed for shipping a long time ago, but minutes away both north and south of the city locals and visitors alike enjoy fine white sands and pleasant resort towns. The adjacent town of Viña del Mar to the northeast is one of Chile's most popular beach cities, as well as a popular suburb with glitzy shopping centers, high-rise hotels and apartments, and bright neon lights that serve modern needs while helping to keep historic Valparaiso historic.

FURTHER READING

Bordorf, Axel, Rodrigo Hidalgo, and Rafael Sánchez, "A New Model of Urban Development in Latin America: The Gated Communities and Fenced Cities in the Metropolitan Areas of Santiago de Chile and Valparaiso," *Cities: International Journal of Urban Policy and Planning*, 24, 5, 2007, pp. 365–378.

Martland, Samuel J., "Trade, Progress, and Patriotism: Defining Valparaiso, Chile, 1818–1975," *Journal of Urban History*, 35, 1, 2008, pp. 53–74.

Webb, Michael "Open City (Valparaiso, Chile)," *Architectural Review*, 1389, November 2012, pp. 40–49.

VANCOUVER, CANADA

Vancouver is an exceptionally beautiful city on the west coast of Canada. It is in southwestern British Columbia and is less than 50 miles (80 km) north of the international border with the United States. It is Canada's largest port city and the principal western terminus of the country's railroad network. A large part of the city is set on a peninsula between the Burrard Inlet to the north and the delta of the Fraser River to the south. The city is known for miles of attractive beaches, dense forests of Douglas fir, Western red cedar, and Western hemlock, many beautiful gardens and parks, and a backdrop of high mountains that retain their snowcaps year-round. Stanley Park near the city's downtown is one of the largest and most beautiful urban parks in North America. There are also many flower and rose gardens that homeowners through the city lovingly maintain in their private yards. An unusual distinction for Vancouver is that one can swim at the beach and ski on high-mountain slopes on the same day because the two are only minutes apart by automobile. Moreover, one can look down on the beach while skiing or up at the snowpack while sunning on the sands. Mountain and water views are spectacular throughout the city, as are the city's famous sunsets. Unlike the rest of Canada, winter temperatures are moderate, although most winter days are rainy or overcast, but weather in spring, summer, and fall is pretty near-perfect. In fact, Vancouver is regarded by many people to be the most beautifully set city in the world.

According to the 2011 census, the population of Vancouver was 603,502 and that of the metropolitan area was 2,476,145. This is the third-largest total among Canada's 27 metropolitan areas after Toronto and Montreal. Because the city is hemmed in by mountains and water, land is scarce and expensive, and the city is densely built-up. It is Canada's most crowded urban center, with a residential population density of 13,540 persons per square mile (5,249 per km^2). Population totals have been increasing steadily in both the city and the suburbs, as many immigrants are attracted to Vancouver. The city has traditionally had a distinctively British flavor, with the majority of residents being of English or Scottish heritage, but the population has now become much more diverse. There is a prominent Chinese minority in the city, including many Hong Kong Chinese who arrived from the former British colony as it reverted to Chinese rule, as well as growing numbers of immigrants from India and other South Asian countries, the Philippines, and elsewhere. Some 52% of Vancouver residents have a first language other than English.

Vancouver's economy has been dominated by the port and the rail freight yards, and exports of lumber, minerals, and grain. The city is also an important financial and corporate center, and center of many industries related to information technology, aerospace, and biotechnology. The city is also a growing center of film production, for which it has been referred to as Hollywood North. Its two largest universities, the University of British Columbia and Simon Fraser University, are not only excellent academically, but also have spectacularly beautiful campuses, the former on a heavily wooded peninsula with picture-postcard views of mountains and sea, and the other splendidly perched on a mountaintop. Because of the city's scenic beauty, tourism is also a major aspect of Vancouver's economy. International tourists from Asia are especially numerous. The port of Vancouver is a base for cruise ships that take visitors north along the beautiful coast of British Columbia and Alaska. In 2010, Vancouver and the nearby mountain resort of Whistler hosted the winter Olympics.

Vancouver consistently ranks highly when compared with cities around the globe in livability. For example, the city was ranked #5 in the world in the Mercer

Vancouver is widely acclaimed as one of the most beautiful big cities in the world. It is a city with ocean beaches and high mountains, all within very easy reach of the city center. (Roman Cybriwsky)

Quality of Life Survey for 2014, #15 in the world in *Monocle's* 2014 Quality of Life Survey, and #3 as the world's most livable city by the *Economist* Intelligence Unit, also for 2014. Moreover, it was the first city to rank in the *Economist's* list of top 10 most livable cities for five consecutive years. The city's strong points in terms of quality of life include the natural beauty of the surroundings, cultural diversity of the population, ample parkland and spaces for sport and recreation, good public transit, good schools for children, good community centers and other neighborhood facilities, and a strong, healthy economy. The city is also walking and bicycle friendly, and ranks highly in urban sustainability. A former industrial area near the downtown known as False Creek has been redeveloped into an especially beautiful waterfront residential and recreation zone that is now a famous case study in the urban planning literature about transition of industrial urban form to post-industrial land uses. Highlights include a mix of housing types in order to attract a diverse population, and considerable open space, and landscaping that suggests the natural environment as it was before urbanization. Nearby, in another part of the former industrial zone, is a new multi-use stadium called BC Place, an entertainment complex called the Plaza of Nations, and Science World, a popular new educational facility.

However, all these pluses have made Vancouver into an expensive city, especially with respect to costs of housing. The prices of homes and apartments had spiraled upward because of rapid population growth and low vacancy rates, and because instead of the familiar "huddled masses" image of immigrants to a new country, many of the arriving immigrants to Vancouver are unusually wealthy. These "millionaire migrants," as they are called in the title of a book about the topic, chose the city (and Canada) because of its attractions, and then inflated the cost of real estate because they were willing and able to pay previously unheard of prices in order to live in the city. In some neighborhoods, rich migrants purchased adjacent properties which they then demolished in order to put up custom-built mansions for themselves. This and other redevelopments in the city's close-in neighborhoods have created what is one of Vancouver's major minus points: the displacement of low- and moderate-income residents, and the conversion of some older neighborhoods into places that only the rich can afford.

FURTHER READING

Delany, Paul, ed., *Vancouver: Representing the Postmodern City* (Vancouver: Arsenal Pulp Press, 2002).

Ley, David, *Millionaire Migrants: Trans-Pacific Life Lines* (Malden, MA: Wiley-Blackwell, 2010).

Wynn Graeme and Timothy Oke, eds., *Vancouver and Its Region* (Vancouver: University of British Columbia Press, 1992).

VIENNA, AUSTRIA

Vienna is the capital and largest city of Austria, a small country in Central Europe and member of the European Union, as well as one of Austria's nine states. The city is located in the northeast of the country on both banks of the Danube River, and is close to the borders of the Czech Republic, Slovakia, and Hungary. The city is officially named Wein, the native German word for Vienna. Vienna's population is 1,794,700 (2015), the seventh-largest total for a city in the European Union, while the Vienna metropolitan area has over 2.4 million residents. The city has a distinguished history and countless historic landmarks, and is sometimes referred to as the "City of Music" because of the who's who of famous musicians and composers who had lived and worked there, as well as the "City of Dreams" because of its association with Sigmund Freud, the celebrated pioneer of psychoanalysis. In 2001, the entire city center of Vienna was designated as a UNESCO World Heritage Site.

Vienna was a northern frontier outpost of the Roman Empire, the de facto capital of the Holy Roman Empire more than a millennium later from 1483 to

1806, and about a century and a half after that the birthplace of the Roman (full disclosure here) who is typing these words. Twice, in the Siege of Vienna in 1529 and in the Battle of Vienna in 1683, the city turned the tide of history by stopping the advance of the Ottoman Empire on Europe. In 1804 it became the capital of the Austrian Empire, and then from 1867 until after World War I, the capital of the Austro-Hungarian Empire. In 1814–1815, the city hosted the Congress of Vienna that met to negotiate a long-term peace plan for Europe in the wake of the Napoleonic Wars and to redraw national boundaries. During the 19th century and then to the eve of World War II in 1938, Vienna was one of the world's preeminent centers of high culture and modernism. It was known for art, architecture, music, science, and socialist politics for which it was referred to as "Red Vienna." The city had had a large Jewish population, but after the Nazi Anschluss (annexation) of Austria, most of the population fled, and the rest, estimated to be about 65,000, perished in the Holocaust. Postwar Vienna evolved into a prosperous corporate and financial center, as well as into a host city for numerous international organizations and conferences, including several organizations of the United Nations, the International Atomic Energy Agency, and the Organization of Petroleum Exporting Countries (OPEC). The city continues to be a leading cultural center known for classical music concerts, opera, and a revival of 19th-century Viennese balls, as well as for its many museums, historical palaces and baroque gardens, universities, and rich café culture. The city attracts more than 12 million tourists a year, and tourism is a major contributor to the economy of Vienna.

The residents of Vienna enjoy many parks, efficient networks of public transportation and highways, excellent medical care, and fine neighborhoods with good housing and excellent local services. There are many trails for bicycling and jogging, and during the warm months there are frequent festivals, street fairs, and outdoor concerts. The population is highly literate and technologically savvy, and generally bilingual (English as well as German) if not multilingual. Immigration from the Balkans region in Europe, Turkey, and other countries is making Vienna even more international. The city is generally clean and safe.

The Intelligence Unit of the *Economist* ranks Vienna as #2 in the world in 2012 behind Melbourne in its ranking of most livable cities. In 2005, it was in a tie for first place with Vancouver in that ranking. The annual Mercer Quality of Living surveys have consistently put Vienna in first place from among hundreds of cities between 2009 and 2014. The Quality of Life Survey by the lifestyle magazine *Monocle* also ranks the city highly, placing it at #6 in the world in 2012. In 2013, the Internet ranking platform "list25.com" rated Vienna at #1 among 25 cities as best for young people. Finally, a 2012 analysis by urban strategist Boyd Cohen concluded that Vienna was "the smartest city on the planet." It was the only city to rank in the top 10 in every category: innovation city, green city, quality of life, and digital governance. The city is often proposed as a model for other cities, and frequently host conferences about city planning, sustainable urbanism, and applications of information technology to urban monitoring and management. Our own observations accord fully with those in published surveys and other favorable commentary: yes, Vienna is a beautiful, elegant, and prosperous city where there is much to do and a very high standard of living.

FURTHER READING

Cohen, Boyd, "The Top 10 Smart Cities on the Planet," *Co.EXIST*, January 11, 2012, http://www.fastcoexist.com/1679127/the-top-10-smart-cities-on-the-planet.
Morton, Frederic, *A Nervous Splendor: Vienna 1888–1889* (New York: Penguin, 1980).
Parsons, Nicholas, *Vienna: A Cultural History* (New York: Oxford University Press, 2008).
Wheatcroft, Andrew, *The Enemy at the Gate: The Hapsburgs, the Ottomans, and the Battle for Europe* (New York: Basic Books, 2010).

ZÜRICH, SWITZERLAND

Zürich is the largest city in Switzerland and one of the world's leading banking centers, as well as the leading business center of the country. It is located in the north-central part of Switzerland on both sides of the Limmat River at the north-western tip of Lake Zürich. The Swiss Alps are less than 20 miles (about 30 km) to the south, and give the city a beautiful backdrop. It was founded by the Romans in about 15 B.C., who gave it the name Turicum. The present name is a corruption of that name. The population of Zürich is about 400,000, while that of the Zürich metropolitan area is a little more than 1.8 million.

Zürich is a very prosperous place, and is very expensive. The Intelligence Unit of the *Economist* lists it as the world's fourth most expensive city in 2015, and Mercer's Cost of Living Survey listed it at #5 in the world in 2014. When the *Economist* listed Zürich as the world's most expensive city in 2012, its write-up referred to the city with the pun ZuRich. We include this very expensive place in our list of 20 most contented cities on earth a bit grudgingly, because we are normally not in favor of places that are disproportionately for the rich, yet we have to acknowledge that because anyone who can afford to live in Zürich should be very happy, the city's population must be highly contented.

Zürich is known worldwide for its banking industry, as well as for insurance and asset management companies. The banks are known for security, stability, excellent service, and for being discreet. Many of the companies are foreign, attracted to the city because of a highly favorable tax regime. Zürich is also the world's largest gold trading center. The city's stock exchange, now known as the SIX Swiss Exchange, was founded in 1877 and is one of the largest stock exchanges in the world. In 1995, it became the first stock exchange in the world to adopt fully automated trading. Other aspects of the economy are tourism, light manufacturing, higher education, and high technology research and development industries. There are about 20 colleges and universities in the city, which is a high number given Zürich's modest population total, and about 60,000 students. Two of the universities, the Swiss Federal Institute of Technology and the University of Zürich, rank among the top universities in the world. The unemployment rate in Zürich as of July, 2012 was a comfortably low 3.2%.Whether it is a plus or a minus we are not sure, but we note that the world headquarters of FIFA, the not-always-popular governing body of the world's favorite sport, football (soccer), is located in Zürich.

The economic success of Zürich is often attributed to the comparative ease of doing business in Switzerland, and to the city's desirability as a place to live for reasons of safety, cleanliness, housing quality, and excellent services. On the first point, we note that the *Global Competitiveness Report for 2014–2015* by the World Economic Forum places Switzerland at #1 in the world, and that a 2014 ranking by *Forbes* has the country at #9 out of 146 countries as being a "best country for business." In terms of Zürich's amenities, we observe that the Mercer Quality of Living Survey has Zürich at #2 in the world from among 221 cities for each of 2010, 2012, 2014, and 2015, always behind Vienna, which is another one of our 20 most contented cities. Furthermore, the city ranks #7 globally in the Quality of Life Survey for 2014 by the lifestyle magazine *Monocle*; and the Intelligence Unit of the *Economist* has ranked the city #11 in the world in 2014 in its Global Livability Ranking. Other accolades include a diverse range: a #1 rating among 23 European cities in air quality by the organization Sootfree Cities; a tie for #5 in the world with Melbourne, Australia, as a best city in the world for students by the consulting company QS; and a #6 ranking among cities worldwide in 2013 by the consulting company ECA International in "Employment Conditions Abroad."

Zürich is a wonderful place to live in or visit. The city is picturesque in terms of both setting and architecture, and is noted for being clean, safe, and orderly. All of its residential neighborhoods have excellent services and infrastructure, and there are many parks, gardens, and other recreation areas for people to enjoy. Public transportation is excellent and dependable, and includes local trains, buses, and an iconic electric tram network that is clean and quiet, and that forms the backbone of local commuting. There are also commuter routes along the river and across Lake Zürich. The main rail station in Zürich is large and modern, and makes much of the rest of Europe easily accessible. There are many festivals and special events each year, ranging from the Weltklasse Zürich, which is a world-class track-and-field event that is sometimes referred to as the Zürich Olympics, the Zürich Marathon, the Zürich Film Festival, and the Street Parade, which is held every August and is one of Europe's largest and most popular outdoor parties. Furthermore, the city offers a rich cultural life that includes opera, ballet, and many theaters, as well as a range of art and other museums. The Zürich Museum of Art, the Swiss National Museum, the Rietberg Museum, and Centre Le Corbusier are but a few of many examples. Zürich also has a rich nightlife scene centered on the Niederdorf district in the city's historic core.

FURTHER READING

Hitz, Hansruedi and Christian Schmid, "Urbanization in Zürich: Headquarter Economy and City-Belt," *Environment & Planning D: Society & Space*, 12, 2, 1994, pp. 167–186.

Koll-Schretzenmeyr, Martina, Frank R. Herhoff, and Walter Siebel, "In Quest of the Good Urban Life: Socio-Spatial Dynamics and Residential Building Sock Transformation in Zürich," *Urban Studies*, 46, 13, 2009, pp. 2731–2747.

Rérat, Patrick, "Gentrifiers and Their Choice of Housing: Characteristics of the Households in New Developments in Swiss Cities," *Environment & Planning A*, 44, 1, 2012, pp. 221–236.

THE 20 LEAST CONTENTED WORLD CITIES

ALEPPO, SYRIA

Aleppo is an historic city in Syria, a conflict-ridden Middle Eastern country with a shoreline on the eastern Mediterranean Sea and land boundaries with Iraq, Turkey, Lebanon, Israel, and Jordan. The city is in the north of the country approximately 75 miles (125 km) from the Mediterranean and about 30 miles (50 km) from the Turkish border. It is on the Queiq River, a small river whose waters have been totally exhausted for irrigation use in both Syria and Turkey. The city has been a prominent center of trade and Islamic cultural life for many centuries, although in recent times it has been somewhat overshadowed in its own country by the national capital Damascus, which is also an ancient city and is better known around the world. Aleppo, however, is Syria's largest urban center, having a population of 2,301,570 (2005) as compared with an estimated 1,711,000 (2011) for Damascus. Both cities are now caught up in the violence of the Syrian Civil War (March 2011–present), and have suffered many causalities and great damage to historic buildings and modern infrastructure. Aleppo continues to be the scene of fierce fighting and has been especially badly destroyed, leading us to include it as one of the world's 20 least contented urban centers.

Aleppo is one of the oldest cities on the planet and has been continuously inhabited for approximately 8,000 years. It had been known for centuries as both a prosperous commercial center and powerful military stronghold, and was the Mediterranean world's terminus of the Silk Road to Central Asia and the Orient. It was annexed by the Ottoman Empire in the 16th century and grew to become its third-largest city after Constantinople and Cairo. The opening of the Suez Canal in 1869 was followed by economic decline in Aleppo, as trade between Europe and Asia began to bypass the city. Another blow to economy was the redrawing of national boundaries in the Middle East after the fall of the Ottoman Empire in 1923. This led to truncation of Aleppo's natural trade hinterland when Turkey was created just to the north, as well as to loss to Turkey of Aleppo's best access to the Mediterranean Sea. Ironically, however, the economic woes helped to preserve Aleppo's historic districts and important landmarks in that the city did not experience as much history-destroying redevelopment and new construction as cities that were economic winners. The historic center of Aleppo was recognized as a UNESCO World Heritage Site in 1986, and in 2006 the city was awarded the distinction "Islamic Capital of Culture." Important landmarks include the Aleppo Citadel, Al-Madina Souq (traditional marketplace), the historic gates of Aleppo, the eighth-century Great Mosque and other old mosques, old churches associated with various Christian denominations, and the ninth-century Central Synagogue of Aleppo.

The Syrian Civil War is a conflict that began in the spring of 2011 during the wave of Arab Spring protests that swept across North Africa and the Middle East at the time and then turned violent when the government of Syrian president Bashar al-Assad responded with deadly force and mass arrests. The protestors had called for more democracy in Syria and an end to Assad's repressive and authoritarian rule. The Free Syrian Army was the first to wage war against the government, followed by a broad coalition of anti-Assad forces known as the Islamic Front. The Islamic State of Iraq and the Levant (ISIL) originated in Iraq and became another combatant, which controls considerable territory in Syria's east, including the country's main oil-producing regions. The government's military forces are large and well equipped, and have managed to keep Assad in power so far (as of this writing) even though the unpopular ruler is reviled in his country and has almost no meaningful support from any country across the world other than Vladimir Putin's Russia. The loss of life has been enormous, and there are millions of displaced persons, about half of whom are living as refugees in countries abroad. Human rights violations abound, as well as reports that Assad's forces have been using chemical weapons against rebels and civilian populations, cluster bombs, and improvised "barrel bombs" filled with shrapnel, oil, and explosives that are dropped from helicopters on settled areas. Both sides also use suicide bombings against their opponents. In addition to death and injuries, the assaults have wrecked buildings, infrastructure, and livelihoods.

What is called the Battle of Aleppo began on July 19, 2012, and is referred to by opposing combatants as "the mother of battles." It is not possible as yet to accurately assess what has happened because the fighting is still in full force, but already thousands have been killed by chemical weapons and barrel bombs, most of the surviving residents have fled, and the historic city is in ruins. There have been innumerable deadly attacks by government forces against public markets, hospitals, and other targets with dense concentrations of civilians. Moreover, the worst might not be over, as the Assad government shows no signs of giving up, but instead seems to be turning up the conflict, prompting fears of more massacres to come. The intensity of the fighting has made it next to impossible for humanitarian aid convoys from abroad to reach Aleppo, and aid workers themselves have been frequent victims of the violence. Analysis of satellite imagery shows that those parts of the city that are in rebel hands have been damaged most severely, as the government has trained missiles and other superior firepower at these neighborhoods. Even if the Assad government was to fall soon and a ceasefire comes into effect, it will be a long time before life in Aleppo returns to normal and the city is rebuilt.

FURTHER READING

Sukkar, Sumia, *The Boy from Aleppo Who Painted the War* (London: Eyewear Publishing Company, 2013).
Sutton, David, *Aleppo: City of Scholars* (New York: Mesorah Publications, 2005).

BAGHDAD, IRAQ

Baghdad is the capital and largest city in Iraq, a Middle Eastern country that has been the scene of considerable warfare and internal strife almost continuously since the Iran-Iraq War of the 1980s. Baghdad itself has been an epicenter of this conflict, and it is for that reason that we have chosen to add it to our list of the 20 least contented cities in the world. We could also have had Iraq on the list of 20 least contented countries, but decided to not double up in this case and to write up only one of the two, either the country or its capital city. We chose Baghdad for convenience, because there was less room for Iraq on our list of countries.

Baghdad is the second-largest city in the Arab world (after Cairo), and the second largest in West Asia (after Tehran). As of 2011, its total population was estimated to be 7,216,040. The city is located on the Tigris River in the heart of what was once Mesopotamia, the "cradle of civilization" for the Western world, and was founded in the eighth century. It became the capital of the Abbasid Caliphate and a major center of learning and trade for the Islamic world. As it prospered, it grew to become quite possibly the largest city in the world in the 10th and 12th centuries, when its population may have reached between 1.2 million and 2 million inhabitants. Then, the city was destroyed by Mongol invasion in 1258 and lost much of its influence until modern times. From 1534 through 1917, Baghdad was under the rule of the Ottoman Empire. In 1920, the city was designated as the capital of the British Mandate of Mesopotamia, and then in 1932 it became the capital of the Kingdom of Iraq. The Republic of Iraq was proclaimed after a coup in 1958 in which the bodies of the former royal family of the country were dragged through the streets of Baghdad. The city prospered in the 1970s, because global prices for oil, Iraq's principal export, reached all-time highs, and there was considerable investment in infrastructure and modernization of the city.

However, in 1980 Saddam Hussein, the country's fifth president, led Iraq into a war against neighboring Iran that lasted until 1988. It cost the country dearly in lives lost, economic impact, and damage to property and infrastructure. That war was followed soon thereafter by the Gulf War of 1990–1991 in which Saddam Hussein ordered an invasion of neighboring Kuwait and its annexation to Iraq. Iraq's military was very quickly defeated by U.S.-led forces in Operation Desert Shield, in which southern Iraq and Baghdad suffered casualties and considerable damage. The damage included deliberate Iraqi draining of wetlands where irrigation agriculture had been practiced, a purposeful oil spill by Iraq into the Persian Gulf, and the setting ablaze of as many as 700 oil wells in Kuwaiti territory. This was followed by an invasion of Iraq in 2003 by a U.S.-led coalition on the claim that Iraq was in possession of weapons of mass destruction. This led to the "Iraq War" that toppled Saddam Hussein's government and resulted in his execution in 2006. The United States officially withdrew from the war in 2011, but violent insurgencies continue, terrorist bombings and suicide attacks are frequent, and there is no place in Iraq that is safe.

Baghdad has suffered disproportionately from the conflicts. The civilian toll included many thousands of deaths and many more thousands injured, as well as the destruction of people's homes and livelihoods. Also, there was considerable physical damage to the city's infrastructure such as roads, bridges, and public buildings, as well as disruptions of electrical service, water supply, and sewage treatment. Even trash collection was disabled, as most of the city's trash trucks had been destroyed in bombing raids or were stolen. The cultural heritage of Iraq was damaged too, as bombs hit mosques, minarets, libraries, and other prominent or historic buildings, and many artistic treasures were looted from museums, palaces, and other buildings. Bombs continue to rock the city almost daily, especially it seems in crowded public places at peak times.

Traffic is a nightmare, as many streets are closed, there are security checkpoints everywhere that stop vehicles and inspect contents, and an entire section of the center of the city, now popularly referred to as the "Green Zone," is cordoned off in an attempt to create a safe neighborhood for the international community such as diplomats, journalists, and aid workers, and for the operations of Iraq's post–Saddam Hussein government. However, that area has also been the target of deadly terrorist attacks. Wherever one lives in Baghdad, stepping out can be dangerous. Public transportation is iffy as to whether or not it will run on a given day, markets lack basic goods, and prices have skyrocketed on whatever is in stock. Many people are out of work and the poverty rate in the city is about 40%. Families double and triple up (or more) in small apartments, many people scavenge through trash for food and usable items, and some even sell their own organs on a black market in Baghdad to earn an income. In the meantime, there are reports of theft and corruption with respect to supplies to aid the needy, and more theft and corruption associated with construction projects to repair the city. Because of the crisis, Baghdad was rated dead last among 221 cities worldwide in the 2010 Mercer quality of life ranking.

FURTHER READING

Marozzi, Justin, *Baghdad: City of Peace, City of Blood—A History in Thirteen Centuries* (Boston: De Capo Press, 2014).

Putz, Ulrike, "Life in Baghdad's Slums: Fighting to Survive in Sadr City," *Spiegel International On Line*, September 1, 2010, http://www.spiegel.de/international/world/life-in-baghdad-s-slums-fighting-to-survive-in-sadr-city-a-715144.html.

Scranton, Roy, "Back to Baghdad: Life in the City of Doom," *Rolling Stone*, July 17, 2014, http://www.rollingstone.com/politics/news/back-to-baghdad-life-in-the-city-of-doom-20140717.

Sessions, David, "This Iraqi Life: 10 Year Later, Baghdad Is a Tough Place to Live In," *The Daily Beast*, March 22, 2013, http://www.thedailybeast.com/articles/2013/03/22/this-iraqi-life-10-years-later-baghdad-is-a-tough-place-to-live-in.html.

BEIJING, CHINA

Beijing is the capital of the People's Republic of China, the world's most populous nation and a giant in the global economy. The city is, therefore, one of the most important and influential cities in the world. Yet, despite China's rise out of poverty and great economic success after the reforms that Premier Deng Xiaoping introduced during his rule from 1978 to 1992, and despite Beijing's many outstanding historical and cultural attractions, the city is a heavily polluted and traffic-choked snarl, and is coming to be barely livable. In the opening words of a recent article about the city, "If you want to be healthy for the rest of your life, don't live in Beijing." Another article quotes the assessment of a Chinese scientific study in its title that China's capital is "barely suitable for life," and reports that the current

Beijing is one of many cities in China with a severe air pollution problem, and one of the most heavily polluted capital cities in the world. The wearing of masks in order to reduce risks to health is common, as is the haze seen in the background. (Hung Chung Chih/ iStockphoto.com)

premier, Li Keqiang, has said that the high levels of smog in the city have given him "a heavy heart." At the time this is being written, the 34th annual running of the Beijing Marathon has concluded with many runners wearing protective masks to cut down on the amount of particulate pollution they would ingest over 26.2 miles (42.2 km) of smog-laden streets and parks.

Truly, something has gone terribly wrong in Beijing. But the problem is nationwide, related to inadequate environmental controls during a time of rapid economic growth, and many other cities in China are also dangerously polluted. Our list of 20 least contented cities in the world has three from China from three different parts of this huge country: Beijing, which is first in alphabetical order, Chongqing, and Ürümqi. Other Chinese cities could have been on our list too, but three is already more than any other country, and we would be playing a broken record over and over about pollution, crowding, more pollution, big construction projects, traffic jams, and still more pollution. That China's once-proud capital has come to be so unlivable is a national embarrassment and scandal.

Beijing has a population of 21,150,000 (2013), and is the second-largest city in China (after Shanghai) and one of the largest in the world. The city is not only the center of government in China, but also the headquarters city of most of China's largest state-owned corporations, the nation's leading financial center, and its principal media center, education center, and transportation hub. The Beijing Capital International Airport is the world's second-busiest in passenger traffic (after that in Atlanta). The city is near the heartland of Han Chinese culture and its history goes back some three millennia. Important historical sites include the Forbidden City, which was the home of China's emperors and their households for nearly 500 years, and just to the north of the city, the most-visited portion of the Great Wall of China. The symbolic center of Beijing is historic Tiananmen Square, located just outside the gates of the Forbidden City, and a cluster of Communist-era (i.e., post-1949) landmarks that ring the square such as the Mao Zedong Mausoleum, the Great Hall of the People, and the National Museum of China. Although the city is greatly modernized and has many tall new buildings, its stands out in China for having retained many of its traditional old neighborhoods called *hutong*, including one near this center that is also a popular tourist attraction. In 2008, Beijing successfully hosted the summer Olympics, for which it had made many improvements to infrastructure and constructed spectacular venues. The games, as well as the opening and closing ceremonies, were a great source of pride for China, although the specter of air pollution menaced the events beforehand and required extraordinary measures such as heavy restrictions on motor vehicle traffic and factory production to make the city breathable.

The major sources of pollution are the city's congested motor vehicle traffic, coal-burning power plants in and near the city, and heavy industry. Not all of the pollutants are locally generated; they come as well from big cities and industrial zones nearby. Air quality is especially poor in winter, which is face-mask season for many Beijingers. The air pollution problem is further complicated by the prevalence of dust storms that are known as Asian dust, yellow wind, and yellow sand, among other terms. They are most severe in the springtime months, and are kicked up by winds travelling across desert sands north and west of the city. Visibility is greatly reduced, it becomes hard to breathe, and afterward everything and everybody is covered with layers of fine grit. The problem is exacerbated by desertification in North China and Mongolia, periods of drought, and the mixing of desert sand with poisonous industrial pollutants. There are various efforts under way to combat the air pollution problem in Beijing, including replacement of coal with natural gas, restrictions on automobile usage, and the planting of a tree belt outside the city, although it is not certain that conditions won't become worse before they become better.

Finally, we note that we have singled out Beijing in this part of the book not just because of its pollution problem, but also because it is the capital city of a repressive country. The well-known brutal suppression of pro-democracy protests by students on Tiananmen Square in 1989 was not just an event from recent history, but also reflects government policy today. Dissent is forbidden. So is even discussion of what took place in 1989, as well as discussion of other sensitive topics in China, such as Tibetan rights, uprisings against Chinese rule in the country's northwest (see Ürümqi), and most criticisms of the Communist Party. The press is not free, the government controls the media, and a "Great Firewall of China" governs access to what computer users can see and read. There are restrictions against religious freedoms too, as well as against political opposition and rival political parties, and penalties are harsh for political and religious prisoners. While these issues are nationwide, we mention them here because Beijing is where China's illiberal policies are implemented and executed.

FURTHER READING

"Beijing 'Barely Suitable' for Life as Heavy Pollution Shrouds China's Capital," *The Sydney Morning Herald*, February 26, 2014, http://www.smh.com.au/environment/beijing-barely-suitable-for-life-as-heavy-pollution-shrouds-chinas-capital-20140226–33ghq.html#ixzz3GnsqDHHt.

Meyer, Michael, *The Last Days of Old Beijing: Life in the Backstreets of a City Transformed* (New York: Walker Publishing Company, 2008).

Minter, Adam, "Why Living in Beijing Could Ruin Your Life," *Bloomberg View*, June 19, 2014, http://www.bloombergview.com/articles/2014–06–19/why-living-in-beijing-could-ruin-your-life.

Wang, Jun, *Beijing Record: A Physical and Political History of Planning Modern Beijing* (Singapore: World Scientific Publishing, 2011).

Wu, Hung, *Remaking Beijing: Tiananmen Square and the Creation of a Political Space* (Chicago: University of Chicago Press, 2005).

CAIRO, EGYPT

Cairo is the capital and largest city in Egypt, a country in the northeast corner of the African continent, and Africa's second-most populous city, after Lagos. It is also one of the most populous and most influential cities in the Islamic world. The city is located on the lower Nile River close to where the main channel breaks up into the distributaries of the delta, and is the hub of a very crowded metropolitan area that extends both up and down the Nile Valley. The population of Cairo is 10,230,350, while that of the Cairo metropolitan area 20,439,541 (2011).

Cairo was founded in about 968 by the Islamic Fatimid dynasty, and became its capital almost exactly two centuries later in 1168. The city is one of the most famous tourism destinations in the world, as it is the gateway to the famous pyramids and the Sphinx just outside the city in the town of Giza, as well as to another complex of pyramids in Saqqara a short distance to the south of Cairo, and to many other monuments from the civilization of ancient Egypt further upriver on the Nile. The city itself is also rich with attractions: the Tahrir Square district in the heart of the downtown and its spectacular Egyptian Museum; the upscale neighborhoods and shopping districts of Gezira and Zamalek on a nearby river island that is named Zamalek; the "Old Cairo" district south of the downtown that includes relicts from Fustat and old Coptic churches; and Islamic Cairo where there are spectacular mosques, the main bazaar of the city, the historic Citadel of Cairo, and old Turkish baths. There are luxurious hotels (as well as cheaper ones), comfortable middle-class neighborhoods, and shopping malls that look fairly much like malls elsewhere and that sell more-or-less the same things. Cairo is also a distinguished center of culture and learning, with great universities and libraries, religious education, the Cairo Film Festival, and a wide range of theaters, music venues, and museums.

However, despite these pluses, we felt compelled to list Cairo among the 20 least contented cities in the world. There are a number of reasons for this. First, the city has been beset recently with considerable social unrest and political instability, and is something of a tinderbox with respect to relations between government and opposition parties, and with respect to the rise of radical Islam. With Tahrir Square as a focal point, there have been frequent mass protests and labor strikes, as well as occasional rioting and deadly violence. Two Egyptian presidents have been forced from office since 2011. The Islamist Muslim Brotherhood has many supporters and aims to make Egypt into an Islamist state. There is a constant threat of terrorism against domestic targets and foreigners alike. Foreign tourists have been harassed, attacked, and even killed, including as recently as 2014. Therefore, the tourism economy has plummeted, leading to unemployment and financial catastrophe in this vital sector of Cairo's (and Egypt's) livelihood, and more unrest among the citizenry.

Second, we observe that life in Cairo is difficult even without the unrest. The city is known for being extraordinarily congested, with extraordinarily high residential densities, highly crowded streets and marketplaces, and nightmarish traffic conditions. City streets and thoroughfares have a reported 4.5 million motor vehicles. The subway system is jammed as well, especially at peak times. The city is covered with an essentially permanent haze, and is known as one of the most polluted big cities in the world. Air pollution is notoriously bad, because not only are there the pollutants from the millions of cars and buses, there is also considerable pollution from industrial emissions and the burning of trash and agricultural chaff. Toxins released into the air by the city's many unregistered lead and copper smelters are especially hazardous. Air pollution levels build up to dangerous levels because there is little rain to wash them away, and because pollutants accumulate along streets between tall buildings. The negative effects to human health from air pollution in Cairo are well documented. Cairo also suffers from water shortages and water pollution, and from inadequate sewer systems that reach capacity levels and then overflow onto city streets.

Finally, we note that although Cairo has a middle-class population and wealthy residents too, it is the poor who are most numerous and whose numbers grow fastest. The metropolitan area has millions of people who live in grossly inadequate housing conditions in informal settlements called *ashwa'iyyat* that are in marginal locations, have no or very poor municipal services, and offer little prospect for gainful employment. The Manshiet Nasser district of the city is an enormous "mega slum" with an estimated 600,000 to 1 million inhabitants, including tens of thousands *zabbaleen*, a word that means "garbage people" in Egyptian Arabic and that refers to the mostly Coptic Christian people who are the informal trash collection system of Cairo. They use donkey carts to take the city's refuse to their particular part of Manshiet Nasser, and live off what women and children can find in picking through the dumps. Elsewhere in the city, as many as 500,000 other impoverished Cairenes live in the tombs and mausoleums of a cemetery nearby that is called the "City of the Dead." Even Cairo's rooftops have sprouted illegal housing for the poor. The situation worsens as Egypt's economy suffers from the country's unrest, and as poor peasants stream to the capital city in hopes of finding a better life.

FURTHER READING

Collett, Michele, "Manshiet Nasser: The Secret Shame of Cairo's Mega Slum," *Scribol*, n.d., http://scribol.com/travel/manshiet-nasser-the-secret-shame-of-cairos-mega-slum.

Goldstein, Eric, "In Crowded Cairo, Even the Rooftops Are Teeming with Life," *Christian Science Monitor*, September 4, 1984, http://www.csmonitor.com/1984/0904/090462 .html.

Jones, Sophia, "Residents of Sprawling Cairo Slum Fear the Government Will Level Their Homes," *The World Post*, April 7, 2014, http://www.huffingtonpost.com/2014/05/07 /egypt-manshiet-nasser-demolition_n_5274375.html.

Sabry, Sarah, "How Poverty Is Underestimated in Greater Cairo, Egypt," *Environment & Urbanization*, 22, 2, 2010, pp. 53–541.

Soueif, Ahdaf, *Cairo: Memoir of a City Transformed* (New York: Anchor Books, 2014).

CARACAS, VENEZUELA

Caracas is the capital and largest city in Venezuela, a country on the north (Caribbean Sea) coast of South America. The city is located in the northern part of the country in an elongated valley just to the south of Venezuela's coastal mountain range, the high and steep Cordillera de la Costa. The central city of Caracas has a population of just over 2 million inhabitants, while the Caracas urban area totals nearly 3.3 million inhabitants. The wider Caracas metropolis (the Caracas Metropolitan Region) totals about 5.2 million residents. In addition to its role as national capital, the city is the leading business center of Venezuela, as well as the cultural capital and principal center of higher education.

Venezuela is one of the world's leading oil-exporting countries, as well as a leading exporter of mineral ores, timber resources, and other natural wealth. Caracas reflects the nation's prosperity in having a bustling business center with soaring corporate and bank towers, as well as a number of very exclusive residential districts where the richest political and business families live. However, Venezuelans have gotten accustomed to referring to oil as "the devil's excrement," meaning that while there are significant riches that come from this black gold, the devil has brought along with the oil a life of crime, corruption, and inequality to the country and its capital city. Wealth is distributed extremely unevenly in both Venezuela as a whole and in Caracas specifically, with the result that the city has a very large number of people who are extremely poor, and enormous slum neighborhoods with miserable living conditions. Many of the poor are refugee migrants from an even poorer countryside. Atop that, the city is one of the most violent places on earth, with constant shootings and gang wars, and a murder rate that is off the charts in comparison to other cities, even cities that also have reputations for out-of-control violent crime. Sadly, Caracas has been likened to a city at war. It is because of the widespread poverty and the astounding crime rates that we have selected Caracas for inclusion on these pages as one of the world's 20 least contented cities.

According to Transparency International's Corruptions Perceptions Index for 2010, Venezuela ranks at #164 out of 178 countries surveyed in level of corruption. The problem exists across many agencies of government, and reaches deeply into the police force, as well as to education, public utilities, health care, and many other aspects of life. The situation with the police is especially distressing. Many people are afraid to report crimes because they know that police work hand in hand with criminals, and believe that complaints will only bring them more harm. According to a 2013 study by the Gallup organization, only 26% of Venezuelans have faith in their local police forces. Moreover, many citizens believe that police are brutal and are more likely to rob people than to help them. Human Rights Watch has reported that one in five crimes are actually committed by police, and that with impunity. The police force in Caracas has reportedly been so criminal that it had to be disbanded and reorganized afresh. This was after accusations that the city's police had a hand in some 17,000 kidnappings, a crime that is common in the city to extort ransom monies.

The Gallup organization reported in 2013 that Venezuela is the most insecure country in the world in terms of crime. Caracas is especially dangerous, and has one of the highest murder rates in the world. Gun ownership is widespread, as are narcotics and narcotics traffickers, and street gangs. There is no part of the city that is safe, but the greatest dangers are in the poor slum areas, the *barrios*, where gangs rule instead of legitimate authority and where police make almost no effort to keep the public safe or to solve crimes. The people of Caracas live in fear. Venturing out after dark is not recommended no matter where. Wealthy people live behind high walls and complex security systems, travel in armored vehicles, and are often accompanied by armed guards. Poorer people seek safety in numbers, and are known to save money and pool resources in the event that they need to rescue someone from kidnappers. Many people, rich and not rich, alter their routines and take different streets as they travel back and forth within Caracas as a precaution against being targeted for crime. Stores such as supermarkets and shopping centers employ a heavy security presence, not to mention jewelry stores, banks, and armored vehicles that convey cash. Petty crime such as pickpocketing is a daily threat, particularly on public transit and other crowded places. A frequently cited story from Venezuela's offshore tourism island of Margarita recounts how firefighters who were called to extinguish a blaze in a shantytown at a landfill site were set upon and robbed by slum residents whose lives they had just saved.

Caracas has many slum neighborhoods and shantytowns. The largest is crowded place of an estimated 1.5 million inhabitants that stretches up steep hill slopes outside the city. It is called Barrio Petare. Houses are perched precariously on unstable terrain, one next to the other and one higher than the other as one ascends the slope. There are few streets, but only footpaths and steps, no public services, little potable water, and only miserable living conditions, capped by gangs, crime, and raw sewage. Fires spread rapidly and take many lives in addition to destroying housing, while during rainy periods, people and their homes are buried in muddy landslides. In addition to squatter slums in peripheral locations such as Petare, Caracas has had what is allegedly the *tallest* slum in the world. This is the so-called Tower of David located amid the skyscrapers of the city center. This unfinished high-rise office building named after developer David Brillembourg has housed as many as 2,500 squatters for more than two decades until evictions in July 2014. It was supposed to have been an opulent structure when it was conceived, but the problems of Venezuela intervened and the building became a yet another symbol of the country's ills.

FURTHER READING

Debaut, Karl, "Poverty and Destitution in the Hills around Caracas," *Socialistworld.net*, July 13, 2006, http://www.socialistworld.net/doc/2375.

Freelon, Kiratiana, "Caracas's Sky-High 'Tower of David' Slum Finally Cleared of Its 2,500 Squatters," *Socialistworld.net*, July, 23, 2014, http://www.socialistworld.net/doc/2375.

Márquez, Patricia, *The Street Is My Home: Youth and Violence in Caracas* (Palo Alto, CA: Stanford University Press, 2002).

Vásquez, Elisa, "'Caracas a Livable City' New Index Says Not on Your Life," *Panampost*, August, 26, 2014, http://panampost.com/elisa-vasquez/2014/08/25/caracas-a-livable-city-new-index-says-not-on-your-life/.

CHONGQING, CHINA

Chongqing, formerly known as Chungking, is a major city located at the confluence of the Jialing River and the Yangtze River (Chang Jiang) near the center of China. It is a river port on the Yangtze. It is an historic city, and was a base in the late 19th–early 20th centuries for foreign commercial interests in China's interior. From 1937 to 1945 the city served as the provisional capital of Generalissimo Chiang Kai-shek and his Kuomintang Chinese Nationalist government. Nowadays, Chongqing is an important manufacturing center and transportation hub, as well as a nucleus for economic growth in the west and center of the country. In 1997 it was separated from Sichuan Province and made into its own municipality, reporting directly to the central government in Beijing.

According to the census of 2010, Chongqing Municipality had a population of nearly 29 million. The city proper, however, numbers about 8 million inhabitants, still huge by any standards and one of the largest urban centers in China. The city is designated as one of China's five National Central Cities, giving it special responsibilities for economic growth and the provision of services in the country, and is one of the three cities, along with Chengdu and Xi'an, that form the West Triangle Economic Zone, a territorial designation that was established in 2009 to promote growth in China's center. The city is located upriver from the new Three Gorges Dam across the Yangtze, an enormous construction project that was completed recently to stimulate economic development in China's interior. Chongqing is expected to benefit in terms of improvements to river transport. Like other cities in China, Chongqing is a world of skyscrapers and new construction that reflects population and economic growth, as well as modernization. There is a distinctive look to the skyline because the city center is itself a confluence of the two rivers and the background is mountainous.

Even though Chongqing has grown recently into a large and prominent city, for which it justifiably takes pride, we include it among the 20 least content cities in the world because the city also reflects some of China's greatest weaknesses. One issue is corruption and shady businesses dealings. A country with a fast-growing economy such as China has lots to tempt dishonest politicians or crooked business owners, and Chongqing has come to be China's "bad apple" in this regard. The city has come to be known for organized crime and for tough gangsters who control many of its businesses and much of its wealth. In 2009, a leading member of China's Communist Party, Bo Xilai, was brought in to clean up. He arrested thousands of crooks, leading to optimism that the gangster days might be over, but then he succumbed to a scandal of his own and is now serving a life term in prison for corruption. His downfall was brought on by the murder in Chongqing in 2011 of British businessman Neil Heywood, with whom Bo was associated. At first the death was declared to be the result of alcohol poisoning, but then former

Neighborliness and street life are hallmarks of all Chinese cities. The two men in this photo from the city of Chongqing are playing a board game called *xiangqi*, or Chinese chess. (Jia He/iStockPhoto.com)

vice mayor and chief of police of Chongqing, Wang Lijun, traveled to the U.S. Consulate and Chengdu with information that Heywood had been murdered and that Bo may have been complicit. Bo's wife, Gu Kailai, has been charged with the murder and was convicted. Such stories can make for great novels or Hollywood movies, but they tear a city apart, harm the economy, and in turn cause harm to every resident.

Also very damaging to Chongqing is its air pollution problem. It is one of the 10 most polluted cities on earth, one of 7 Chinese cities on this dubious list. Culprits include heavy industry such as the Chongqing Iron and Steel Company, South West Aluminum, which is Asia's largest aluminum smelting and refining plant, and the automobile and motorbike industries, of which Chongqing is a China leader. The city burns considerable coal, leading to particulate pollution, sulfur dioxide pollution, and acid rain. There is also increasing pollution from automobile exhausts. All this is made worse by Chongqing's form as a city in river valleys surrounded by steep slopes. High humidity and other environmental factors made the city foggy on as many as 100 days per year, earning the Chongqing the nickname "Fog City." The fog is itself polluted. A recent scientific study conducted in Chongqing has concluded that pollution has resulted in a decline in sperm quality among resident men, leading to decreases in fertility.

Another critical problem is traffic congestion. The city is squeezed for space as is, given its location in valleys between steep slopes, but traffic conditions are made worse by more people and more automobiles, narrow roads, and few opportunities to build new ones or to widen existing streets. Where road construction does take place, it is typically at the expense of residences and businesses that have to be cleared to make way. The city's many bridges are traffic choke points. There has been some relief from new expressways and ring roads, as well as from construction of tunnels through mountains, but it seems that Chongqing is learning the lesson the hard way that that more you build or readjust a city to accommodate the automobile, the more automobiles there will be. There is investment in rail and subway transit as well, but they too are crowded, and the trajectory in China is for automobile ownership to continue growing as the population prospers. Unfortunately, bicycles and motorbikes are not as practical in Chongqing as they are in other Chinese cities because of hilly conditions and winding, narrow roads. Chongqing's traffic congestion adds to air pollution and to individuals' stress levels, and is also a costly impediment to efficient economic productivity.

FURTHER READING

Danielson, Eric N. "Chongqing," in *The Three Gorges and the Upper Yangzi* (Singapore: Marshall Cavendish/Times Editions, 2005, pp. 325–362).

Doyle, Christopher, "Air Pollution Lowers Sperm Quality," *Environment*, February 25, 2014, http://www.abc.net.au/environment/articles/2014/02/25/3951119.htm.

Watts, Jonathan, "Invisible City," *The Guardian*, March 15, 2006, http://www.theguardian.com/world/2006/mar/15/china.china.

CIUDAD JUAREZ, MEXICO

Ciudad Juárez (Juarez City; formerly known as Paso del Norte), is a city of just over 1.5 million inhabitants (2013) in Chihuahua State, Mexico, at the border with the United States. It is on the right bank of the Rio Grande, which Mexicans know as Río Brave del Norte, just south of El Paso, Texas. The combined metropolitan area of the two cities is about 2.7 million, making Ciudad Juárez–El Paso the second-largest metropolitan area at the U.S.–Mexico border, after that of Tijuana–San Diego. The city is very fast growing, as Mexican citizens from the interior and migrants from Guatemala, Honduras, and El Salvador further south move there because of jobs, and because the city is a gateway for legal and illegal entry to the United States. In 2010, the population of Ciudad Juárez was 1.3 million, in 2000 it was 1.2 million, and in 1990 it was 790,000. The city was founded by Spanish Franciscan friars in 1659 as a mission settlement, and then grew as a trading post between Spanish settlements on either side of the Rio Grande.

Like Tijuana and other cities on the Mexican side of the international border, Ciudad Juárez was once sustained by short-visit tourism from the United States and gambling, but has since grown to become an important center of manufacturing in the global economy. It is home to some 300 factories called *maquiladoras* (assembly plants) owned by American, Japanese, and European corporations who take advantage of cheaper wage rates in Mexico and less oversight than in home countries about working conditions and environmental concerns. There are also Mexican-owned companies. The companies also enjoy infrastructure improvements such as good highways and serviced pad sites, and free passage across the international border for parts, raw materials, and finished products. The factories are generally labor intensive and employ a workforce that is disproportionately female. Automotive components (including leather upholstery) and electronics are the two biggest sectors of the manufacturing industry, but there are also firms that produce plastics, medicines, and packaging, among other products. The first *maquiladoras* in Ciudad Juárez opened in 1965. Their numbers increased dramatically after the implementation of the North American Free Trade Agreement in 1994, with the result that manufacturing has become the mainstay of the local formal economy. More than 222,000 workers are now employed in the city's factories (2013).

We include Ciudad Juárez on our list of 20 least content cities in the world mostly of the city's very serious crime problem. The city is reported to have the highest murder rate in the world. Most famously, Ciudad Juárez is the site of the grisly "Juárez femicides," the tragic case of at minimum 370 young women, mostly workers in maquiladoras, who were found murdered in the city since the 1990s. Many of them had been tortured and their bodies mutilated. Another 400 women are missing in Ciudad Juárez under circumstances similar to those whose bodies had been found. The vast majority of the crimes are unsolved, and young women, especially factory workers, live in fear and take extraordinary precautions in going to and from their jobs. Simply riding the bus is not safe enough, because on remote routes women have been sexually assaulted and killed by bus drivers. Even where there have been arrests and convictions for individual murders, there is uncertainty about guilt because police have been accused of working in haste and using questionable methods to extract confessions and testimony from witnesses. An often-cited theory as to why so many women have been killed in Ciudad Juárez relates to traditional male patriarchal beliefs that women's work is in the home and resentment of women who are independently employed. A sad icon of the city is pink crosses that stand where bodies of the murdered had been found.

There is considerable gang violence in Ciudad Juárez as well. The city is base for the Juárez Cartel, one of the largest and bloodiest drugs trafficking organizations in Mexico. The gang also traffics in human beings and smuggles people across the international border to the United States, as well as engages arms trafficking, extortion, and kidnapping for profit. The gang members murder rivals and honest police without remorse, and use decapitation as a trademark to spread fear. Many police officers take bribes to not interfere with gang activities. The armed wing of the Juárez Cartel is called La Linea, and the gang's main rival to control the flow of cocaine and other drugs into the United States is the Sinaloa Cartel, an equally violent gang that was founded in the Mexican state of Sinaloa and that has claimed Chihuahua as part of its turf. Because of the gang wars, many people with a choice have left Ciudad Juárez and moved elsewhere for safety, and many businesses have shuttered. The worst might be over, as there was a peak in bloodshed in 2009–2010 and there is now an apparent truce between rival cartels, but the city is still very dangerous, and the gruesome femicides that made Ciudad Juárez famous around the world are still unsolved and continue.

The rapid industrial growth in Ciudad Juárez has brought jobs to many poor Mexicans, as well as increased profits for corporations. The city itself is much changed because of the new economy, with worsening problems of traffic, the worst air pollution along the U.S.–Mexico border, and substandard housing conditions, infrastructure, and social services in informal settlements called *colonias* where the poorest residents live. Young people often feel that they lack opportunities to get ahead, and turn to gangs and illicit business for social and economic security. Corruption is endemic. Community leaders, journalists, politicians, and law enforcement officials who try to make things better often wind up dead for getting in the way of drug lords. Even so, there are brave citizens and political leaders who work hard to turn things around, and to make Ciudad Juárez a more livable city. Still, however, social problems are many in this formerly sleepy border town that has been turned in a short time into a sprawling metropolis of laborers in the global economy at the doorstep to the United States.

FURTHER READING

Bowden, Charles, *Murder City: Ciudad Juárez and the Global Economy's New Killing Fields* (New York: Nation Books, 2010).

Rodriguez, Teresa and Diana Montané, *The Daughters of Juárez: A True Story of Serial Murder South of the Border* (New York: Atria Books, 2007).

Waldorf, Brigitte, "Localized Effects of Globalization: The Case of Ciudad Juárez, Chihuahua, Mexico, *Urban Geography*, 25, 2, 2004, pp. 120–138.

DHAKA, BANGLADESH

Dhaka is the capital and largest city of Bangladesh, a poor and crowded country in South Asia. It is one of the largest, fastest-growing, and most crowded cities in the word, and is also mostly poor. There are more than 7 million inhabitants in the city proper and 15 million in the metropolitan area. More than 80% of the metropolitan population lives below the poverty line, making Dhaka one of the world's largest concentrations of poor people on the planet. Poverty and environmental problems in the countryside continually push people off the land, sending as many as 400,000 new migrants to Dhaka every year, if not more. There is insufficient housing and employment for everyone, with the consequence that most new arrivals are relegated to residence in squatter settlements in marginal locations. Those who find employment do so mostly in what is called the informal sector where pay is typically meager and uncertain. The city has a growing middle class as well, as Bangladesh is finding footing in the global economy, particularly in the readymade garment (RMG) industry. There are better neighborhoods with good housing and good schools, but so far this is just a small part of the total picture in Dhaka. Sadly, the city's major characteristics are extreme crowding and poverty.

Increasingly, poor migrants who come to Dhaka arrive as environmental refugees. Bangladesh is extremely flood-prone because of heavy monsoon downpours in the June-to-October wet season, and because there are many large river channels in the country (most notably distributaries of the Ganges and Brahmaputra Rivers). Also most of the country is extremely flat and low-lying. Despite being an inland city, Dhaka itself is at less than 20 feet (6 meters) above sea level. For centuries, the flooding was a blessing because it replenished soils and watered farm fields, but now the floods are much more severe, causing farmers to lose both their crops and their lands. The increased flooding is because of greater population densities in the highlands where Bangladesh's rivers have their upper courses, and because of global climate change that brings on coastal flooding and saltwater incursions. Farmers and villagers are driven from their lands, and swell the country's cities. Dhaka attracts these migrants like a magnet, because it is the largest city and capital, and is located in the very center of the country, where it is accessible to the largest number of people. The city itself, however, is flooded more often, deeper, and for longer periods, so that for many residents, especially the poor who live in the most flood-prone neighborhoods, the misery continues.

Dhaka is called the "rickshaw capital of the world," although Kolkata, which is located in India near the border with Bangladesh, could also make a claim for the title. In both cities, rickshaws were once pulled by human power, but *rickshaw wallahs* have been replaced by bicycle-powered rickshaws and, more recently, by rickshaws with small engines powered by compressed natural gas. City officials in both Dhaka and Kolkata prefer motorized rickshaws because they are faster

Workers at a brick factory in Dhaka, Bangladesh, load bricks on a bicycle for delivery to purchasers. Labor is inexpensive in Bangladesh, and tasks that might otherwise seem inefficient when done by hand can actually be cost-effective. (Dmitry Chulov/iStockphoto.com)

and help keep traffic flowing on crowded roadways, but they are more expensive for drivers to purchase and more expensive for passengers to ride, so they are not as popular with the city's poor. Bicycle rickshaws have been banned from major roads and the central commercial districts of both cities, and serve primarily residential areas. In Dhaka, there are an estimated 400,000 rickshaws at work in the city, which calculates to an astounding one rickshaw for every 37.5 residents, including children and rickshaw drivers themselves. Only about 85,000 of the 400,000 rickshaws are licensed. City government wages a continual war with the owners of others in order to reduce the oversupply and the resultant street congestion, and orders occasional massive rickshaw round-ups. One can see tens of thousands confiscated bicycle rickshaws piled up in Dhaka's impoundment lots, but it seems that almost as soon as an illegal rickshaw is taken off the streets, another takes its place. Rickshaws are a prime source of employment for poor migrant males who have no other options for work. The work is hard and dangerous. Moreover, most drivers do not really work for themselves but for rickshaw bosses who take a large percentage of fares collected. The popularity of rickshaws in Dhaka is explained by the fact that fares are low and that passenger ride under a canopy that protects them from rain or sun. In the wet season, rickshaws can outperform motor vehicles because their high wheels are able to move through flooded streets. Fares are higher during these times, but hazards to drivers' health are much greater because they work in dangerously polluted waters.

There are as many as 5,000 slum neighborhoods or "clusters of slum housing" in Dhaka with a total population of well over 3 million. These areas are notorious for crowded living conditions, ramshackle dwellings, poor sanitation, and polluted water supplies, as well as high incidences of disease. Some neighborhoods are temporary, because they are in zones of annual flooding, but population pressure causes them to be built anew when waters recede. There are often slum clearance programs by municipal government, both to eradicate the worst living conditions and to clear land for other uses such as building construction and the widening of streets. This adds to the uncertainly faced by slum dwellers, who feel that they are unwanted and have no place to go. At the same time, there are many laudable efforts by government and by NGOs (nongovernmental organizations) to aid people in slum neighborhoods by providing health care, potable water, sanitation infrastructure, informal education programs, and financial assistance such as micro-credit for starting small business, among other steps. Among the lessons learned in problem-plagues cities like Dhaka is that solutions to poverty have to concentrate on the country as a whole, especially the countryside where investment and economic opportunities have been notoriously lacking, because improvements to the city itself, including economic development, simply cause more poor people to flood the city.

FURTHER READING

Begum, Sharifa, "Pulling Rickshaws in the City of Dhaka: A Way Out of Poverty," *Environment and Urbanization*, 12, 2, 2005, pp. 11–25.

Faruque, Dr. Cathleen Jo and Dr. Muhammad Samad, *The Invisible People: Poverty and Resiliency in the Dhaka Slums* (Frederick, MD: America Star Books, 2008).

Paul, Bimal Kanti, "Fear of Eviction: The Case of Slum and Squatter Dwellers in Dhaka, Bangladesh," *Urban Geography*, 27, 6, 200, pp. 567–574.

DONETSK, UKRAINE

Donetsk is an industrial city in eastern Ukraine that is occupied at the time of this writing by Russian troops and Russia-backed militants in a war against Ukrainian sovereign territory. It was never a great city to begin with, as it has been badly scarred by decades of mining and industry, and is badly polluted, but now that the city is the center of a deadly conflict and the target of missiles fired from one direction and the other, it was an easy choice for inclusion on our list of 20 least contented cities of the world. The city is presently in the control of the self-proclaimed Donetsk People's Republic, which depends on Russia for arms and supplies, although the Ukrainian government intends to win it back. Before the current conflict, the population of Donetsk was estimated to be 953,217 (2013), the fifth-largest total among cities in Ukraine, and the metropolitan area had over 2 million residents. The war, however, has greatly reduced both numbers, as refugees have left from the city itself and the surroundings to seek safety elsewhere. Although we have no reliable statistics, it seems clear that the number of refugees is well over 100,000 and that most of them have resettled in other parts of Ukraine. Many others have gone to Russia, and some have found their way to other countries in Europe.

Donetsk was founded in 1869 when eastern Ukraine was part of the czarist Russian Empire and John Hughes, a businessman from Wales, opened coal mines and built a steel plant. The settlement was named Yuzovka, a Russian-language corruption for Hughesovka ("Hughes's town"), although a smaller settlement that had existed there previously was named Aleksandrovka. The new industrial town attracted Welsh immigrants and prospered as a steel-making city and the hub of the Donbas, a critically important mining and heavy industrial district in the southern Russian Empire and later the Ukrainian Soviet Socialist Republic of the Soviet Union. In 1924, the Soviet leadership renamed the city after Stalin, first "Stalin" in 1924 and then "Stalino" in 1929. Because of the importance of its industrial base, the Germans completely destroyed the city as they advanced across Ukraine in World War II. The name "Donetsk" was adopted in 1961 as part of the de-Stalinization program in the Soviet Union at the time. The new name is taken from a local river, the North Don. During the Soviet period, Donetsk and its region were settled by transplants from Russia who were brought in as laborers. They also russified eastern Ukraine, and replaced the millions of Ukrainians who had perished in the 1932–1933 forced famine during Stalin's collectivization of Ukrainian farm lands.

The industrialization of Donetsk and the Donbas ("Don Basin") region in general came with a very steep environmental cost. The terrain was originally flat steppe and rich in agricultural productivity, but with time the land was disturbed by coal mining. There are shaft mines as well as strip mines, and huge piles of mine waste in all directions. Locally, these conical mountains of slag are called *terakony*. Not only are they unsightly, but they also contribute to groundwater and stream pollution, and create landslides in heavy rains. Donetsk is dotted with *terakony*. Furthermore, there are great labyrinths of mine tunnels and shafts directly below the city. Mine accidents occur often with deadly results, while above ground subsidence creates havoc with building foundations, roads, and rail lines. The air is foul too, because of emissions from steel mills and other industries. The local economy depends on mining and heavy industry, and the local culture is taught to lionize miners and industrial workers (e.g., the beloved local professional football [soccer] squad is called *Sakhtar*, the "miners"), but the bottom line is that Donetsk was made into a foul city. Neither Soviet government nor the government in independent Ukraine after 1991 ever did much to improve the city, as

Donetsk is a large industrial city in eastern Ukraine. The photo is of a coal miner after a day of work in a pit beneath the city, and is from a happier time, as now Donetsk and the region around it are caught in a war that was initiated by Russia in order to separate the area from Ukraine. Many people have died and much of the city is in ruins. (EdStock/iStockphoto.com)

the emphasis always seemed to be on industrial production instead of quality of life. As a result, many Donetsk neighborhoods have unpaved streets that turn to black, coal-dust mud in rainy periods and when winter snows melt, and houses that are no better than aging wooden cottages with outhouses in back and pumps to draw water from below ground. The planned apartment block neighborhoods for miners and industrial workers that the Soviets had built are especially low in quality and dilapidated. There are graffiti everywhere, and public spaces indoors and outdoors are in awful shape. The main streets of the city have a Soviet look, with grave government buildings, and spacious squares marked with statues that honor V.I. Lenin and other former Soviet leaders, industrial workers, and heroes of the war against Germany. There are new shopping malls, upscale hotels, and a beautiful new stadium for the Shakhtar team too, but these add up to only a small part of Donetsk. Most of the people are too poor to enjoy these points of luxury, and most of the city and all of the other industrial cities nearby are pretty much the same: sacrificed for the benefit of Soviet industry.

The post-Soviet period (after 1991) was marked by a chaotic period during which state property became privatized, and the rise of well-connected oligarchs who came to control entire industries and acquired fabulous fortunes. Donetsk became an especially corrupt city and stronghold of corrupt politicians. It was the home base of Viktor Yanukovych, a former street thug who won election to Ukraine's presidency in 2010, and who was eventually run out of office in February 2014 by the Maidan revolution of 2013–2014 in the national capital, Kyiv, and other Ukrainian cities. He and his associates had amassed huge personal fortunes from the national treasury and planned to move the country back into the Russian fold. His ouster from office was a victory for the Ukrainian people, but it caused Russia's Vladimir Putin to turn to Plan B in an attempt to control Ukraine, the hijacking of Crimea in March 2014, followed by the war in Ukraine's east that has destroyed much of Donetsk and turned many of its residents into refugees. There were especially hard-fought battles for control of Donetsk's beautiful new international airport. The result was many lives lost by pro-Russian separatists and Ukrainian forces alike, and the total destruction of the airport itself.

FURTHER READING

Kuromiya, Hiroaki, *Freedom and Terror in the Donbas: The Ukrainian-Russian Borderland, 1870s–1900s* (Cambridge: Cambridge University Press, 1998).

Motyl, Alexander J., "A Free Donetsk?" *World Affairs*, January 10, 2014, http://www.worldaffairsjournal.org/blog/alexander-j-motyl/free-donetsk.

Reid, Anna, *Borderland: A Journey through the History of Ukraine* (Boulder, CO: Westview, 1997, pp. 46–69).

Siegelbaum, Lewis H. and Daniel J. Walkowitz, *Workers of the Donbass Speak: Survival and Identity in the New Ukraine, 1989–1992* (Albany: State University of New York Press, 1995).

Taylor, Alan, "The Battle for Donetsk," *The Atlantic PHOTO*, October 13, 2014, http://www.theatlantic.com/photo/2014/10/the-battle-for-donetsk/100831/.

DUBAI, UNITED ARAB EMIRATES

Dubai is simultaneously a prominent Middle Eastern city in a country named the United Arab Emirates and one of the seven emirates, that is, political territories that are ruled by dynastic Islamic rulers called *emirs*, that comprise the UAE. The country is in the southeast of the Arabian Peninsula and borders the Persian Gulf, while Dubai is on the Persian Gulf in the northeast of the UAE. The urbanized part of the emirate of Dubai runs along the shoreline. The area has a hot desert climate and the terrain is covered with fine sand comprised of crushed shells and coral. There are high sand dune ridges located inland from the built-up area of Dubai. The city is the largest in the UAE, with a population of 2,106,177 (2013). Most residents are foreigners, as Emiratis make up only about 17% of the total, and Indians are, in fact, the majority population in Dubai, making up about 53%

of the total. Pakistanis are in third place with 13.3% of the population, and Bangladeshis are in fourth place with 7.5%. The vast majority of these South Asians, as well as many other foreigners in Dubai, are laborers or service workers. We say more about them here.

Dubai is a fast-growing city with a fast-growing economy and a fast-rising skyline. As recently as 1900 the city's population was only about 10,000, and in 1960 it was only 40,000, but then over the latter half of the 20th century, the city was purposefully developed to be a hub for global business and trade, and it grew at an extraordinarily rapid rate. Oil revenues are responsible for part of the growth, but unlike other states along the Persian Gulf, Dubai is not especially rich in oil resources. Oil accounts for only about 5% of the Emirate's revenue. Dubai's strategy, instead, has been to exploit its geographical location between the large economies of Europe and those of Asia, and to specialize in trade, high-end and specialty retailing, business services, and tourism. The city is also tied economically to North America, a major consumer of oil from the Arabian Peninsula, and Africa, the Indian Ocean coast of which is relatively nearby. A large new port built in 1979 and the establishment of the Jebel Ali Free Trade Zone nearby helped to attract foreign companies to Dubai where they could benefit from various tax

A large public space outside a large new shopping mall near the Burj Khalifa, the world's tallest building. Dubai is a rapidly growing city with countless new buildings and attractions for residents and visitors alike. (Roman Cybriwsky)

advantages, modern infrastructure, and comfortable living conditions for expatriate employees. As the city developed, it became one of the world's most ambitious construction projects—ever—and a showpiece of architecture and urban design that can be described only as amazing, unique, and over-the-top. The most famous structure is the 2,722-feet (830-meter) high Burj Khalifa, which was completed in 2010 and is the world's tallest man-made structure. Other landmarks are the Burj Al Arab, a hotel building shaped like a traditional Middle Eastern *dhow* (a sailing vessel), and said to be the most expensive hotel in the world; Palm Jumeirah, a huge offshore residential and commercial development that is shaped like a palm tree; and World Islands, a yet unfinished series of man-made islands about 2.5 miles (4 km) offshore in the Persian Gulf that extend for about 5.6 miles (9 km) by 3.7 miles (6 km) and are shaped like individual countries on a giant map of the world. The city has beaches, an indoor ski slope, camel racing, traditional Middle Eastern markets, and some of the largest and most spectacular shopping malls in the world. All of it a sight to behold, and tourists come from all over the world to see and enjoy.

The business strategy of Dubai and its urban plan are the responsibility of the Sheikh Mohammed bin Rashid Al Maktoum, the all-powerful *emir* of Dubai. The Al Maktoum family has ruled Dubai since 1833, and makes all the decisions. In this case, the decisions have produced an exceedingly impressive and prosperous city seemingly out of nothing, and have given Emirati citizens a strong economy, excellent services, including health care and education, and ample opportunities to enjoy life. Many Emiratis enjoy racing ATVs in the desert, betting on camel races, hunting with falcons, traveling around the globe, and shopping, shopping, shopping. Many foreign expats live very well in Dubai too, with high pay, luxurious housing, and excellent benefits and services for their dependents. Tourists also have a blast, as we have said.

Then why is Dubai on this list of least contented world cities, and not among the most contented cities instead? Here, we return to the South Asian workers mentioned earlier, and to other foreigners such as Iranians, Palestinians, and East Africans, whose lot in the city is miserable. They have come from poverty to work, and work is what they do. Typically, they labor in gangs, in uniforms in the hot sun, put in long hours for low pay, and at the end of the day are transported by labor gang buses to camps outside the city where they are housed. There are no amenities there, and often only metal barracks with bunk beds one next to the other. But even if there were amenities, there would be little time to enjoy them, because the next morning the bus awaits to take them to the work site. There is little time off and almost no opportunity to enjoy Dubai. Sometimes workers are cheated of their wages. That is how Dubai was built and that is how it stays clean and green thanks to a silent army of foreign sweepers, trash collectors, gardeners, and irrigators of golf courses. That is the story about male laborers. Foreign women labor in

Dubai too as home maids and hotel room sheet changers, in kitchens, and in child care. They, too, are kept on a short leash, often by employers who hold their passports. Moreover, some women have been trafficked to Dubai, and are trapped as sex workers. Until the practice was stopped in about 2005 because of an international outcry, Dubai also employed very young and very slight boys from Pakistan and India as camel jockeys at the camel races. Now there are remote-controlled robots that whip the camels during races.

Exploited workers represent the majority of people in Dubai. They are not citizens, and they are not tourists—they are simply exploited for labor like slaves. There are no ifs ands, or buts about it: the good life in Dubai (and a few other places in the world that work similarly) is on the backs of people who, quite emphatically, are not contented. Open criticism of these conditions is not allowed in Dubai, and an essay such as this one can result in denial of entry to the UAE the next time we travel there. There is no democracy in Dubai, and the 17% of the population that has a great deal, as well as high-living foreigners, knows to keep silent about the unfairness around them lest they lose the comforts they have.

FURTHER READING

Ali, Syed, *Dubai: Gilded Cage* (New Haven, CT: Yale University Press, 2010).

Davidson, Christopher, *Dubai: The Vulnerabilities of Success* (New York: Columbia University Press, 2009).

Krane, Jim, *City of Gold: Dubai and the Dream of Capitalism* (New York: St. Martin's Press, 2009).

DZERZHINSK, RUSSIA

Dzerzhinsk is a city that not many people outside Russia have heard of, but those who know it and those who have studied its history of industrial production and pollution know that it is one of the most heavily polluted places on the planet and that it is extremely dangerous to health. It is a terrible place even by the standards of Russia, which has many gravely polluted and ugly industrial cities, and where many public services are neglected and antiquated. Yet, the city is not in some remote corner of the vast country, but is located in Russia's European heartland, on the Oka River about 250 miles (400 km) east of the national capital, Moscow.

Dzerzhinsk has origins that date to 1606 and was once known as Rastyapino. It became a prominent urban center during the 1920s and 1930s when it was built up under the authority of the Soviet Union with military-strategic industries and was officially classified as a secret city. That means that it was closed to foreigners, closed to Russians without official business and permissions, and was not shown on maps or discussed in encyclopedias and other sources. There were other cities of this category as well in the secretive Soviet state. Adding to the darkness about the city is its name: Dzerzhinsk was named in 1929 after Felix Dzerzhinsky (1877–1926), a noted Bolshevik Revolutionary leader who became the first chief of the Cheka, the notorious Soviet secret police (and precursor of the NKVD and the KGB) that was responsible for tens of thousands of summary executions of suspected political enemies and class enemies. He is, therefore, associated with the worst of the Red Terror and his name is highly controversial. While other Russian cities have "softened" their names away from communist leadership (e.g., Leningrad reverted to St. Petersburg and Stalingrad became Volgograd), Dzerzhinsk seems stuck in the past and retains its name.

It is the chemicals industry that made Dzerzhinsk so polluted, most notoriously the manufacture of chemical weapons such as lewisite, an organoaresnic compound that acts as a blister agent and lung irritant, and yperite, also known as sulfur mustard gas. The manufacture of chemical weapons started in 1941 in World War II, and ended in 1965. The hazards, however, remain because huge quantities of waste containing high levels of arsenic were buried on factory grounds and have not been removed. A specific dump site in the city is referred to as a "white sea" of chemical wastes. Likewise, the most dangerous of the factories have not been fully disassembled and are hazardous sites. The environmental agency in the city of Dzerzhinsk estimates that some 300,000 tons of hazardous chemical waste were dumped in the city between 1930 and 1998. The city still has some 38 large industrial facilities and continues to be a leading producer of chemicals, including cyanide in a factory that dates to 1915 and various munitions and explosives.

Reliable data are hard to come by, but the New York–based Blacksmith Institute, now named Pure Earth, a non-for-profit international organization that monitors environmental hazards worldwide, has listed Dzerzhinsk among the world's 10 most polluted places. Its report cites persistent dioxins, sarin, lewisite, sulfur mustard, hydrogen cyanide, phosgene, and lead as the most dangerous chemicals, and adds that the city's water is contaminated with dioxins and phenol at levels that are reported to be 17 million times the safe limit. Such information prompted the Guinness Book of World Records to name Dzerzhinsk as the world's most polluted city in 2007. Because of the pollution, life expectancy rates in the city are extraordinarily low: 42 years for men and 47 years for women as reported by the Blacksmith Institute. Furthermore, in 2003 the death rate is said to have exceeded the birth rate by 260%. Local sources in Dzerzhinsk have disputed the Blacksmith report, saying that pollution is "moderate" by Russian standards, that life expectancy rates are much higher, and that there is continual progress in cleaning up the toxins, but other sources continue to stress that the environment is seriously polluted. High levels of phenol in the air are said to be the main contributor to high cancer rates of the eyes, lungs, and kidneys, and to resultant deaths. A study that was published in 2013 reported that residents who live near industrial and mining areas have much higher rates of chronic coughing with sputum than people living further way, but also concluded that all residents of Dzerzhinsk are at risk in their city.

Whatever the pollutants, it is indisputable that Dzerzhinsk is a city in trouble. Its population is plummeting. According to the 2010 census, the city's population was 240,742; in 2002 it was 261,334, and in 1989 it was 285,071. (Before then, the city was closed and the Soviet Union did not produce census data for the city.) The decline is because of more people are dying than are being born, very few people chose to move in, and large numbers chose to move out. Young people leave the city in disproportionate numbers, many being attracted to the glamor of Moscow or opportunities to leave Russia altogether, and the overall population of the city ages as a result. On inspection, Dzerzhinsk is not an appealing city, industrial decline and industrial pollution aside. It was laid out by Soviet city planners in a rigid of radial streets with trolley lines that radiate like wheel spokes from a central square, and large expanses of dull, unadorned, identical apartment blocks with few amenities. The Soviet priority was always industrial production, and investments in housing and good neighborhoods lagged. Other Soviet-built cities have similar characteristics, but in the case of Dzerzhinsk there is a statue of the murderous Felix Dzerzhinsky still standing in the central square.

FURTHER READING

"Environmental Disaster in Dzerzhinsk," 2011, http://survincity.com/2011/02/environmen tal-disaster-indzerzhinsk/.

Specter, Michael and Stanley Greene, "The Most Tainted Place on Earth," *New York Times,* 147, 51062, February 28, 1998, p. 48, 5pp.

JAKARTA, INDONESIA

Jakarta is the capital and largest city of Indonesia, a sprawling archipelago nation in Southeast Asia. The city is on the northwest coast of the island of Java, Indonesia's most populous island, and is an important port and business center in addition to being the center of government for the world's fourth- most populous nation. According to official estimates for 2012, Jakarta has a population of 9,761,407 inhabitants, the highest total for a city in Southeast Asia. The Jakarta metropolitan area, which is known by the awkward name Jabodetabek, has a population of more than 28 million, and is the world's second-most populous metropolitan area after that of Tokyo. "Jabodetabek" comes from combining the first syllables of the main cities in the metropolis: Jakarta, Bogor, Depok, Tangerang, and Bekasi. In colonial times, the city was the capital of the Dutch East Indies and was named Batavia. Jakarta is in many ways a great urban center that reflects Indonesia's rapid economic growth and diverse cultural traditions, but it, along with the sprawling urban areas that adjoin it, is a crowded and chaotic urban mess and a nightmare for city planners. We know firsthand that life can be very difficult in Jakarta, and therefore have included the city on our list of the 20 least contented cities in the world. We could have listed Manila or Bangkok, or Medan or Surabaya elsewhere in Indonesia, instead of Jakarta for this list, but chose Jakarta to stand for them all because it is so enormous and its problems area so grave.

Some of the most serious problems are environmental. Jakarta occupies a low-lying marshy plain that faces Jakarta Bay in the Java Sea. The inland zones are hilly, but closer to the sea Jakarta is extremely flood-prone from overflowing rivers during the summer rainy season. Entire neighborhoods get flooded during this time, as do key roadways and interchanges, and the city's traffic becomes a nightmare. The problem is becoming worse as Jakarta sinks of its own weight into the muck, bringing more and more of the city below sea level. Withdrawal of groundwater exacerbates the subsidence. The floods of 2007 inundated 70% of the city and killed 57 people. The city was inundated again in 2008 and the airport was closed. There was major flooding again in 2012 and 2013. Engineers are considering a network of dikes to hold back the bay and dams to regulate the flow of rivers, as well as improvements to canals and the dredging of rivers.

The city also suffers from severe traffic congestion. The mass transit system is grossly underdeveloped, and it is only now that a modern rail system is being constructed. Subways are impossible because of ground conditions. A network of highways and boulevards was constructed to accommodate motor vehicle traffic, but key roads are often hopelessly jammed and what should be routine travel within the city seemingly takes forever and becomes exhausting. A "stop-start" index named after the motor vehicle product Castrol has revealed that of all cities in the world, Jakarta has the worst traffic conditions. Furthermore, many cars, buses, and motorbikes are noisy and lack adequate exhaust systems, so air and noise pollution are chronic problems. Vendors walk among the cars stalled in traffic and sell everything from snacks and bottled water, to cigarettes, newspapers, and lottery tickets. Even walking can be problematic, as sidewalks are often crowded with street vendors and food stalls, and with illegally parked cars. Many of the city's poor live in informal settlements that have sprung up at the urban outskirts. For them, getting into the city is especially costly and time-consuming.

A representative photograph of Jakarta shows a dramatic skyline of impressive office and residential towers as a backdrop to a view of crowded low-rise *kampungs* (neighborhoods) with the city's iconic red-tile roofs. The contrast is meant to reflect Jakarta rising from poverty. However, what we and other observers have observed is that in Jakarta (and the other cities named earlier), wealth and privilege push against poverty and displace the poor who are then forced to find accommodations elsewhere. It is not just a matter of a space to live, but also about making a living, as many street vendors and small stalls are displaced by a modernization of the city that zones them out in favor of shopping centers. Likewise, inexpensive informal "taxi" systems such as *ojek* (back of a motorcycle), *becak* (bicycle rickshaw), and bajaj (three-wheeled auto rickshaw) are often zoned out of key districts of the city and off busy thoroughfares because they are seen as inappropriate for the modernizing city. This, too, takes work away from the struggling poor, as well as an affordable service that other poor Jakartans depend on. A book by anthropologist Lea Jellinek called *The Wheel of Fortune* describes these conflicts in detail. It was published in 1991, but is still accurate today, as more and more poor Indonesians stream into the capital city in search of opportunity, and find that modern Jakarta does not want them.

Finally, we note that the city is beset with political and religious conflict, and with protests and demonstrations that occasionally become violent. Indonesia is rich in oil and other natural resources, but there is considerable government corruption and favoritism in the economy that results in grossly unequal distribution of wealth. Widespread poverty has increased people's anger and also exacerbated crime. The Intelligence Unit of the *Economist* has calculated a Safe Cities Index that is based on four variables, digital security, health security, infrastructure security, and personal safety, and found that Jakarta ranks last in the world in 2015 out of 50 prominent cities that were surveyed.

FURTHER READING

Abeyasekere, Susan, *Jakarta: A History* (New York: Oxford University Press, 1987).

Cybriwsky, Roman and Larry R. Ford, "Jakarta," *Cities: International Journal of Urban Policy and Planning*, 18, 3, 2001, pp. 199–210.

Firman, Tommy, "From 'Global City' to 'City of Crisis:' Jakara Metropolitan Region under Economic Turmoil," *Habitat International*, 23, 4, 1999, pp. 447–466.

Jellinek, Lea, *The Wheel of Fortune: The History of a Poor Community in Jakarta* (Honolulu: University of Hawaii Press, 1991).

Rukmana, Deden, "The Megacity of Jakarta: Problems, Challenges and Planning Efforts," *Indonesia's Urban Studies*, March 29, 2014, http://indonesiaurbanstudies.blogspot.com/2014/03/the-megacity-of-jakarta-problems.html.

KARACHI, PAKISTAN

Karachi is the largest city in Pakistan, the second-largest city in the world when "city" is defined by official municipal limits, the largest city in the Muslim world, and the world's seventh-largest metropolitan area. It was Pakistan's first capital when the country became independent in 1947 and remained so until 1959 when the seat of government was moved to Rawalpindi during construction of the new permanent capital city, Islamabad. The city continues to be Pakistan's leading financial, industrial, and media center, as well as the country's main port. There are many pluses to Karachi, as reflected in nicknames such as "the bride of cities" and "city of lights," the latter reportedly because of active nightlife, but the combination of explosive population growth, excessive crowding, and many serious social and environmental problems has caused us to include it in this group of 20 least contented cities in the world.

Karachi was once a much happier place. Although now few people would think of freely visiting the city for almost any reason, much less for a holiday, in the 1960s and 1970s Karachi was a busy hub of international tourism, and especially an important stop on the backpackers' "hippie trail" from Europe through Turkey, Afghanistan, and on to India and Nepal. It offered low prices, a nightlife scene replete with bars, popular music, dancing, alcohol, and hashish, as well as recreational beaches on the Arabian Sea. It was a place to rest after overland treks through mountains and desert. The city was safe, and foreigners had no worries about terrorists, political kidnappings, and outbreaks of rioting. But all that began to change in the 1980s when Karachi began to grow out of control, and political unrest coupled with religious and ethnic conflict began to tear the city apart. Conditions worsened from the 1970s onward as the Middle East exploded with wars and revolutions in nearby countries such as Iran, Afghanistan, and Iraq, and with the rise of Islamic fundamentalism in the region. Pakistan was sucked into the fighting as a supply route for arms and a staging place for new recruits for the conflicts, and was torn internally between being an ally of the United States and the conflicting demands of radical Islam. Karachi drew ever greater numbers of destitute refugees from the wars, and spiraled downward to become a poor, overcrowded, and dangerously politicized metropolis. There are still some fine neighborhoods and new subdivisions where life is comfortable for those who can afford to surround themselves with heavy security, but the core of the city has become an unstable pit of poverty and sectarian strife.

If anything, the city is now famous for periodic outbreaks of bloody rioting. This history began with the partition of India and Pakistan as the British colonialists left South Asia in 1947, and the rioting that ensued between Muslims and Hindus. This tragic episode was soon followed by conflict between Karachi's locals, the so-called Sindhis from Pakistan's Sindh Province of which Karachi is capital, and the city's Mohajir population, Muslims who had settled in the city after they were forced to flee India during its partition into separate countries for Muslims and Hindus. Other ethnic groups were also drawn into the city's conflicts, most notably the city's Pashtun minority, a people from the Pakistan-Afghanistan borderland, as well as students, laborers, and various political parties from time to time, irrespective of ethnicity. Conflict has been an annual occurrence in the city, with major riots resulting in multiple deaths in at least the following years after 1947: 1986, 1988, 2007, 2010, and 2012. A 2012 article by Sabir Shah in a major Pakistani newspaper has counted 91 major terrorism incidents in Karachi in 64 years since 1947 and 30 times during this period when the city was under imposed curfew. As an indicator that the violence is more recent than historic, the article notes that two-thirds of these incidents have taken place since the September 11, 2001, attack against the World Trade Center in New York City. Karachi has also had more than its share of political assassinations. The gangland-style killing of member of Parliament Raza Haider on August 2, 2010, set offs riots that left scores dead, while on February 13, 2103, a beloved social worker among the city's poor, Parveen Rehman, was gunned down apparently by mobsters who had long threatened to kill her because of her tireless work to protect impoverished neighborhoods from being torn down by shady land developers.

Reliable data are hard to come by for Karachi, especially about the city's poor people, but it is estimated that about one-half of the city's population is impoverished and that an equal number of people live in illegal or "irregular" neighborhoods that are called *katchi abadis*. Translated as "temporary settlements," they arose with the influx of population to the city in 1947 and proved themselves to be anything but temporary. Some of the older squatter communities have since petitioned successfully to be legally recognized, but new ones are being established every year with an influx of poor migrants, and their numbers and total number of inhabitants are growing. The mushrooming of *katchi abadis* is seen as an impediment to economic progress and modernization in Karachi, and there is considerable support among the middles class of the city and local business leaders to raze them so that something else can be built in their place. Consequently, the poor are continually at risk of being evicted from their dwellings; helping them stay in their homes in a famous slum neighborhood called Orangi Town is what got Ms Rehman killed. Diseases are commonplace in Orangi Town and other *katchi abadis*, as most residents live in overcrowded conditions without adequate fresh water and sanitation.

FURTHER READING

Gayer, Laurent, *Karachi: Ordered Disorder and the Struggle for the City* (Oxford: Oxford University Press, 2014).

Inskeep, Steve, *Instant City: Life and Death in Karachi* (New York: Penguin Books, 2012).

Pakistan Institute of Legislative Development and Transparency (PILDAT), "Ethnic Conflict in Sindh: October 2011," http://www.pildat.org/publications/publication/Conflict_management/EthnicConflictinSindhOctober2011.pdf.

Shah, Sabir, "91 Major Incidents of Terrorism Haunted Karachi in 64 Years," *The News*, May 4, 2012, http://www.thenews.com.pk/Todays-News-6–106417–91-major-terrorism-incidents-haunted-Ka.

KINSHASA, DEMOCRATIC REPUBLIC OF THE CONGO

Kinshasa is a city with enormous problems. Were it not for the fact that our 20 most discontent cities in the world are listed here in alphabetical order, where Kinshasa falls approximately in the middle, it would be listed at or near the top of the world's most miserable cities. With a population of more than 9 million, this capital city of the Democratic Republic of the Congo (DRC) is the third-largest urban center on the African continent and one of the largest concentrations of abject poverty in the entire world. Additionally, the city is severely lacking basic necessities for most of its residents, including fresh water, sanitation, decent housing, and public transportation. Yet, the DRC is enormously rich in natural resources, especially mineral wealth where it is a world leader, from which its population could live well. Instead, for decades the natural wealth of the country has been appropriated by corrupt political elites and by foreign mining companies. For this reason, we not only discuss the city here as among the worst in the world, but also in a separate section of this book we discuss the country as a whole as one of the world's least contented.

Although Kinshasa has more than 9 million inhabitants, it is not yet a century and a half old, meaning that population growth rates are extraordinarily high. The city was founded in 1881 as a colonial trading post at a strategic point along the lower reaches of the Congo River by Henry Morton Stanley, and was named Léopoldville after Belgium's King Leopold II, for whom the vast territory along the Congo was a personal possession and source of immense personal wealth. In 1966, after colonial rule ended, it was renamed Kinshasa after a village that had preceded the colonial city. Today the sprawling city is a great mix of African tribal groups and languages, especially Lingala, a Bantu-family tongue that dominates a significant part of the DRC near Kinshasa and some neighboring countries, but the official language of the country and the language of interethnic communication remains French from the Belgian period. In fact, Kinshasa is the largest French-speaking city in the world after Paris. There is, however, considerable French vocabulary that is of local origin and that is not heard in standard French. Residents call their city "Kin" for short, and are themselves "Kinois," a French word that is also common in English usage about the city. As expressed in a popular guidebook to the DRC (Lonely Planet series), locals once referred to Kinshasa as Kin la Belle ("beautiful Kinshasa"), but after the city became overwhelmed with poverty, population growth, and urban problems, they darkly redubbed the city Kin la Poubelle, "Kinshasa the trashcan."

The ecological conditions in Kinshasa are truly problematic. Other than rainwater, the water supply for most of the population is the Congo River and its tributaries, which is also where the sewage of the city and surroundings winds up. Few streets are paved, and during the wet season most are muddy messes infused with sewage and other waste. Mounds of trash abound in the city and attract vermin, flies, and other insects. The city smells as a result. The air is further polluted by dry-season dust, and by the belching of black smoke from countless microbuses, motorbikes, pickup trucks, and automobiles with deficient exhaust systems. The city is noisy, too, from the motor vehicles and urban crowding. The hot and steamy tropical climate adds to the miseries.

The social environment is equally problematic. Poverty is endemic. Most people live in poor, crowded conditions in shantytown neighborhoods without basic services or amenities. While some areas manage to improve with time as long-term residents work together to upgrade community facilities and their own dwellings, in much of Kinshasa the trajectory is downward with ever more crowding as population increases with continually heavy rural-to-urban migration. The city sprawls endlessly without plan, and merges imperceptibly with villages and farm plots at the margins. Crime is a major problem, as Kinshasa is considered to be one of the world's most dangerous cities. Public officials and police are widely corrupt, and many enter their professions not to serve the public but to extract bribes. It seems that nothing gets done in the city without payoffs, shakedowns, and tips. The city is also notorious for street children, many of whom are orphans or refugees from domestic violence and abuse. About 20,000 youngsters under the age of 18 live on the streets and survive by begging or by working odd jobs such as street vending.

Vendors are everywhere in the city, competing for space equally with potential clients and other vendors, and are loud and persistent with calls to passerby to note their wares. Their incomes are minimal, and prospects for meaningful improvements in how they live are slim. In order to survive on a day-to-day basis, people learn to be creative and entrepreneurial, and to work extremely hard. In their own, French words for how they live, Kinois rely on their own *débrouillardise*, meaning resourcefulness, in order to *se débrouiller*, "to get by" or "to manage." Another term comes from the Lingala language: *kobeta libanga*. It originated during the time of forced labor under Belgian colonization, and means "to break stones." Today, the term refers to the fact that people will do any work available to get by.

Yet, Congolese continue to migrate to Kinshasa in great numbers, reflecting that the lure of the city is strong because life is even harder in the countryside. Each year, hundreds of thousands of new arrivals are added to the city's total. This adds even more demand for services and facilities that are already way short in supply: affordable schools, housing, employment opportunities, transportation, and medical care—even water and simple foodstuffs. There are prosperous Congolese who live in beautiful houses in exclusive neighborhoods under very strong security, as well as some exclusive shopping centers and entertainment places for those with money. There is also a vibrant intellectual life, as the city has three universities and an art school, and a tradition of excellent popular music and dance performances with local cultural infusion. On the whole, however, Kinshasa is a city with enormous problems and millions of residents whose lives are mired in poverty. A number of other African cities have similar problems, including Brazzaville, the 1.4 million population capital of the Republic of the Congo that is across the Congo River from Kinshasa and within sight, but we have singled out Kinshasa because of its distressing combination of enormous, fast-growing population and miserable conditions.

FURTHER READING

De Boeck, Filip and Marie-Françoise Plissart, *Kinshasa: Tales of the Invisible* City (Leuven, Belgium: Leuven University Press, 2014.

Draper, Robert, "Kinshasa: Urban Pulse of the Congo," *National Geographic*, September 2013, http://ngm.nationalgeographic.com/2013/09/kinshasa-congo/draper-text.

Shiner, Cindy, "Congo-Kinshasa: A City's Modern March of Hope," *allAfrica*, June 11, 2012, http://allafrica.com/stories/201206111872.html.

Trefon, Theodore, *Reinventing Order in the Congo: How People Respond to State Failure in Kinshasa* (London: Zed Books, 2005).

LAGOS, NIGERIA

Lagos is a giant city in Nigeria, a country in West Africa that is the continent's most populous nation, the seventh-most populous country in the world (2014 population: 178,516,904), and recently the fastest-growing country among the world's 25 most populous nations (2013–2014 population change: +2.82%). The city itself has a population of 17,390,000 (2013 estimate), about one-tenth of the nation's total. It is not only the most populous city and metropolitan region in Nigeria, but also the most populous city by far on the African continent and one of the biggest in world, ranking at #5 by at least one definition. Because of extra fast growth, it is poised to rise soon to #2 in the world, behind only Tokyo, which is far ahead of all other metropolitan areas in the world in population. Lagos is swollen with people and traffic almost beyond belief, and is considered to be among the most hectic and least livable cities on earth. In 2014, the intelligence unit of the *Economist* ranked Lagos as the third-worst city on the planet, after #1 Dhaka and #2 Port Moresby, cities that are also discussed on these pages as among the world's least contented places.

Lagos is located in southwestern Nigeria on the Atlantic coast where it is a major port. It grew from an indigenous African (Awori) settlement that was given the name Eko in 15th century when it was part of the Benin Empire, and was remade into "Lagos" by Portuguese explorers near the end of the century. The name means "lakes" in Portuguese, and refers to the lagoons that the Portuguese encountered when seeing Eko, as well as to the city of Lagos in Portugal from whence the country's navigators sailed. In the 19th century the city was incorporated into England's empire in Africa, and in 1914 it was designated to be the capital of Britain's Colony and Protectorate of Nigeria. It remained capital after Nigerian independence in 1960 until 1991 when the capital was relocated to a specially built new city in the interior, Abuja. One of the reasons for moving the capital from Lagos was that the city had become too big and unwieldy, and planners had recommended decentralization of its economic functions to slow its growth. The city's unwieldiness is exacerbated by its site, which has proven to be inappropriate for a giant metropolis. Lagos is a series of islands, lagoons, sand bars, and a peninsular mainland that is tied together by bridges. Such geography assures that traffic will always be a nightmare, that time and money will be forever lost in the city's famous "stand-stills," that stagnant water will accumulate the worst of pollutants, and that even the beaches where tides wash in and out will be dirty. The hot and steamy tropical climate worsens the sanitations situation and enables the spread of disease.

Nigeria is one of the world's leading petroleum-exporting nations, and the wealth that is generated from this and other businesses is evident in Lagos alongside the city's many problems. The Central Business District, located on Lagos Island, is booming and modern, with tall skyscrapers, fine restaurants and hotels, and other trappings of a successful global city. Nearby are desirable neighborhoods with nice apartments and hotels, a lively nightlife, and one of the best music scenes in the world. Some of the prestige neighborhoods are near beaches. But even the rich get caught in traffic, and cannot escape the foul air, incessant noise, and high humidity of the outdoors.

The other Lagos is poor. A recent article in *Nigerian Tribune* reports that more than 11 million people, representing nearly three-quarters of the city's population, reside in slums. One of the most famous slums, indeed in all of Africa, is called Makoko. It grew from a fishing village on Lagos Lagoon near the heart of the city, and is now home to more than 100,000 people living in ramshackle wooden houses on stilts in the water and connected to one another and the rest of the city by rickety gangways and small boats. These areas often lack adequate freshwater resources and basic sanitation, utilities, and even roads, have poor-quality housing, are overcrowded, and are often located at remote distances from job centers and other opportunities to get ahead. Crime and drug abuse are common, while police are corrupt and do little to make people feel safer. Instead, the slums are the domain of the so-called area boys or *agberos*—gangs of street children and teenagers who steal, extort money from locals and strangers alike, operate protection rackets, and act as informal security forces to protect neighbors from everyone but themselves. Such gangs roam the business center too. Indeed, street crime is a problem everywhere in Lagos, and the city is one of the world's most dangerous places to live or do business.

There are many laudable investment projects that are intended to fix Lagos, but Nigeria is one of the most corrupt countries in the world, and whatever new

Many women in African cities such as Lagos, Nigeria, work as street vendors. This woman is selling bread in her neighborhood. (Fridah/iStockphoto.com)

bridge or roadway is built, new water and sewer lines are installed, or industrial district is unveiled, there has been corruption at every step and enormous cost overruns. A new district of the city that will be built along the city's shoreline and is to be called Eko Atlantic promises to be a showpiece, but will almost certainly make the rich richer, be fraught with corruption, and not help the poor. Nigeria could be a much better place if corruption were to be brought under control. Other problems loom, not the least of which are that the terrorist group Boko Haram is causing great harm in northern Nigeria, and its effects are hurting the economy nationwide, including Lagos where the group could spread its campaign of bombings and kidnappings; and that the Ebola virus has recently spread to the city from nearby countries and could be truly devastating.

FURTHER READING

Adadibu, Afolabi A. and A. A. Okekunle, "Issues in Environmental Sanitation in Lagos Mainland, Nigeria," *The Environmentalist*, 9, 2, 1989, pp. 91–100.

Campbell, John, *Nigeria: Dancing on the Brink* (Lanham, MD: Rowman and Littlefield, 2013).

"Lagos and Its Slum Population, *Nigerian Tribune*, September 13, 2013, http://www.tribune .com.ng/news2013/index.php/en/editorial/item/21436-lagos-and-its-slum-population .html.

Whiteman, Kaye, *Lagos: A Cultural History* (Northampton, MA: Interlink Books, 2013).

MARSEILLE, FRANCE

Marseille is the second-largest city in France, after Paris, and an important port on the Mediterranean Sea. According to the census of 2011, its population is 850,636, while that of the metropolitan area is 1,720,941. The metropolitan area ranks third in France, after Paris and Lyon. The city is very cosmopolitan, as the port of Marseille has been a gateway to France for immigrants from diverse countries for many centuries. The city has also been important as a port-based commercial center and as a base for the French navy. It has a picturesque setting and a pleasant climate, and is a popular destination for tourism. However, the city also has social and environmental problems that are among the worst in Europe, and has therefore landed on our list of 20 least contented cities in the world.

We singled out France in another section of this book as one of the 20 least contented countries in the world, citing the country's growing racism against immigrants and increasing religious and ethnic conflicts as principal reasons. Our thinking about Marseille is the same: here is a charming place that is rich in history and culture, but that is unacceptably torn socially and increasingly divided between rich and poor, native and newcomer. We welcome Europe's increasing diversity and applaud immigration policies that give people from poor countries a chance for a better life. But too many people in Marseille and France act as if Europe needs to be defended from people who look different and have different cultures. The Europeans who think this way are discontented because they see unwelcome immigrants in their midst, while the immigrants themselves are discontented because of a lack of welcome and open hostility against them. We are sorry to see such divisions in Marseilles and its country, because both are great places otherwise.

In many respects, Marseille is an impressive and enjoyable city. It has a charming old port district with interesting shops and restaurants and lively street life, historic sites such as the Château d'If on a small offshore island that was the setting for Alexandre Dumas's brilliant novel *The Count of Monte Cristo*, the beautiful Cathedral of Sainte-Marie-Majeure, and a dramatic natural shoreline away from the center that is noted for steep-walled inlets of the sea that are called *calanques* in the local Occitan language. The beautiful church Notre-Dame de la Garde stands guard over the city from a hilltop nearby that once housed a true defensive fortress. The cultural life of Marseille includes opera and classical ballet, as well as hip-hop music, for which the city is an acknowledged mecca, and modern dance. There is a lively arts scene, as there has been for centuries, and a vibrant nightlife. Yachts and cruise ships dock in the city's modern harbor, while a short distance away, the working waterfront is busy with the trade of France. The world can thank Marseille for bouillabaisse.

These scenes contrast with the reality of the city's immigrant districts. Marseille continues its historic role as a gateway to Europe, and because it faces North Africa across the Mediterranean where France once had a colonial empire, the city now attracts many immigrants from across the water. The main nationalities are Algerians, Comorians, Tunisians, and Moroccans, but there are also Senegalese and other West Africans, Turks, and other ethnic groups, and Islam is the immigrants' dominant religion. An estimated 30% or more of the current population of Marseille is Muslim. While life for many immigrants is an improvement from the poverty or civil unrest that they had left back home, for many others the new life in the south of France is also hard and fraught with dangers. Most immigrants live in massive apartment blocks at the urban periphery that are known as *cites* where housing conditions are poor and overcrowded, and where the landscape is heavy

Marseille is on the coast of France across the Mediterranean Sea from North Africa. The city has many immigrants from across the waters, as shown in this photo of a Muslim woman and her children on a city bus. The Mediterranean Sea is in the background. (Joel Carillet/iStockphoto.com)

with litter, graffiti, and broken-down industrial plants. There are few jobs, and youth unemployment is 40% or more. Drugs and violence are increasingly common, as is anger among disaffected youth and political-religious radicalization. The city has been called the most dangerous city in France and even the most dangerous in Europe. It has also been referred as the murder capital of Europe because of a spate of killings in recent years between rival drug gangs. Marseille has also been called the "Chicago" of France, not because of many outstanding qualities of America's "Second City," but because of associations with gangsters, gang killings, and drugs. As a port city, Marseille has indeed been a conduit for drug smuggling, as was made widely known by Hollywood in the 1971 blockbuster movie *The French Connection*.

An article that was published in 2000 in *Harper's* refers to Marseille as the venue of a "new French Revolution," meaning that it is in this city specifically that Europe is being remade first and most dramatically. Marseille is a fast-changing city with new residents and new cultures, but unfortunately far too many of the newcomers remain on the outside. There are, of course, many good people among natives and newcomers alike who work together to ease tensions and enhance opportunities for poor migrants, but there are also those on both sides who hate the other and make Marseille an unhappy place. A new museum that opened in 2013 could help to change things. It is called MuCEM for Museum of European and Mediterranean Civilizations, and is dedicated to cultural and artistic exchanges between the old and new cultures of France, and to the building of mutual respect between residents of an increasingly diverse country.

FURTHER READING

Kornblum, William, "Letter from Marseille," *Dissent*, January 17, 2015, http://dissentmaga zine.org/online_articles/letter-from-marseille-environmental-justice.
Tayler, Jeffrey, "Another French Revolution: In Marseilles, Europe Confronts Its North African Future," *Harper's*, 301, 1806, November 2000, pp. 58–66.

PORT MORESBY, PAPUA NEW GUINEA

Port Moresby is the capital and largest city of Papua New Guinea, a country that occupies the eastern half of the Island of New Guinea and some offshore islands in Oceania north of Australia. The country is extremely diverse culturally, with hundreds of ethnic groups and languages, as well as extraordinarily rich and diverse in flora and fauna, and rich in mineral and timber resources. However, most Papua New Guineans are very poor, as the nation's wealth is highly concentrated and few citizens benefit from the richness of their environment. Port Moresby is also rich in cultural diversity, because as capital it attracts migrants from all parts of the country, but it reflects the country's economic inequalities and is mostly poor. Unemployment is as high as 60%. The city is also among the most dangerous in the world in terms of violent crime. Of 372 cities that were compared according to crime index by the Numbeo database, Port Moresby is second-worst in the world (after Pietermaritzburg, South Africa; mid-2014). Because of the poverty and high crime risks, Port Moresby is on many lists of "least livable" cities in the world (e.g., Intelligence Unit of the *Economist* ranks the city 139th in livability from 140 cities rated, ahead of only Dhaka, Bangladesh), and is therefore included here in our list of the 20 least content cities in the world (as is Dhaka).

The population of Port Moresby is officially estimated to be about 364,000 (2011), more than double that of the next city in the country, Lae (155,000). This is almost certainly an undercount, however, as population has grown extremely rapidly in Port Moresby in recent years, with innumerable unregistered and uncounted migrants from countryside provinces continually moving to the city, and the true total might be as high as double the official total and headed toward 1 million. A 2010 report by the United Nations gave a conservative estimate of 400,000 as the city's population. In 2000, Port Moresby had a population of 254,000, in 1990 it was 196,000, and in 1980 it was 124,000. As a result of such growth, there is not sufficient housing in the city, and new arrivals are forced to live in crowded conditions in marginal districts by doubling and tripling up, and by building new shacks in unplanned squatter communities next to other new shacks. An estimated 45% of the population lives in such informal communities, if not more, without adequate sanitation, refuse collection, access to clean water, transportation to the urban center, social services, and other basic needs. The newest migrant slums are at the city's edges, as urbanization expands outward toward hills behind the city, as well as in some cases on stilts along the coastline, as Port Moresby is a port city on the Coral Sea. During low tide, the urban shoreline is covered with layers of litter and garbage that had been beached by retreating waters.

The socioeconomic divide in Port Moresby is chasmic. The minority of the city's population with high incomes is disproportionately from foreign countries, as opposed to native citizens, who are posted as expatriates in Port Moresby by global companies, particularly those that extract resources such as minerals, oil and gas, and timber. Their housing is very expensive, also because of limited supply, and is heavily guarded by high walls, barbed wire, CCTV, and private security guards. There are also many foreign aid workers associated with the United Nations and various nongovernmental organizations that fight poverty and other social problems. They, too, live in protected compounds and rarely go out after dark because of the threat of crime. There is virtually no nightlife in the city. Offices, hotels, shopping centers, and other places where people with money gather are also very heavily secured. Barbed wire and razor wire seem to be everywhere, but street-lighting is scarce. Carjacking is always a threat, as is kidnapping for ransom. Therefore, people who can afford automobiles prefer to live near to where they drive, and venture out after dark in convoys. The majority of foreigners are from Australia, given the country's nearness and historic ties to Papua New Guinea, but there are also those from Europe, North America, and Japan, among other parts of the world. In recent years, Chinese business investors have come to Port Moresby too.

The crime threat in Port Moresby (and in other parts of Papua New Guinea) is mostly from violent criminals called *raskols*, a Tok Pisin (Pidgin English) word taken from the word "rascals." Their gangs are based in the city's squatter settlements and are called raskol gangs. At first their criminal activities focused on burglaries and other theft, but the gangs are now more numerous and more violent, and traffic in narcotics, and commit murder and rape. Weapons, including guns, are often homemade. Domestic violence against women is common in Port Moresby and prevalent throughout Papua New Guinea, and is often excused in court because of drunkenness on the part of the male. Rape is also common, with more than one-half of the women in the country reporting that they had been victims of sexual assault at least once. In some regions, almost every woman has been a rape victim. Children are also vulnerable to sexual assault. The perceived high risk of crime on squatter settlements has impeded provision of services in these neighborhoods, as workers such as trash collectors, teachers, and bus drivers often refuse to work in these areas.

Other problems in Port Moresby include a high level of HIV-AIDS infection, tuberculosis, malaria, and other diseases. The city's largest public hospital reports that AIDS is the leading cause of death for adult men. The health crisis is compounded by a shortage of hospitals, clinics, and medical personnel, as well as by the city's environmental crises such as water shortages and inadequate or nonexistent sewage and trash disposal. According to a United Nations report about the city, medical clinics have had to close at times because of vandalism or theft. Alcoholism and drug addiction are common, especially among men. Schools are poorly equipped and overcrowded, and many students enter adulthood poorly prepared for employment. Responsibilities for child-rearing, education, and earning an income to sustain households fall disproportionately on women.

FURTHER READING

U.N. Habitat, Regional and Technical Cooperation Division, *Papua New Guinea: Port Moresby Urban Profile* (Nairobi: United Nations Human Settlement Program, 2010), http://www.fukuoka.unhabitat.org/projects/papua_new_guinea/pdf/Port_Moresby_March_2010.pdf.

Zimmer-Tamakoshi, Laura, "Patterns of Culture in the Tower of Babel: Letters from Port Moresby, Papua New Guinea," *Journal de la Société des Océanistes* [*Journal of the Society of Oceanists*], 103, 1996, pp. 163–171, http://www.persee.fr/web/revues/home /prescript/article/jso_0300–953x_1996_num_103_2_1987.

SOCHI, RUSSIA

Sochi is a small but famous city on the Black Sea coast of Russia. It is in a region known as Krasnodar Krai, and can be considered to be at the boundary of Europe and Asia if one agrees that the crest of nearby Caucuses Mountains forms the continental divide. The city has a subtropical climate and has been a popular beach resort in Russia from late in the 19th century. No other part of Russia is as warm. Yet, even though most of the rest of Russia is as wintery as any place on earth, this temperate city recently hosted the 2014 winter Olympics, as the mountains behind the coast are high enough to support skiing and other snow sports. It is the preparation of Sochi and its surroundings for the Olympics, as well as the spectacle of the games and opening/closing ceremonies, that has made Sochi globally famous. It is the unprecedented corruption that was associated with Olympics construction, the shoddiness of much of the work, and the high-handed nature of the entire project that has caused us to include the city as one of the world's 20 least contented urban centers.

According to the 2010 Russian census, the population of Sochi is 343,334. The coastal strip where Sochi is located has been settled for many centuries by various ethnic populations, most notably the Circassians who had their land taken away by Imperial Russian expansionism in the early 19th century. A Russian fortress that was erected at the mouth of the Sochi River in 1838 marks the start of the area as a Russian settlement. Because of the climate, Sochi was developed as beach resort during the decades just before and after 1900 for the elites of czarist society. The area came to be referred to as the Caucuses Riviera. The Soviets also favored Sochi during their decades in power. Joseph Stalin, who ruled Russia from 1922 to 1952, and who was from the nearby Soviet Republic of Georgia, built his dacha in Sochi. It is now a historical landmark and museum. The city was also noted for several large, neoclassical-style sanatoria that were built for the enjoyment of the Soviet elite. With the collapse of the Soviet Union in 1991, Sochi lost some of it cachet, as well-healed Russians began to travel abroad for their holidays, and this small city became more of a middle- or working-class resort.

Sochi won the right to host the 2014 winter Olympics and the 2014 winter Paralympics following a vote by the International Olympics Committee in Guatemala City on July 4, 2007. It beat out two finalist cities, Pyeongchang, South Korea and Salzburg, Austria. There was controversy from the start about the choice, because an extraordinary amount of construction and other preparation would be needed to make this Russian "Riviera" suitable for winter sports, and because of credible reports that Russian mobsters had threatened the life of Salzburg's bid coordinator in an attempt to scare him from the competition. Russia's President Vladimir Putin made an unusual personal appearance at the Guatemala City meeting to press his country's case. There were also concerns about possible terrorism at the games, given Sochi's nearness to restive Islamic populations in the Caucuses region and Russia's recent wars in the area, and about the safety of gay-lesbian athletes and visitors, given Russia's official homophobic policies. Thankfully, the worst did not happen on either count.

The estimated budget for the games was to be US$12 billion, which exceeded the cost of the previous (2010) winter Olympics by $4 billion, but the final cost escalated to an unprecedented $51 billion, making these games by far the most expensive Olympics ever. The 2008 summer Olympics in Beijing had cost $44 billion, but the numbers of events and numbers of expected visitors were much higher than in the case of the Sochi games. A post-games comparison reveals that the cost of the Beijing Olympics was $132 million per event while that of the Sochi games was $540 million per event. The leaders of many countries, most notably in North America and West Europe, announced that they would not attend such a costly extravaganza and sent lower-ranking officials in their place.

The high costs for Sochi were because there was so much to be built—not just the venues for the sporting competitions, but also hotels, athletes' housing, and transportation facilities. A 28-mile (45-km) road and rail link from Sochi to the high-altitude games site at Krasnaya Polyana cost nearly $7 billion, making it the world's most expensive stretch of rail and asphalt. The construction contract was awarded without bids, and went to a close friend of President Putin. Before long, Russian pride at hosting the games was tempered by realization that citizens would bear the cost via the national treasury, and that those who were closest to the president were making enormous profits. Sochi residents found themselves to be in the way of nonstop, speeded-up construction, and were permanently displaced from their homes. Construction workers also became discontented victims, because they were forced to work extraordinarily long shifts as deadlines loomed. In the end, many were never paid as bosses stole their wages. Boris Nemtsov, an opposition politician who happened to be born in Sochi, referred to his home city's Olympics as "an unprecedented thieves' caper" and "a festival of corruption, a festival of human-rights violations, a festival of destroying the environment, and a festival of destroying the only subtropical region in Russia." (Nemtsov was murdered in Moscow on February 27, 2015.) It became clear after the games that Putin's plan for Sochi was to make it into an upscale resort for Russia's rich and powerful—a sort of gentrification at public cost with the Olympics as a tool. However, many of the intended construction projects were never completed, and much of what was built now has no use and is a white elephant. Some new streets and buildings are already falling apart from poor workmanship. In fact, a year after the Olympics, Sochi resembles a ghost town. The fact that Russia snatched Crimea from Ukraine just days after the Sochi Olympics ended, leading to a bloody war, is also a part of Sochi's dark legacy.

FURTHER READING

MacKinnon, Mark, "In Sochi, Anger and Controversy of Olympic Proportions," *The Globe and Mail*, January, 7, 2014, http://www.theglobeandmail.com/sports/olympics /in-sochi-anger-and-controversy-of-olympic-proportions/article16227652/?page=all.
Walker, Shaun, "The Sochi Olympics Legacy: 'The City Now Feels Like a Ghost Town,'" December 17, 2014, http://www.theguardian.com/sport/2014/dec/17/sochi-olympics-legacy-city-feels-like-a-ghost-town.

ÜRÜMQI, CHINA

Ürümqi has a population of 2,988,715 (2010 census) and is the 42nd-largest city in the People's Republic of China, a vast country with many cities with multiple millions of people. The city stands out from the others for being the largest city by far in China's vast western region, and its economic and cultural capital. It is also the political capital of the Xinjiang Uyghur Autonomous Region of the PRC, China's biggest administrative district. The area is strategically important because of abundant oil, natural gas, and mineral resources, and because it borders eight foreign countries, including India with which the border is disputed. Furthermore, Xinjiang as a whole is a very sensitive region in terms of ethnic and religious tensions within China, and has many different minority populations and ethnic regions. Although Ürümqi was founded by Han Chinese, much of the territory nearby is the home of the Uyghur people, a Turkic ethnic group that, in China, numbers more than 10 million people. Many Uyghurs object to Chinese rule and have taken part in political movements in favor of independence. This has led to bloodshed in the region and tension between Uyghur natives and Han settlers. Other distinctions for Ürümqi are that it is located further from any sea than any other large city in the world, and that a particular point just to the southwest of the city is considered to be the geographical center of Asia. There is a monument there to that effect.

"Ürümqi" means "beautiful pasture" in Mongolian. In history, the city was a major trade center along the Silk Road, and then a frontier settlement for Han Chinese moving west. It is now much like any other big Chinese city: modern, increasingly prosperous, and fast-growing with a skyline of tall building pushing upward. It is clogged with people, including more and more new migrants who have come for the jobs, and traffic, including both cars and bicycles. There are many new high-rise housing developments, shopping centers, and industries. There is no longer a "beautiful pasture" in this desert oasis city that has been turned into a concrete metropolis, but there are some beautiful parks and squares, and oases of air-conditioning. However, despite the city's pluses, Ürümqi also reflects much of what is wrong in China today: unsustainable urban growth, major environmental issues, and political and religious repressions by the Chinese government. There are outbreaks of violence and bloodshed. In these respects, Ürümqi and its surrounding Uyghur homeland resemble another border ethnic region nearby with aspirations for independence, Tibet and its capital city Lhasa. We could have written about Lhasa on these pages too, but are limited to a total of 20 most discontented cities only, and have decided to let Ürümqi represent the dark aspects of modern China that are seen as well in Lhasa.

A little more than three-quarters (75.3%) of the population of Ürümqi is Han Chinese, while Uyghurs comprise the largest minatory at about 12.8%. The rest of the population is made up of many other ethnic groups, the most populous of which are the Hui. By contrast, the Xinjiang Uyghur Autonomous Region is 46.4% Uyghur in population and 39.0 Han, indicating the dominance of Han migrants in the region's prosperous capital city and, by extension, concentration of Uyghurs and other ethnic minorities in more traditional, poorer rural regions. This is one source of the conflict in and around Ürümqi: Han Chinese have taken over the region, its resources, and its economic benefits to the disadvantage of local populations. The other dimension is that Uyghurs have more in common culturally, linguistically, and in terms of shared Islamic faith with other minorities in Xinjiang, as well as with the national populations of neighboring and other nearby Central Asia countries (Kazakhstan, Kyrgyzstan, Tajikistan, Afghanistan, Pakistan, and Turkmenistan) than with Han China. As a result, many Uyghurs would like to see the establishment of an independent "Uyghuristan," or separatism in the form of either a pan-Turkic or pan-Islamic state. For at least 20 years, China's military has tried to suppress a separatist movement in Xinjiang that is known as the East Turkestan Islamic Movement. There have been many violent confrontations, including bombings, suicide attacks, and other terrorist acts carried out by the separatists, and violent police action in response. The cycle of violence was stepped up in advance of the 2008 Beijing Olympics in order to gather international attention for the Uyghur cause, and has not abated since, as major incidents involving many deaths take place almost routinely multiple times per year in Ürümqi and other cities in Xinjiang.

The environmental problems in Ürümqi are also very serious. To start with, there is nowhere near the needed water to sustain such growth, as Xinjiang is a semi-desert area and water shortages are routine. For the time being, a new water diversion project called the Irtysh- Ürümqi Canal that China built at enormous cost in the first decade of the 21st century has eased the difficulty by taking water from the Chinese headquarters of the mostly Russian-Siberian Irtysh River that flows into the Arctic Ocean and diverting it southward. The air pollution problem is even worse. Incredibly, this remote desert city is now one of the planet's 10 most polluted cities as reported from a 2013 study by China's Tsinghua University and the Asian development Bank. (Six of the other 10 most polluted cities are in China too, including the national capital Beijing which is also on these pages as one of the 20 least contented cities in the world.) The New York–based former Blacksmith Institute, now named Pure Earth, cited Ürümqi as one of the world's most polluted spots as far back as 2007. The main pollutants are sulfur dioxide from industrial emissions, as well as aerosols and soil dust kicked up by urbanization and construction. In winter, the pollution haze is so thick that it affects air traffic. Needless to say, such air pollution affects human health too, causing sickness and premature death.

FURTHER READING

Demetre, Andrew, *Drinking and Driving in Ürümqi* (New York: Strangers Gate Books, 2013).
Deng, Wen and Xiaolei Zhang, "Ürümqi," *Cities: International Journal of Urban Policy and Planning*, 28, 1, 2010, pp. 115–125.
Millward, James A., *Beyond the Pass: Economy, Ethnicity, and Empire in Qing Central Asia* (Stanford, CA: Stanford University Press, 1998).

VENICE, ITALY

Yes, Venice, the beloved city in Italy that is visited by millions of tourists each year to see the Piazza San Marco and the canals, to ride in a gondola, and to experience the joys of the "Republic of Music"—that Venice is in this book as one of the 20 *least* contented cities in the world! It is a great and historic city, to be sure, and well worth the visit, even at Venetian prices, and some other book might have it at the top in a comparison of cities, but the truth is that Venice is a city with great problems, and it is fair to say that its residents are less than fully contented. It is from the standpoint of the people who live in Venice that we make our judgment about the place, and not from the standpoint of the short-term visitor. The tourist is awed and then goes elsewhere; the resident Venetian knows the painful fact that the future of the city is uncertain and that the present is impractical.

Venice is located in the marshy Venetian Lagoon of the northern Adriatic Sea between the mouths of the Po and Plave Rivers, and comprises 117 small, low-lying islands separated by canals and bridges. The present population of the city is about 270,000, while that of the historic core is about 60,000. The city was a major maritime power in the Middle Ages and a wealthy trading port that bridged the European world with the worlds of Byzantium, Islam, North Africa, the

Middle East, and distant Asia. It is the city of Marco Polo, the famed 13th-century merchant traveler. The city is also intimately associated with the Crusades and Europe's wars against the spread of Islam. During the Renaissance and afterward, Venice was prominent in art, architecture, and music, with some of the most prominent paintings being scenes of Venice itself such as the remarkably bright and detailed *veduta* that were executed by native son Canaletto in the early 18th century. Venice is undeniably a beautiful and romantic city that for many people with a basis for comparison is a world favorite. It is listed as a UNESCO World Heritage Site in its entirety, lagoon and all.

Our first reason for listing Venice as a least contented city is that all the grandeur is in danger of being lost. Despite centuries-old expert construction on closely spaced water-resistant wooden piles, the city is slowly sinking into the lagoon because of its own weight, with foundations of many buildings and old ground-floor levels already permanently under water. The subsidence problem was exacerbated in the 20th century when water was withdrawn for industrial uses in the Venice area by artesian wells. As the city sinks, high water comes in with the strongest tides and floods the city. During such episodes, tourist zones

The famous historic city of Venice, Italy, is plagued with environmental problems, not the least of which is that the city is sinking under its own weight into the muck of the island on which it was built at the same time as sea levels rise. The result is low-level flooding during periods of high tide. The photo shows tourists in Venice's St. Mark's Square wading across the waters of the public plaza. (Valeriya Potapova/Dreamstime.com)

such as the Piazza San Marco have elevated wooden walkway above the flood line. There have been costly studies to find ways to save Venice from the sea, and costly proposals for flood walls and floating pontoons that would stretch across entrances to the lagoon and be drawn closed as necessary. Also, much of the historic architecture of the city is in disrepair. A wonderful nonfiction book about Venice called *City of Falling Angels* is so named because ornate mortar reliefs that adorn old buildings around the city are crumbling and are succumbing to the pull of gravity.

Second, we note that Venice is frequently so overrun with tourists that the city becomes unpleasant for visitors and locals alike. As many as 50,000 tourists visit the city each day and about 3 million in a given year, overwhelming local facilities and crowding main attractions. While this might be a boon for people who make their living off tourists, it can be a nightmare for other Venetians who have to put up with noise, crowding, and litter, as well as unpleasant for visitors whose experiences in the city are diminished by the same noise, crowding, and litter. In peak seasons, visitors complain that what they saw in Venice was other visitors. Prices are artificially high under such circumstances, and all too many tourists report that in the net, they consider Venice to be one giant tourist trap. We can also add that many of the people who own homes or apartments in Venice are wealthy foreigners who are attracted by the uniqueness and fame of the city, but who spend only part of their time in the historic city. When they are in Venice, they do not want their surroundings to be overrun with gawking tourists. These rich property owners have driven up the prices of real estate to the point that ordinary Venetians find it difficult to afford to live in the city, and are displaced by rising rents. Ironically, many of the people whose livelihoods depend directly on tourism such as restaurant workers, guides, and museum staff cannot afford to live in Venice, and are commuters instead. Large cruise have been banned from Venice because of the nuisance of so many arrivals at one. The city has also enacted restrictions against rolling suitcases because of the annoying sound that they make when tourists drag them on cobbled walkways and over bridges.

Finally, we note that the charming city of islands and canals is not a very practical place for modern living. For example, the comforts of living quarters can be diminished by historic preservation requirements that forbid certain modern updates. Similarly, residents complain that high prices in local shops force them to shop on the mainland for groceries and other needs, and then to lug their purchases some distance by hand to get home. They also complain that many local needs are not available in Venice, as the businesses on the city's islands cater more to the tourist market than to everyday household items. We can also say that it probably is no fun living in a damp place where the basement is permanently flooded with still water, and where the canals outside your windows stink. Yes, one of the secrets of Venice that the tourism industry likes to keep quiet is that sewage has to go somewhere in this city, and that that somewhere is the celebrated canal network.

FURTHER READING

Ackroyd, Peter, *Venice: Pure City* (New York: Random House, 2009).
Berendt, John, *City of Falling Angels* (New York: Penguin Books, 2005).
Madden, Thomas F., *Venice: A New History* (New York: Viking, 2013).

3

The Most and Least Contented U.S. States and Cities

As we explained in the introduction, we had decided early on to treat the United States separately in this book. Your author is an American, as is the book's publishing company, and it seems prudent to steer away from comparing the country or its cities with other countries and foreign cities because of the possible appearance of a conflict of interest. Other rankings do, in fact, include the United States or other home countries in their analyses, but ours is not strictly or mechanically quantitative as are many of the others. Furthermore, as we have already discussed, our topic is imprecise, leaving us all the more open to criticism for our choices.

Within the United States we decided to list the five most contented states and the five least contented states, meaning that 10% of the 50 states are listed in each of the two groups. That is an appropriate fraction, we think. As for cities, we chose to list 10 in each of the two categories, most contented cities and least contented cities. As with global cities, there was no lower limit of population to be considered, so some of the places that we selected are quite small. The population range is from just under 40,000 for Atlantic City, New Jersey, to 1,445,632 for Phoenix, Arizona. Both cities are in the least contented group. And as we did in our global analyses, we sought to have regional representation across the United States in our choices of most contented and least contented states and cities. Our choices are listed next and do indeed show a mix of North, South, East, and West, as well as Heartland.

The methodology paralleled that of the countries and global cities analysis. We used various kinds of data, including the results from various rankings of

Table 3.1

5 Most Contented U.S. States	5 Least Contented U.S. States
Colorado	Arizona
Hawaii	Louisiana
Minnesota	Mississippi
New Hampshire	New Jersey
Oregon	Texas

Table 3.2

10 Most Contented U.S. Cities	10 Least Contented U.S. Cities
Austin, Texas	Atlantic City, New Jersey
Boulder, Colorado	Beaumont-Port Arthur, Texas
Burlington, Vermont	Camden, New Jersey
Charleston, South Carolina	Detroit, Michigan
Des Moines, Iowa	Flint, Michigan
Minneapolis, Minnesota	Memphis, Tennessee
Provo, Utah	Niagara Falls, New York
Pittsburgh, Pennsylvania	Phoenix, Arizona
San Francisco, California	St. Louis, Missouri
Seattle, Washington	Stockton, California

U.S. states and cities, authoritative books and articles, information from the news media, and our own considerable travels across the country, in order to come up with ever-shorter lists of the states and cities before making our final choices. Key rankings that we consulted included the following:

Livability's Best Places to Live. The editors and writers of Livability consulted with many experts as they travelled across the United States in compiling a list of the best small- and medium-sized cities in the country to live. They considered more than 2,000 places in coming up with a ranking of the top 100. The ranking is updated and published annually, most recently in 2015. Livability is a private company that for 25 years has worked with communities across the United States to help them find ways to attract and retain businesses and residents by showcasing their strengths. http://livability.com/best-places/top-100-best-pla ces-to-live/2015.

Livability's Best Places for Families. Among criteria that the editors of Livability considered in rating places with respect to how well they met family needs were the number of other households in the community with children, the crime rate, the quality of schools, school graduation rates, programs for children, the cost of living, and the average time of commuting for parents. http://livability .com/top-10/families/10-best-cities-families/2015.

Livability's Best Places for Retirees. The editors of Livability determined the best places to retire by looking for areas that have an active population and ways to say active. They also considered natural amenities, a temperate climate, and the number of golf courses as pluses. Another factor was the conduciveness of a community for walking. The most recent ranking was for 2014. http://livabil ity.com/top-10/retirement/best-places-retire/2014.

Businessweek.com's Best Places to Live. With assistance from Bloomberg Rankings, Businessweek.com has evaluated 100 of the largest cities in the United States to determine which ones are the best places to live. The criteria included leisure attributes (the number of restaurants, bars, libraries, museums, professional sports teams, and acres of parkland by population), education attributes (school performance, the number of colleges, and graduate degree holders), economic factors (income and unemployment data), crime rates, and air quality. The first ranking was conducted in 2011 and the second was in 2012. http://www.bloomberg.com/bw/slideshows/2012–09–26/americas-50-best-cities.

Gallup-Healthways Well-Being Indexes for U.S. Cities and States. Indexes of well-being are calculated separately for U.S. states and cities each year from data obtained from structured interviews with thousands of U.S. residents across the country. Well-being is based on healthy behaviors, emotional health, personal fitness, abstinence from smoking, and living in a place where one can learn new and interesting things. http://www.usatoday.com /story/money/2014/02/20/healthways-wellbeing-most-content-states/5624043/; http://www.usatoday.com/story/money/business/2014/02/23/most-miserable-states/5729305/; and http://www.usatoday.com/story/news/nation/2014/03/25 /gallup-cities-well-being/6828197/.

There were many difficult decisions along the way as we made our choices, particularly with respect to states. For example, on the most contented side, there was a close call between Utah and Colorado for representation from the West, between Minnesota and both Wisconsin and Iowa from the Midwest, between New Hampshire and Vermont in the Northeast, and between Oregon and Washington on the West Coast. Some of the final choices were swayed by city choices: for example, we settled on New Hampshire instead of Vermont in part because one of our most contented cities is Burlington, Vermont, and we settled on Oregon instead of Washington because Washington is represented with the city of

Seattle as one of our choices for the most contented cities list. With respect to the least contented states, we were sorry to have to select three states from the South-Central region for the final list of five, but the data were persuasive: this is the poorest region of the United States, and all of the states there, including Arkansas, Alabama, Tennessee, and Oklahoma, rank low or on the low side in various rankings that deal with health, education, income, and other quality of live measures. Kentucky and West Virginia were also finalist-candidates for the least contented states list, as were Florida and California, two populous states with considerable in-migration. We noted that both of these sunny states suffer from overdevelopment and chronic traffic snarls, as well as environmental problems, natural hazards, and other problems.

Our list of 10 most contented cities would have been easy to expand, as there are a number of other excellent cities with many amenities and high standards of living. We hesitated to add yet another community where a major university was prominent presence because the present list already has three such cities: Austin, Boulder, and Provo. It would have been nice to include Madison, Wisconsin, Ann Arbor, Michigan, State College, Pennsylvania, and Ames, Iowa too, but too many college towns are too many college towns. Other possible cities for the plus list include Asheville, North Carolina, Portland, Oregon, and Napa, California. On the least contented side of the ledger, there is unfortunately no shortage of American cities that are in trouble. Therefore, that list could have been expanded too, particularly with down-at-the-heels industrial cities such as Cleveland and Youngstown, Ohio, Wheeling, West Virginia, and Gary, Indiana. Paterson and Trenton, New Jersey, are in the same category, but we already have two cities from that state on the list, as well as the state itself on the list of five least contented U.S. states. In the South-Central region, we could have added Baton Rouge and Shreveport, Louisiana, although to some extent the Beaumont-Port-Arthur, Texas, metropolitan area stands for these two cities with problems of industrial pollution. Finally, there is no shortage of cities in California that are broke and poor in addition to Stockton. Our next choices may have been Fresno and Modesto.

THE 5 MOST CONTENTED U.S. STATES

COLORADO

For many Americans, Colorado is a dream state because of its beautiful Rocky Mountains and reputation for wide open spaces, and personal and economic freedoms. Furthermore, many of those who are inclined to prefer cities are inclined to prefer Denver, the state capital and one of America's more beautiful and more popular cities. The state has farms, ranches, cities, mines, and mountains, as well as national parks, ski slopes, cowboy lore, military installations, and as of 2014, legalized marijuana for personal use by adults. Its University of Colorado is one of the top public universities in the United States. The state appears to have something for everyone, as it accommodates both the very conservative military city of Colorado Springs and the very liberal university city of Boulder with its borders. Colorado is one of the most rapidly growing states in the United States, having increased it population from about 2.2 million in 1970 to 4.3 million in 2000, to an estimated 5.4 million in 2014.

Comparative rankings confirm that Colorado is a contented state. We observe that it was rated at #7 among the 50 states in a 2013 Gallup survey of people's well-being, with especially good scores for low obesity rates and low rates of diabetes, and low chances of heart attack by most of the population, and at #4 in the Gallup-Healthways poll for 2014 of happiness by state. We also report that

Colorado is perhaps best known for its Rocky Mountains, but a large part of the state is agricultural, and cattle ranching is a big business. The National Western Stock Show is a major trade fair for cattle breeders that is held annually in Denver, the state's capital. The photo shows a parade from the opening of the fair in 2012. (Arinahabich08/Dreamstime.com)

Colorado's schools rank sixth in the country in overall quality, and that the state ranks fourth among the 50 states in an index of science and technology. The state is fifth in the country as a place for business as reported for 2014 by *Forbes* and seventh in economic competitiveness in 2013 by the National Association of Manufacturers and the Council on Competitiveness. It is also a rather green state, ranking at #13 out of 50 states. There is a very strong environmentalist movement in the state and a population that is dedicated to preserving the natural beauty of both the mountains and the western canyon lands, but there are also great demands on the state's limited water supplies by ranchers and farmers. The city of Denver is to be commended for enlightened urban development policies such as light rail system and support for bicycling.

HAWAII

For many people, Hawaii is paradise. That is certainly the case for the many tourists from the rest of the United States and many foreign countries who vacation there, and for the great many young couples in love who choose the state for their honeymoons. It is also a dream place to retire, if one can afford it. Yes, Hawaii is expensive, but the price includes warm weather year-round, sunny days almost every day, palm trees swaying in the breezes, beautiful beaches, and lush greenery on windward mountain slopes. It is a beautiful state, and one that is diverse geographically, socially, and economically. There are dry zones in Hawaii too, in the rain shadow of mountains, as well as active volcanoes and hot-flowing lava. There are cattle ranches, as well as pineapple and sugar plantations. There is a very large U.S. military presence, especially on Oahu, the island with Pearl Harbor that is famous from World War II. Oahu also has Honolulu, the state capital and largest city, and the Waikiki Beach area, the state's largest and most congested zone of tourists. There are very quiet places in Hawaii too, including secluded beaches, secret waterfalls, and scenic mountain trails.

Hawaii has a very diverse population. According to the 2010 U.S. Census, 24.7% of the population is white, 38.6% is Asian, 10.0% is Native Hawaiian or other Pacific islander, 1.6% is African American, and 23.6% is of two or more races. The large Asian population includes many Filipino Americans and Japanese Americans. A difficult problem is that many Native Hawaiians and other residents of Pacific Island heritage are disproportionately poor, and are priced out of much of the housing market in the state, which has been inflated by high demands for Hawaii living by rich people from the mainland and from countries abroad. This poses hardships, but there is still contentment with the knowledge that Hawaii is home, that they have community, and that they are the custodians of the islands' cultures, language, music, and song. The state ranks first in the country in overall health, according to a 2014 survey by the United Health Foundation. It also ranks high in social tolerance and life satisfaction. In paradise, that is to be expected.

MINNESOTA

Minnesota is known for its 10,000 lakes, frozen winters, and its unofficial state bird, the biting mosquito. The state is also known for friendly people, good food, and a high quality of life, and is a good fit for designation as one of the most contented states in the United States.

In addition to the lakes that are advertised on the state's license plates, Minnesota has farms, forests, cities, and mines. The state's population is nearly 5.5 million, about 60% of whom live in the Twin Cities metropolitan area. Minneapolis is the larger of the two with a population of about 400,000, while St. Paul next door, the state capital has about 295,000 people. A tangle of suburbs and freeways surrounds these two main cities. The metropolitan area is home base for a number of prominent companies: Target, General Mills, 3M, US Bancorp, and Best Buy, among others. Rochester, a smaller city in southern Minnesota, is home to the famed Mayo Clinic, one of the world's leading hospitals and medical research centers. The North Woods area has tourism, logging, and the Mesabi Iron Range, long a leading source of iron ore for American industry. The ports of Duluth and Two Harbors nearby on Lake Superior were the main ports for ore vessels.

A Gallup-Healthways poll for 2014 showed Minnesota to be the second-most contented state overall (after Utah). The state was ranked at #3 in overall health in 2014 by the United Health Foundation. In 2014, its poverty rate by household was 8.1%, the fourth-lowest in the United States. In February 2015, the unemployment rate as reported by the U.S. Bureau of Labor Statistics was 3.7%, the fourth-lowest in the United States. Minnesota's schools were rated at #8 in overall quality among 50 states in a 2014 study by WalletHub, and a Milken Institute ranking for the same year has the state at #12 in its State Tech and Science Index. The state ranks sixth in the country in per capita philanthropy, and seventh in the country in social tolerance as measured in 2011 by the *Daily Beast*. The state has fairly low crime rates and ranks 49th out of 50 states in incarceration rates. Its guns are used for hunting.

NEW HAMPSHIRE

New Hampshire was one of the first of the original 13 colonies to rebel against British rule, and has maintained a spirit of independence ever since. At least that is what the bold motto on the state's licenses plates, "Live Free or Die," is thought to mean. And indeed, the state does think independently: it has no general sales tax and no personal income tax other than on interest and dividend incomes. What holds back a potential torrent of penurious settlers from other states is that property taxes are high in New Hampshire, so that the state's bills can be paid.

New Hampshire is not very big nor populous, but it is certainly beautiful. Much of the state is forested and mountainous, with clear lakes and streams and ample opportunity for outdoor recreation. In winter the state is a skiers' paradise, and in autumn it is spectacular with the colors fall foliage and picture-postcard New England villages. The southern part of the state is urbanized, as it is part of the Boston, Massachusetts, metropolitan area and where the state's largest city, the historic mill town of Portsmouth is found. The small state even has a stretch of ocean shoreline and some beaches. Among the high rankings that New Hampshire has in comparison with other states is #4 in overall quality of the state's school systems, #4 again in educational attainment as measured by percentage of adults who have successfully completed high school, and #5 in the overall health of the population as reported for 2014 by the United Health Foundation. Not surprisingly, the state ranks high (at #4) in personal freedoms. The state is lowest in

Former New York governor George Pataki meeting face to face with voters in a local café on June 24, 2015, to explain why he should be the Republican Party's nominee. Every four years, New Hampshire gains wide attention as candidates for the U.S. presidency test the political waters in preparation for the nation's earliest primary elections. (AP Photo/Jim Cole)

the United States in incidence of poverty, and among the top seven states in low unemployment.

Every four years, this small and lightly populated state enjoys national and even global attention as the site of the first Democratic and Republican Party primaries of the presidential campaign season. Doing well or not doing well in New Hampshire can make or break a candidacy, so politicians spend huge sums to drum up votes. For New Hampshirites, the spending is a boon to the economy and the balloting in the primaries gives them the privilege of a disproportionately influential voice over who gets to run for president. And, of course, New Hampshirites often like to show their independence by voting against favorites in the race, just to mix things up.

OREGON

Oregon is always mentioned favorably when American states are being compared, and Oregonians are among the most contented of any state population. Their slice of America is remarkably beautiful, green, and unspoiled, fairly lightly settled in most parts, and strongly protected by strict environmental laws and a popular culture of respect for the land. It was the Lewis and Clark Expedition of 1804–1806 and then the explorers of the 1810 Astor Expedition that first informed Americans about the beauties of the far West and the richness of Oregon, and it was the Oregon Trail of the 1830s to about 1869 that brought the first thousands of settlers across perilous terrain to build new lives in the fertile Willamette River Valley and elsewhere in the territory. Migration to this poplar state has continued ever since, with the result that Oregon's population is now almost 4 million. Portland (population 609,456; metropolitan area 2,314,554) is the largest city, while the capital is Salem, population 160,614, the state's second-largest city.

Oregon is apparently the origin of the pejorative portmanteau "Californication," a new word that has recently evolved into semi-popular usage to describe mindless land development and environmental recklessness. It was first used by Oregonians in an environmentalist warning to protect the state from the destructive processes that were changing California to the south. Slogans based on "Don't Californicate Oregon" have appeared on bumper stickers in other states where rapid growth has become an issue. A similar sentiment was expressed in early 1971 when the then-governor of Oregon Tom McCall said in a national television interview "Come visit us again and again. But for heaven's sake, don't come here to live." This was a unusual thing to say at the time by a government official who would normally be expected to promote growth and seek investment, but McCall reflected the sentiments of many Oregonians who were drawn to the state by its beauty and wanted to keep it that way, even if it meant shutting the door behind them after they have entered. Thus, the state has some of the first and most stringent environmental protection laws such as those that govern recycling of wastes and protecting the coastline from development. In a 2007 survey published in *Forbes*, Oregon was rated #2 in the country as a green state, just barely behind #1 Vermont. Portland is often ranked at or near the top of American cities in sustainability, being known for its light rail system, bike share program, and many parks, among other qualities.

THE 5 LEAST CONTENTED U.S. STATES

ARIZONA

Even though the state has many wonderful attractions such as the Grand Canyon, beautiful deserts and mountain ranges, and many days of sunshine and blue skies, and even though there are a great many residents who absolutely love where they live and think that Arizona is best, we have decided that Arizona should be designated as one of the five least contented states in the United States. Every other state has beautiful attractions too and residents who love where they live, but few states have suffered the environmental problems that Arizona faces because of fast growth and overdevelopment, and few states are as riven socially as this, the last state of the contiguous 48 states to be admitted into the Union (on Valentine's Day, 1912).

We acknowledge that the state ranks highly on some comparative measures (e.g., #11 out of 50 states in personal and economic freedoms in 2013 as measured by researchers at George Mason University; #22 overall as a best state for business as reported by *Forbes* in 2014), but are troubled by low scores and low rankings. For example, in 2014 some 15.2% of the Arizona's households were living below the poverty line, the ninth-highest percentage among the 50 states, and in February 2015, the state's unemployment rate was 7.0%, the seventh-highest in the nation. The state of the Arizona economy was rated at #32 out of 50 states by *Business Insider* in 2014. Arizona's many Native American and Hispanic residents face the greatest economic hardships. Furthermore, the state has the 6th-highest rate of violent crime in the United States, has the 6th-highest incarceration rate, and ranks 11th in the number of executions of convicted prisoners. Its schools rank 43rd in the country in overall quality. Only 84.2% of adults have graduated from high school, a #37 ranking in the United States. We also observe that Arizona ranks 46th out of 50 states in philanthropic giving per capita. In a quantitative study conducted in 2011 by the *Daily Beast*, Arizona came out at #43 among American states in level of social tolerance. The state has a record of vocal opposition to immigration and amnesty for immigrants, as well as vocal opposition to same-sex marriage, and has faced economic boycotts as a result. The state has also opposed celebration of Martin Luther King, Jr. Day.

Finally, even though Arizona is beautiful, we see the state as unsustainable with its high demands for water for agricultural and urban uses. A combination of prolonged drought, high demands by farmers and ranchers, and fast-growing population has brought the state to the edge of water supply crisis. Runoff from chemically enriched agriculture worsens the water situation. The explosion of population in the Phoenix and Tucson areas has produced unsustainable urban sprawl, with still more demands for water and a reliance on automobile-dependent living. Air pollution is especially bad in the Phoenix area. In another section of this chapter, we discuss Phoenix as one of America's least sustainable cities.

LOUISIANA

Put aside the uncomfortably hot and humid summer climate and the frequent hurricanes that bring the state so much destruction, and put aside also the long coastline along the Gulf of Mexico with swamps instead of beaches, and we still give Louisiana lots of negative marks. We like New Orleans, but mainly as a place to visit and then leave, and enjoy the state's unique blends of cultures, cuisines, and music, but a state that is so rich in oil and industry should not be so poor.

According to the U.S. Bureau of the Census, in 2014 fully 18.4% of Louisiana's households were living below the poverty line, the 2nd highest percentage among the 50 states. Only Mississippi next door had a higher incidence of poverty. Likewise, the state ranks high in unemployment. According to the most recent data from Bureau of Labor Statistics at the time of this writing (data for February 2015), Louisiana had an unemployment rate of 6.7%, the fourth highest rate in the country. We are disappointed also to see that the state ranks 48th out of 50 states in the overall health of the population as reported for 2014 by the United Health Foundation, ahead of only its neighbors Arkansas and Mississippi. Furthermore, the city has the fifth-highest rate of violent crime among the 50 states, and ranks first in incarceration rate. It carries out the death penalty. The school systems of Louisiana rank #48 out of 50 states in overall quality, and the state is at #45 in percentage of adults who have completed high school. A recent state law assures teachers in public school that they are free to teach that global warming does not exist and that if it does exist, it is not influenced by human activity. They may also tell children that evolution is no more than an unproven theory. The state's rating for competitiveness in business is #43 out of 50. It ranks near the bottom in the United States as well in environmental quality and sustainability, as a sizable chunk of the state is a petrochemical alley along the lower Mississippi River. The state ranks in the top 10 in the United States in worst roads and bridges. And, sad

Oil is big business in Louisiana, and so is agriculture. The photo is a benign view of an oil rig in a field of cane sugar. Happily, the two coexist here, but often the oil industry causes pollution to the state's farms, bayous, and offshore waters, creating not only environmental damage but also wrecking livelihoods. (Anne Power/Dreamstime.com)

to say, Louisiana compares poorly with other states in being charitable, as it ranks 45th out of 50 states in per capita philanthropic giving.

MISSISSIPPI

There is an unkind adage in use in the United States, especially in the South, that says "Thank God for Mississippi." Instead of the literal meaning that we should be thankful to the Almighty for such a wonderful state, the saying means that we rejoice that we are not the worst, and that there is always Mississippi to bring up the bottom in comparative rankings of states. We are sorry that it is so, but it is true: Mississippi is almost always at or near the bottom among the 50 states no matter what the criterion.

Our own research reveals that Mississippi is last as a "best state" for business as reported for 2014 by *Forbes*, ranks worst in the health of its population as reported for 2014 by the United Health Foundation, and worst in health care. More than 30% of the state residents and nearly one-quarter of its children are classified as obese. Furthermore, the state is worst again in the overall quality of its school systems. It ranks 49th in the percentage of adults who have successfully completed high school. Only Texas ranks lower. The state ranks fairly high (#31) in rate of violent crime, and #2 in the country in incarceration rate. Unemployment is the second highest in the nation: 7.0% as of February 2015, the most recent information that was available from the U.S. Bureau of Labor Statistics at the time of this writing. The state has the highest teenage birth rate in the country, more than 60% above the national average. Mississippi ranks low (#38/50) in social tolerance as reported in 2011 by the *Daily Beast,* and in 2004 passed an amendment to the state constitution that bans same-sex marriages by a margin of 86% to 14%, the largest margin of any state. The constitution of the state of Mississippi stipulates that "no person who denies the existence of a Supreme Being shall hold any office in this state." Finally, we report that Mississippi has some of the worst roads and bridges in the country.

NEW JERSEY

"I would say some nasty things about New Jersey, but my mother taught me to never speak unkindly about the dead." That is an old New Jersey joke. There are probably more jokes said about this small state than about any other state in the country, and perhaps more than about any other state in the whole world. There is no good reason for this, as New Jersey is a fine state, as well as a state with some problems, just like any of the other 49 members of the Union. The explanation might be as simple as the fact that New Jersey is wedged between two large cities, New York City and Philadelphia, for whom the state is something of a backyard or the "other side of the tracks." For many New Yorkers and Pennsylvanians, New Jersey is where you go to buy cheaper liquor and cheap gasoline. Drivers do not get out of their cars at gas stations to pump their own; attendants do the work for you, and still the price of gas is a bargain. New Jersey is also the way to drive between the New York and Philadelphia, or up and down the Northeast Corridor in general, so many people's images of the state are shaped by what they see along the New Jersey Turnpike. They forget the greenery along most of the roadway's length, but remember the sights and smells of the oil refineries and chemical plants near New York. Another joke is that the reason it says "Garden State" on the New Jersey license plates is because "Refineries, Pollution, Toxic Waste, Broken-down Cities, and Corruption" won't fit.

New Jersey is a state of contrasts. We have written up two of the state's cities, Atlantic City and Camden, elsewhere in this book as places with great problems, but also know the state is one of the nation's wealthiest in income levels, and has one of the largest concentrations of engineers, physicians, scientists, and other highly educated professionals anywhere in the world. Hey, Albert Einstein lived in New Jersey! It might be almost true that nothing but crime grows in Newark (or Camden or Trenton or Elizabeth), but much of the state is actually densely forested, and in the north there are verdant low mountains. The Atlantic coast of New Jersey is wonderful, with wide beaches, pleasant resort towns, and great

Unionized construction workers at a rally to support union jobs at a site where a rail tunnel is to be built. New Jersey has a stronger labor union presence than most states. (Ramin Talaie/iStockphoto.com)

summer fun. We like New Jersey, but we also know it well: a history of mobsters and corrupt politicians (in New Jersey everything is legal as long as you don't get caught), very high real estate taxes and high costs for car insurance, costly storms from the sea, long traffic jams, and lots of pollution. There are many prosperous suburbs, to be sure, but the cities are generally the nation's worst: forgotten, thrown away, and to be avoided. But if they serve the needs of commuters to New York, for example, Hoboken and parts of Jersey City, then they become gentrified.

TEXAS

Probably more than any other state, Texas has vocal local supporters who love their state, proclaim their state pride, and even voice opinions that they would be happy to secede and form their own independent country, as it was from 1836 to 1846 as the Republic of Texas. The state is, after all, only one of two U.S. states to have been an independent nation before joining the Union, the other being the Kingdom (and later the Republic) of Hawaii. Texans like that their state is big (it is the second in size in the United States), and they like to boast about big cars, big ranches, big churches, big hair, big high school football stadiums, big steaks, big belt buckles, big pickup trucks, and big school rings, among other big things. They also like their new slogan, "Don't Mess with Texas," which reflects Texas swagger even though it was created originally (in 1985) as a campaign against roadside litter. Texas is a fast-growing state, with a population of about 27 million, the second-highest total in the United States after California and nearly three times what it was in 1960.

We understand the pride that Texans have in their state, but also think that some of them might not be too happy if they think badly about the rest of the country. We also deduct happiness points because Texas is big on inequality. That is, the state ranks highly in business competitiveness (#6 among 50 states as a "best state" for business in 2014 as published in *Forbes*, and #2 in the country in 2013 in competitiveness as measured by the National Association of Manufacturers and the Council on Competitiveness), and has an enormous economy that is based on oil and petrochemicals, national defense, high technology, and agriculture, among other fields, but it also ranks high in poverty. According to data from the U.S. Census Bureau for 2014, 16.2% of Texas household live below the poverty line, the fifth-highest percentage among the 50 states after Mississippi, Louisiana, New Mexico, and Alabama. There are especially large concentrations of poverty in the poor cotton-growing regions of East Texas, and along the Rio Grande, where Texas faces Mexico, as well as in all of the state's big cities from inner-city Houston in the east to El Paso in the far western corner. African Americans and Hispanics are especially likely to be poor. This contrasts with the showy world of big mansions at the end of long driveways that can be found in the exclusive suburbs of Houston, Dallas, and other cities.

We also take Texas to task for high crime rates, for having the fifth-highest incarceration rates in the United States, and for executing the most death-row prisoners by far of any state. Many Texans own guns and are extremely vocal against any proposals for gun control. We ask how contented can they possibly be?

THE 10 MOST CONTENTED U.S. CITIES

AUSTIN, TEXAS

Austin is the proud capital of the boisterously proud state of Texas, and is thought by many to be the best city in the state by far, as well as the best city in the entire south-central region of the United States. Among other pluses, Austin is home to the University of Texas, one of the largest and best universities in the country in both academics and athletics, has an exceptionally lively, creative, and diverse music scene with numerous live venues, recording studios, and music festivals, and an exceptionally strong downtown by the standards of suburbs-oriented Texas. In contrast to other cities in the state, Austin's downtown has a high density of residential occupancy, with many new apartment and condominium buildings, reflecting a high demand for living in the city center. The urban core is anchored economically by employment in state government, the university, museums and other cultural institutions, and a booming nightlife area that features good restaurants and live music. Lady Bird Lake, an artificial lake on Austin's River, the Colorado River of Texas, is an attractive outdoor recreation spot in the city center. The city's nicknames include "Silicon Hills" in reference to Austin's prominence in the high technology industry, and "Live Music Capital of the World." The city is also known as a regional center for live theater, and for the film industry, of which the annual Austin Film Festival is a highlight.

Austin is a quintessential "Sunbelt" city, meaning that is has grown considerably in recent decades with the large-scale north-to-south shift of the American population. It has become one of the fastest-growing urban centers in the United States. With a population of 885,400 (2013), it ranks 11th in size in the country, having surpassed San Francisco with the 2010 census, and is headed for the top 10. In Texas, the city ranks fourth in size. The present total is more than double the population of as recently as the mid-1980s (1980 population: 345,498, U.S. rank = 42nd; 1990 population: 472,020, U.S. rank = 27th). In 1950, the census year that is considered to be a starting point for mass suburbanization in the United States and the north-to-south regional shift, Austin had 132,459 residents and ranked 72nd in size. The majority of Austin's population is white (68.3%), while Hispanics or Latinos (of any race) are the largest minority and the fastest-growing population group. The five-county Austin metropolitan area has a population of 1,883,051 (2013) and ranks 35th in the United States. The suburban zone has been the fastest-growing part of the metropolis, and has, more-or-less, the look and feel of prosperous middle-class suburbs anywhere in the United States.

Austinites, as they are known, are generally proud of their city and think of it as an exceptionally fun and fine place, and often protest against urban development plans that would erode the city's distinctive character. The slogan "Keep Austin Weird" reflects some of the spirit of the city. Among the many distinctions that Austinites like to point about their city is that it consistently ranks highly on comprehensive surveys that compare cities, and that it ranks highly on many individual variables. For example, Austin was ranked #1 among big cities for jobs and #9 for business and careers by *Forbes*; #2 in cities that people are moving to by *Financial Times*; #2 as a best place to succeed with technology startups; #2 in 2006 as best city among big cities as a place to live by *Money* magazine and #3 in 2009; #10 as the best place to live for recent college graduates by Rent.com; and a great place to retire by *CBS Moneywatch*. The Travel Channel has called Austin America's best college town. The city's unusually broad appeal is further underscored by a #6 rating as a vegetarian-friendly city by GrubHub Inc., *and* by both

Couples dancing to the Cornell Hurd band at a popular night spot named Jovita's in Austin, Texas, which is known for its lively music scene. (Will van Overbeek/National Geographic Creative/Corbis

a #5 ranking by *U.S. News* as a barbeque city and a #13 ranking by *Travel and Leisure* as "America's Best Burger City." Our own inquiries in Austin, as well as among Americans elsewhere who have traveled to the city, confirm that the city is unusually popular: "I didn't know that Texas could be so cool," was the comment of one impressed visitor, while a resident transplanted from the U.S. Northeast once proclaimed "I've come here and I never, ever want to go elsewhere."

The most popular neighborhood in Austin for shopping, music, and nightlife is the South Congress area, SoCo, centered on South Congress Avenue. Nearby is St. Edwards, a residential area that was described in a review of the city's residential districts as "home to artists, musicians, gardeners, and the terminally quirky—some of Austin's best-known personality types." It offers a mix of housing types, ample greenery, a sense of Austin history, and a friendly, small-town feel. St. Edward's University, a private, Catholic, liberal arts institution known as the "other university" in town, is in this neighborhood. Another popular area is Hyde Park, near the University of Texas. It is listed on the National Register of Historic Places, and is home to many undergraduate and graduate students, and university faculty and staff, as well as other Austinites. There are also many restaurants, cafes, bars, and various unique shops in this neighborhood.

A closer look reveals that Austin is, in fact, probably not for everyone, and that its popularity is based on being an island of different culture within the wider culture of the Texas and the south-central states. Specifically, Austin is a very liberal place in a conservative, red-state environment. We are not arguing that one is better than the other, but simply that liberal Austinites are a self-selected population that gravitated to this island, where they built up an alternative urban culture that keeps them content. That urban culture, in turn, continually attracts new migrants with like minds, keeping the city continually different. Other Texans might also enjoy the city's music, restaurants, and of course University of Texas football, but for them, the city is sarcastically the "People's Republic of Texas" that votes Democratic in a solidly Republican state, and that is not as pro-business as they think it should be. Indeed, one of the characteristics of the island that is Austin is opposition by many residents to American corporate culture and the transformation of cities and city neighborhoods by big businesses for profit. Instead, many Austinites prefer to support small, locally owned businesses with individual character, and efforts to keep the city distinctive and affordable. Not surprisingly then, Austin is often a battleground about land use issues between business interests that want to capitalize on the city's fast growth and preservationists who do not want the city to become like every other city in America. Within the metropolitan area, it can be said that Austin proper is the liberal cultural island, while the surrounding suburbs are more conservative, like Texas as a whole. We note that the suburban population is generally content too, as it is also self-selected with many migrants from other regions attracted by the city's strong economy, high quality of life, and geographical advantages: generally warm climate without a severe winter, and a surrounding landscape of beautiful rolling hills, open spaces, and endless sky.

FURTHER READING

Long, Joshua, *Weird City: Sense of Place and Creative Resistance in Austin, Texas* (Austin: University of Texas Press, 2010).
Wolfe, Alexandra, "The New Tech Town: Austin," *Departures*, May–June 2013, http://www.departures.com/articles/the-new-tech-town-austin.

BOULDER, COLORADO

Boulder, Colorado, is not a city for every taste, but for the most part the people who have chosen to live in Boulder swear by it and consider it to be a wonderful place to live and a world apart from most other communities in the United States. They certainly prefer Boulder to the many places in Colorado with which Boulder clashes in culture and lifestyle. Put simply, Boulder is a liberal city socially and politically that is dominated by a large public university, the University of Colorado, and that strongly supports a liberal social agenda that includes strong rules for environmental protection, women's and minority group rights, women's rights to choose about abortion, legalization of marijuana, same-sex marriage, and various other liberal and LGBTQ issues. The city differs from much of the rest of state where voters tend to support conservative candidates and conservative issues, and think of Boulder almost as foreign territory or an island of different thinking. For them, the city is "the People's Republic of Boulder." In this book, an example of a highly contented, conservative city that balances the attention given here to Boulder is Provo, in the neighboring state of Utah.

Boulder was founded in 1858 as a frontier settlement at the foot of the Rocky Mountains in what would become, in 1876, the new state of Colorado. The town was designated by the legislature as the site for the state's public university, which was opened in 1877, and it grew in large part in tandem with the growth of the university and university-affiliated businesses and research centers. The many amenities of the Rocky Mountains nearby also helped Boulder prosper, as many people attracted to the outdoors and mountain sports chose this city as a place to study and to live, and to invest in businesses. The city is only 25 miles (40 km) from Denver, the much larger city that is Colorado's capital, so it benefits from the many attractions and events that are found there, including the large Denver International Airport which is only 45 miles (72 km) from Boulder. Because it is in the shadows of a larger metropolis with sprawling suburbs, Boulder needs to plan carefully for growth in order to retain its distinctive urban character.

Boulder first appeared in the U.S. Census in 1870 when it had a population of 343. It has grown with every census count since, sometime spectacularly, and now numbers about 100,000 people. The 2010 census counted 97,385 residents, while an estimate for 2013 says that the city's population is 103,166. This is the 11th-largest total in Colorado. The Boulder Metropolitan area is more populous, however, with a population 294,567 inhabitants in 2010. Because of the University of Colorado, which has a student enrollment of 31,702 (Fall 2013), the city's population is younger on the average than that of many other communities. According to the 2010 census, Boulder's median age was 28.7 years as compared to the national median age of 37.2 years. Likewise, because of the student population, a disproportionate number of Boulder's residents do not live in family-type households with children, but live either alone or with unrelated housemates and are renters rather than homeowners.

Other than the University of Colorado, which has some 10,000 faculty and staff and is Boulder's largest employer, the city is home to numerous scientific institutes, especially those concerned with atmospheric research, polar and mountain environments, environmental monitoring, and research about space. Therefore, there are many highly educated scientific specialists in the city, and it has a commensurate income and salary structure. A recent proposal by Google to greatly expand its workforce in the city would add to the economy, but there are concerns on the part of city residents that housing will become less affordable because of "Google gentrification." The city also attracts outdoors enthusiasts, nature lovers, and people with strong commitments to environmental protection and sustainability. It is a mecca for outdoor sports such as hiking, marathon running, and rock climbing. The Flatirons is an iconic rock formation at the city's edge that is particularly popular among climbers. Furthermore, Boulder is one of the most bicycle-friendly cities in the United States. The city also attracts a young population of vagabonding backpackers, attracted to Boulder's mountain setting, young population, independent music scene, and liberal attitudes, and has had problems with unruly behavior, drug abuse, and homeless beggars. In the 1960s, Boulder was one of America's most popular hippie meccas. Today, visitors and locals alike enjoy strolling along the Pearl Street Mall in the heart of Boulder's downtown, and sampling local restaurants, pubs, and interesting shops. The street is an urban revitalization project from the 1970s and is regarded as being highly successful both commercially and aesthetically.

Boulder has received considerable favorable mention in comparison with other American cities. For example, as reported by MoneyWatch News on March 17, 2011, Boulder was ranked #1 in a Gallup survey in overall well-being among American cities and as the happiest city in the United States. Likewise, portfolio.com employed census data to study "brain power" in the 200 largest metropolitan areas in the United States and reported that Boulder ranks first in having a highly educated workforce: 82.5% of adults have attended college and 26% of the city's residents hold master's, doctoral, or professional degrees, both figures being the highest in the country. In another comparative study, *Forbes* reported in 2009 that Boulder is #1 among America's "top 25 towns to live well," citing the ease of doing business in the city as a major advantage. *Forbes* also lists Boulder as one of the best cities in the United States for business and careers (2013). Other rankings show Boulder to be "LGBT family-friendly," #8 among the top 10 American cities for artists, #6 according to *AARP Magazine* among the top 10 cities to live and retire, and the best city in America in which to raise an "outdoor kid" according to *Backpacker Magazine*.

FURTHER READING

Dougherty, Conor, "A Google Gentrification Fight That Doesn't Involve San Francisco," *International New York Times*, December 28, 2014, http://bits.blogs.nytimes.com/2014/12/28/a-google-gentrification-fight-that-doesnt-involve-san-francisco/?partner=rss&emc=rss&_r=0.

Pettem, Silvia, *Boulder: Evolution of a City* (Boulder: University Press of Colorado, 2006).

BURLINGTON, VERMONT

Burlington, population 42,417, is the largest city in Vermont. The Burlington metropolitan area, which also includes the cities of South Burlington and Winooski, has a population of 204,796, about one-third of the population of the state. We had considered listing Vermont as one of the five most contented states in the United States, because it clearly is an outstanding place with a high quality of life, but decided to spread the glory and make room for our sixth-ranking state, and to let Burlington speak for Vermont. The city is in the northeastern part of the beautiful "Green Mountain State" on the eastern shore of Lake Champlain, across which is northeastern New York State. The Canadian border is 45 miles (72 km) to the north.

Burlington was founded in 1785, and grew initially as a port on Lake Champlain and as a lumbering and manufacturing center. The University of Vermont was established in 1791 by Ira Allen, one of the Green Mountain Boys of the American Revolution and a founder of the state of Vermont, and is one of the oldest universities in the United States. In 1862 it became the state's Land Grant university. The town's early prosperity is reflected in a number of historic buildings that remain today, including the 1816 Unitarian Church, the classical 1840 Follett House, and the Victorian Howard Opera House, the Richardson Building, and the Masonic Temple. Today, the University of Vermont and the University of Vermont Medical Center are this small city's two largest employers. They give Burlington the feel of a college town. There is also a manufacturing base in Burlington that, historically, has been led by G.S. Blodgett Company, a maker of ovens for restaurant kitchens. Today, Burlington is known as the home of the Ben and Jerry's brand of ice cream, the Vermont Teddy Bear Company, Burton's Snowboards, the Bruegger's chain of bagel-centered bakery-cafés, the Seventh Generation paper products company, and the Burlington Chocolates. The list is remarkable because they are all fairly recent, locally founded small businesses that made good by producing high-quality products within a framework of socially and environmentally responsible business practices. Thus, these businesses reflect the progressive nature of Burlington and the state of Vermont, independent thinking, and local traditions for hand-crafting. Another example of the distinctive social-political culture in both Burlington and Vermont is Bernard (Bernie) Sanders, the state's current junior U.S. senator. He is a self-described democratic-socialist, which in itself would guarantee that he would never be elected in most states in the United States, and a successful former four-term mayor of Burlington who ran against Democratic and Republican parties' candidates as a socialist.

We chose to list Burlington as one of America's 10 most contented cities because our own observations agree fully with what we have heard and read about the city: here is a wholesome, picturesque, and exceedingly friendly New England town that is green and healthy, a paradise for college students, ideal for raising a family, and also a great place to settle down in as a retiree. In 2010, *Forbes* praised Burlington as one of the "prettiest" towns in America and featured a photograph from downtown Burlington on its cover. The accompanying article says that "Burlington has it all," with charms that include "a brick pedestrian marketplace, Vermont's iconic white steeples and rolling hills that spill down toward a lively, green waterfront on Lake Champlain." In recommending the city to retirees, the magazine *AARP* noted that Burlington met its specific criteria for what makes a community livable: "new urbanism, smart growth, mixed-use development, and easy-living standards." Among those who have recommended Burlington as a place for families is *National Geographic*. Its writers cited the picturesque background for a host of family-fun outdoor activities, as well as buying ice cream at the shop where the Ben & Jerry's got its start and a personalized teddy bear at the popular Vermont Teddy Bear Factory. In 2009, *Children's Health Magazine* wrote that Burlington was the best city in the country in which to raise a family. In 2006, the city was rated among the top cities in the country for health by *Men's Health* magazine.

Burlington is a town for four seasons. Vermont winters can be long and brutal, and the wind from across Lake Champlain bites deeply, but Burlington in the snow is holiday-card beautiful. Residents enjoy ice fishing in the lake and skating, and take their children to hockey practices and games. The fabulous ski slopes of Vermont are only a short drive away. As winter ends, there is a beautiful spring for hiking and biking, fishing, boating and other sports, while in summer Burlington enjoys boating and swimming in the lake, and camping in nearby state parks. The colors of autumn are legendary, and Burlington enjoys another busy tourist season as people from a wide area in the United States East travel to New England to enjoy the peak of fall foliage. The white-steeple charm of the New England town is a draw for visitors year-round, and not surprisingly, tourism is a big business in Burlington. The city's Church Street Marketplace, a four-block long pedestrian mall with shops and restaurants, is a very pleasant public space and another of Burlington's popular attractions.

FURTHER READING

Martin, Mary L. and Dinah Roseberry, *Greetings from Burlington, Vermont* (Atglen, PA: Schiffer Publishing, 2007).

Soifer, Steven, *The Socialist Mayor: Bernard Sanders in Burlington, Vermont* (Westport, CT: Bergin & Garvey, 1991).

CHARLESTON, SOUTH CAROLINA

Charleston is the oldest city in South Carolina and the second-largest city in the state after the capital, Columbia. It was founded in 1670 and was originally named

Charles Town in honor of King Charles II of England. Before the Revolution, it was the largest and most important city in the American colonies south of Philadelphia, and was known for its busy port and prosperous traders. The slave trade was especially lucrative, as were the plantations near the city where slaves toiled for their owners to raise rice, cotton, and indigo for export. An island in Charleston Harbor named Sullivan's Island was the disembarkation point for an estimated 40% of the approximately 400,000 slaves who were brought from Africa to British North America. The first shots of the American Civil War were fired at Fort Sumter in Charleston Harbor on April 12, 1861. Charleston never regained national prominence after the South's loss in that war, and struggled economically and with race relations for decades afterward. It was poor as well for much of the 20th century, and depended heavily on nearby military bases to support the local economy. Now the city is a prosperous business center once again, serving a fast-growing coastal region in South Carolina where there are many tourist resorts and retirement communities. It has a charm of its own that is based on historic ambience and distinctive local cultural flavors, and has evolved into one of America's most popular cities to visit. We include Charleston as one of our 10 most contented cities in the United States because of its charm, its rebound in economy, and the pride that city residents take in their community.

Charleston was the fourth-largest city in the United States in the first national census in 1790 and was still in the top 10 in 1840, but its rank and influence slipped as country shifted its growth westward and developed its powerful industrial base in the Northeast and Midwest. The city now has a population of 127,999 (2013 estimate), and ranks at exactly #200 in size in the United States. The three-county metropolitan area that focuses on Charleston ranks #76 in the country and has an estimated 712,200 residents. The population is growing at a fast rate both in the city and in the surroundings because of a stronger local economy and the lure of warmer temperatures and coastal amenities, but Charleston is a much smaller city in rank than it was in the past. The racial makeup of the city is 70.2% white and 25.4% African American. This contrasts with the historical pattern in which Charleston had an African America majority population. The change came with migration of African American residents to Northern cities and, more recently, the migration of white Americans to the Sunbelt. Gentrification of historic neighborhoods has also been a factor in Charleston's changing social geography.

The center of Charleston is the old city which is located on a peninsula formed by the confluence of two local rivers, the Ashley and the Cooper. Proud Charlestonians like to say that it is in their city that the Ashley and Cooper Rivers come together to form the Atlantic Ocean. An historic defensive seawall called the Battery is located at the point of the Charleston peninsula, and is a focus of the city's tourism. There is a promenade along the wall, from which there are views of historic Fort Sumter and the retired aircraft carrier from World War II, the USS *Yorktown*, among other landmarks, as well as a number of the elegant antebellum

In addition to charming historical architecture and distinctive cultural traditions, Charleston, South Carolina, offers ocean beaches and waterfront recreation. This photo shows a man fishing from the pier at Folly Beach. (Brian Patterson/Dreamstime.com)

mansions for which the city is so famous. Other stately homes, including the iconic "Rainbow Row" of old homes and the distinctive "Pink House," are on streets nearby. The intersection of Broad and Meeting Streets is called "the Four Corners of Law" because the four corners have buildings that represent federal, state, local, and ecclesiastical authority: a federal courthouse, the old capital of colonial South Carolina, city hall, and historic St. Michael's Church. The term is said to have been coined in the 1930s by Robert Ripley, the creator of *Ripley's Believe It or Not*. The Charleston Museum, founded in 1773, is the oldest museum in the United States and is dedicated to the history of the city and the so-called South Carolina Lowcountry.

But Charleston is more than old buildings and landmarks. It is also a city of unique blends of culture and traditions that set it apart from all other cities, and that add to the city's appeal. The city's cuisine is known for locally grown rice as a staple and for seafood, and includes dishes such as gumbo, she-crab soup, and fried oysters. Some of Charleston's fine restaurants are listed among the top choices for dining in America. Charleston also has rich traditions of live theater and music, and is known for classics such as "Charleston Rag," the Charleston dance craze that swept America in the 1920s, the opera "Porgy and Bess," and the various iterations of the early 20th-century Jenkins Orphanage Band that were comprised of orphaned African American boys who had been taught to play donated instruments. There are also distinctive dialects and word pronunciations that are associated with Charleston. Many of these and other cultural traits are rooted in the African American Gullah culture of the Sea Islands along the South Carolina coast.

The combination of historical architecture, rich local culture, and friendly people has made Charleston into the tourist mecca that it is today. Among the accolades that the city has received is "America's Most Friendly [City]" by *Travel + Leisure* and *Condé Nast Traveler*, and "the most polite and hospitable city in America" by *Southern Living* magazine. Indeed, there is a danger of too much success in Charleston's new life, as gentrification has followed on the heels of the city's popularity, displacing older, lower-income residents and furthering the transition of the city to a racial mix that does not accurately represent the city's history.

FURTHER READING

Gessler, Diana Hollingsworth, *Very Charleston: A Celebration of History, Culture, and Low-country Charm* (Chapel Hill, NC: Algonquin Books, 2003).

Rosen, Robert N., *A Short History of Charleston* (Columbia, SC: University of South Carolina Press, 1997).

DES MOINES, IOWA

Des Moines is the capital and largest city of the state of Iowa. It is located in Polk County in the center of the state at the confluence of the Des Moines and Raccoon Rivers where the U.S. War Department's Fort Des Moines once stood for about four years in the 1840s to protect frontier settlers from local Indians. It became an industrial center later in the 19th century based on local coal reserves and completion of railroad linkages to Chicago and to growing settlements in Iowa and places west. Sufficient wealth was generated by the end of the 19th century for the city to afford a fine ensemble of public buildings in the downtown that today forms the core of the Civic Center Historic District. As with other American cities, economic restructuring and globalization resulted in industrial decline and growing urban problems by the mid-20th century, and Des Moines was forced to reinvent itself in order to reverse a falling jobs base and stem population loss. The city has done so in admirable fashion, and is now one of America's most pleasant cities and among the healthiest economically.

Des Moines has consistently earned high rankings in recent years in comparisons on a wide variety of criteria with other American cities. For example, rankings for 2014 include best city in the United States for young professionals by *Forbes*, #2 as the best place in the United States for business, by *Forbes* again, and #6 as the most family-friendly U.S. city, by *Forbes* still again. Furthermore,

MarketWatch ranked the city in its list of top 10 cities for young home buyers, *Fortune* identified Des Moines as the #1 city with "Up-and-Coming Downtowns," ZipRecruiter listed it in the top 5 cities for finding jobs, and Beyond.com ranked the city as one of America's top 10 for finding jobs. *Vocativ* has identified Des Moines as the #4 LGBT-friendly city in America. A Gallup survey in 2012 ranked the Des Moines metropolitan area as #7 in the United States in community optimism, with 73.0% of respondents saying that their town is becoming a better place to live.

The population of Des Moines is about 207,510 (2013), and that of the metropolitan area is estimated to be about 594,600 (2014). The estimate for 2013 and last three census counts, 1990, 2000 and 2010, show successive population increases for the city after two decades of loss in the 1970s and 1980s, with a likely uptick in population growth rate more recently, mostly because the city is become stronger economically and more attractive (annexation of new territory to city limits also figures into the total population). Des Moines residents have known for a long time that theirs is a fine city for living, and exhibit strong pride in their home town as well as a sense of commitment to continually improve the city's appearance and public services. As the new economy of the Des Moines area evolves and employees and managers are transferred to the area from other parts of the United States, Des Moines is coming to be better known and the secret is out: if you want a city that is not too big and not too small, and that is a great and safe place to raise a family, and where living costs are very manageable, then Des Moines might be just the perfect place for you. Many people, including jobs transplants to the city that we talked to from supposedly more sophisticated cities such as New York, Chicago, and Boston, swear by Des Moines, and acknowledge that until they had moved there, they did not know about "Des Moines cool." Returning residents too speak about a "new Des Moines," in which neighborhoods that were once run-down and scary are now hip and progressive, and where young people at the cutting edge of new developments in their chosen careers rave about the city and choose to live and invest in its core.

The new economy of Des Moines is based on white-collar jobs in the services sector, most especially in insurance, banking and finance, and the publications industry. In fact, the city has been referred to as the third-largest "insurance capital" in the world, and the Hartford of the West, referring to the insurance city of Hartford, Connecticut, in the eastern United States. Major companies include the Principal Financial Group, whose 45-story office tower in the downtown of Des Moines is the tallest building in Iowa, Nationwide/Allied Insurance, and Wellmark Blue Cross Blue Shield, while in banking and finance there is Wells Fargo Bank, Des Moines' largest private employer. The Meredith Corporation, founded in 1902, has been a leading publishing company for more than a century, famous for magazines with "American heartland" values that cater especially to mass-market women's readership, including *Better Homes and Gardens* and *Family Circle*. The city's economy is also closed tied to the farmlands of Iowa and other states in the Midwest, with offices of companies that sell farm machinery, seed, and fertilizers, as well as insurance companies and banks that specialize in farmers' needs and agribusiness. Des Moines is also growing as a center of medical care, information technology, higher education, and the arts.

The city has a vibrant cultural scene, including theater, ballet, opera, and other performing arts, and outstanding museums, including the Des Moines Art Center and Salisbury House, an English-style residential mansion with a superb collection of art from around the world and valuable books that had been collected by the early 20th-century cosmetics magnate from Des Moines, Carl Weeks and his wife Edith. The city also has many parks, bicycle trails, and recreation centers, as well as a zoo and a botanical garden. Gray's Lake Park near the downtown is especially popular. The city has tree-lined streets and lush-green neighborhoods, and a full range of healthy and educational activities for children. There are also popular music festivals and fun local neighborhood events. Three wonderful seasons more than make up for harsh midwestern winters. The East Village neighborhood is a funky blend of historic buildings, trendy apartment living, and interesting restaurants, pubs, and cafés, shops, and nightlife. The area caters especially to a younger crowd. Every four years, Des Moines gains national and international spotlight as the principal campaign and media center for the Iowa political primaries, crucial testing grounds for both Democrat and Republican candidates who hope to become president. Locals enjoy the attention, as well as the benefits that the elections season bring to the area's economy.

FURTHER READING

McCue, Craig S., *Des Moines (Then & Now)* (Mount Pleasant, SC: Arcadia Publishing, 2012).
Ream, Michael, *Insiders' Guide to Des Moines* (Guilford, CT: Globe Pequot Press: 2011).

MINNEAPOLIS, MINNESOTA

Minneapolis is the largest city in Minnesota and the larger of the state's "twin cities," Minneapolis and St. Paul. The city's population is 400,070 (2013 estimate), and that of the combined Minneapolis-St. Paul metropolitan area is about 3.5 million, the 16th largest total for a metropolitan area in the United States. The city is on both banks of the upper reaches of Mississippi River near where the larger waterway is joined by the Minnesota River, and has nicknames that include City of Lakes, Mill City (because of a long history of flour milling at the Mississippi's St. Anthony

Falls), "Mini-Apple," and the Twin City because it abuts another prominent city, St. Paul, the state's capital. It is widely regarded to be among the most livable of the larger cities in the United States, which is why we list it here among America's 10 most contented urban centers. Indeed, our accolades apply to the entire Twin Cities area, including the smaller twin, St. Paul, 2013 population 294,873.

There is a saying that it is hard to get people to move to Minneapolis, but even harder to get them to move away once they have lived there. The former reflects the relative isolation of the city from other big metropolitan areas in the United States and the brutally cold winters of Minnesota, while the latter is said to be a response to the city's extra measures of friendliness and high quality of life. Among other pluses, Minneapolis is a city with many parks and lakes that support an active, outdoors lifestyle for probably a higher fraction of residents than in most other cities, even in the dead of winter. Rather than dreading the cold and ice, Minneapolitans are drawn to frozen lakes for skating, ice hockey, and the ever-popular ice fishing, and to parks and trails for cross-country skiing and snowy vistas. In warm weather there are ball games, picnics, and neighborhood festivals in local parks, as well as open-air concerts and other events. The terrain is more or less flat, so bicycling and jogging are popular activities too. The park system of Minneapolis has been called the best-designed, best-financed, and best-maintained in the United States.

Our choice of Minneapolis for these pages was also influenced by a flattering article about the city by Derek Thompson in a recent issue of the *Atlantic*. Entitled "The Miracle of Minneapolis," the article lauds the city for being both prosperous and affordable. This is a rare combination for urban centers in the United States, where the pattern, unfortunately, has been for housing prices to rise out of proportion as an economy grows, making it difficult for middle-class and poorer people to afford decent housing. An important ingredient for this success, according to Thompson, is a "fiscal equalization" law that was passed in 1971 that required all political jurisdictions in the Twin Cities area to share tax revenues, so that poor areas without a strong tax base would not fall far behind in an ability to provide residents with good services. Such a law is rare in urban America, although it would be a good model nationwide, because it has helped to make Minneapolis into city with fewer glaring inequalities between neighborhoods, as well as fewer deprived neighborhoods. A companion to that legislation was another law, this one passed in 1976 and also disappointingly rare across the United States, that has required all jurisdictions in the metropolitan area to take on their fair share of housing construction for the poor and middle classes. This has resulted in a city with fewer so-called gilded ghettoes. The economic benefit of such social engineering is that people can afford to continue living in the city they enjoy as it gains in prosperity, and that Minneapolis has had an opportunity to grow its own businesses from the bottom up into large corporations. The city is, therefore, distinguished as a successful incubator of new companies that grow, pay taxes, and stay. The giant retailing chain Target was founded in the Minneapolis area in 1962 and is now one of five Fortune 500 companies that is headquartered in the city.

Another recent article about the city, this one in a *Huffington Post* site about healthy living, discusses what the rest of America can learn from the Twin Cities about living well. It notes that the Minneapolis-St. Paul area has been rated as the fittest city in the United States (2012) by the American College of Sports Medicine, that nearly 83% of residents were active every single day, and that more than one-half of the area's residents got at least the government-recommended 30 minutes of moderate exercise every day. The article also points out the Minneapolis-St. Paul area has the lowest unemployment rate of any metropolitan area in the United States, and argues that there is better mental health as a result. Furthermore, Minneapolis-St. Paul is reported to be among the "top three most literate cities" because of many bookstores, high levels of newspaper circulation, and a proclivity for reading. This in turn is said to result in "better sleep, better cognitive function and improved stress release."

Stone Arch Bridge across the Mississippi River in the center of Minneapolis was once a railroad bridge, but is now used only by bicyclists and pedestrians. Jogging across the bridge is popular too. The photo was taken on July 4, 2014, U.S. Independence Day, and shows the city skyline in the background and part of the historic flour milling district at the river's edge. (Jacek Sopotnicki/Dreamstime.com)

Finally, we note that Minneapolis (and St. Paul) has become increasingly diverse in population makeup in recent decades, and has made great strides in acculturating immigrant groups into the wider community. Historically, the urban population was overwhelmingly white, with a noticeably heavy admixture from the Scandinavian countries, but from the mid-20th century the metropolis began attracting increasing numbers of African Americans, Latinos, and Asians. The largest communities in the United States of Hmong immigrants and immigrants from Somalia live in the Minneapolis area despite the fact that they come from regions of where there is no winter weather. Most of them arrived in the United States as extremely poor and under conditions of extreme hardship, and without knowledge of English or American ways. The added diversity has enriched the city culturally, and added various religious and ethnic festivals, and ethnic restaurants and cuisines to the routines of city life in Minneapolis-St. Paul.

FURTHER READING

Aamont, Gregg, *The New Minnesotans: Stories of Immigrants and Refugees* (Minneapolis: Syren Book Company, 2006).

Nathanson, Iric, *Minneapolis in the Twentieth Century: The Growth of an American City* (St. Paul: Minnesota Historical Society Press, 2009).

Thompson, Derek, "The Miracle of Minneapolis," *The Atlantic*, 315, 2, March 2015, pp. 20–32.

"What the Twin Cities Can Teach Us about Living Well," *Huffpost Healthy Living*, November 18, 2013, http://www.huffingtonpost.com/2013/11/18/minneapolis-health-happin_n_4213678.html.

PITTSBURGH, PENNSYLVANIA

Pittsburgh is the second-largest city in Pennsylvania and the largest city in Appalachia. It is located in the western part of the state where the Alleghany and Monongahela Rivers come together to form the Ohio River, and was founded at that strategic confluence in 1764 as Fort Pitt. It prospered as the settlement frontier expanded west of the Appalachian Mountains in the early United States, and was a busy departure point for settlers and goods moving west via the Ohio River on locally built vessels. In the 19th century, the city became one of the premier industrial centers in the United States. Its growth was based on coal reserves in nearby Pennsylvania and West Virginia mines, and iron ore shipped via the Great Lakes to ports on Lake Erie that were, in turn, connected to Pittsburgh by rail. In the late 19th century, the city became America's undisputed #1 steel-making city, and soon accounted for between one-third and one-half of all steel that was manufactured in the country during a time of robust national expansion. The city also produced aluminum, glass, food products, and many kinds of machinery, including electrical machinery. The population grew with immigrant labor from Europe and, in the 20th century, stepped-up migration of African Americans from the South. At the same time, the city's air became notoriously polluted, and Pittsburgh earned a wide reputation as smoky city covered in soot.

The Pittsburgh of today is quite different. The steel mills and other heavy industrial establishments have closed because of economic restructuring and global competition, so the pollution is much abated and the city's famed hills are now green instead of black. There was considerable unemployment and economic hardship when deindustrialization took place, and many Pittsburghers left the city to seek work in other parts of the country. However, now the city has succeeded in developing a prosperous postindustrial economy that is based on white-collar jobs in corporate offices and financial institutions, as well as in high technology, higher education, the arts, tourism and hospitality, and other fields. For much of the 20th century the city was America's third-ranking corporate headquarters center, ranking behind only the much larger New York and Chicago in numbers of important companies having headquarters there. Among the giant corporations in Pittsburgh are U.S. Steel, PNC Financial Services, PPG Industries, and H.J. Heinz. Their headquarters' skyscrapers are among the 30 or so tall buildings in Pittsburgh's compact yet impressive downtown, an area that is commonly called the Golden Triangle after the historic river confluence where Pittsburgh was founded. The city also has a number of prestigious universities, led by the University of Pittsburgh and Carnegie Mellon University, both in the city's East End, and Duquesne University. The University of Pittsburgh Medical Center is another major employer in the city.

Like many American cities, Pittsburgh recorded its peak population in the 1950 census, just before the decades of deindustrialization and suburbanization would take their greatest toll. At that time the city's total was 676,906, more than double today's total 305,841. In its heyday, the city ranked 8th in the United States in size, but it is now 62nd. There is a large area of suburban development around Pittsburgh, as well as many nearby formerly industrial towns in the immediate vicinity, so the Pittsburgh urban area is much more populous: 1,733,853 as of the most recent census (#27 in the United States), while the metropolitan region totals 2,360,867 residents and ranks as the 22nd-largest American metropolitan area. The thinned-out population of the Pittsburgh central city has meant less crowding in old industrial neighborhoods and a higher quality of life for a much larger fraction of the city's residents. Housing is among the most affordable among cities in the United States, with many homes being spacious and enjoying fine views from hill slope and hilltop locations. There is a strong element of neighborhood cohesion in the city, bonded by ethnic ties, and many old neighborhoods are known for their histories of immigrant laborers and the ethnic churches, other ethnic institutions, and ethnic traditions that they endowed the city. In addition to

African Americans, the city's main ethnic groups include Germans, Poles, Italians, Irish, Ukrainians, and Ruthenians. The city also has a sizable Jewish population.

In some ways, Pittsburgh is an undiscovered American treasure. The old reputation of industrial smoke and respiratory ills is in the past, as is the crisis of economic decline, and there has been a full-fledged urban renaissance that is as yet not fully known across America. Old neighborhoods that were once depressed are now trendy homes to well-paid young professionals in a bustling post-industrial economy, and formerly dilapidated shopping streets are now lined with popular bars and restaurants, art galleries, and fine shops. Some of the old mill districts have been put to new uses, including riverside parks, shopping areas, and residences. The city has even become a popular location for making movies and television productions, and has the largest soundstage in the United States outside New York and Los Angeles. Unique landscape elements include historic hillside neighborhoods, 446 bridges, and 712 outdoor pedestrian staircases. The city's residents take pride in the urban past, and celebrate the city's new strengths. An unabashed Pittsburgh lover has called his book about the city *The Paris of Appalachia*, while two other local writers entitled their self-published profile of the city no less than *Pittsburgh: The Greatest City in the World*. The local professional sport's teams, notably the Pittsburgh Pirates baseball club, the Pittsburgh Steelers football team, and the Pittsburgh Penguins hockey franchise, have avid fan followings that also speak of Pittsburgh pride. Those who have looked closely at the new Pittsburgh are impressed: the city has been rated as "America's Most Livable City" by *Places Rated Almanac*, *Forbes*, and the *Economist*. Pittsburghers could have told them that, because they are a contented population indeed, but many also want to keep a lid on the new charms of their city lest the word gets out too widely and the city becomes spoiled all over.

FURTHER READING

Kidney, Walter C., *Pittsburgh Then and Now* (San Diego: Thunder Bay Press, 2004).
Martin, Sean Elliot and Heath Curran, *Pittsburgh: The Greatest City in the World* (CreateSpace Independent Publishing Platform, 2009).
O'Neill, Brian, *The Paris of Appalachia: Pittsburgh in the Twenty-First Century* (Pittsburgh: Carnegie Mellon University Press, 2009).

PROVO, UTAH

Provo is located in north-central Utah, about 43 miles (69 km) south of Salt Lake City, the state's capital and largest city. It is set beautifully in the Utah Valley against the front of the Wasatch Mountains, and is most famous as the home of Brigham Young University, an excellent university with more than 30,000 students that is operated by the Church of the Latter-Day Saints (LDS), commonly known as the Mormon Church. According to the 2010 census, the city had 112,488 residents, making it the third-largest city in Utah. To the north is the smaller city of Orem. The Provo-Orem metropolitan area had 526,810 residents, the third-largest total for a metropolitan area in the state of Utah. The city is one of the fastest growing in the United States, with percentage increases in population between 10-year census counts always in the double digits from the first counts in 1860–1870 to the counts in 1990–2000. Population growth slowed between 2000 and 2010 to about 7.0%, but was still well above the average for American cities. An estimate for 2103 shows the city's population at 115,919, up 3.1% from 2010.

The city was founded as a frontier outpost called Fort Utah in 1849 by 33 Mormon families, and has always been an overwhelmingly Mormon city. At present, about 98% of the population belongs to the LDS Church, making Provo the most homogeneous city in the United States of its size in terms of religious identity. In addition to being the base of Brigham Young University, the city is the site of the largest LDS Missionary Training Center, a Mormon temple, and a second temple that is being constructed on the site of an historic Mormon tabernacle that had been destroyed by fire. The city is also very homogeneous racially, as 84.8% of the population is white. African Americans make up only 0.7% of the population, and are outnumbered by Pacific Islanders who comprise 1.1% of the total. They come from a part of the world where the Mormon Church is very active. Other than the college student population, which is young and primarily single, Provo is a city with many families that have a relatively large number of children (e.g., four or more). This characteristic is tied to Mormonism, which values large families, and helps to explain the fact that the Provo-Orem metropolitan area has the largest-sized houses, on the average, of any metropolitan area in the United States: 1,980 square feet.

Even though Provo has an unusually homogeneous population in terms of religious makeup and race, residents like to point to aspects of the population that reflect diversity. Specifically, because many city residents have spent time abroad as Mormon missionaries, there is an unusually large number of people who speak languages other than English as second languages, as well more knowledge within the population about foreign cultures and a diversity of interesting foreign travel experiences. The city also boasts a number of restaurants with authentic cuisine from other cultures as another side benefit of Mormon mission activity abroad.

Provo is said to be the most conservative of American cities with a population of 100,000 or more. The conservatism is based on the teachings and ways of living of the LDS Church, which dominates the city culturally. Examples of Mormon influence are that there are few bars in the city and other places that sell alcohol, comparatively few smokers, significantly less consumption of carbonated beverages, coffee, and other caffeinated drinks, and comparatively few people with

tattoos. Furthermore, standards of dress and personal grooming in Provo are conservative and clean-cut, including among young students on the Brigham Young
University campus. The university itself, excellent as it in many fields, has been
criticized for promoting conservative LDS viewpoints too strongly at the expense
of open exchange of ideas and freedoms for opposing thought. Therefore, for us
Provo is something of a balance on our list of 10 most contented cities in the
United States to Boulder, Colorado, which we describe on a different page as a
very liberal city. Both cities have highly self-selected populations, meaning that
most residents are there by choice, and we expect that many people who are contented in one of these cities might not like the other city very much, even though
both are beautiful and are noted for outdoors activities.

Provo is widely recognized as a great, safe, and beautiful place to live. It has
fresh air and countless recreation opportunities, especially in the outdoors where
there are mountains, lakes, streams, bike trails, and nearby ski slopes, among
other attractions for a healthy lifestyle. *Outside Magazine* consistently ranks it
among the top places to live in America, most recently (2014) as second-best in
the country after Duluth, Minnesota. The city is also ranked second-best (after
Bloomington, Indiana) in work-life balance by NerdWallet, #3 for business and
careers by *Forbes*, and #1 as a start-up hub. After considering seven categories of
variables ranging from income to housing affordability, quality of education, and
crime rates, *Forbes* has rated the city third in the United States (after Grand Rap-
ids, Michigan and Boise, Idaho) for raising a family. A Gallup survey in 2012 rated
Provo as the #1 city in the United States in community optimism, with 76.0% of
respondents saying that their town is becoming a better place to live.

The economy of Provo is usually strong. There are relatively high incomes and
an unemployment rate of only 3.2% (September 2014), which is considered to be
very low. In addition to the university and the missionary training center, major
employers include a number of growing companies that were founded in Provo:
Ancenstry.com, a genealogy research company; Nature's Sunshine Products, makers of vitamins and encapsulated herbal products; Nu Skin Enterprises, a maker
of skin care products; and Novell, a large software company that has helped to
bring a Silicon Valley type of economy to the Utah Valley.

FURTHER READING

Clark, Jayne, "The Road to Happiness Leads to Provo," *USA Today*, April 25, 2014, p. 04d.
Prall, Derek, "Provo, Utah: Best Place in the Country?" *American City & County Exclusive
    Insight*, April 2, 2014, p. 7.
Waterman, Bryan and Brian Kagel, *The Lord's University: Freedom and Authority at BYU*
    (Salt Lake City, UT: Signature Books, 1998).

SAN FRANCISCO, CALIFORNIA

San Francisco is a beautiful and historic city on the Pacific Coast of California on a peninsula between the ocean and San Francisco Bay. It is an important port and industrial city, a major corporate and financial center, and an extremely popular destination for domestic and international tourists. Many people, San Franciscans and visitors alike, say that this "City by the Bay" is their favorite city, citing everything from climate to picturesque charm, and from distinctive and diverse cultures to characteristics of the economy as reasons. We agree that San Francisco steals hearts, and know that many of its residents have settled there specifically because they have fallen in love with the city. Therefore, it was an easy choice for us to include the unusually popular city on our list as one of the 10 most contented urban centers in the United States.

According to an estimate for 2014, the population of San Francisco is 852,469, making it the 5th most populous city in California, and the 14th largest in the United States. The city is part of a much larger metropolitan area that includes the larger city of San Jose to the south and Oakland across San Francisco Bay to the east and that totals about 8.6 million inhabitants. With a population density of 18,187 people per square mile (7,022 per km²), San Francisco itself is one of the most crowded cities in the United States, second only to New York City. The crowding is because of a combination of the city's confined space at the tip of a peninsula and its popularity, as well as because it is an older city that predates America's love affair with the automobile. The city was founded in 1776 as a Spanish mission and garrison outpost, and began to grow into a great city with start of the American era and the California Gold Rush of 1849. It was a boom-town with a sudden influx of migrants, and distinguished Victorian architecture that reflected prosperity. A great fire in 1906 was a temporary setback that opened a door for Los Angeles in the south to outstrip San Francisco for preeminence on the West Coast, but the city soon recovered to become the metropolis of northern California. It attracted immigrants from many countries of Europe and Asia, and later from south of the U.S. border, as well as migrants from all parts of the United States, and became one of the most diverse cities in the country. The city's China-town neighborhood is one of the nation's largest. San Francisco has a large number of information technology companies and is one of the nation's smartest cities.

In the 1960s, San Francisco became a major focus of social change and protest. It was a capital of the hippie counterculture, the Sexual Revolution, and American protests against involvement in the Vietnam War. It also became strongly identified with the gay rights movement, and is one of the world's most gay and lesbian-friendly cities. Its Castro neighborhood is one of the world's largest and most famous gay neighborhoods. The city is also known for progressive liberal politics, for a high degree of political participation and high voter turnouts, and for strong support for environmental initiatives and sustainable living. The environmentalist Sierra Club was founded in San Francisco in 1892, and is one of many organizations in the city that are dedicated to environmental causes. Far more than most American cities, especially in the West, people in San Francisco and the Bay Area depend on public transit or bicycles to get around, and eschew automobile lifestyles. The Bay Area Rapid Transit system (BART) that connects the city with communities east of the bay and the San Francisco Municipal Railway system (Muni) that provides transportation within the city itself are two of the best and most popularly used public transit systems in the country. The city is also known for its bridges, most notably the Golden Gate Bridge, and for its iconic cable car system that runs up and down the city's streets with unusually steep slopes. The city has more than 200 parks, as well as many miles of beachfront and other areas for recreation at the waterfront. There are also a rich architectural heritage, an especially vibrant nightlife, many cultural institutions such as museums and theaters, and a full array of festivals and street fairs that celebrate the

The Golden Gate Bridge and the gay couple walking hand in hand are both icons of San Francisco, California's "City by the Bay." (Carlos Alvarez/iStockphoto.com)

city's many ethnic groups, the LGBT community, as well as various religious and national holidays. There is never a shortage of things to do in San Francisco.

There are problems in San Francisco, to be sure, but many of them are the result of the city's popularity: shortages of available housing units and high costs for rent, heavy traffic in specific parts of the city, and throngs of tourists. High demand for urban space has stimulated urban development, which in turn has made the city even more densely built-up. Gentrification is widespread and has reduced the supply of affordable housing. There are many homeless people in the city, some displaced from where they had lived by high prices and others drawn to San Francisco along with their economic or personal problems because of the city's weather, many charms, and traditions of liberalism. Although many San Franciscans are fed up with these problems, there is more of a desire to stay and fight for a better city than to abandon the metropolis for greener pastures. For many people, it gets no greener than the "City by the Bay."

FURTHER READING

Beitel, Karl, *Local Protests, Global Movements: Capital, Community, and State in San Francisco* (Philadelphia, PA: Temple University Press, 2013).

Hartman, Chester, *City for Sale: The Transformation of San Francisco* (Berkeley: University of California Press, 2002).

Solnit, Rebecca, *Infinite City: A San Francisco Atlas* (Berkeley: University of California Press, 2010).

SEATTLE, WASHINGTON

Seattle is the largest city in the state of Washington and in the American Pacific Northwest, and one of the largest and most important cities on the U.S. Pacific coast. It is located on an isthmus between Puget Sound, an inlet of the Pacific Ocean, and Lake Washington, and is an important rail terminus on the U.S. West Coast and port. The city is also a gateway from the 48 contiguous states to Alaska, both by ship and by air. It was founded in the early 1850s, and grew subsequently over various "boom and bust" cycles that began with the processing of local timber resources. Other chapters in economic history include service center for the 1893 Klondike Gold Rush in Alaska, then shipbuilding, followed in turn by aircraft manufacturing, and more recently by high-technology companies and a "dot-com" boom led by companies such as Microsoft, Amazon, and T-Mobile. Biotechnology is also a strong sector. Seattle's University of Washington is the largest of several higher education institutions in metropolitan area, and is also a major employer with wide impact.

The population of Seattle is 652,405 (2013 estimate), the 21st-largest city total in the United States, while that of the Seattle metropolitan area totals about 3.6 million inhabitants, making it the 15th-largest metropolitan area in the country. After a period of decline in the 1960s and 1970s when Boeing Aircraft, the city's largest employer at the time, lost critical government contracts and some real estate agents with a dark sense of humor put up a billboard that read "Will the last person leaving Seattle—Turn out the lights" in response to the exodus that followed job losses, the population of the city is once again on the rise. In 2013, it was reported to be the fastest-growing major city in the United States, led by the city's prosperous technology companies and a strong services sector, and a wide reputation for being a great place to live. The Seattle area's most famous residents are native-son William (Bill) Gates, founder of the Microsoft Corporation and one of the richest men in the world, and his wife Melinda, who live in a beautiful waterfront home in the suburb of Medina on the opposite shore of Lake Washington from the city core. Historically, the population of Seattle was overwhelmingly white, but in recent decades the city has become more diverse racially and ethnically, with about one-third of the population being of minority races. Asians, led by Chinese, are the most numerous minority group.

The city is especially appealing to lovers of the outdoors, as Seattle is a green city with many parks and trails, beautiful neighborhoods and recreation opportunities along Lake Washington, and beautiful residential and recreational islands in Puget Sound that are made close to the city center by ferry services. Furthermore, the city is near the Cascades mountain range and prominent mountain peaks such as Mt. Rainier and Mt. Baker, and the richly green old-growth mid-latitude rainforests and rugged shorelines of Olympic National Park. The city's "Emerald City" nickname comes from the deep green hues of the natural surroundings. For some, the rainy winters of Seattle are a problem, as there are few days of sunshine, although the mountains nearby do offer excellent skiing. However, Seattle's summers are near-perfect with sunny and dry weather and temperatures that are never too hot. In addition to the aforementioned skiing, popular outdoor activities include hiking, biking, camping, mountain climbing, hunting, fishing, and boating.

People are also attracted to Seattle because the city is a leader in advancing sustainable urban lifestyles in the United States, and also because it is an open and tolerant city with generally progressive government. It was the first large American city to have elected a female mayor, Bertha Knight Landes in 1926, and presently has an openly gay mayor, Ed Murray, and a socialist member of city council, Kshama Sawant. Seattle voters have also voted to support same-sex marriage and legalization of marijuana, and their city councilors have passed legislation to ban use of plastic bags in the city (as of July 2012), to raise the minimum wage to a nation's highest $15 per hour (in June 2014), and replaced celebration of Columbus Day with Indigenous People's Day to honor the city's Native America minority (as of October 2014). The LGBT population of Seattle is reportedly one of the highest per capita in the United States, ranking in this category alongside San Francisco. According to a 2012 estimate by the U.S. Census Bureau, Seattle leads the nation in percentage of same-sex households, at 2.6%. Seattle is also a leader in revitalization of older neighborhoods and vibrant city life, urban public transit, people walking or biking to work, and alternative music styles and clothing fashions. It is known as the home of grunge music.

Having said all this, it is not surprising to see Seattle at or near the top of various rankings of American cities on a wide variety of criteria. For example, it was presented as the #2 city in the United States as a place to live (after San Francisco) in a 2012 survey by *Bloomberg Business*, and ranks consistently among the nation's most sustainable urban centers. A long list of such accolades for the city (along with the appropriate references) is given by the Seattle Office of Economic Development on the city's website. Examples from 2013 and 2014 include second-best city for today's college graduates (CNBC); third best for women entrepreneurs (*Geekwire*); #1 smartest city in North America (*Fast Company*); fifth-best tech start-up city (*Entrepreneur*); #3 in job satisfaction in America (Glassdoor); and #3 as a gay-friendly U.S. city (*Nerdwallet*).

FURTHER READING

Conrad, Alex, "America's 50 Best Cities," September 28, 2012, http://www.bloomberg.com/bw/slideshows/2012–09–26/americas-50-best-cities.

Klingle, Matthew, *Emerald City: An Environmental History of Seattle* (New Haven, CT: Yale University Press, 2007).

Sale, Roger, *Seattle: Past to Present* (Seattle: University of Washington Press, 1976).

Sanders, Jeffrey Craig, *Seattle and the Roots of Urban Sustainability: Inventing Ecotopia* (Pittsburgh, PA: University of Pittsburgh Press, 2008).

THE 10 LEAST CONTENTED U.S. CITIES

ATLANTIC CITY, NEW JERSEY

Atlantic City is located on Absecon Island off the Atlantic coast of southern New Jersey. It is an ocean-side resort city with beautiful wide beaches, as well as a casino gambling mecca, having more casinos than any city in the United States outside Nevada. However, the city is very seriously down on its luck, and has been for some time. There is a semblance of glamor with showy casino-hotels and bright lights, but for the most part, the city is depressed economically and poor. It is because of the dissonance between the pleasures of the beaches and casinos and the distressed neighborhoods just blocks away that we were compelled to include Atlantic City on this list of 10 least contented U.S. cities. The population of Atlantic City is about 39,551 (2013 estimate).

Atlantic City was once a splendid place. The city dates back to 1853 when the first beach-side hotel was built, and was developed specifically to be a resort town. In 1854, a railroad connected the city with Philadelphia, stimulating a seasonal tourism industry. The immodestly named United States Hotel was owned by the railroad company, and was the largest hotel in the country with 2,000 rooms. Within 20 years, some 500,000 summer visitors were traveling to Atlantic City by rail. More and more hotels were erected in a line along the beach, and in 1870 the first boardwalk was built to help keep sand out of hotel lobbies. The city focused at first on the Philadelphia market, as it only 60 miles (97 km) to the west, but as Atlantic City's popularity grew it became a resort for New York City too, as well as for the Middle Atlantic region in general. In 1921, Atlantic City held the first Miss America pageant, initially as a gimmick to extend the tourism season into September. The pageant became an annual event that brought considerable publicity (both good and bad) to the city. During the 1919–1933 period of Prohibition in the United States, Atlantic City came to be associated as well with mob bosses and racketeers, as liquor kept flowing in the city's restaurants and nightclubs, and gambling took over many of its back rooms.

The fortunes of Atlantic City are reflected in its population totals. The city first entered the U.S. Census in 1860 with a total of 687 residents. It then grew quickly, and peaked in 1930 with a population of 66,198. The declines afterward were fairly small until the urban crisis decades of the 1960s and 1970s, when the city lost 19.6% of its population and an additional 16.0%, respectively, to a total of 40,199 in 1980. This was a time when Americans began to journey to Florida or the Caribbean Islands for their beach vacations, and when cities, even a smallish beach resort like Atlantic City, came to be associated with crime and poverty, and were to be avoided. Furthermore, racism played a role too, because as Atlantic City's population came to have increasing numbers of African Americans, there was white flight to whiter places, just like in American cities in general. When the Democratic Party's National Convention was held in Atlantic City in 1964 (to nominate Lyndon B. Johnson and Hubert Humphrey), America saw a beat-up city on national television, and Atlantic City's reputation plummeted. With growing competition from resorts elsewhere, Atlantic City fell on hard times, and once-elegant hotels began to close and be demolished. Even the Miss America Pageant left the city, choosing Las Vegas from 2006 through 2013. In order to rebuild the economy, New Jersey voters approved legalization of casino gambling in 1976, with the first new casino opening in 1978 and others following immediately thereafter. There were new jobs and increases in population in Atlantic City and commuter communities nearby, but soon enough the hopes would be dashed as casinos were opened up and down the East Coast, including right in the heart of Philadelphia, and Atlantic City once again had more competition than it could handle. As a result, many casino construction and expansion projects were cancelled, and several once-prosperous casino-hotels were closed. Once again, there is gloom in Atlantic City and outmigration.

What is left unsaid in this analysis is that the city's poorest neighborhoods are just blocks away from the economic crisis at the beachfront, and are having crises of their own. These are disproportionately minority-group neighborhoods, as the city is 26.7% white, 38.3% African American, and 30.5% Hispanic or Latino of any race (2010 census), and their residents who work in the casino-hotel services industry are the first casualties of job loss. About one-quarter of the city's population lives below the poverty line, including more than 36% of all children (population under age 18). The city has many public housing projects and substandard dwelling units, as well as boarded-up shops on streets that once thrived with business. Even new shopping developments are in trouble, as there are many fewer customers than developers had planned for. All over the city, there are vacant lots and entire vacant blocks where homes and businesses once stood. Developers had bought up land in anticipation of profits to come, but for now prospects are dim. Some owners fail to pay real estate taxes, adding to the impoverishment of city government and cutbacks in city services and employees. Crime rates are high, and some city streets almost in the shadows of the high-rise casino-hotels

Casino gambling came to Atlantic City in 1978 in an effort to revive the economy of a faded resort town on the Atlantic coast. There was promise for a time, but as more and more communities around the country opened casinos, there was too much competition and several casinos were forced to close. The photo shows the entry to one of the city's casinos, where inside visitors can forget the rest of the world and play games of chance as long as their cash and credit hold out. (Meinzahn/iStockphoto.com)

along the waters have become zones for drug-dealing and prostitution. There is crime in city government too, as corruption has long been a problem. New Jersey, too, has a reputation for corruption. There are new proposals to fix the city with new commercial projects, but Atlantic City has seen this before, and its poorest residents have learned to believe that whatever the benefits that result, they will not be for them.

FURTHER READING

Johnson, Nelson and Terence Winter, *Boardwalk Empire: The Birth, High Times, and Corruption of Atlantic City* (Medford, NJ: Medford Press, 2010).

Simon, Bryant, *Boardwalk of Dreams: Atlantic City and the Fate of Urban America* (New York: Oxford University Press, 2006).

Van Meter, Jonathan, *The Last Good Time: Skinny D'Amato, the Notorious 500 Club, & the Rise and Fall of Atlantic City* (New York: Crown Publishers, 2003).

BEAUMONT-PORT ARTHUR, TEXAS

The Beaumont-Port Arthur twin-city metropolitan area is located along the Gulf of Mexico in eastern Texas, and has a population of 388,745 as of the 2010 census. It is the 10th-largest metropolitan area in Texas by population, and is located immediately east of the Houston-Sugar Land-Baytown metropolitan area, the state's second largest. Beaumont is the larger city with a 2010 population of 118,296, and is the county seat of Jefferson County, while Port Arthur, which is also in Jefferson County and is located closer to the gulf, has a 2010 population of 53,818. Both cities registered peak populations in the 1960 census count, but have declined since in numbers, Port Arthur considerably more steeply. The metropolitan area as a whole continues to grow in population, but not as rapidly as other metropolitan areas in fast-growing Texas.

Both Beaumont and Port Arthur owe their growth to oil production and petrochemical refining. The cities had been founded more than 50 years apart in the 19th century (Beaumont is older), but they were significant locally only until the historic January 10, 1901, Spindletop oil strike at a well in the southern part of Beaumont. That particular strike revealed the largest deposit of oil in the world up until that time and ushered in the Texas Oil Boom that was to forever change not only the region, but also the profile of Texas and the national economy. The two small towns quickly became boomtowns with skyrocketing population growth as speculators poured in and oil jobs were plentiful, and the region was transformed into a landscape of oil derricks, refineries, pipelines, tank farms, and port facilities. Locally, the area came to be called the "Golden Triangle" because the main industrial zone was located mostly within a triangle formed by the centers of Beaumont, Port Arthur, and a third city in the metropolitan area, Orange. A number of the major oil companies in the United States have facilities in the region, and the area's main port, located in Port Arthur on an estuary that is called Sabine Lake, is along the lower bends of the Sabine River, consistently ranks among the top five ports in the United States in tonnage. The port is continually being updated and expanded, with major addition in the works to refining capacity and facilities being planned to for handling shipments of liquefied natural gas.

The growth, however, has brought various problems to the area, not the least of which has been very serious air and water pollution. This is one of the main reasons why we list Beaumont-Port Arthur as one of the 10 least contented American cities. According to the Toxics Release Inventory of the U.S. Environmental Protection Agency, Jefferson County, Texas, ranks among the very worst communities in the nation for air pollution by chemicals known to cause cancer, birth defects, and reproductive disorders. Health problems are worse in African American neighborhoods than in white districts, because whites tend to live further from refineries and upwind, while it is segregated African American neighborhoods that are nearest the refineries and in harm's way. An award-winning article about this issue by Ted Genoways cites Port Arthur as a case of environmental racism, as white city leaders made the decision some decades ago to located public housing projects built with federal dollars right next to the refineries, knowing that the overwhelming percentage of residents would be low-income African Americans. He refers to Port Arthur specifically as an American Sacrifice Zone: air, land, and waters that are routinely poisoned so that Americans elsewhere can enjoy the benefits of oil and gasoline. There have been numerous explosions and fires over the years at the area's refineries, oil spills into the waters, releases of toxic gas, and frequent burn-offs that foul the air and cause cities to smell. Exxon Mobil, Invista, and other oil companies in the area have been fined on numerous occasions by the state of Texas and the federal government for emissions violations and catastrophic accidents.

We also include Beaumont-Port Arthur on these pages because of social problems. Despite the profitability of the oil industry, unemployment is high in both communities as port and refining jobs are increasingly automated. According to census data from 2010, about 17.6% of families in Beaumont and 22.2% of residents live below the official poverty line. In a study published in 2014 by Wallet Hub, the Beaumont-Port Arthur metropolitan area ranks dead last among the nation's 150 largest metropolitan areas in education as measured by both educational attainment and quality of education. A key finding was that only 17.1% of adults have a college education. The Gallup-Healthways Well-Being Index for the same years ranks Beaumont as "America's sixth most miserable city," while another study, albeit one about which some hard questions about methodology can be raised, conducted at the University of Vermont concluded from a content analysis of some 10 million tweets sent from across the United States that Beaumont is the saddest city in the country. The researchers noted that the word choice of tweets from Beaumont was especially heavy with curse words and short on what they call "happy words," and argued that this reflects a bad mood in the city. Other problems in Beaumont-Port Arthur are higher crime than in most other communities in high-crime Texas, and occasional devastating hurricanes such as Rita in 2005 and Ike in 2008 that sweep ashore from the Gulf of Mexico and cause much damage to life and property.

FURTHER READING

Genoways, Ted, "Port Arthur, Texas: American Sacrifice Zone," *On Earth*, August 26, 2013, http://archive.onearth.org/articles/2013/08/if-built-the-keystone-xl-pipeline-will-end-in-one-toxic-town.

Lerner, Steve, "Port Arthur, Texas: Public Housing Residents Breathe Contaminated Air from Nearby Refineries and Chemical Plants," *The Collaborative on Health and the Environment*, http://healthandenvironment.org/articles/homepage/1008.

CAMDEN, NEW JERSEY

Camden, population 77,344 (2010 census; 2013 estimate 76,903), is a deeply troubled small city that is getting smaller. It is located in southern New Jersey directly across the Delaware River from the center of the much larger city of Philadelphia, Pennsylvania. It is New Jersey's 12th-largest city, and one of several in the state with very severe urban problems, including the capital city Trenton, the casino-seaside resort community of Atlantic City, the formerly industrial cities of Paterson, Bayonne, and Jersey City, and others. We single out Camden for this list of 10 least content American cities because its decline has been especially severe, and because it stands out not just in New Jersey but also in the United States as a whole for poor government, high rates of poverty and unemployment, large-scale deindustrialization, and severely distressed neighborhoods. According to the Neighborhood Scout ratings service, which utilized uniform FBI crime data in its reports, Camden was ranked the third-most dangerous city in the United States in 2014 in violent crime. It was #2 in 2013 and #5 in 2012.

Camden's peak population was registered in the census of 1950 at 124,555. This was just at the time when mass suburbanization and accelerated deindustrialization began to transform many American cities for the worse. During its heyday in the first half of the 20th century, Camden was the headquarters and factory city for RCA Victor, the largest manufacturer of phonographs and phonograph records in the world; the Campbell Soup Company, which made use of local agriculture production in "Garden State" New Jersey; and the New York Shipbuilding Corporation, maker of powerful warships for the U.S. Navy and employer of as many of 40,000 workers when business was at a peak. Of these three employers, two are no longer in business and have vanished from Camden entirely, while

Campbell Soup still maintains corporate headquarters in the city and has invested heavily in its redevelopment efforts, but has also shut local production facilities. As a result of plant closings, population plummeted and Camden was left with a landscape of vacant factory buildings, vacant houses, and vacant lots. Other neighborhoods were bulldozed to clear the way for construction of wide-swath highways through the city, which then had the effect of not just moving traffic, but also hastening suburbanization and the city's economic decline.

According to data for 2011, about 45% of Camden's population was living below the poverty line. This is one of the highest rates for any city in the United States. The median household income was $21,191, the lowest of all cities that the U.S. Census Bureau included in its survey. In so many words, those who could afford to have left Camden, leaving behind a population that is disproportionately poor. Poverty data correlate with racial-ethnic characteristics of the population, as most of the poorest residents are either African American or Hispanic. Camden was once an overwhelmingly white city, but became increasingly African American in the 1950s–1970s as whites moved to the suburbs and blacks moved to the old neighborhoods that were left behind. The city then became increasingly Hispanic as well, as migrants from Puerto Rico and other parts of Latin America moved to the city. While many African Americans migrated to the city at a time when Camden was already hemorrhaging jobs, most Hispanics arrived at a time when, except for certain skilled professions, secure jobs with decent pay and benefits were almost nonexistent. According to the 2010 census, 48.1% of Camden's population is African American and 47.0% is Hispanic or Latino of any race (i.e., some of the city's black population is also counted as Hispanic). Persons of Puerto Rican ancestry account for 30.7% of Camden's total, one of the highest percentages of any city outside Puerto Rico itself. From time to time, racial tensions flare in Camden, adding to the city's woes.

The poor quality of government in Camden is seen in the fact that since the 1980s, three mayors of the city have been found guilty and set to prison for political corruption. The first was Angelo Errichetti who was convicted of accepting a $50,000 bribe along with three other individuals in an FBI sting operation; the second was Arnold Webster, once the superintendent of Camden's public schools, who was convicted in 1999 of continuing to pay himself from school system funds at the same time that he was being paid separately to be mayor; and the third was Milton Milan, who was sent to federal prison in 2000 for soliciting bribes, skimming money from a political action committee, and laundering drug money. In 2009, Wayne R. Bryant, a state senator who had previously represented Camden, was sent to prison for bribery while in office and for accepting no-show jobs to inflate his pay and future pension. The city's finances have long been a mess, not just because of declining revenues caused by lower population and an eroded business base, but also because of corruption and poor recordkeeping. The city continually finds itself with budget deficits and near bankruptcy, and has been forced again and again to cut costs by reducing services to the population. This has included reductions in the numbers of police officers and firefighters in Camden, as well as cutbacks in schools and social services. From 2005 to 2012, the state government of New Jersey ran Camden's schools and police department, because the city lacked both funds and competence. From 1985 to 2009 when it was closed to make way for other redevelopment, a portion of the Camden riverfront directly adjacent to the Benjamin Franklin Bridge to Philadelphia (where some of the New York Shipbuilding facilities had been) was the site of Riverfront State Prison, a highly visible testament to the city's crime problem.

However, not all is bad in Camden: the city's Cooper University Hospital is an excellent medical center and important employer; Campbell's Soup has built a handsome new headquarters complex within city limits; and the Camden campus of Rutgers University has sparked much redevelopment in the city's downtown and is also a leading employer. In 2004, a main building of the RCA Victor Company, the iconic Nipper Building in the heart of downtown, was renamed The Victor and converted to high-end condominiums. With the prison out of the way, the once-industrial Camden riverfront is ripe for more new projects. Already, there is Campbell's Field, an attractive minor league baseball stadium, the Adventure Aquarium, and the Susquehanna Bank Center, a pleasant venue for outdoor concerts. Each is an increment in remaking a city that has fallen, but the road ahead is still long and Camden is still a deeply troubled city.

FURTHER READING

Gillette, Howard, Jr., *Camden after the Fall: Decline and Renewal in a Post-Industrial* City (Philadelphia: University of Pennsylvania Press, 2006).

Morgia, Lindsay and Thomas J. Vicino, "Waterfront Politics: Revisiting the Case of Camden, New Jersey's Redevelopment," *Urban Research & Practice*, 6, 3, 2013, pp. 329–345.

Taibbi, Matt, "Apocalypse, New Jersey," *Rolling Stone*, Issue 1198/1199, December 19, 2013, pp. 70–77.

DETROIT, MICHIGAN

Detroit is the largest city in Michigan and is most famous as the center of the American automobile industry. Its nicknames include Motor City and the Automobile Capital of the World, as well as Motown, associated with a genre of popular music that originated there, and Renaissance City, associated with a landmark building complex in the city's downtown and Detroit's struggle to reverse urban decline. The city is located on the Detroit River, a wide channel that connects Lakes Huron and Erie, and is across from Windsor, Ontario, Canada. It is a port city on the Great Lakes—St. Lawrence Seaway.

As reported in the 2010 census, the population of Detroit was 713,777, the 18th-largest total among cities in the United States. It has since shrunk to 681,090 (2013 estimate). The city used to rank as #4 in the country, in 1920 when its population was 993,678, behind only New York City, Chicago, and Philadelphia, and it had a peak population in 1950 when there were 1,849,568 inhabitants and the city ranked fifth in the United States. The population decline is the largest of any major city in the United States in absolute numbers, and is due to both the migration of many, mostly middle-class residents to suburbia over much of the 20th century, as well as to outmigration from the Detroit area altogether because of economic decline and people's searches for jobs in other parts of the country. In percentage terms, Detroit's decline was second only to that for St. Louis, Missouri. In the decade 2000–2010, the loss of population in Detroit was especially precipitous, about 25% of the base, and the city plummeted from #10 in rank in the United States to #18. The Detroit metropolitan area (U.S. portion only) has a population of 4,292,060, owing to a large suburban zone, and ranks 14th in the United States.

Detroit is a poster child for urban failure in the United States. It was once a booming industrial city, but with declines in the automobile industry that came

Detroit, Michigan, has lost considerable population over every decade since the 1950s and has many vacant buildings and vacant lots. The photo shows a scrap collector at work in a neighborhood near the city center where there are plans to erect a new hockey arena and a retail complex. The projects are costly, but are touted as investments in economic development for the future. (AP Photo/Carlos Osorio)

with major oil crises in 1973 and 1979 and skyrocketing prices for gasoline, coupled with competition from Japanese and European auto makers for the U.S. and global markets, high labor costs, and some notably poor business decisions in the auto industry, the economy unraveled and people left. Simultaneously, Detroit constructed a number of freeways through the city to serve suburban commuters that, unfortunately, cut through and destroyed previously fine neighborhoods. Other neighborhood decline came as a result of racial tensions and some of America's worst urban race riots. A disproportionate number of those who stayed in the declining city were African American, which led to still more population decline because of white flight. The result is a racial mix of 82.7% African American and 10.6% white residents. By contrast, the majority of people in the suburban ring are white, and many suburbs are almost wholly white. Other American metropolitan areas have similar racial geographies, but the Detroit metropolitan area is more strongly segregated than most and the city of Detroit is more heavily African American than most American cities.

Economic decline and outmigration by middle-class Detroiters has left the city disproportionately poor, as well as disproportionately African American, and presented the city with many problems and challenges that are associated with poverty and unemployment. For example, the city has a high welfare burden, high rates of default on home mortgages, and high rates of tax delinquency. About one-half of all Detroit homeowners fail to pay their real estate taxes. This has fed a revenue crisis for city government, making it difficult for city agencies to provide quality services, including essential services such as schooling and police and fire protection. On July 18, 2013, Detroit became the largest city in U.S. history to file for bankruptcy. It has since submitted a financial plan to become solvent, and now operates in the black, albeit with great difficulty and many layoffs of city workers. Other problems associated with poverty and unemployment include one of the highest crime rates of any city in the United States (another of Detroit's nicknames has been "Murder Capital of the United States), high rates of narcotics addiction and alcoholism, domestic violence, and a landscape of boarded-up houses, businesses, churches, and other buildings. Throughout the city there are great expanses of vacant lots where buildings once stood. Indeed, the city aggressively demolishes empty buildings in order to combat a problem of dangerous arson-for-fun fires that has plagued the city, and to reduce the costs of servicing neighborhoods where population has been greatly thinned out. There are many industrial buildings, including large car plants from the past, that stand in ruins and are being overrun by weeds, and that often attract hobbyist "ruins photographers" and amateur industrial archaeologists. The nearby city of Flint, Michigan, has many similar characteristics, and is also included on these pages among the 10 least contented cities in the United States.

As Detroit considers its future, it plans to concentrate remaining residents into fewer neighborhoods, and to find new uses for empty spaces such as parkland, urban agriculture and community gardening, and redevelopment for reindustrialization and other economic gains. Much of the city is now a clean slate that that can be used for creative remaking of urban space. Downtown Detroit has received a lot of attention in city planning, beginning with the construction of Renaissance Center in the 1970s at the riverfront. This is a large and once-glitzy office, hotel, and retailing complex that centers on the headquarters of the General Motors Corporation that is meant to herald urban revitalization. Unfortunately, its gleaming towers are often photographed in juxtaposition with scenes of urban decay, showing just how great a challenge Detroit faces. There are, however, some notable successes in the city's downtown, including a rise in nightlife, theaters, and fine restaurants, some thriving ethnic communities, new condominiums for prosperous residents, and a great new ballpark for the city's beloved Detroit Tigers baseball team.

FURTHER READING

Austin, Dan and Sean Doerr, *Lost Detroit: Stories behind the Motor City's Majestic Ruins* (Charleston, SC: The History Press, 2010).

Binelli, Mark, *Detroit City Is the Place to Be: The Afterlife of an American Metropolis* (New York: Picador, 2013).

Le Duff, Charlie, *Detroit: An American Autopsy* (New York: Penguin, 2013).

FLINT, MICHIGAN

Flint is a distressed industrial city in southeastern Michigan about 66 miles (106 km) northwest of Detroit. Like Detroit, its rise to prominence and its economic decline is tied to trends in the American automobile industry. Flint was founded in 1819 and grew initially as a frontier lumbering town. It then manufactured carriages and other vehicles, and in 1908 began manufacturing automobiles after William Crapo Durant founded the General Motors Company in the city. For many years thereafter, the city prospered as the maker of Buicks and Chevrolets, as well as automobile parts such as spark plugs, but increasing competition from foreign automobile makers and changes in the geography of automobile assembly within the United States brought depression to Michigan, and in the 1980s General Motors closed most of its factories in Flint. This brought hard times to the city and high unemployment, and resulted in population loss, housing abandonment, and huge vacant spaces where once-busy factories had stood. The former "Buick City" site is one of the largest vacant industrial tracts in the United States.

According to the census of 2010, the population of Flint was 102,434. It has since dropped below the 100,000 mark to an estimated 99,763 in 2013. Both figures represent a steep drop from the city's peak population of 196,940 that was recorded in the census of 1960. The population has declined with every census count since because of outmigration in response to the loss of jobs. Many former residents, especially African Americans, moved to the South, where there were family roots, while others moved to the Sunbelt states more generally to find footholds in a stronger economy. Homeowners faced extra difficulties, because the collapse of the manufacturing economy undermined the city's real estate market, causing large drops in house values and a spike in defaults in mortgage payments. Neighborhoods that were once content and lively quickly became depopulated slums with dilapidated housing that would soon be bulldozed away. Fires in empty houses were also commonplace. Attempts to reverse the decline by building a new economic base (e.g., investment in the University of Michigan-Flint, attempts to stimulate a tourism and conventions economy) have been only partly successful at best, and Flint continues to be among the country's most problematic cities.

Because of a declining tax base, the municipal government of Flint is woefully short of funds, as well as borrowing capacity, and relies on help from state and national governments. For residents of Flint, this has meant increases in taxes and major cutbacks in the services that taxes pay for, including education, policing, and other vital areas. The demolition of vacant housing is also a cost-saving measure, as it reduces the number of properties that require utilities and municipal services and creates maintenance-free empty land. In addition, there have been sharp declines in the numbers of city workers over the years, as emergency layoffs seem to have become almost routine. Even the police department has been cut back, this despite the fact that Flint is suffering from a very serious crime problem. The city is acknowledged to be one of the most dangerous cities in the United States in terms of murder and other violent crime. It has long ranked in the top five of most dangerous cities in America as measured by uniform FBI crime statistics, and in 2011 it was alone at the top in violent crime per capita. According to *Forbes*, the city was #6 in the United States in 2012 as "most violent city for women." In 2013, Flint was called the "most dangerous city in America" by *Business Insider* based on FBI crime data. The city also suffers high rates of theft, vandalism, drug addiction, alcoholism, and other social problems. Racial segregation is also a problem. More whites have moved out of the city than blacks, with the result that, like Detroit, Flint is a majority African American city.

The woes of Flint have been made widely known by local-born filmmaker and social critic Michael Moore, beginning with his famous *Roger & Me*, a 1989 documentary about the summary shut-down of General Motors plants in the city by GM chairman Roger Moore. The film centers on Moore's futile attempts to secure an interview with Smith, who clearly does not want to talk to him, to discuss the impact of unemployment on the city's citizens, as well as on the city's once-proud history and insights to people's lives as they face eviction from their homes and uncertain income prospects. *Pets or Meat: The Return to Flint* was a 1992 follow-up that focused on people's economic hardships. It took its title from a vignette about a formerly well-paid automobile worker who was reduced to raising rabbits as either pets or meat in order to feed her family. Other Michael Moore movies have also shown the distressed aspects of Flint, as have other movies and books. Gordon Young's recent book compares memories of growing up in the city with the harsh realities that he encountered after returning from the West Coast to his hometown: devastated neighborhoods, crime, and government ineptitude, among other ills, but also dedicated citizens who fight against the odds to bring the city back.

Unfortunately, Flint has become something of the poster child for urban economic collapse and the troubles that people face as a result. A metaphor for the city's fall is the story of its tallest building, the 19-story Genesee Towers, a modernist office structure that included eight floors of parking space. It was completed to much fanfare in 1968 just before the onset of crisis in American automobile industry, lost its last major tenant in 1985, was condemned as unfit for habitation in 2004, and was then demolished by implosion near the end of 2013.

FURTHER READING

Dandaneau, Steven P. Flint, *A Town Abandoned: Michigan, Confronts Deindustrialization* (Albany: State University of New York Press, 1996).

Flinn, Gary, *Remembering Flint, Michigan: Stories from the Vehicle City* (Mount Pleasant, SC: History Press, 2010).

Hamper, Ben, *Rivethead: Tales from the Assembly Line* (New York: Warner Books, 1986).

Young, Gordon, *Teardown: Memoir of a Vanishing City* (Berkeley: University of California Press, 2013).

MEMPHIS, TENNESSEE

Memphis is an historic city on the Mississippi River in the southwestern corner of Tennessee. It was founded in 1819 on a relatively flood-free bluff above the Mississippi to be a river-based trade center, and was named after an ancient capital city on the Nile in Egypt. It was a major port on the Ohio-Mississippi Rivers during the U.S. steamboat era, and later a busy rail hub. The early business of the city centered on cotton produced by the slave-based plantation economy of the U.S. South, as well as on the slave trade itself. Just before the Civil War, Memphis was the fifth-largest city in the South, with a population of 22,623 (1860 census). The city's population is now 653,450 (2013 estimate), the largest total in Tennessee and of any city on the Mississippi River, and the 20th-largest total in the United States. The Memphis metropolitan area has 1,316,100 residents (2010 census), and is the second-largest metropolitan area in Tennessee after that of Nashville, and the 42nd-largest in the United States. The population of Memphis had increased significantly with every census count since the city's founding except for the 1870s, when there were deadly outbreaks of yellow fever, and for most decades from the 1980s onward, when the city registered population losses that reflect a period of urban problems and decline.

Our choice to include Memphis on our list of 10 least contented American cities is based on these problems. At the top of our list is the fact that Memphis has one of the highest crime rates of any city in the United States. Despite recent declines in crime as in other American cities, it is consistently ranked in the top 10 of the most dangerous places in the country, and in some years since 2000 has ranked at #1 or #2 in violent crime. In 2011, City-Data.com ranked the city at #10 on its gloomy-sounding list of "Cities you don't want to live in," citing the high crime rates as well as the comparatively poor health of Memphians. The city ranks high in obesity, diabetes, and hypertension, among other health problems. Also, we note that Memphis is one of the most segregated cities in the United States, with black-white segregation ranking at #15 in the country for the municipality and #20 for the metropolitan area, as determined from 2010 census data in a study by urban scholars John Logan and Brian Stults. As recently as the 1970 census, Memphis was 60.8% white, but since then white flight has caused a reversal in the city's makeup and Memphis now approaches a population mix that is two-thirds African American. The city has a high poverty rate. About one in five residents live below the poverty line, children and African Americans disproportionately so. Another problem is dirty air and littered streets. Indeed, the city has been ranked as one of the dirtiest cities in the United States, being pegged at #9 in this category by *Travel + Leisure* magazine in 2012. The magazine *Country Home*, which publishes a ranking of greenest cities in the United States, has Memphis way down on its list for 2007: #339 out of 379 cities surveyed.

A metaphor for troubles in Memphis is the city's iconic Pyramid, which has itself been besieged with difficulties. Built in 1989–1991 and originally named the Great American Pyramid, this 321-feet (98 meters; equivalent of 32 stories)-high, glass-sheathed pyramid-shaped structure near the city's downtown on banks of the Mississippi River was constructed to be a grand new symbol of urban revitalization. The design was chosen to echo the pyramids in Egypt. There was originally supposed to be a cluster of three pyramids, but only one was built. It is the sixth-tallest pyramid in the world, after four in Egypt and the Luxor Hotel in Las Vegas. The intended use was as a 20,142-seat arena for the city's University of Memphis and professional Memphis Grizzlies basketball teams. However, there were problems from the start, beginning with a flooded arena floor on opening night because of inadequate drainage pumps and the need for sandbags to save the electrical system, and ending with both basketball teams leaving the arena in 2004 to play instead in the newly opened FedEXForum after finding the Pyramid to be an unsatisfactory home. The structure then sat in darkness without tenants for almost a decade while various proposals were put forward for how to use it. Among the many ideas that were floated were aquarium, casino, shopping mall, and a mid-America branch for the Smithsonian Institution. The Pyramid is currently being retrofitted to be a super-large Bass Pro Shops emporium, complete with archery range, shooting range, and laser arcade, as well as duck pond, in addition to sports retailing. However, the project is well behind schedule, and might not be as successful as investors hope.

Whatever happens with the Pyramid, it is certain to be one of the curiosities of Memphis for visitors. Tourism is important part of the city's economy. Among the present attractions are the Lorraine Motel where Dr. Martin Luther King, Jr., was assassinated by a gunshot in 1968; Graceland, which is the former home of singer Elvis Presley, and the Pink Palace Museum which contains a replica of the first Piggly Wiggly store, the nation's first self-service supermarket. Memphis also offers Beale Street, an historic avenue of blues clubs that is being invaded by mass-market chain businesses and kitsch retailing. Happily, the street has great music festivals. The city is well served by highways that make it accessible for visitors, but that ironically have simultaneously contributed to the demolition of historic neighborhoods and hastened white flight to distant suburbs. Today Memphis is a major hub for FedEx Express shipping. As a result, Memphis International Airport ranks as the #2 busiest cargo airport in the world after that in Hong Kong.

FURTHER READING

Lauterbach, Preston, *Beale Street Dynasty: Sex, Song, and the Struggle for the Soul of Memphis* (New York: W.W. Norton & Company, 2015).

Rushing, Wanda, *Memphis and the Paradox of Place: Globalization in the American South* (Chapel Hill, NC: University of North Carolina Press, 2009).

NIAGARA FALLS, NEW YORK

Niagara Falls, the torrents of cascading water on the Niagara River at the international border between state of New York and the Canadian province of Ontario, is a natural wonder of the world that is visited by between 20 and 30 million tourists each year. However, within blocks of the beautiful state park that is part of the tourist zone, the city of Niagara Falls, New York, is run-down and economically distressed, and is a world apart from what visitors come to see. Niagara Falls, New York, is also a world apart from its partner city in Ontario, Canada, also named Niagara Falls, which has more attractions for visitors to enjoy, better and cleaner neighborhoods, and less crime and other social problems. For visitors, it is a must to view the falls from both the American and Canadian sides, because the scenery is spectacular from both directions, but for most people the preferred place to stay, to eat, and to visit other attractions that spin off the main tourist attraction is Niagara Falls, Ontario, the acknowledged better of the two falls cities.

The cities named Niagara Falls are different not just because they happen to be in different countries, but because of differences in strategic planning and investment decisions that were made locally decades ago about how best to exploit the falls for economic advantage. Both cities understood that water power from the falls could be a stimulus for efficient generation of electricity and the development of an industrial economy, and responded accordingly, growing into significant centers of electro-chemical and electro-metallurgical industrial production. Both cities also saw that there was money to be made from tourism, and invested in infrastructure for that economy too, but unevenly. The Canadian city invested earlier and more heavily, while in the American city, more chips were on manufacturing and tourism was secondary. When global economic restructuring eroded the American and Canadian industrial economies, Niagara Falls, Ontario, was quicker to adapt to a mostly tourism economy by investing in access roads, hotels, casino gambling from the mid-1990s, and other lures. The Americans came later with less. Moreover, Niagara Falls, New York, also made some unfortunate planning decisions for revitalizing the city center that probably did more harm than good. Most specifically, an ill-conceived urban renewal project in the 1960s resulted in demolition of the historic Falls Street tourist district near the Niagara Falls State Park, leaving vacant lots in place of the kinds of attractions for visitors that the city's Canadian counterpart was building. A casino did come later, the Seneca Niagara Casino in 2004 on the site of a demolished convention center, but it has done little to reverse the city's fortunes. Indeed, it is sovereign Native American territory within the city, rather than a direct part of the Niagara Falls, New York, tax base. In the meanwhile, also in 2004, the Canadian city opened Niagara Fallsview Casino Resort overlooking Horseshoe Falls, a massive and glitzy $1 billion casino complex that has become the region's single largest income producer.

The population of Niagara Falls, New York, was estimated to be 49,468 in 2013. From the first census for the city in 1870, the city had always been bigger than its Canadian counterpart (first recorded in the Canadian decennial census in 1881), and reached a peak population with the 1960 census at 102,394. Because of industrial decline and associated outmigration to regions with better jobs opportunities, the total has declined with every census count and intercensal estimate since then. At the time of the 1980 census (1981 for Canada) the two Niagara Falls cities were approximately equal in population (71,384 in New York and 70,960 in Ontario), but the Canadian city has since outstripped its American counterpart and now totals 82,997 (2011). The different trajectories in population are reflected in the price of housing, which is much lower in New York, and in the fact that Niagara Falls, New York, has run-down neighborhoods with empty and abandoned housing, boarded-up storefronts, and vacant lots where houses and business once stood. There are better areas too, such as the Deveaux neighborhood near the Niagara escarpment, but on the whole, the New York city has the look and feel of a declined American Rust Belt city. As has happened elsewhere in postindustrial cities in the United States, the largest population decline has been with the white population, which has moved to other regions in disproportionate numbers, resulting in ever-higher fractions of minority population. As of 2010, about 21.9% of the city's total was African American.

In 1978, Niagara Falls, New York, experienced a calamitous event in which a neighborhood called Love Canal was discovered to have been built on toxic industrial landfill and was dangerous to residents' health. Its residents had to be relocated to other areas at federal government expense, a first in the establishment of the Superfund law that protects American citizens from previously unknown environmental hazards. The city had also gotten bad publicity nationally in having been a center of organized crime and vice over much of the first half of the 20th century, and of corruption on the part of labor union officials and local politicians, including at least one mayor, more recently. Although crime rates and perceptions of dangers from crime are higher for nearby Buffalo and Rochester, New York, both of which are also declined industrial cities and significantly larger, Niagara Falls suffers from excessive crime and gun violence, drug abuse, racial and ethnic tension, and other social problems. It has been rated as #53 on NeighborhoodScout's top 100 most dangerous cities in the United States for 2013 and as the most dangerous city in New York State in 2014 in another survey, one by mylife.com. There are important efforts to improve the city and to take better advantage of the spectacular natural wonder that is its neighbor, but for now, Niagara Falls, New York, continues to struggle.

FURTHER READING

Laskow, Sarah, "Have the Politics Finally Lined Up for a (U.S.) Niagara Falls Revival?" *Capital (New York)*, June 5, 2014, http://www.capitalnewyork.com/article/albany /2014/06/8546232/have-politics-finally-lined-us-niagara-falls-revival?page=all.

Mah, Alice, *Industrial Ruination, Community, and Place: Landscapes and Legacies of Urban Decline* (Toronto: University of Toronto Press, 2012).

PHOENIX, ARIZONA

Phoenix, population 1,445,632 (2010 census), is the capital of the state of Arizona, the most populous state capital in the United States, and the sixth most populous city in the country. The city's first census was in 1870, when it registered 270 inhabitants, and it was incorporated in 1881. It has grown rapidly ever since and with an estimated total of 1,513,357 in 2013, and will soon catch Philadelphia for the #5 spot and then vie for #4. The population growth rate has averaged about 4% per year over the last four decades. Despite the fact that many Americans and foreign immigrants want to live in Phoenix and move there, we include Phoenix on our list of 10 least content American cities because it has serious problems that stem from rapid growth and overdevelopment, and because the city is, arguably, the least sustainable in the United States. This is an especially significant shortcoming, because the United States itself has an overly large environmental footprint, even on a per capital basis. Unfortunately, Phoenix reflects some of the worst trends in urban development in the United States, as well as wasteful aspects of American lifestyles and resource usage.

Phoenix is at the edge of the Sonoran Desert in south-central Arizona in the broad valley of the Salt River. In various directions beyond are low mountain ranges. Because of the dry climate, there are perennial worries about water supply and frequent shortages. This is all the more so because of the large population base in Phoenix and rapid rate of growth, and because the city competes for its water with irrigation needs in surrounding farmlands, which are, in fact, one of the underpinnings of the urban economy. Yet, Phoenix residents consume water as if there were no desert, and wash their cars, fill swimming pools, and water their lawns and gardens as if there were no limits to water supplies. Some water, such as that used to irrigate the city's many excellent golf courses, is recycled from previous uses, but for the most part, Phoenix and the rest of Arizona exhaust available supplies and are constantly on the edge with respect to where tomorrow's water supplies might come from.

At first, Phoenix made use of water supplies from the Salt River, thanks to federally funded dams and reservoirs that were erected early in the 20th century to promote settlement and agriculture, and then added supplies from the Gila River (a tributary of the Salt) and the Colorado River, which also supplies Las Vegas, Los Angeles, and other urban centers in the dry Southwest, as well as ever-deeper wells. Bad habits followed, with the result that capita water usage in Phoenix is about 20% more than that in Los Angeles, which also consumes water far too prodigiously. The irony here is that Phoenix, whose name suggests a city rising from the ruins of a previous civilization, is actually on the ruins of ancient Hohokam Indian settlement—a population that inhabited the same desert area for hundreds of years, building irrigation canals and water reservoirs to sustain its own agriculture and clustered settlements, until that society crashed because of water shortages. Many critics think that Phoenix, and Arizona more generally, are headed down the same unsustainable road to environmental and economic disaster. Pro-growth forces in Phoenix, on the other hand, look to engineering-technological solutions funded by American taxpayers as a whole to bring more water from additional sources their way.

Phoenix is also unsustainable in its sprawl. It is one of the most spread-out of all American cities, with wasteful and inefficient usage of land, and inadequate planning and management about where to build what as the city grows. The result is a landscape of bland sameness across the metropolis, with occasional better-designed areas and noteworthy architecture only here and there. An even worse result is that the metropolis is extremely dependent on the automobile and freeways, because distances are great and public transportation can do only so much in a landscape of sprawl. The streets of Phoenix are arranged in a rigid grid and are wide to accommodate many cars, while the freeway system is one of the largest and fastest-expanding networks in the country, totaling some 1,405 lane miles across the metropolis in 2005. Nevertheless, there are traffic jams at busy times, resulting in demands by drivers for more roads and more lanes. Not only does dependence on the automobile consume fossil fuels and contribute to global heating, it also creates a heat island in the Phoenix metropolis, making an already-hot place even more uncomfortably hot. Because of the basin setting of the metropolis, there is also an uncomfortable build-up of air pollution on days without wind or rain. The city has been ranked by *Health* magazine as the fourth most polluted in the United States in terms of air quality. There is a bus system in the metropolis and a new (2008) light rail line called METRO that connects downtown Phoenix with the nearby communities of Tempe and Mesa, and there are plans for expansions. However, this is just a drop in the bucket in comparison to transportation patterns in Phoenix overall, and the unhappy truth is that most of the ridership on city buses is by people with no other choice (e.g., they cannot afford to buy a car but need to get to work). Buses do not run frequently on most routes, and few bus stops have shelters from the searing heat. Thus, while some cities in the world are people-friendly in providing excellent public transit and opportunities for bicycle commuting, spread-out Phoenix is friendly to cars, oil companies, and land developers who covert desert land and farms outside the city to distant suburbs.

Phoenix also has very serious crime problems, and has long been one of the most violent and dangerous cities in the United States. Some of the reasons include easy availability of guns, great social disparity and poverty, social and ethnic tensions, and the trafficking of both human beings and narcotics across Arizona's border with Mexico by brutal gangs. Because of the drugs trade, Phoenix has been called the "Kidnapping Capital of the United States." Inner-city neighborhoods are plagued by gang violence. Joe Arpaio, the controversial Sheriff of Maricopa County, Arizona, in which Phoenix is located, calls himself "America's toughest sheriff," and has made a national (and even international!) reputation for himself in chasing after illegal immigrants in his jurisdiction, as well as for unyielding insistence without proof that U.S. president Barack Obama was born outside the country. He is popular with white voters and has been elected to his post six times. The Maricopa County Jail that Arpaio oversees is said to be one of the toughest and largest prisons in the United States. Land fraud has long been a problem in Phoenix, as there is considerable money to be made in turning desert into development tracts, with the result that the Phoenix area is sometimes referred to as the "Tainted Desert," a word pun on the beautiful Painted Desert in the northern part of Arizona.

While the thrust of our discussion is to explain why we include Phoenix in this "bottom 10" list, we close by noting that, of course, Phoenix has many positive aspects too, and by acknowledging once again, as we did at the top, that many Phoenix residents love their city (and their cars, single homes, and green lawns). The city and some of its suburbs are especially popular as places for Americans and Canadians to retire. The deserts and mountains around the city are truly beautiful, and there are ample opportunities for enjoyment of the outdoors. The city itself has many cultural institutions, sports teams, golf courses, and other popular attractions, as well as a generally strong economy that, in addition to agriculture, is based on defense industries, electronics, education, and finance, among other sectors.

FURTHER READING

Ross, Andrew, *Bird on Fire: Lessons from the World's Least Sustainable City* (New York: Oxford University Press, 2013).

Shermer, Elizabeth Tandy, *Sunbelt Capitalism: Phoenix and the Transformation of American Politics* (Philadelphia: University of Pennsylvania Press, 2013).

VanderMeer, Philip, *Desert Visions and the Making of Phoenix, 1860–2009* (Albuquerque: University of New Mexico Press, 2011).

ST. LOUIS, MISSOURI

St. Louis is located on the Mississippi River in Missouri, near where the Missouri River joins the Mississippi. The city was founded by French fur traders in 1764, and was named after King Louis IX of France. It became part of the United States with the Louisiana Purchase of 1803, and then figured heavily as a base for American exploration and settlement of the West. It became an important hub of river transport during the steamboat era of the early 19th century, and grew to become one of the country's largest cities. In 1850 it became the first city west of the Mississippi to be among the 10 largest U.S. cities, when its population was 77,860 and rank was #8, and by the 1870 census it rose to #4 in rank in the United States and a population of 310,864. Immigrants came from Germany, Italy, and other countries and worked in the city's industries. The population of St. Louis peaked in 1950 at 856,796, when the city again had a #8 rank in the country. Then, because of sub-urbanization and deindustrialization, the population declined with every census count and population estimate afterward. Its population now is about 318,976 (2013 estimate), only a little more than the 1870 total, and its rank in the United States has tumbled to #58. The suburban area is much bigger than St. Louis, and totals 2,810,056 residents, the country's 19th-largest metropolitan total.

We include St. Louis on our list of 10 least contented U.S. cities because its decline from prominence and prosperity has been steeper than most other American cities. This has resulted in an extra-large population flight from the city, and numerous urban problems such as unemployment, crime, and declining neighborhoods. There are some fine parts of the city, to be sure, as well as a number of commendable social programs and urban redevelopment projects that have resulted in urban improvements, but as a whole the city is one of America's most troubled urban centers. The dramatic 630-foot (192-meter) high Gateway Arch on the Mississippi River near the downtown and the charming new ballpark for St. Louis baseball Cardinals nearby are two of the more prominent examples of urban revitalization in St. Louis. However, much of the city remains distressed, and some neighborhoods continue to decline. A famous symbol of the downfall is the city's large Pruitt-Igoe public housing project that had opened in 1954 with great promise to help the poor, but quickly became a dangerous slum and had to be totally demolished only a short while later in the mid-1970s. Today, St. Louis is a strongly segregated city that is about 50% African American and 40% white. About one-quarter of residents live at incomes below the poverty line and about one-in-five houses are empty because of depopulation. The city's tax base has been shrinking, making it difficult for government to provide services such as schooling and police and fire protection. Even though there has been a steady decline in recent years in crime, the crime rate is still significantly higher than the national average, and the city ranks in the top 10 in the United States in violent crime.

Our choice of including St. Louis in these pages is also driven by at least two "least contented" communities in the metropolitan ring around the city: the once-booming but now distressed industrial city of East St. Louis across the Mississippi in the state of Illinois; and the suburban town of Ferguson, Missouri, that has recently become a prominent symbol of racial tension in the United States. East St. Louis had once prospered as a stockyards and meatpacking center, as well as other industry, and grew to a peak population in 1950 of 82,366. Its decline afterward was even more precipitous than that of St. Louis, with a result that the total now is less than one-third of what it had been: 27,006. The city was affected not only by suburbanization and deindustrialization but also by racial tensions and rioting, white flight, and by the construction of freeways through once-decent neighborhoods. The goal was to improve access to downtown St. Louis, but the result was the displacement of East St. Louis residents and stepped-up suburban growth on the Illinois side of the river. At least one-third of the population is poor and nearly 100% of residents are African Americans. Areas of businesses and homes became vacant lots overgrown with weeds and wild grasses, such that it is said that the native prairie has returned to what was once urban East St. Louis. Street gangs roam what is left of the city and crime is extremely high. According to data from the FBI, the murder rate is at least double that of other high-murder cities such as Gary, Indiana, and Detroit, and is even higher than that of Honduras, the country with the highest murder rate in the world.

Ferguson is an inner suburb in St. Louis County, to the north of downtown St. Louis. As of the 2010 census, its population was 21,203. The town had been 99% white as recently as 1970, but whites began to move out as African American seeking better housing and neighborhoods moved in, and the area is now

Ferguson, Missouri, an inner suburb of St. Louis, Missouri, was the scene of the shooting death on August 9, 2014, of an unarmed young African American male named Michael Brown by a white police officer. The incident was followed by angry demonstrations against police brutality and racial profiling, some of which became violent. This photo is of a peaceful rally in Ferguson in support of racial justice. (Kevin Duke/Dreamstime.com)

approximately two-thirds African American. It can be classified as a blue-collar suburb. Ferguson became international news when on August 9, 2014, a white police officer shot and killed an unarmed African American youth, 18-year-old Michael Brown, resulting in days of vociferous protests by angry African American residents and their supporters, as well as rioting, and then protests and civil disorder again several months later when a grand jury decided not to indict the police officer in the young man's death. Racial tensions have been high in Ferguson and the St. Louis area since, and "Ferguson" has entered the American vocabulary as a word connoting violence and racial profiling by police against African Americans. The protest slogan "Hands up, don't shoot" originated with the killing of Michael Brown and has spread across America as a statement against police brutality.

FURTHER READING

Gordon, Colin, "St. Louis Blues: The Urban Crisis in the Gateway City," *St. Louis University Public Law Review*, 33, 1, 2013, pp. 81–91.

Hamer, Jennifer, *Abandoned in the Heartland: Work, Family, and Living in East St. Louis* (Berkeley: University of California Press, 2011).

Theising, Andrew J., *Made in USA: East St. Louis* (St. Louis, MO: Virginia Publishing, 2013).

STOCKTON, CALIFORNIA

Stockton is a city in the San Joaquin Valley in north-central California, and the county seat of San Joaquin County. The area is part of California's Central Valley and is one of the most important agricultural districts in the United States. Leading crops include grapes, cotton, nuts, vegetables, and citrus fruits. The city is a market and service center for the surrounding farmlands, and a regional transportation hub. It is where the caterpillar tractor originated. In 1937, the city gained notoriety for labor unrest among employees in the city's canneries, and was the scene of the bloody Spinach Riot of that year, a critical moment in U.S. labor history. Stockton was named in honor of Commodore Robert F. Stockton, a U.S. naval officer who is credited for securing California for the United States in the Mexican-American war, and is identified as the first city in California to not have a Spanish or Native American name. The population of Stockton is 300,899 as of 2014, the 13th-largest total in California. Unlike many other U.S. cities, Stockton has never registered a population loss between census counts, and has continued to grow with every tally starting with 1860, the year of city's first appearance in the census.

Stockton has an ethnically diverse population. The farms in the surrounding area, as well as canneries and other food processing plants in the city, attracted hopeful workers from all parts of the United States, as well as immigrants from Asia and Latin America. The city's population makeup as of the 2010 census is Hispanic of any race 40.3%, white 37.0%, Asian 21.5%, and African American

12.2%, plus small percentages of other races. (The total adds up to more than 100% because many Hispanics are double-counted as both Hispanic and white.) Mexican Americans are the single largest ethnic group, comprising 37.0% of the city's total, while the largest Asian ethnic group is Filipinos, with 7.2% of the population. Non-Hispanic whites comprised 22.9% of the city's population in 2010, down sharply from 57.1% in 1980. These data show that Stockton is increasingly a city of people of color. Many of the people are poor. Farm work does not pay much, and is seasonal, so incomes are low and sporadic. A 2011 article in the *Huffington Post* lists Stockton as one of the 10 poorest suburbs in America. Why "suburb" we do not know, as we think of Stockton as a medium-sized city and not a suburb, but the numbers that the article cites are telling nonetheless: overall poverty rate in 2010, 16.4%; change in median household income 2007–2010, –9.4%; and change in poor population 2000–2010, +56.4%.

Stockton is a poor city not just because of low wages in agriculture, but also because the city still feels the effects of the 2007 subprime mortgage financial crisis. The city led the United States in foreclosures that year, with mortgages on one of every thirty homes in default, and home process plummeting. From

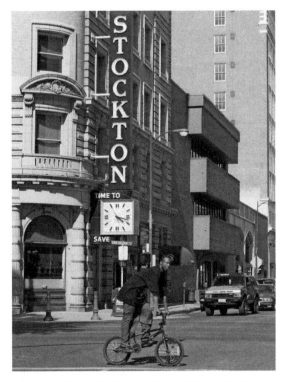

Stockton, California, is one of the cities in the United States that has been most strongly affected by the home loan foreclosure crisis. (Justin Sullivan/iStockphoto.com)

September 2006 to September 2007, the value of a median-priced house in Stockton declined an astonishing 44%, wiping out people's home equity and bringing the value of many homes to a value significantly lower than the money owed on it. The collapse in real estate values undermined the city's property tax base, and in July 2012, Stockton became the biggest city in the country to file for bankruptcy. It has since been surpassed in that dubious category by another one of our least contented cities, Detroit. There is now a city sales tax to help fund the Stockton's exit from bankruptcy. Unemployment remains high, which also has a negative effect on the real estate market and tax revenues. Negative publicity from the bankruptcy has slowed investment in the city and economic growth, which in turn has speeded outmigration by those with a choice about where to live and work. In this way, Stockton becomes not only increasingly a city of people of color, but also a city of increasing poverty. Cultural traditions value large families and many children, but the sad result is that it is children who live in poverty in the most disproportionate numbers. With poverty, there are increases in crime, and with poverty among the young, there are increases in juvenile delinquency, substance abuse, and gang activity. Stockton is widely known to have some of the most violent street gangs in the country.

There are some rankings of Stockton that put the city in an especially unflattering light. For one, in February 2012, *Forbes* ranked Stockton as the eighth most miserable city in the United States, largely because of the devastating effects of a sharp decline in home values and high unemployment. In the same year, the city was ranked the 10th most dangerous in America in terms of crime and the 2nd-most dangerous city in California, after Oakland. The National Insurance Crime Bureau reported that the city ranked seventh in the United States in auto theft per capita. A Gallup poll in 2010 rated Stockton in a tie for first place with Montgomery, Alabama, as the fattest city in the United States, with an obesity rate of 34.6%; and in 2013 Stockton was rated in a study conducted at Central Connecticut State University as the third-least literate city in the country with a population of at least 250,000, behind Bakersfield, California, and Corpus Christi, Texas. We are aware that there are people who take great pride in Stockton and who work hard to make the city a better place, and commend them for some laudable urban development projects and efforts to advance the arts and grow the economy. However, the last decade or so has been very hard on the city, and Stockton is, unfortunately, still some distance away from urban contentment.

FURTHER READING

Bradford, Harry, "10 Suburbs with the Highest Poverty Rates: Census," *Huffington Post*, September 23, 2011, http://www.huffingtonpost.com/2011/09/23/suburbs-poverty-rates_n_978058.html.

Chakrabortty, Atidya, "Stockton, California: 'This Economy Is Garbage,'" *The Guardian*, November 2, 2012, http://www.theguardian.com/world/2012/nov/02/stockton-california-economy-is-garbage.

Mabalon, Dawn Bohulano, *Little Manila Is in the Heart: The Making of a Filipna/o-American Community in Stockton, California* (Durham, NC: Duke University Press, 2013).

Appendix A

Summaries of Country Rankings

Table A1 Human Development Index, 2014 Report, Data for 2013

Top 20 Countries	Bottom 20 Countries
1. Norway	168. Haiti
2. Australia	169. Afghanistan
3. Switzerland	170. Djibouti
4. Netherlands	171. Ivory Coast
5. United States	172. Gambia
6. Germany	173. Ethiopia
7. New Zealand	174. Malawi
8. Canada	175. Liberia
9. Singapore	176. Mali
10. Denmark	177. Guinea-Bissau
11. Ireland	178. Mozambique
12. Sweden	179. Guinea
13. Iceland	180. Burundi
14. United Kingdom	181. Burkina Faso
15. Hong Kong	182. Eritrea
16. South Korea	183. Sierra Leone
17. Japan	184. Chad

(Continued)

Table A1 (Continued)

Top 20 Countries	Bottom 20 Countries
18. Lichtenstein	185. Central African Republic
19. Israel	186. Democratic Republic of the Congo
20. France	187. Nigeria

Source: Human Development Report, 2014, United Nations Development Programme. http://hdr.undp.org/sites/default/files/hdr14-report-en-1.pdf.

Table A2 Overall Life Expectancy by Country, 2012

Top 20 Countries and Years	Bottom 20 Countries and Years
1. Japan, 87	179. Malawi, 51.55
2. Andorra, 84.2	180. South Africa, 51.20
3. Singapore, 84	181. Nigeria, 50.26
4. Hong Kong, 83.8	182. Somalia, 50.24
5. San Marino, 83.5	183. Equatorial Guinea, 50.10
6. Iceland, 83.3	184. Mali, 49.99
7. Italy, 83.1	185. Cameroon, 49.97
8. Sweden, 83	186. Angola, 49.62
9. Australia, 83	187. Burundi, 48.81
10. Switzerland, 82.8	188. Mozambique, 48.77
11. Canada, 82.5	189. Chad, 48.52
12. Spain, 82.5	190. Democratic Republic of the Congo, 47.42
13. New Zealand, 82.1	191. Swaziland, 47.36
14. Luxembourg, 82	192. Afghanistan, 47.32
15. Israel, 82	193. Zambia, 46.93
16. Norway, 81.9	194. Guinea-Bissau, 46.76
17. Austria, 81.5	195. Zimbabwe, 46.59
18. France, 81.5	196. Sierra Leone, 46.26
19. Netherlands, 81.5	197. Lesotho, 46.02
20. Ireland, 81.4	198. Central African Republic, 45.9

Source: CIA World Fact Book: https://www.cia.gov/library/publications/the-world-factbook/rankorder/2102rank.html and United Nations, World Population Prospects: The 2012 Revision: http://esa.un.org/wpp/.

Table A3 Infant Mortality Rate, Estimates for 2013 (Number of Deaths of Infants Aged One Year and under per 1,000 Live Births)

Top 20 Countries	Bottom 20 Countries
1. Monaco, 1.81	169. Ivory Coast, 61.66
2. Japan, 2.17	170. Uganda, 62.47
3. Bermuda, 2.47	171. Gambia, 67.63
4. Singapore, 2.59	172. Zambia, 68.58
5. Hong Kong, 2.89	173. Haiti, 69.69
6. Iceland, 3.17	174. South Sudan, 69.97
7. France, 3.34	175. Liberia, 70.93
8. Finland, 2.28	176. Republic of the Congo, 72.45
9. Anguilla, 3.42	177. Equatorial Guinea, 73.12
10. Norway, 3.47	178. Mozambique, 74.63
11. Malta, 3.62	179. Democratic Republic of the Congo, 74.78
12. Belarus, 3.67	180. Sierra Leone, 74.95
13. Czech Republic, 3.67	181. Burkina Faso, 78.30
14. Andorra, 3.73	182. Angola, 81.75
15. Ireland, 3.78	183. Chad, 91.94
16. Switzerland, 3.80	184. Guinea-Bissau, 92.66
17. Israel, 4.03	185. Central African Republic, 95.04
18. South Korea, 4.10	186. Somalia, 101.91
19. Denmark, 4.15	187. Mali, 106.49
20. Austria, 4.20	188. Afghanistan, 187.50

Source: CIA World Fact Book: https://www.cia.gov/library/publications/the-world-factbook /fields/2091.html and United Nations, World Population Prospects: The 2012 Revision: http://esa.un.org/unpd/wpp/Excel-Data/mortality.htm.

Table A4 WHO Ranking of Health Systems, 2000

Top 20 Countries	Bottom 20 Countries
1. France	171. Equatorial Guinea
2. Italy	172. Rwanda
3. San Marino	173. Afghanistan
4. Andorra	174. Cambodia

(Continued)

Table A4 (Continued)

Top 20 Countries	Bottom 20 Countries
5. Malta	175. South Africa
6. Singapore	176. Guinea-Bissau
7. Spain	177. Swaziland
8. Oman	178. Chad
9. Austria	179. Somalia
10. Japan	180. Ethiopia
11. Norway	181. Angola
12. Portugal	182. Zambia
13. Monaco	183. Lesotho
14. Greece	184. Mozambique
15. Iceland	185. Malawi
16. Luxembourg	186. Liberia
17. Netherlands	187. Nigeria
18. United Kingdom	188. Democratic Republic of the Congo
19. Ireland	189. Central African Republic
20. Switzerland	190. Burma

Source: World Health Organization, The World Health Report, 2000: http://www.who.int/whr/2000/en/whr00_en.pdf.

Table A5 Gross Domestic Product (at Purchasing Power Parity) per Capita

Top 20 Countries

International Monetary Fund (2014)	World Bank (2011–2013)	CIA (1993–2013)
1. Qatar	1. Qatar	1. Qatar
2. Luxembourg	2. Luxembourg	2. Liechtenstein
3. Singapore	3. Kuwait	3. Monaco
4. Brunei	4. Singapore	4. Luxembourg
5. Kuwait	5. Brunei	5. Singapore
6. Norway	6. Norway	6. Norway
7. United Arab Emirates	7. United Arab Emirates	7. San Marino
8. San Marino	8. Switzerland	8. Switzerland

(Continued)

Top 20 Countries

International Monetary Fund (2014)	World Bank (2011–2013)	CIA (1993–2013)
9. Switzerland	9. Saudi Arabia	9. Brunei
10. United States	10. United States	10. United States
11. Saudi Arabia	11. Netherlands	11. Hong Kong
12. Bahrain	12. Ireland	12. Canada
13. Ireland	13. Austria	13. Australia
14. Netherlands	14. Oman	14. Austria
15. Australia	15. Sweden	15. Kuwait
16. Austria	16. Germany	16. Netherlands
17. Sweden	17. Bahrain	17. Ireland
18. Germany	18. Denmark	18. Sweden
19. Taiwan	19. Australia	19. Iceland
20. Canada	20. Canada	20. Taiwan
#1 = $Int. 143,427	#1 = $Int. 136,727	#1 = $Int. 102,100

Bottom 20 Countries

International Monetary Fund (2014)	World Bank (2011–2013)	C.I.A. (1993–2013)
168. Haiti	166. Burkina Faso	176. Haiti
169. Mali	167. Uganda	177. Nepal
170. Kiribati	168. Gambia	178. Ethiopia
171. Rwanda	169. Mali	179. Guinea-Bissau
172. Burkina Faso	170. Sierra Leone	180. Mozambique
173. Gambia	171. Rwanda	181. Afghanistan
174. Ethiopia	172. Comoros	182. Guinea
175. Comoros	173. Madagascar	183. Mali
176. Togo	174. Guinea-Bissau	184. Togo
177. Madagascar	175. Togo	185. Madagascar
178. Guinea-Bissau	176. Ethiopia	186. South Sudan
179. Guinea	177. Guinea	187. Malawi
180. Eritrea	178. Eritrea	188. Central African Republic
181. Mozambique	179. Mozambique	189. Eritrea

(Continued)

Table A5 (Continued)

Bottom 20 Countries

International Monetary Fund (2014)	World Bank (2011–2013)	C.I.A. (1993–2013)
182. Niger	180. Niger	190. Niger
183. Burundi	181. Liberia	191. Liberia
184. Liberia	182. Democratic Republic of Congo	192. Burundi
185. Malawi	183. Malawi	193. Somalia
186. Dem. Rep. Congo	184. Burundi	194. Zimbabwe
187. Central African Republic	185. Central African Republic	195. Dem. Rep. Congo
#187 = $Int. 607	#185 = $Int. 604	#195 = $Int. 400

Note: The money figures given here are in current Geary-Khamis dollars, more commonly known as international dollars (Int$).

Source: International Monetary Fund: http://www.imf.org/external/pubs/ft/weo/2015/01/weodata/index.aspx; World Bank: http://data.worldbank.org/indicator/NY.GDP.PCAP.PP.CD; CIA: https://www.cia.gov/library/publications/the-world-factbook/rankorder/2004rank.html.

Table A6 Legatum Prosperity Index, 2014

Top 20 Countries	Bottom 20 Countries
1. Norway	123. Zimbabwe
2. Switzerland	124. Mauritania
3. New Zealand	125. Nigeria
4. Denmark	126. Ethiopia
5. Canada	127. Pakistan
6. Sweden	128. Iraq
7. Australia	129. Syria
8. Finland	130. Sudan
9. Netherlands	131. Liberia
10. United States	132. Angola
11. Iceland	133. Guinea
12. Ireland	134. Sierra Leone
13. United Kingdom	135. Haiti

(*Continued*)

Top 20 Countries	Bottom 20 Countries
14. Germany	136. Togo
15. Austria	137. Afghanistan
16. Luxembourg	138. Yemen
17. Belgium	139. Burundi
18. Singapore	140. Democratic Republic of the Congo
19. Japan	141. Chad
20. Hong Kong	142. Central African Republic

Source: The Legatum Institute, The 2014 Legatum Prosperity Index, http://www.li.com /docs/default-Source/publications/2014-legatum-prosperity-index.pdf.

Table A7 World's Lowest Literacy Rates by Country, 2013

Percentage of Population Aged 15 and Over That Can Read and Write

Bottom 20 Countries

1. Timor-Leste	58.60%
2. Mauritania	58%
3. Bangladesh	57.70%
4. Papua New Guinea	57.30%
5. Guinea-Bissau	55.30%
6. Pakistan	55%
7. Haiti	52.90%
8. Bhutan	52.80%
9. Gambia	50%
10. Benin	42.40%
11. Guinea	41%
12. Senegal	39.30%
13. Ethiopia	39%
14. Chad	35.40%
15. Sierra Leone	35.10%
16. Burkina Faso	28.70%
17. Niger	28.70%
18. Afghanistan	28.10%

(Continued)

Table A7 (Continued)

Percentage of Population Aged 15 and Over That Can Read and Write

Bottom 20 Countries

19. Mali	27.70%
20. South Sudan	27%

We do not give a top 20 list for this variable because many more than 20 countries have a literacy rate that approaches 100%.

Source: CIA: https://www.cia.gov/library/publications/the-world-factbook/fields/2103.html
UN Human Development Report: http://hdr.undp.org/en/content/adult-literacy-rate-both-sexes-ages-15-and-older.

Table A8 Transparency International's Corruption Perceptions Index, 2014

20 Least Corrupt Countries	20 Most Corrupt Countries
1. Denmark	156. Cambodia
2. New Zealand	156. Myanmar
3. Finland	156. Zimbabwe
4. Sweden	159. Burundi
5. Norway	159. Syria
6. Switzerland	161. Angola
7. Singapore	161. Guinea-Bissau
8. Netherlands	161. Haiti
9. Luxembourg	161. Venezuela
10. Canada	161. Yemen
11. Australia	166. Eritrea
12. Germany	166. Libya
13. Iceland	166. Uzbekistan
14. United Kingdom	169. Turkmenistan
15. Belgium	170. Iraq
16. Japan	171. South Sudan
17. Barbados	172. Afghanistan
17. Ireland	173. Sudan
17. United States	174. North Korea
21. Chile	174. Somalia
21. Uruguay	

Source: Transparency International, The 2014 Corruption Perceptions Index, http://www.transparency.org/cpi2014.

Table A9 Index of Economic Freedom, 2015

Top 20 Countries	Bottom 20 Countries
1. Hong Kong	159. Solomon Islands
2. Singapore	160. Uzbekistan
3. New Zealand	161. Burma
4. Australia	162. Ukraine
5. Switzerland	163. Bolivia
6. Canada	164. Kiribati
7. Chile	165. Chad
8. Estonia	166. Central African Republic
9. Ireland	167. Timor-Leste
10. Mauritius	168. Democratic Republic of the Congo
11. Denmark	169. Argentina
12. United States	170. Republic of the Congo
13. United Kingdom	171. Iran
14. Taiwan	172. Turkmenistan
15. Lithuania	173. Equatorial Guinea
16. Germany	174. Eritrea
17. Netherlands	175. Zimbabwe
18. Bahrain	176. Venezuela
19. Finland	177. Cuba
20. Japan	178. North Korea

Countries 1–5 are classified as "free."

Countries 6–20 are classified as "partly free."

All of the Bottom 20 countries are classified as "repressed."

Source: The 2015 Index of Economic Freedom, http://www.heritage.org/index/ranking.

Table A10 Democracy Index, 2014

Top 20 Countries	Bottom 20 Countries
1. Norway	148. Azerbaijan
2. Sweden	149. Yemen
3. Iceland	150. Zimbabwe
4. New Zealand	151. Afghanistan
5. Denmark	152. United Arab Emirates
6. Switzerland	153. Sudan

(Continued)

Table A10 (Continued)

Top 20 Countries	Bottom 20 Countries
7. Canada	154. Uzbekistan
8. Finland	155. Eritrea
9. Australia	156. Tajikistan
10. Netherlands	157. Laos
11. Luxembourg	158. Iran
12. Ireland	159. Guinea-Bissau
13. Germany	160. Turkmenistan
14. Austria	161. Saudi Arabia
15. Malta	162. Democratic Republic of the Congo
16. United Kingdom	163. Syria
17. Uruguay	164. Equatorial Guinea
18. Mauritius	165. Chad
19. United States	166. Central African Republic
20. Japan	167. North Korea

Source: Intelligence Unit of The Economist, The Democracy Index: http://pages.eiu.com/rs/eiu2/images/Democracy-Index-2012.pdf.

Table A11 World Press Freedom Index, 2014

Top 20 Countries	Bottom 20 Countries
1. Finland	161. Kazakhstan
2. Netherlands	162. Rwanda
3. Norway	163. Bahrain
4. Luxembourg	164. Saudi Arabia
5. Andorra	165. Sri Lanka
6. Liechtenstein	166. Uzbekistan
7. Denmark	167. Yemen
8. Iceland	168. Equatorial Guinea
9. New Zealand	169. Djibouti
10. Sweden	170. Cuba
11. Estonia	171. Laos
12. Austria	172. Sudan

(*Continued*)

Top 20 Countries	Bottom 20 Countries
13. Czech Republic	173. Iran
14. Germany	174. Vietnam
15. Switzerland	175. China
16. Ireland	176. Somalia
17. Jamaica	177. Syria
18. Canada	178. Turkmenistan
19. Poland	179. North Korea
20. Slovakia	180. Eritrea

Source: Reporters Without Borders, World Press Freedom Index 2014, http://rsf.org/index 2014/en-index2014.php.

Table A12   Satisfaction with Life Index, 2006

Top 20 Countries	Bottom 20 Countries
1. Denmark	159. Chad
2. Switzerland	160. Ivory Coast
3. Austria	161. Niger
4. Iceland	162. Eritrea
5. The Bahamas	163. Rwanda
6. Finland	164. Bulgaria
7. Sweden	165. Lesotho
8. Bhutan	166. Pakistan
9. Brunei	167. Russia
10. Canada	168. Swaziland
11. Ireland	169. Georgia
12. Luxembourg	170. Belarus
13. Costa Rica	171. Turkmenistan
14. Malta	172. Armenia
15. Netherlands	173. Sudan
16. Antigua and Barbuda	174. Ukraine
17. Malaysia	175. Moldova
18. New Zealand	176. Democratic Republic of the Congo

(Continued)

Table A12   (Continued)

Top 20 Countries	Bottom 20 Countries
19. Norway	177. Zimbabwe
20. Seychelles	178. Burundi

Source: Satisfaction with Life Index, University of Leicester, http://www.eurekalert.org/pub_releases/2006–07/uol-uol072706.php.

Table A13   Level of Happiness Index, 2010–2012

Top 20 Countries	Bottom 20 Countries
1. Denmark	137. Sri Lanka
2. Norway	138. Gabon
3. Switzerland	139. Malawi
4. Netherlands	140. Cambodia
5. Sweden	141. Chad
6. Canada	142. Yemen
7. Finland	143. Afghanistan
8. Austria	144. Bulgaria
9. Iceland	145. Botswana
10. Australia	146. Madagascar
11. Israel	147. Senegal
12. Costa Rica	148. Syria
13. New Zealand	149. Comoros
14. United Arab Emirates	150. Guinea
15. Panama	151. Tanzania
16. Mexico	152. Rwanda
17. United States	153. Burundi
18. Ireland	154. Central African Republic
19. Luxembourg	155. Benin
20. Venezuela	156. Togo

Source: The World Happiness Report, 2013, John Helliwell, Richard Layard, and Jeffrey Sachs, http://unsdsn.org/wp-content/uploads/2014/02/WorldHappinessReport2013_online.pdf.

Table A14 Best Countries for Business

Top 20 Countries	Bottom 20 Countries
1. Denmark	127. Malawi
2. Hong Kong	128. Bolivia
3. New Zealand	129. Tajikistan
4. Ireland	130. Laos
5. Sweden	131. Gabon
6. Canada	132. Iran
7. Norway	133. Cameroon
8. Singapore	134. Zimbabwe
9. Switzerland	135. Mauritania
10. Finland	136. Ethiopia
11. Netherlands	137. Algeria
12. Belgium	138. Gambia
13. United Kingdom	139. Yemen
14. Slovenia	140. Venezuela
15. Iceland	141. Angola
16. Australia	142. Haiti
17. Taiwan	143. Myanmar
18. United States	144. Libya
19. Luxembourg	145. Chad
20. Germany	146. Guinea

Source: *Forbes*, Best Countries for Business, http://www.forbes.com/best-countries-for-business/list/#page:1_sort:0_direction:asc_search.

Table A15 Global Competitiveness Index, 2014–2015

Top 20 Countries	Bottom 20 Countries
1. Switzerland	125. Gambia
2. Singapore	126. Libya
3. United States	127. Nigeria
4. Finland	128. Mali
5. Germany	129. Pakistan
6. Japan	130. Madagascar

(*Continued*)

Table A15 (Continued)

Top 20 Countries	Bottom 20 Countries
7. Hong Kong	131. Venezuela
8. Netherlands	132. Malawi
9. United Kingdom	133. Mozambique
10. Sweden	134. Myanmar
11. Norway	135. Burkina Faso
12. United Arab Emirates	136. Timor-Leste
13. Denmark	137. Haiti
14. Taiwan	138. Sierra Leone
15. Canada	139. Burundi
16. Qatar	140. Angola
17. New Zealand	141. Mauritania
18. Belgium	142. Yemen
19. Luxembourg	143. Chad
20. Malaysia	144. Guinea

Source: World Economic Forum, Global Competitiveness Index, 2014–2015, http://reports
.weforum.org/global-competitiveness-report-2014–2015/.

Table A16 Sustainable Society Index, 2014

Human Well-Being

Top 10 Countries	Bottom 10 Countries
1. Finland	142. Togo
2. Iceland	143. Nigeria
3. Germany	144. Niger
4. Japan	145. Republic of the Congo
5. Sweden	146. Mozambique
6. Denmark	147. Papua New Guinea
7. Norway	148. Madagascar
8. Austria	149. Central African Republic
9. Hungary	150. Chad
10. Ireland	151. Democratic Republic of the Congo

United States = #40

(*Continued*)

Environmental Well-Being

Top 10 Countries	Bottom 10 Countries
1. Guinea-Bissau	142. Netherlands
2. Malawi	143. Belgium
3. Nepal	144. Australia
4. Mozambique	145. South Korea
5. Central African Republic	146. Kuwait
6. Zambia	147. Turkmenistan
7. Rwanda	148. United Arab Emirates
8. Dem. Republic Congo	149. Saudi Arabia
9. Burkina Faso	150. Qatar
10. Burundi	151. Oman

United States = #139

Economic Well-Being

Top 10 Countries	Bottom 10 Countries
1. Norway	142. Jordan
2. Sweden	143. Guiana
3. Switzerland	144. Gambia
4. Denmark	145. Togo
5. Estonia	146. Burundi
6. Luxembourg	147. Zimbabwe
7. Australia	148. Yemen
8. Czech Republic	149. Guyana
9. Finland	150. Mauritania
10. Slovenia	151. Sudan

United States = #96

Source: Sustainable Society Foundation, Sustainable Society Index, http://www.ssfindex .com/.

APPENDIX B

SUMMARIES OF WORLD CITIES RANKINGS

Table B1   Mercer's Quality of Living, City Rankings, 2015

Top 20 Cities	Bottom 20 Cities
1. Vienna	211. Dhaka
2. Zürich	212. Lagos
3. Auckland	213. Abuja
4. Munich	214. Dushanbe
5. Vancouver	215. Ouagadougou
6. Dusseldorf	216. Tripoli
7. Frankfurt	217. Antananarivo
8. Geneva	218. Niamey
9. Copenhagen	219. Bamako
10. Sydney	220. Damascus
11. Amsterdam	221. Nouakchott
12. Wellington	222. Conakry
13. Bern	223. Kinshasa
14. Berlin	224. Brazzaville
15. Toronto	225. Sana'a
16. Hamburg	226. N'Djamena
17. Melbourne	227. Khartoum
18. Ottawa	228. Port au Prince

(Continued)

Table B1 (Continued)

Top 20 Cities	Bottom 20 Cities
19. Luxembourg	229. Bangui
20. Stockholm	230. Baghdad

Source: Mercer, 2015 Quality of Living Rankings, http://www.imercer.com/uploads/GM /qol2015/h5478qol2015/index.html.

Table B2 EIU Livability Ranking, Best and Worst Cities, 2014

Top 10 Cities	Bottom 10 Cities
1. Melbourne	131. Abidjan
2. Vienna	132. Tripoli
3. Vancouver	133. Douala
4. Toronto	134. Harare
5. Adelaide	135. Algiers
6. Calgary	136. Karachi
7. Sydney	137. Lagos
8. Helsinki	138. Port Moresby
9. Perth	139. Dhaka
10. Auckland	140. Damascus

Source: The *Economist*, Intelligence Unit, http://www.eiu.com.

Table B3 *Monocle's* Quality of Life Survey, Best World Cities, 2014

Top 20 Cities
1. Copenhagen
2. Tokyo
3. Melbourne
4. Stockholm
5. Helsinki
6. Vienna
7. Zürich
8. Munich
9. Kyoto
10. Fukuoka

(*Continued*)

Top 20 Cities

11. Sydney

12. Auckland

13. Hong Kong

14. Berlin

15. Vancouver

16. Singapore

17. Madrid

18. Paris

19. Amsterdam

20. Hamburg

Source: *Monocle*, Quality of Life Survey, 2014, http://monocle.com/film/affairs/quality-of-life-survey-2014/.

APPENDIX C

SUMMARIES OF U.S. CITIES RANKINGS

Table C1 Livability's Top 10 Best Places to Live, Small–Medium-Sized Towns, 2015

1. Madison, Wisconsin
2. Rochester, Minnesota
3. Arlington, Virginia
4. Boulder, Colorado
5. Palo Alto, California
6. Berkeley, California
7. Santa Clara, California
8. Missoula, Montana
9. Boise, Idaho
10. Iowa City, Iowa

Source: Livability, Top 100 Best Places to Live, http://livability.com/best-places/top-100-best-places-to-live/2015.

Table C2 Livability's Top 10 Best Cities for Families, 2015

1. Overland, Park, Kansas
2. Plano, Texas
3. Holland, Michigan
4. Carmel, Indiana
5. Leesburg, Virginia

(Continued)

Table C2 (Continued)

6.	Chandler, Arizona
7.	Naperville, Illinois
8.	Bentonville, Arkansas
9.	Rockville, Maryland
10.	St. George, Utah

Source: Livability, 10 Best Cities for Families, http://livability.com/top-10/families/10-best-cities-families/2015.

Table C3 Livability's Top 10 Best Cities for Retirees, 2014

1.	Springfield, Missouri
2.	Knoxville, Tennessee
3.	Bellevue, Washington
4.	Largo, Florida
5.	Wheat Ridge, Colorado
6.	Honolulu, Hawaii
7.	Albuquerque, New Mexico
8.	Tucson, Arizona
9.	Missoula, Montana
10.	Coeur d'Alene, Idaho

Source: Livability, 2014 Best Places to Retire, http://livability.com/top-10/retirement/best-places-retire/2014.

Table C4 Businessweek.com's 10 Best Places to Live, 2012

Selected from among the 100 Largest Cities in the United States

1.	San Francisco
2.	Seattle
3.	Washington, D.C.
4.	Boston
5.	Portland, Oregon
6.	Denver
7.	New York City
8.	Austin

(Continued)

Selected from among the 100 Largest Cities in the United States

9. San Diego

10. St. Paul

Source: Bloomberg Business, America's 50 Best Cities, http://www.bloomberg.com/bw/slide shows/2012–09–26/americas-50-best-cities.

Table C5 Gallup-Healthways Well-Being Index by City, 2014

Top 10 Cities	Bottom 10 Cities
1. Provo-Orem, UT	180. Evansville, IN-KY
2. Boulder, CO	181. Mobile, AL
3. Ft. Collins-Loveland, CO	182. Shreveport-Bossier City, LA
4. Honolulu, HA	183. Columbus, GA-AL
5. San Jose-Sunnyvale-Santa Clara, CA	184. Beaumont-Port Arthur, TX
6. Ann Arbor, MI	185. Hickory-Lenoir-Morganton, NC
7. Naples-Marco Island, FL	186. Spartanburg, SC
8. San Luis Obispo-Paso Robles, CA	187. Redding, CA
9. San Francisco-Oakland-Fremont, CA	188. Charleston, WV
10. Lincoln, NE	189. Huntington-Ashland, WV-KY-OH

Source: USA Today, Gallup Ranks Best and Worst Cities for Well-Being, http://www.usato day.com/story/news/nation/2014/03/25/gallup-cities-well-being/6828197/.

Table C6 America's Greenest Cities, *Popular Science*, 2008

Top 10 Cities	Green Score
1. Portland, OR	23.1
2. San Francisco	23
3. Boston	22.7
4. Oakland, CA	22.5
5. Eugene, OR	22.4
6. Cambridge, MA	22.2
7. Berkeley, CA	22.2
8. Seattle	22.1

(*Continued*)

Table C6 (Continued)

Top 10 Cities	Green Score
9. Chicago	21.3
10. Austin	21

Source: *Popular Science*, America's Greenest Cities, http://www.popsci.com/environment/article/2008–02/americas-50-greenest-cities?page=1%2C1.

Table C7 U.S. Cities with the Worst Air Pollution, *Health* Magazine, 2015

Bottom 11 Cities
1. Visalia, CA
2. Los Angeles
3. Phoenix
4. Hanford, CA
5. Fresno
6. Pittsburgh
7. Bakersfield, CA
8. Birmingham, AL
9. Cincinnati
10. Louisville
11. Modesto, CA

Source: *Health*, 11 US Cities with the Worst Air Pollution, http://www.health.com/health/gallery/0,,20490855,00.html.

Appendix D

Summaries of Rankings of U.S. States

Table D1 Gallup-Healthways Well-Being Index by State, 2014

Top 10 States	Index	Bottom 10 States	Index
1. North Dakota	70.4	41. Louisiana	64.9
2. South Dakota	70	42. Oklahoma	64.7
3. Nebraska	69.7	43. Missouri	64.5
4. Minnesota	69.7	44. Tennessee	64.3
5. Montana	69.3	45. Arkansas	64.3
6. Utah	69.1	46. Ohio	64.2
7. Colorado	68.9	47. Alabama	64.1
8. Hawaii	68.4	48. Mississippi	63.7
9. Washington	68.3	49. Kentucky	63
10. Iowa	68.2	50. West Virginia	61.4

Sources: *USA Today*, America's Most Content States Have Good Jobs, Health, http://www.usatoday.com/story/money/2014/02/20/healthways-wellbeing-most-content-states/5624043/ and *USA Today*, Report: The Most Miserable States in the USA, http://www.usatoday.com/story/money/business/2014/02/23/most-miserable-states/5729305/.

Table D2 Ranking of U.S. States by Business Competitiveness, CNBC, 2014

Top 10 States	Bottom 11 States
1. Georgia	40. Louisiana
2. Texas	40. New York (tie)
3. Vermont	42. Vermont
4. Nebraska	43. New Jersey
5. North Carolina	44. Pennsylvania
6. Minnesota	45. Maine
7. Washington	46. Connecticut
8. Colorado	47. Alaska
9. Virginia	48. West Virginia
10. North Dakota	49. Hawaii
	50. Rhode Island

Source: CNBC, America's Top States for Business 2014, http://www.cnbc.com/id/101758236.

Selected Bibliography

Abbott, Mary Lu and Annette Fuller, *America's 100 Best Places to Retire* (Houston, TX: Vacation Publications, Inc., 2003).

Diener, E., J. F. Helliwell, and D. Kahneman, eds., *International Differences in Well-Being* (New York: Oxford University Press, 2010).

Economist Intelligence Unit (EIU), *A Summary of the Liveability Ranking and Overview*, August 2014, http://www.eiu.com.

Florida, Richard, *The Rise of the Creative Classes* (New York: Basic Books, revised edition 2014).

Florida, Richard, *Who's Your City?: How the Creative Economy Is Making Where to Live the Most Important Decision of Your Life* (New York: Basic Books, 2009).

Helliwell, John, Richard Layard, and Jeffrey Sachs, eds., *World Happiness Report* (New York: Earth Institute, 2013).

Janssen, Sarah, ed., *The World Almanac and Book of Facts 2015* (New York: World Almanac, 2014).

Knox, Paul, ed., *Atlas of Cities* (Princeton, NJ: Princeton University Press, 2014).

Konrad, Alex, "America's 50 Best Cities," *Bloomberg Business*, September 28, 2012, http://www.bloomberg.com/bw/slideshows/2012–09–26/americas-50-best-cities.

Kotkin, Joel, "Why the 'Livable Cities' Rankings Are Wrong," *Forbes*, August 11, 2009, http://www.forbes.com/2009/08/10/cities-livable-elite-economist-monocle-rankings-opinions-columnists-joel-kotkin.html.

Lapierre, Dominique, *The City of Joy* (New York: Warner Books, 1985).

Lonely Planet, *The Cities Book: A Journey through the Best Cities in the World* (Melbourne: Lonely Planet, 2009).

Moretti, Enrico, *The New Geography of Jobs* (New York: Houghton Mifflin Harcourt, 2012).

National Geographic, *World's Best Cities: Celebrating 220 Great Destinations* (Washington: National Geographic, 2014).

O'Leary Morgan, Kathleen and Scott Morgan, *City Crime Rankings, 2015* (Thousand Oaks, CA: CQ Press, 2015).

O'Leary Morgan, Kathleen and Scott Morgan, *State Rankings, 2015: A Statistical View of America* (Thousand Oaks, CA: CQ Press, 2015).

Prescott-Allen, Robert, *The Wellbeing of Nations: A Country-by-Country Index of Quality of Life and the Environment* (Washington: Island Press, 2001).

Smith, Dan, ed., *The Penguin State of the World Atlas, 2012,* 9th edition (London: Penguin Books, 2012).

Sperling, Bert and Peter Sander, *Cities Ranked and Rated* (Hoboken, NJ: Wiley, 2007).

Sustainable Society Foundation, *Sustainable Society Index,* 2014 (The Hague: Sustainable Society Foundation, 2014).

Vázquez, José Juan, Sonia Panadero, and Esther Rivas, "Happiness among Poor Women Victims of Intimate Partner Violence in Nicaragua," *Social Work in Public Health,* 30, 1, 2015, pp. 18–29.

World Economic Forum, *Global Competitiveness Report,* 2014–2015, http://reports.wefo rum.org/global-competitiveness-report-2014–2015/.

INDEX